Patronage Copy No.   391

This book was made possible by
the support of Patrons who pre-paid for their
copies. This copy was subscribed for by

PROFESSOR WILLIAM B. LONG

....

to whom sincere thanks are expressed

Lou Warwick

....
Lou Warwick

THEATRE UN-ROYAL

Or "THEY CALLED THEM COMEDIANS"

A HISTORY OF THE THEATRE, SOMETIME
ROYAL, MAREFAIR, NORTHAMPTON (1806-84
and 1887)

Written and published

by

LOU WARWICK

Obtainable from the Publisher at 54 St. George's Avenue,
Northampton, and from

C. B. SAVAGE, 99 Kettering Road and 41 St. Giles Street,
Northampton.

W. MARK & CO. (1935) LTD., 27 The Drapery, Northampton.

R. HARRIS & SON, 6 Bridge Street, Northampton.

PREEDY'S, 51a Abington Street, Northampton.

For Greta
&
Nigel

. . . and hopefully dedicated to the idea that history can be serious without being too frightfully solemn

RUNNING ORDER

THE EARLIEST PLAYBILL surviving of the Theatre, Marefair, is this one of 1808 during the brief management of Mr. Mudie, with his company from the Theatre Royal, Windsor. Mr. Richer, the tight rope walker, was the brother-in-law of Mr. Watson, manager of the Cheltenham Company.

(Northampton Public Library)

THE VISUAL REPRESENTATIONS

OVERTURE

. . . AND BEGIN
HERE PLEASE

*The manager of this production makes his most
'umble overtures to his audience and explains how it
all came about through the strenuous urgings of Mr.
Cecil Madden, M.B.E. He also extends his most
respectful thanks to others who have helped to get the
show on the road.*

FIRST
THINGS
FIRST . . .

My very first duty in introducing this theatre book must be to touch fore-lock as humbly as an old-time provincial theatre manager did to the "nobility, gentry and public in general" who formed his audience, and to thank the Patrons who made the book possible.

Indeed that form of address is not inappropriate in the present context for there are members of the "nobility, gentry and public in general" among the subscribers you will find listed at the end of this volume.

Thank you Your Graces Bedford and Buccleuch*; thank you earls, lords, ladies, baronets and sirs; thank you libraries, schools, drama groups and universities; thank you to that man with whom I used to play partner nap Sunday lunchtimes and who also coughed up in advance the necessary sum to help make this book possible; thank you that young lady who used to type my letters and make my tea at work on the Northampton and County Independent and who not only helped with some of the typing for the book but who also, when sales were slow and I was temporarily pessimistic, said she would have one "if it will help".

Thank you one and all. And now, having paid a year or more in advance for your tickets and taken your seats, you are waiting for the curtain to go up, the page to turn, to see whether you must applaud, boo or yawn.

My second duty, therefore, must be to apologise in advance for the short-comings of the production. I do this most humbly, for they arise from the shortcomings of the producer, who does not claim to be God's gift to litera-ture, let alone theatre literature.

I am a provincial journalist who simply chanced to be given the job of doing theatre "crits" because no-one better was available at the time. This was at Northampton Repertory Theatre. From there I was later translated to the local variety house, the New Theatre. When they closed the "New" and pulled it down I thought that it was a stupid and short-sighted thing to do and that the least I could do for the place where I spent so many happy hours was to write a book about it.

How to raise the cash to do so was the problem. I hit upon the idea of employing the old method of patronage. It worked, but not without some

---

* Since this was written, I regret to hear of the death of the Duke of Buccleuch, and, to my knowlededge of five other Patrons, Mr. Wilfrid S. Church, Mr. George Foster, Mr. Ben Harries, Alderman Jim Lewis and Miss Joan Wake.

anxious moments and I resolved at the time never to try it again. It was Cecil Madden, M.B.E., who caused me to break that resolution. After "Death of a Theatre" appeared in 1960 I had persistent letters from him urging me to fill another gap in the town's theatre history. He wanted me to research the early years of the town's Theatre Royal and Opera House (now Repertory Theatre) but somehow I got interested instead in the town's vanished and totally forgotten theatre in Marefair.

Thus it was a case just opposite to that of the New Theatre, where I attempted to ensure that its memory did not fade: in the present instance the story had already been forgotten and to conjure up the people who built it, played in it, lost money in it, gave concerts in it, held religious services in it and made political speeches in it, I had to start from scratch—virtually from the two words "Theatre Royal".

Even when I became so interested that I felt I must carry on and write the story, my ambition was limited to the idea of a few duplicated copies. But Cecil Madden kept urging me to have a go—by letter, we have never met or even spoken on the telephone—until at last I said that if he would send £3 and become the first subscriber, I would have a try. The money came by return of post, late in November, 1972, and I was committed to badgering a further 399 people to trust me with their three quids plus postage.

In setting out on the project I resolved that, apart from the invaluable, indeed vital, monetary co-operation of the Patrons, I would not seek financial assistance elsewhere. The very fact that they were not asked makes me all the more grateful for two sums of £50 which pleasurably surprised me from Northampton Amateur Operatic Company (the letter enclosing their cheque was one of the last charitable acts of the late Mr. Ben Harries, their chairman) and from Northampton Mercury Company (i.e. my "Boss" firm).

There are other people I must thank most sincerely. So many have helped on the factual side that it is not possible to list them all; indeed I do not know many of their names. This particularly applies to those patient and helpful persons who staff our libraries and reference libraries throughout the world. I am especially indebted to Mr. J. A. J. Munro, Northampton's Chief Librarian; Mr. J. B. Stafford, Reference Librarian; Miss Marion Arnold, Local History Librarian; and Mrs. Julia Thornton and Miss Susan Brumhill, Reference Library Assistants. They are all at Northampton and I can only hope that all the others who have helped me, from Bedford, Beds., to Boston, Mass., will mentally add their names to the list.

At the start of his career as an actor, Mr. Brian R. Carter, of Milton Malsor, kindly filled in some hours between auditions in cataloguing for me the British Museum's fine collection of Northampton playbills, of which xeroxes have since been acquired by Northampton Public Library.

But the person I need to thank most for factual assistance is Miss Joan Wake, who was responsible for preserving the "letters in a sack", including theatrical correspondence, which were such a help in writing the Jackman story (from Page 119). It is sad indeed that this remarkable lady died the very day on which I was passing the final proof of this page, requiring me to make the thanks posthumous. Miss Wake, who had the strongest possible sense of history, wrote: "I am so pleased to know that material of real value has turned up in the 76 sacks full of records I found in the solicitor's office 30 or 40 years ago. It is a great satisfaction to see my action bearing fruit in this way." She also left me instructions on what to do with her copy of the book if she died before it came out but added, "Do hurry up—I want to read it." I am so sorry to be too late.

Valuable co-operation in distributing leaflets was given by the Society for Theatre Research and Miss Kathleen Barker, the society's joint secretary, was most helpful with sound advice on sources of information.

For some very speedy proof-reading I am most grateful to Mr. Victor Hatley, Librarian of Northampton College of Technology and College of Art, who kept a special eye open for local history "boobs" (and not in vain!), and to Mr. Harry Greatorex, of Swanwick, Derbyshire, whose field was that of the theatrical history contained in the book (apart, of course, from that newly researched). Special thanks are due to Mr. T. Osborne Robinson, of Northampton Repertory Theatre, for the drawing on Page 33 and to Mr. Bryan J. Douglas for the curtain photographs on Page 227. Mr. Ray Hedley, of Garden City Press Ltd., has been extremely co-operative, giving personal attention and useful advice. So too have Mr. George Hoare and Mr. Robert Hoare, of Hoare and Cole Ltd., who made most of the blocks. Again, as with "Death of a Theatre", the ever-willing Mr. Ken Nutt acted as co-trustee of the cash involved, so that I was at all times unable to abandon the project in favour of a trip abroad.

Nor must I forget to tender my respects to my predecessors, the generations of Northampton journalists through whose writings over 250 years we are enabled to re-enact a past which would otherwise be buried beyond resurrection.

Last but not least I must thank Mrs. Greta Warwick and Master Nigel Warwick for tolerating the not inconsiderable inconveniences of a household where a book is being written...

All the opinions, comments, etc. in this book are my own. Patrons, proof-readers and other helpers do not, of course, necessarily share them.

But I hear a few cat-calls. "Get on with it!" Curtain up, then, on the Theatre Un-Royal...

PROLOGUE

DRAMA THAT SMELLED

...how The Drama "began" in Northampton 250 years ago, for the entertainment of the Quality and diversion of the Gentry. How some of its early roots were bedded in horse manure. Pointing out that Skipping is preferable to Yawning. And explaining why tickets for a Roger Kemble performance came to be on sale at the County Gaol.

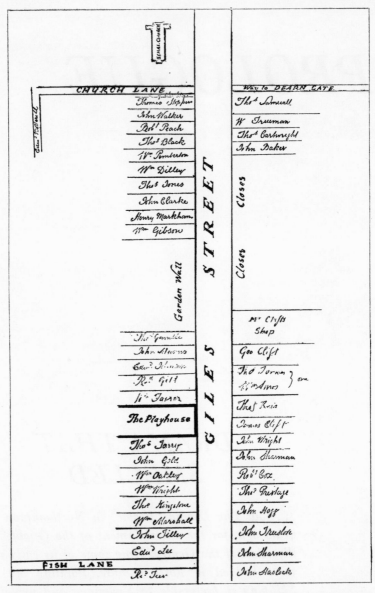

THE SITE of the early theatre—here termed the Playhouse—is shown in the plan drawn by an "election agent" in 1768. See Page 20. (*Northampton Public Library*)

DRAMA THAT SMELLED

Our Theatre Un-Royal died—or rather, faded away—nearly a century ago and for at least fifty years past it has been as unrecollected as the majority of the drama performed in it. It is a forgotten theatre where plays now long forgotten were produced. Likewise the names of nearly all the comedians—that was what they called actors and actresses in the old days—are meaningless to the Northamptonians of 1974.

Yet the building in Marefair was Northampton's theatre for nearly seventy-eight years. If this book serves to make it a little less forgotten; to give it its rightful place in the town's history, however lowly that place may be, it will have achieved its object. A parallel purpose is to do honour in whatever degree they deserve to the thespian fraternity who managed it and performed in it, especially to Old Henry Jackman, whom I have come to know as a close acquaintance, if not a friend, although he died seventy-two years before I was born.

Who was Tom Robertson, whose Lincoln Company opened the theatre and whose name was once a by-word for honesty in theatrical management? Was the sister of Manager Mudie, of Windsor, really a child star or a dwarf with a large family? How was it that Old Henry Jackman came to be buried almost in the centre of Northampton? Was George, the mystery man of the Jackman brood, the odd man out who rebelled against the family tradition of the stage? Why did several managers of the Marefair theatre go bankrupt? Was Chevalier Byron, the only known manager to have thrown a bailiff out of the theatre, an amusing fool or a devious rogue?

These are some of the questions we shall be pondering. Hopefully the answers will not prove uninteresting, not only to that minority of Britons whose hobby is theatriana, but also to the general reader, especially those who are curious about the history of the town in which the theatre was situated.

Criticism may be expected from both camps. The theatre-reader may well contend that there is too much about railways, diaries, over-full grave-yards, toping, incendiary underwear and other apparently extraneous matters; while the Average Northamptonian, if there be such an animal, may mutter as he ploughs through meaningless lists of actors' names and unheard-of plays. If you are firmly in either camp I can only suggest that you take a little exercise, in skipping.

But at least the nature of the questions listed indicates that however much times may have changed, human nature and conflict have altered scarcely at all.

However, the purpose of the Prologue is not to repeat the Overture, but to act as an introduction to the events leading up to the opening of a new theatre in Northampton on Monday, May 5, 1806.

The first printed record of dramatic performances in the town comes almost precisely 250 years ago, in October, 1721, when the Northampton Mercury reported that "for the entertainment of the quality, there will be a play each night at the Talbot Inn by Mr. Toller's Company which now being compleated and made one of the best companies that ever was in the country will continue for some time to perform the most celebrated tragedies and comedies now acted at the theatres in Drury Lane and Lincoln's Inn Fields".

This does not mean that drama suddenly began in Northampton in October, 1721. To take just two instances, there had almost certainly been some form of acted amusement when Richard Coeur de Lion came to Northampton Castle for Easter in 1194 and when Henry III kept the festival of Christmas there in 1218.

Northampton's recorded drama began in 1721 simply because the Northampton Mercury newspaper had been founded the previous year.

In 1723 the paper chronicled the visit of a company including a Mr. Berriman and a Mr. Phipps to the Hind Inn, Northampton, and mentioned their performing *The Spanish Fryar or The Double Discovery* (many pieces had alternative titles) and *Hamlet, Prince of Denmark.*

Four years later the "Comedians from Bath" were in town. They were said to have been expected some time and "are now arrived from the Rt. Hon. the Lord Leigh's (where they had been detained some time) and intend to give our gentry an evening's diversion or two before they go to Banbury Races. There were a vast concourse of people to see their performances at Warwick." Many companies were careful to time their visits to coincide with race meetings, fairs, assizes, etc.

AT the THEATRE at Brixworth, in Northamptonshire, by Mr. JACKSON's Company of Comedians, on Monday, January 23, will be presented

LOVE in a VILLAGE.

In which will be introduced a STATUTE for the HIRING of SERVANTS.
To conclude with a DANCE by the Characters.
To which will be added,

MISS in her TEENS.

On Wednesday, January 25, will be presented,

King RICHARD the Third.

To which will be added,

DAMON and PHILLIDA.

And on Friday, January 27, will be presented,

The WAY to KEEP HIM.

To which will be added,

HOB in the WELL: Or, The COUNTRY-WAKE.

THEATRE IN A BARN? It seems a likely venue for this 1769 performance in the Northamptonshire village of Brixworth. (*Northampton Mercury*)

The following year, 1728, a Company of Comedians from the Theatre Royal itself (Drury Lane) paid a July visit to the town (venue not named) presumably during the summer break in their London engagements. Their selection of pieces included two which could be termed "daring". *The Provok'd Husband* was an eighteenth-century comedy which was recalled in the Northampton Daily Echo in 1922 when it was said that it would certainly not be approved today. In today's today, fifty years later, the wheel of taste and standards has turned again and almost anything goes in entertainment. The second "daring" production was *The Beggar's Opera* with Macheath's

> *"Since laws were made for every degree*
> *To curb vice in others as well as in me*
> *I wonder we've not better company*
> *Upon Tyburn Tree.*
>
> *But gold from law can take out the sting*
> *And if rich men like us were to swing*
> *T'would thin the world such numbers to string*
> *Upon Tyburn Tree."*

. . . daring in another direction, in cocking a snook at dishonesty in high places, especially in government.

In 1729 they paid a return visit and in 1730 there was a company from "both the theatres in London" who played at the Talbot Inn.

The first time that a Northampton building records a claim to being a "playhouse" is in 1735 : "We hear that a company of Comedians from the Theatres in Drury Lane etc. are coming to this place to divert the gentry with their performances this summer and that they have taken the New Playhouse in Abington Street for that purpose." This prior mention is the only one. There are no further advertisements and no reports of the performances.

The old saying about a rose smelling as sweet by any other name applies to playhouses, possibly in reverse. Though the new place was called a "playhouse" it was probably only an inn room with verbal garnish. As Sybil Rosenfeld notes in her *Strolling Players* : "At worst the company tramped with their belongings on their shoulders . . . and the first barn which receives them answers their purpose." The title "playhouse" or "theatre" could cover a multitude of dingy premises.

The year of this first mention of a playhouse in Northampton saw an attempt to put on the Statute Book a law placing all playhouses outside the legal pale, except a couple in London and a few others holding the Royal permission and sanction (or "Patent"). The drama was looked upon as permissive, revolutionary, and a menace to corrupt Government.

When the Bill was considered, one of the few who took the trouble to protest was a country manager named Tony Aston who pointed out that it would be a great loss to the country gentlemen to be deprived of their playhouses. He foretold an outcry from frequenters of marts, fairs, horse

2—TU * *

races, and cock matches who would be robbed of their customary dramatic diversions. "The country now is regularly entertained at great expense with good plays and waggon loads of scenes and adapted habits," he puffed away and forecast that "If all the country actors must promiscuously suffer by this Act I question if there is wood enough in England to hang them all."

The Bill did not become law but after Henry Fielding's *The Historical Register* the following year, a less concealed attack on corruption, a further attempt was made to throttle the playwrights and in 1737 Walpole's infamous Act virtually outlawed all "legitimate" drama, if that is not too contradictory a way of putting it.

On the oath of a credible witness an actor was liable to be adjudged a rogue and vagabond, to be fined and his property distrained upon, and if he had no property, which was more than likely, to be put in gaol with hard labour for up to six months. If the fine was paid, half went to the informer and half to the poor.

This penal legislation might have been expected to put an end to provincial acting, to have dropped a curtain on drama outside the capital and a few other towns, but England being what it is and Englishmen being what they are, this was not the result. It was no more comprehensively effective than the Industrial Relations Act is today. If Britons do not like a law they ignore it as far as possible.

For one thing, as manager Aston had forecast, along with other members of the quality, the country magistrates did not want to be deprived of their amusements; so they normally turned a blind eye in the court; and continued to cast a couple of appreciative eyes in the theatre.

Entirely "legitimate" plays, such as *Macbeth*, which might be bastardised in the eyes of the law if performed as Shakespeare intended, could beat the restrictions by the introduction of half-a-dozen songs, turning the performance into a "burletta".

Or a manager might "give away" the plays, but charge admission for the short musical items given before and after them. If you go to Bedford's Museum, on that town's beautiful embankment, you will find playbills hanging there of around 1780 relating to performances in the "New Theatre, in the George Yard". These were announced as "concerts of vocal and instrumental music" but this was a device for, to take one instance, "between the parts of the concert will be performed (gratis) a comedy call'd 'The Wonder, A Woman Keeps a Secret', also a pantomime interlude".

Not until six years after the Act, December, 1743, did the Abington Street Playhouse announce a further season, in the first theatrical "display" advertisement in the town's history, which included the reassurance "N.B. Great care will be taken to make the house warm and commodious for the reception of the gentlemen and ladies that intend to honour us with their company."

But the previous year came an announcement of the first "significant" playhouse in the town, when, in June, 1742,* "Mr. Jones Company of Comedians from the theatres in London have taken for a playhouse the

* Not 1736 as stated in my previous book, *Death of a Theatre*.

riding house of this town. The place is fitted up to the best advantage in a theatrical manner."

"Fitted Up" is the pertinent phrase. In towns which did not yet boast a permanent theatre, any structures, however lowly or apparently unsuitable, were used. I have mentioned barns and inns (where an assembly room or the inn yard might serve); there were also cowsheds, stables ... and at Northampton it was the riding house. It never does to take the word "Theatre" at its twentieth-century face value, as I did in the case of a Peterborough embankment "theatre" on one occasion, until stopped short by an announcement that the roof had been fitted with a new canvas! This was the booth type of "theatre".

In the case of a riding house, as at Northampton, it may be imagined that all would not be sweetness in the atmosphere as equestrian odours mingled with the smoke of the candles which served for illumination and the odours of the great unwashed in the pit, in days long before under-arm sprays.

In 1756 the Warwick Company of Comedians visited this smelly theatre and one Wednesday night some of the gallery seats fell down. "Providentially," reported the Mercury, "no damage was sustained. They are now so effectually repaired and such due and proper care has been taken to make them safe and firm that no such misfortune need again be feared."

Miss in Her Teens was in the Warwick Company's repertoire, showing that the expression "teens" is not a twentieth-century invention but is over 200 years old.

Seasons were played at this theatre in the Riding House, situated in the Riding, between Abington Street and St. Giles Street, by the Durravan Company of Comedians, who operated on what later crystallised into the Nottingham and Derby Circuit.

In former times the method of publicising performances was to parade, beating a drum, and making announcements and handing out bills at strategic points. In 1764 Durravans announced with dignity, however: "This company use no drum but bills will be properly distributed the day preceding the play." A Mr. Robertson, a name of significance, was then in the company.

Their first season had begun in May, 1762, following which their next call was at Litchfield; they subsequently appeared at Derby from November, 1763, to February, 1764. At Leicester they performed at a theatre on Coal Hill.

When they turned up at Northampton again in May, 1768, it seems evident from their announcement that they would present *The Stratagem* at the New Theatre, St. Gyles Street, that either new premises were being used (which is most likely) or that the old ones had been considerably tarted up, for apart from the usual claims such as that "the house will be fitted up in a more elegant and commodious manner than any Thing of the Kind that has been seen in this town" and "that the house will be lighted in the manner of the London theatres" there was a highly significant change. In addition to the pit and gallery there were now boxes. These were at 3s, with the pit at 2s. and the gallery 1s. It was always a step up the ladder when a theatre boasted boxes, as it then became more attractive to the nobility and gentry.

The question of whether the theatre was in the Riding or St. Gyles (or St. Giles) Street is complicated by the fact that these streets are parallel and only a few yards apart.

We are indebted to a political source for a street guide which seems clearly to place the theatre in St. Giles Street in 1768. This was the year of an election which was the most notable, or notorious, in the history of a town which has had much political tumult. That year the Earl Spencer and the Earls of Northampton and Halifax are said to have spent a quarter of a million pounds on "election expenses". Earl Spencer is said to have thrown in the contents of his cellar. The result strained the finances of all three families.

The Whigs were led at this election by Edward Bouverie, of Delapre Abbey, where the "letters in a sack" which are part of the properties of Act Two are now stored. The house is now a repository of historical records.

To aid in the battle to capture the voters of 1768, someone in charge of polling them drew up a street map to show where they were to be found. The theatre is clearly shown, not because a vote was to be had there but as a point of identification.

In his "Rambles Roundabout" written in 1866, George De Wilde, editor of the Northampton Mercury from 1830–71, noted: "The Playhouse occupied the site of the houses opposite Castilian Street. It had been a malting and had been newly adapted for the purposes of the children of Thespis."

From the Durravan Company season in Northampton of 1771 there survives a record of a speech of thanks made by Mrs. Glocester on June 2 during the benefit night for her and her husband. It is a fair reflection of the deferential attitude of those on stage to their betters in the seats, more especially in the boxes :

> *"When I look round this crowded house and see*
> *Each generous heart that appears for me*
> *Who by their presence striving to abate*
> *The unpleasing rigours of a Wanderer's Fate*
> *Heavens how I feel! My grateful soul would pay*
> *In more than words the Favors of this day*
> *To you (the gallery) and you (the pit) and chiefly YOU (Mrs.*
> *   Thursby's box) my friends*
> *I humbly bow—you've gained your generous ends*
> *You always strive in every different part*
> *By well tim'd praise t'assure my doubting heart*
> *You strove at last nor here you strive in vain*
> *To fill an empty purse quite full again*
> *We'll fear no more th'imperious Landlord's frown*
> *But pass with cheerful heart from Town to Town*
> *And yet believe me ladies from this place*
> *I cannot go but with a lingering pace*

With you my grateful heart would still reside
Regardless of its interest or pride
But duty calls, my Husband's strict command
Bids me away to Shakespear's native land
And we poor folks in spite of all our wit
Must to our husbands, yes we must submit
To Rank alone, the Privilege is given
To break that vow that's registered in Heaven
This world's a stage; to different scenes I go
Unconscious if they lead to joy or woe
Ah should I meet the critic's surly rage
How should I sigh for this good natur'd stage
Where o'er my faults a friendly curtain's thrown
And I am praised for merits not my own
Yet let me boast that free, quite free from Art
I've one perfection—'tis a grateful heart."

That season appears also to have been a farewell for the Durravans, though not for all the actors who comprised their company.

Mrs. Carleton, who came with her husband's company in 1772 and 1773, appears to have been a remarkable lady. After playing some favourite tunes on the "much admired musical glasses" she took to the slack wire. She was, it was claimed, "The admiration of all London being the first female that ever attempted the wire." She was not content merely to walk and balance upon it but would also "play upon the violin, the tabor and pipe, the guittar, toss the balls, and beat a set of trevailles on the drum, all standing with one leg upon the wire".

Next came Roger Kemble, head of the famous theatrical family, who announced that he had long wished for the opportunity of entertaining the town and "flatters himself that his performers will not only appear respectable ON the stage but will prove themselves an ornament to the profession OFF".

For their seasons, Mr. and Mrs. Kemble took a house near St. Giles Square. Of the other members of the company Mr. Smith, prompter, and Master Smith lodged at Mr. Cliff's in Abington Street, Mr. and Mrs. Sidney at the Black Lion Inn, lower down St. Giles Street, an inn still surviving today and where the ghosts of some of these old actors are said to appear on occasion. The Kembles ran seasons in 1774, 1778 (when you could for one night book seats at the County Gaol, this being a benefit night for debtors in prison) and 1781. Their 1778 season included the farce *All the World's a Stage* by Isaac Jackman, about which more later.

For a brief period in 1787 Northampton had another fit-up theatre. It was because he was unable, for reason unstated, to secure the use of the St. Giles Street house that Signior Scaliogni improvised at Mr. Joshua Stevenson's large warehouse in Church Lane, alongside the ancient round church of the Holy Sepulchre, to present his "celebrated exhibition of dancing dogs", along with a comic performance by Mr. Saunders, of the Theatre,

Sadlers Wells, Paris and Edinburgh, a comic opera, rope dancing, a pantomime and the slackwire—all in the same bill!

Later that year Mr. Pero, who had now assumed control of the Nottingham and Derby Company, ran a season at St. Giles Street from July to October including a pantomime in which Harlequin leaped through "a hogshead of real fire".

Partial relief from the legal restrictions on the theatre came in 1788 with an Act empowering magistrates to license theatrical presentations in the provinces for sixty days at a time, though no second licence was to be granted until eight months had elapsed after the first nor to any place within the same jurisdiction within six months. There were up till this time a mere handful of "legal" theatres, in the provinces, those which had been granted Royal patents.

The Pero Company were back in 1790, announcing that their May–June season could last only three weeks because they had to move on to Stamford on June 22. A Mr. Robertson was in the company.

Then came two seasons by Mr. Beynon's Company. That of 1793 lasted an extraordinary and apparently illegal length from June 17 to the following January, even allowing for a break from July 31 to September 19, during a summer so hot that many post horses expired on the road. In 1796, Mr. Palmer of Drury Lane was a guest with the Beynon Company.

That really is the end of the Prologue. But we cannot end in such a tame manner. To do so would be an anti-climax, something never to be permitted in matters theatrical.

It is a bold man who tries to sum up seventy years of a nation's history in a 100-word paragraph but about the period we are now concerned with a valiant attempt has been made by Professor Harold Perkins in his *Origins of Modern English Society, 1780 to 1880*, published in 1969.

He wrote as follows: "Between 1780 and 1850 the English ceased to be one of the most aggressive, brutal, rowdy, outspoken, riotous, cruel and bloodthirsty nations in the world and became one of the most inhibited, polite, orderly, tender-minded, prudish, hypocritical. The transformation diminished cruelty to animals, criminals, lunatics, and children (in that order), rid the penal code of 200 capital offences, abolished transportation, and cleaned up the prisons, turned Sunday into a day of prayer for some and mortification for others; bowdlerised Shakespeare, Gibbon, and other obscene classics and *almost gave a death blow to the English stage*."

ACT
THE
FIRST

THE EARLY YEARS

... in which the Northampton stage is taken successively by Mr. Tom Robertson, of the Lincoln Circuit; Mr. Mudie and his little sister, from Windsor; Mr. J. Simms, of Birmingham and Manchester; that Napoleon of the drama, Mr. Robert William Elliston; Mr. Francis Raymond, who took his company thence to open a new theatre at Stratford-upon-Avon; Mr. Stewart, of Bath; Messrs. Parry and Hamilton; Mr. Scott; and the enterprising Mr. Simpson, later of Birmingham fame.

THE FIRST advertisement for the Marefair Theatre (*Northampton Mercury*)

Scene One

THE MAN FROM LINCOLN

Into the picture of Northampton theatre there stepped next the notable company of the Lincoln Circuit, managed by Mr. Thomas Shaftoe Robertson and Mr. Robert Henry Franklin, who were adding Northampton to a tour which included Lincoln, Newark, Boston, Grantham, Wisbeach (as it was then spelt), Huntingdon, Peterborough and Spalding.

Robertson and Franklin made a happy team, which had not always been the case with Lincoln Company partnerships. When Robertson's widowed mother had handed over her interest in the circuit to him as a coming-of-age present, the other manager, with a two-thirds share, was a Mr. Miller.

"This partnership of Miller and Robertson lasted a stormy ten or twelve years," recalled Robertson in a letter from Newark on December 1, 1803, "during which time such frequent dissensions arose that it became necessary to separate". It was as a result of the rows between the two that the company "lost" Lynn (Kings Lynn) where they had performed for nearly forty years. The magistrates of Lynn decided to give the licence instead to the Norwich Company. In place of Lynn, Huntingdon was substituted in the Lincoln tour. Miller sold his two shares to Robertson for £1,200 and he in turn sold a half of the property to Mr. Franklin for £900.

The result was gratifying. "Robertson and Franklin" was noted for its unanimity and understanding—Miller and Robertson for the contrary.

Perhaps it was because Franklin was a "gentleman" that he was so easy to get on with. Son of a Sheriff of County Limerick, Ireland, and a member of a landed family, he had been a classical student at Trinity College, Dublin, before feeling the call of the stage, on which he proved a capable and versatile performer.

A word or two about the prior history of the "Lincoln" would not be out of place, though I do not propose to set down all the material I have available in view of the fact that Squadron-Leader John Richards, of Oakham, is researching the Circuit for a thesis and therefore its full ascertainable history will emerge later.

The founder of the company in about 1750 was a Dr. Herbert, who was so absent-minded that when fighting a duel on stage he was known to forget which combatant was to succumb. On one recorded occasion he "died" in error, only to be reminded stridently by his wife, presumably from the wings, "Curse your old soul, it's the child that's to die, not you!" Herbert got up, re-fought the duel and was this time the victor, to the ironic cheers of the audience.

Those who took part in the subsequent management of the circuit included that great character James Augustus (Jemmy) Whitely, about whom there is a fund of tales to be told, but no room to tell them here. One of his claims to fame was the authorship of a book of bawdy songs, so outrageous that after his death on September 13, 1781, his relatives went round buying up the copies to restore the family reputation.

It was Jemmy Whitely who introduced a Robertson into the Lincoln. Whitely found he had too much on his plate, being involved also in the management of the Nottingham and Derby Circuit which at various times embraced Derby, Worcester, Nottingham, Wolverhampton, Retford, and Stamford. It must be remembered that the itinerary was not fixed, but could be added to or changed according to circumstances.

As his deputy on the Lincoln Circuit, Whitely introduced James Shaftoe Robertson, who afterwards bought Jemmy's share. Robertson's family hailed originally from Perthshire, Scotland, but his father became a senior servant of Lord Clive or Lord Powis in the area of Ludlow, where James was born, probably in 1723. He went to Ludlow Grammar School, but ran away at seventeen to go on the stage. While acting at Loughborough, he married Miss Ann Fowler. The three children of the marriage were Thomas Shaftoe; James, who became a manager on the Nottingham and Derby Circuit; and George, who became a printer and stationer at Peterborough.

Six or eight weeks after his birth at Alford, Lincs, Tom Robertson was riding in a hand basket carried by his mother, behind his father, on a horse the twenty-eight miles to the season at Boston, sleeping all the way.

Throughout life he had the Churchillian knack of dropping off for a snooze at any odd moment. This led to an alarming happening when, as a six-year-old fairy in a pantomime at Lynn, he had to ascend to the top of the house, in a chariot where, once up in the air he had to remain until the end of the show.

"Feeling myself easy and comfortable I fell asleep," he later recalled. "Had I by any accident overbalanced myself I must have fallen out and inevitably been dashed to pieces as the height was considerable. The performance being over the sceneman forgot to wind me down and I was left. At supper my father and mother, missing me, supposed I was in bed but on inquiry found I was not and their agitation and consternation was wound up to the highest pitch by recollecting that I was certainly left in the chariot. In this distress my father immediately went to the stagekeeper's lodgings, called him out of bed, took a lanthorn to the theatre. In fear and despair I might have fallen out, with trembling steps he approached the stage but was relieved by not seeing me and by the hope I was in the chariot. He got to the crank and slowly let me down and found me fast as a church.

"Being of a rather passionate nature he directly knocked me out of the chariot which awakened me and brought me to my senses. . . . I shew'd an early inclination to sleep and even in my maturer years have never been noted for wakeful sprightliness."

In later years tribute was paid to Robertson by the actor F. C. Wemyss, who crops up later in the book, but who is here quoted for his opinion of a manager who was also a friend : "Mr. Robertson was regarded more like the father of a family than the director of a theatre : and were I asked, to point out a strict and justly honest man, Mr. Thomas Robertson, the Lincoln manager, would be that man."

Wemyss gave an insight into the manager's honest dealings with his actors. "It was a rule with him that all forfeiture of salary, for neglect, belonged to the actors and should on no account be allowed to find its way into the manager's pocket. The forfeits, therefore, were cheerfully paid and a fund created from which actors in distress were occasionally relieved and from which members of the company derived a source of gratification and social intercourse—a supper being given regularly each year." If the fund was insufficient the manager dipped into his own pocket.

Fines were imposed under a set of rules which varied from company to company. One regulation charged 2s. 6d. for an actor's dog being on stage during rehearsal; if during a performance, twice as much. Wearing stage costume (if it belonged to the company) out of the theatre was also subject to a fine. Some managers were far less honest than Robertson, using their authority to levy fines as a second source of income.

Mrs. Robertson also came in for praise from Wemyss. A pregnant remark about her is made in the memoirs of Fred Belton who says she was a fine actress of the Siddonian School and, "When asked why she preferred the provinces her lofty reply was 'I would rather reign in Hell than serve in Heaven'." She was the former Miss Frances Ross, daughter of Mrs. Brown, who had appeared at the Theatre Royal, Covent Garden, and whose style of acting was said to have set a pattern for the famed Royal mistress, Mrs. Dorothy Jordan. The marriage took place a few years after Robertson's mother had handed him her share in the company.

Robertson wrote with great affection of his wife : "It has been observed that a superior genius for the stage is hereditary in the family of Mrs. Brown. Mrs. T. Robertson is well-known to possess that genius in an extraordinary degree and being the wife of the manager of the circuit is the only tie that occasions her continuance in a provincial theatre. The Lincoln Circuit never had such an actress and to her talents and exertions the Circuit has arisen to a fame it never before possessed."

The arrivals of the Robertsons at Newark were watched as a young boy by Belton who became an actor himself and in 1880 wrote these *Random Recollections of an Old Actor*.

"Crowds gathered and I was on all possible occasions one of the number. Great was the excitement when the waggon was unpacked. A wooden gate made of laths, but looking like a real wooden gate, appeared. This gate was indispensable, being used in a then popular piece called 'The Turnpike Gate'. But wonders reached their climax when we gazed upon a 'real' horse which turned out to be a small pony used by Mrs. Robertson in a piece called 'Queen Elizabeth'. Young as I was I pitied the poor beast when

I saw it at night on the stage with Mrs. Robertson's portly figure in long train, feathers and furbelows. The prettiest sight was the appearance of Mr. Robertson's son as the youthful page who held the 'untamed fiery steed'."

As the time referred to is early nineteenth century Belton's memory or knowledge of the Robertson family tree appears to be at fault here for to the best of my knowledge Mr. and Mrs. Tom Robertson had no children.

A custom of free admission which I have not found referred to anywhere else—"In those days a free night was given to the public and called a house-warming"—is referred to by Belton who also gives an indication of one of the possible reasons why Shakespeare figured on the programmes : "In 'Hamlet' the low comedian threw off the traditional three-and-twenty waistcoats before he commenced to dig Ophelia's grave which caused immoderate laughter as each phase of the waistcoating pattern was more grotesquely developed than its predecessors."

Belton also records a Shakespearian scene in which humour figured unexpectedly. It has nothing whatever to do with the Robertsons as it concerned the company of a manager named Beverley; it is not linked with Newark or Northampton, taking place as far away as Wigan, in Lancashire. It has not the slenderest claim to be recounted for relevance, but having found a good story, I must tell it, rather like some comedians I have known.

"Those were the days. We laugh when we see Hogarth's picture of the strolling players but many things not 50 years ago have been enacted as ludicrous. In Wigan, a little town, the juvenile leading lady, a good actress and a very pretty woman and a young mother was cast to play Juliet. Her baby had been placed in the dressing room for security but just before the balcony scene the young tyrant became unruly and a mother's tact hit upon a soothing syrup. She nestled the infant to her breast and from that moment the young villain became silent as a mouse. Being called she hastily mounted the rostrum that supported the supposed balcony throwing a lace scarf over her shoulders, which concealed the little suckling; and leaning over the balcony with her other arm pensively placed upon her cheek she looked the picture of innocence and beauty. The scene opened and went glowingly. But Alas! Juliet has to appear and disappear three times and in her effort to do so gracefully she stumbled against the iron brace that held up the frail structure. Down fell the balcony and lo! the love-lorn maiden was discovered with a baby at her breast—seated on a tub that served for a stool. At her foot, accidentally placed there by a thirsty carpenter, was a quart pot; the said carpenter was discovered on all fours, steadying with his back the rickety structure above. Shrieks of laughter from all parts of the house greeted the tableau and of the play no more was heard that night."

All Belton's recollections here are in the section of his book covering the years 1815–22.

Time now to return from the Recollections Circuit which has taken us rather far away from Northampton and get back to the Lincoln Company's entry into Northampton.

The first "Lincoln" season at Northampton was at the Old Theatre in St. Giles Street and began on Thursday, April 25, 1799, with *Everyone has his Fault* and *The Agreeable Surprize*. Later came *The Castle Spectre*, with which the company were to open the new theatre seven years later, *The Stranger*, *Lover's Vows*, *Heir at Law*, *He's Much to Blame*, *Secrets Worth Knowing*, *False and True*, *Laugh When You Can*, *The Jew and the Doctor*, *Botheration*, *The Secret*, *The Will*, *The Poor Soldier*, *The Way to Get Married* and *The Sultan*.

What's that you say? Never heard of them? That's just the point. Little of the drama then being written or produced has survived. It is as lost an era, artistically speaking, as if it never existed.

There were only three advertisements during the season, which ended on Thursday, June 6, apart from the customary farewell one : "The managers return their most sincere acknowledgments to the Ladies and Gentlemen of Northampton and the public at large not only for the support the theatre has been honoured with but for the politeness and candour they have so universally met with during the season and they beg leave to add that it shall always continue to be equally as it is at present their unremitting study to merit the patronage of a public to whom they are bound by the warmest gratitude and the most heartfelt respect."

You had to know your place in those days and an actor's was well down the social scale.

In April, 1800, the company were back for a further six weeks season with a number of the same plays and a few more you may never have heard of : *Pizzaro*, *Little Bob and Little Ben*, *The Birth-Day*, *The Neglected Daughter*, *Ways and Means*, *The Prize*, *The Deaf Lover*, *The Romp*, *Wives as They Were and Maids as They Are*, *The Irishman in London*, *The Wise Men of The East*, *No Song No Supper*, *Speed the Plough*, *Fortune's Frolicks*. And there were *The School for Scandal*, *The Rivals* and *Macbeth*.

During the first season, only the managers had been named in the newspaper advertisements (no playbills survive) but during the second season company members named included Messrs. Brown, Twiddy, Cooper, Wright, Rutley, Evans, Walcot, Messrs. Stanari and Tilliard (musicians), Mr. and Mrs. Tuthill, Mr. and Mrs. Elliott, Mrs. Kendall, Miss Chapman, Miss Bullen, and of course Mrs. Robertson, the manager's wife.

Robertson and Franklin were still the managers at the time of the Northampton season of 1802, from April 26 to June 7, and one of the company members was a Mr. J. Franklin, presumably the co-manager's son. Other players not mentioned two years earlier were Mrs. Brunton, Mr. and Mrs. Clarke, Mr. Stanley, Mr. and Mrs. Mason and Mr. and Mrs. Wilde.

Usually the last night of the season was reserved for the benefit of the manager or when there were two, the senior manager. Thus it was usually Mr. Robertson's prerogative. But the last night of 1802—it was *The Winter's Tale* with Mr. Robertson as Leontes—was for Mr. Franklin. It was to be the very last Northampton benefit night for him, because at Peterborough aged but thirty-two, he "paid the debt of nature", as his partner picturesquely recorded his death. In 1803 there was no theatrical season at Northampton though there were plays at Wellingborough, at what was described as the New Theatre, by Mr. Lacy, from the Theatres Royal, London, lasting apparently from the beginning of May to mid-June; and

at Daventry, Northants, earlier in the year, when the theatre was burnt to
the ground, as I shall mention later.

John Bull or An Englishman's Fireside opened the Northampton
Lincoln season of 1804, with Mr. Robertson as sole manager. Tickets and
places for the boxes for what was to be the last season at the Old Theatre
were to be taken of Mr. Wright (presumably the before mentioned member
of the company, and probably the treasurer) at Mr. Parbery's, Upholsterer,
in Abington Street.

There were three Shakespearean choices that year, *As You Like It* on
May 7, *Hamlet* on June 1 and *Romeo and Juliet* on June 9.

The audience probably did not realise that *Romeo and Juliet* was the
very last play to be performed in the Old Theatre, or Playhouse, in St.
Giles Street, for it was not until the following December 8 that the Mercury
carried an advertisement seeking support for the new theatre project.

But on the last but one night of the 1804 season Robertson wrote a letter
to a theatrical friend named Winston who was compiling material about,
and drawings of provincial theatres, for publication in monthly instalments
under the title of *Theatric Tourist*. The letter to Winston, datelined
"Theatre, Northampton, June 1804" which is reproduced in part (four
lines have been deleted), contains the following:

"Inclosed with this I have sent you drawings of Huntingdon and Newark
Theatres. . . . I was in hopes to have sent you at the same time a drawing
of Peterborough Theatre but that is not yet done. I shall be there on Sunday
as we finish here tomorrow and commence our season at Peterborough on
Tuesday . . . I hope the publication answers your expectations. . . . I am in a
great bustle from being the close of our campaign here. Northampton
Theatre is so bad a building that a drawing of it would disgrace a publication. Next season I shall open a new theatre." (*Page 35.*)

Now we know why Northampton needed a new theatre—the old one was
a disgrace. The advertisement for the new theatre project which appeared
on December 8, 1804, said that it was being undertaken because "complaints
had long been made of the want of a proper theatre in the town". This was
six months after Robertson wrote his letter so he evidently had foreknow-
ledge of the scheme, which was put forward by Robert Abbey, one of the
Coroners for the County, who had also supervised the old theatre.

Besides making uncomplimentary remarks to Winston about the
Northampton Theatre, Tom Robertson also sent to him further details of
it and, of other theatres of the Lincoln Circuit.

From Newark on December 1, 1803, he supplied facts about all the
theatres:

NORTHAMPTON: "Still remains as it has been for many years
temporary. When full contains upwards of £30, situated in St. Giles Street.
The season six weeks commencing in May every second year."

LINCOLN: "Has been built upwards of 40 years and has undergone
very little improvement. It is situated in the Kings Arms Inn yard. Will
hold between £60 and £70. The season commences in the Race Week in the
beginning of September and continues two months."

NEWARK: "Was in its first state temporary where the Methodist

Chapel now is in Balderden Gate, only pit and gallery. About 30 years back a new theatre was built by the late Job Brough Esq. with front boxes and which at several times underwent alterations. This year it has undergone a total alteration and enlargement—circular boxes, upper and lower, and allowed to be a most handsome and elegant provincial theatre. It is situated in Middlegate, calculated to contain when filled between £60 and £70. The season six weeks commencing in November."

GRANTHAM : "In its first state was a rude temporary building of pit and gallery in Westgate. Thirty years back a more convenient one was built in the Market Place but no boxes. Ten years back front boxes were added. In 1800(?) the lease being out a handsome new theatre with circular upper and lower boxes was built by Joseph Lawrence. It is situated at the bottom of (blank). When full will contain about £50. Season five weeks commencing in December."

BOSTON : "Was a temporary pit and gallery in a granary in the Market Place. Twenty-six years ago one was built by the Corporation within a few yards of the old temporary one and at that time esteemed handsome, having front boxes but being found for several years past much too small for its improving spirits and population a new one on the most improved plan is about being built by subscription. The present theatre, when filled to inconvenience, will hold about £40. Season six weeks commencing latter end of January."

WISBEACH : "Was for several years at the end of the town on the road to Spalding and from its inconvenient situation when the lease was out about ten or twelve years back a new one was built in the centre of the town at the back of York Row, the property of Mr. Robertson. When full it will hold upwards of £40. The season six weeks commencing in March."

HUNTINGDON : "Was for many years temporary in a barn. Four years back an elegant theatre at the back of the George Inn was built by subscription with lower and upper boxes, planned by Mr. Rowles, nephew to Mr. Holland, the architect of Drury Lane. When filled will contain about £50. The Lincoln Co. attends the Race Week and every second year."

PETERBOROUGH : "Was for many years pit and gallery noted for being dirty and inconvenient. A handsome commodious theatre was built four years back by subscription within a few yards of the old one. Contains when full about £50. Season seven weeks commencing in June."

SPALDING : "Is on the same ground that it has been for upwards of 40 years. It has undergone various alterations. Ten years ago boxes were added. It is in the White Hart Inn Yard. When full upwards of £40. Season one month commencing August."

Mr. Robertson added that prices through his circuit were boxes 3s.; pit 2s.; gallery 1s. Half-price, for admission to the latter part of the evening, was taken at every town.

From Grantham on January 9, 1805, he told Winston that the engraving of the theatre there had been a good deal admired—"I have put it in the stationer's window and showed it to some principal people. They all like it, but confound them, they haven't the spirit to order any numbers. I hope that other parts of my circuit will patronise the work a little better."

Alas, it was the same story not only throughout the circuit but throughout the country. Not enough people supported Winston's valiant and imaginative effort to put on the record all the provincial theatres of the country (except those that were too disgraceful!) and after eight monthly issues with twenty-four pictures of theatres the series came to an end. Notes for some of the unpublished numbers survive. From the *Theatric Tourist* comes the picture of the Theatre Royal, Windsor, which is reproduced on Page 37, as the home theatre of Robertson's successor at Northampton.

There was similarly luke-warm support for the new theatre project at Northampton. The sum of £1,500 was needed, in sixty shares of £25, and at first the idea was to have a tontine, a system by which the survivor takes all, but some did not like this idea and in the end a normal share system was substituted.

Even so on March 23, 1805, Robert Abbey had to issue an ultimatum that as a number of people had not come forward with their promised payments, "unless the subscription is completed by the sixth day of April the design will be wholly given up and the premises immediately appropriated to other purposes". Evidently the impasse was avoided because on May 25 tenders were invited for erecting the theatre.

Meetings to formulate the plans were held at The George Hotel, atop Bridge Street and opposite All Saints Church. The first had been on January 16, 1805, and others followed to wrangle over the details. Shareholders were to have an absolute right, transferable, with a free admission ticket to the boxes for every £25 share. Abbey told them that a "handsome rent" had been agreed with the manager.

Abbey was evidently a very keen theatre-goer. An Attorney-at-Law, he had been a Coroner since February, 1782, succeeding W. Jackson on his death. In November, 1794, Abbey was a member of a committee set up to assist in recruiting a somewhat curious military formation—a regiment of "Fencible Infantry". With Major John Kerr as their Commanding Officer they were to be 1,000 strong and to serve only in Great Britain and the Channel Islands. In fact they were given the same thankless task that the British Army has in Northern Ireland today—of keeping the factions apart and struggling to keep an uneasy peace. Ten companies were posted to Armagh. The Militant Catholics of that day called themselves "The Defenders" while the extremist Protestants were the "Peep O' Day Boys". Both indulged nightly in murder, rape and arson. The Fencibles were there at the time of the Irish Rebellion of 1798. [Major Kerr, a son of the eminent physician Dr. Kerr, later became a general.]

We know that Robert Abbey was a horseman (indeed, who of the quality would not be in those days—being in the saddle would be just as normal to them as being at the wheel of a Rover 2000 today) because in December, 1794, his servant William Stanton had an accident while exercising Abbey's horse—"He imprudently rode him over a hedge near Wootton when, owing to the slipperiness of the ground, the horse fell with him and his foot being entangled in the stirrup he was dragged a considerable distance and so dreadfully mangled that he was taken up speechless and expired in a few minutes." Presumably Abbey had to sit at the inquest on his own servant.

INTERIOR of the Theatre, Marefair, drawn by Osborne Robinson, specially for this book. It is a "conception" as no pictures survive of the theatre. The scene is from "The Castle Spectre" on the opening night May 5, 1806. See pages 33–4.

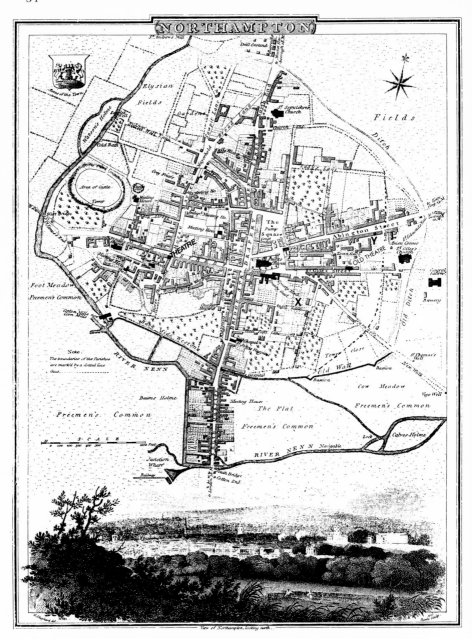

THE MAREFAIR THEATRE is marked "Theatre" on this map of Northampton at the time it was built, succeeding the St. Giles Street Playhouse, indicated here as "Old Theatre". "X" marks the site of the future Theatre Royal and Opera House (built in 1884) and "Y" of the future New Theatre (1912-60).

THE LETTER (opposite) was written on the last day but one of performances at the Old Theatre. See Page 30. (*Lincoln Public Library*)

Sir

Inclosed with this I have sent you Drawings of Huntingdon & Newark Theatres — I am ashamed that I have been so long a time in procuring them, but it is owing to the Negligence of the Draughtsmen — I sent them repeatedly Letters & at last I have received them — I was in hopes to have sent you at the same time a Drawing of Peterbro Theatre, but that is not yet done — I shall be there on Sunday — as we finish here tomorrow & commence our Season at Peterbro on Tuesday — & being on the Spot I'll take care that it shall be completed — I have not order'd any more Numbers than that which you sent me at Wisbeach — therefore if you please to be so good to direct any of your Booksellers to send me the remainder of the Numbers that are out directed to me Theatre Peterbro Northamptonshire I hope the Publication answers your Expectations & with my sincere wishes for its success

I am Dr Sir
Yours
T. Robertson

Theatre Northampton
June 14th 1804

I am in a great bustle being the Close of our Campaign here —
Northampton Theatre is so bad a Building that a Drawing of it would disgrace a Publication — Next Season I shall open a new Theatre —

ST. JOHN'S HOSPITAL, subject of an ancient charity and pictured here in the early 19th Century, owned the site of the Marefair Theatre. (*Northampton Public Library*)

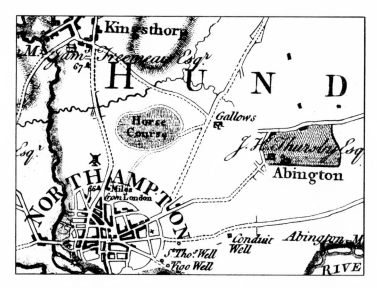

A MAP OF THE NORTHAMPTON AREA at the time the Marefair Theatre was opened. Note the site of the Gallows near the Horse Course (now the Racecourse). Executions took place there until 1818. See Page 68. (*Northampton Public Library*)

THE THEATRE ROYAL, WINDSOR, a true "Royal theatre" (i.e. holding the Royal patent) from which came Mr. Mudie, second manager of the Northampton Theatre. The picture is from Winston's "Theatric Tourist". (*British Museum*)

CHARLES MATHEWS in the role of Somno in "The Sleepwalker" in which he appeared at Northampton in 1815. See Page 60. (*National Theatre*)

THRAPSTON, 1813, Playbill of a season by J. Simms, then manager of the Northampton Theatre. See Page 57. (*Photo by Cyril E. Diamond*)

R. W. ELLISTON, lessee of the Theatre Royal, Drury Lane, and of the Northampton Theatre from 1818–21. The engraving is from a portrait by Samuel De Wilde, the theatrical artist, who was the father of George James De Wilde, editor of the Northampton Mercury from 1830 to 1871. (*Picture by courtesy of Harry Greatorex*)

MADAME TUSSAUD
brought figures of the French
Royal Family, who died by
guillotine, to Northampton in
1824. See Pages 81–2. (*From
pastel by George Fisher*)

SULBY HALL, one-time home of George Payne, the great gambler, was the childhood home of Northampton's former M.P., Mr. R. T. Paget. The drawing is by George Clarke. The hall, which is now demolished, was pictured on a back-drop scene when George Payne was in the theatre audience in 1833. See Pages 102–3. (*Northamptonshire Record Office*)

IRA ALDRIDGE, the "African Roscius", appeared at Northampton in 1831 and 1846. See Page 99.

EDMUND KEAN, seen here as Sir Giles Overreach in "A New Way to Pay Old Debts", was brought to Northampton by Elliston in 1820. (*Enthoven Collection*)

The design for the new theatre decided on by Abbey and the share-holders sounded quite splendid—"on the lines of London's Haymarket Theatre". There were to be two tiers of boxes, a pit and a gallery. It is the statistic for the pit which gives the game away as to how small it was to be—"a pit with 12 rows of benches covered with matting".

Tip-up upholstered seats were far into the future, of course, but for a mind's eye view of the size of the auditorium imagine twelve backless park benches set fairly closely one behind the other. This was the size of the floor area from stage to centre boxes. It should also be added that boxes then were not what they are today but were of larger size and accommodating a mixture of people.

Looking at the site now—the theatre was where the widened Horseshoe Street now runs—it is difficult to see how any sort of theatre at all could be perched upon that tiny site. In this respect, however, it must be borne in mind that the street itself was exceedingly narrow compared with modern streets. See the road plan which is reproduced to confirm this. It was, indeed, originally called Crow and Horseshoe *Lane*. (*Page 232*.)

But whatever the limitations inside, it is clear that the promoters could have done more to gild the lily by at least having an attractive exterior. Northampton's new theatre must have been just about the plainest in the country, skimped for cheapness. No pictures survive of it in use as a theatre, only of it in its latter days as shop premises. One is tempted to ask why George Clarke, the Northamptonshire man who drew so many streets and corners, mansions and market places, buildings and squares, did not sketch this particular corner. The question is on reflection self-answering; it just was not an attractive thing to put on paper. They were not yet calling it the Theatre Royal, but un-royal it certainly was.

Even within its limitations it must have been a vast improvement on the old "disgraceful" theatre, or it would not have been undertaken. It has also to be remembered that all things are relative and times change. What one generation considers a luxury the next finds run-of-the-mill and the generation after that intolerable. One age considers a good well of water in the garden a real amenity; the next demands water on tap; the third requires hot and cold water; while the great-grandchildren demand bathrooms in duplicate with shower rooms and bidets. By present day standards the Theatre Royal and Opera House in Guildhall Road (better known as the Repertory Theatre) is bijou but when it was erected in 1884 to replace the Marefair theatre it was looked upon as spacious, by comparison.

So the theatre project went forward. Between its mooting and completion one of the most famous naval battles in British history took place. On November 9, 1805, the Mercury reported: "Providence has blessed His Majesty's Navy with a most signal victory over the Combined Fleets of our enemies but it has been thought fit to chasten our exultation by depriving us of a man whose very name was a tower of strength—Admiral Lord Nelson was killed in action." The funeral of the hero of Trafalgar was to be re-enacted ad nauseam on the stage of the Northampton theatre, as of others throughout the country. The opening night was May 5, 1806, and the play *The Castle Spectre*.

Mr. Robertson's Lincoln Company had some 7,000 Northamptonians from whom an audience could be drawn, not to mention the rural area around the town, including a number of country seats of noblemen and gentry whose support theatre managers were always desperately keen and obsequious to obtain.

A reference to the street map reproduced, of 1807, gives an idea where the theatre was situated with regard to what was then little more than an overgrown village, where most people knew each other and the common people scarcely ever left the town to see what lay beyond.

The theatre stood on the corner of Marefair and Crow and Horseshoe Lane, about mid-way between the central and focal church of All Saints, rebuilt after the Dreadful Fire of Northampton in 1675 which had wiped out most of the town, and the site of the former Northampton Castle, where Thomas Becket, Archbishop of Canterbury, had stood trial in 1166. Another notable building within sight of it was the Church of the Holy Sepulchre. One of the four round churches left in England, it was built by Simon de Senlis in the twelfth century as a thank-offering for his return from the Crusades.

The town was a very tiny place compared with the Northampton of today, which has a population of 130,000. But it was on the verge of a population explosion as is the town of today. The nineteenth century saw Northampton grow twelve-fold in population, from 7,020 in 1801 to 87,021 in 1901. When the theatre opened in 1806 there were about 7,700 in the borough. This grew as follows: 8,427 in 1811; 10,793 in 1821; 15,349 in 1831; 21,242 in 1841; 26,657 in 1851; 32,813 in 1861; 41,168 in 1871; and 51,881 in 1881.

Thus the theatre of 1884, when it closed, had about 53,000 Northamptonians from whom it could draw its audiences—seven times as many as when it opened. This nineteenth-century growth was a "natural" one, resulting from the efforts of builders, building societies and people wishing to live in more airy and pleasant surroundings, whereas today's Expansion is a forced, artificial growth.

The Mercury was predictably warm about the opening night: "Our new theatre was opened on Monday night last with a very neat and appropriate address delivered by Mr. Robertson. The play of *The Castle Spectre* and the after-piece of *The Weathercock* were afterwards performed in a style that justly merited the spontaneous and reiterated plaudits of the audience, which was numerous and genteel, and which could not fail being extremely gratifying to the feelings of the manager and the whole of the performers. Two comic songs given with great humour by Messrs. Norman and Adamson added to the evening's entertainment and from the well-known liberality and active exertions of the manager in bringing forward the newest and most popular pieces—the excellence of the performers—and the excellence and general accommodation of the theatre, we doubt not but it will be well attended during the season.

"The subscribers to this undertaking are deservedly entitled to the thanks of every liberal-minded person, as they have not only been the means of ornamenting the town with another public building but of combining rational amusement with its growing prosperity."

A good deal of which can be taken with a pinch of salt. If the audience was orderly it was exceptional. The performers as a whole were more likely to be competent than excellent. As to whether the theatre building was an ornament . . .

No frank account of the first night, or indeed of any performance of the first seasons, exists but we can turn to a contemporary account of a visit to the Chichester Theatre by Lord William Pitt Lennox, fourth son of the fourth Duke of Richmond and Lennox. He was ten when he was first taken to the theatre and he never forgot it. The year was 1809 and George Frederick Cooke was the star visitor in the role of Shylock.

"The house was crowded to the roof and the discordant sounds that issued from the occupiers of the gallery perfectly astounded me. The good old green curtain was down and a man in a carpenter's dress was lighting six tallow candles that were stuck into wet clay and partly screened by dirty tin shades. At last after a great deal of yelling, shouting, hallooing, catcalling during which the roaring of lions, warbling of cats and screech-owls, with a mixture of the howling of dogs were judiciously imitated, the curtain rose."

Confusion was not confined to the auditorium on this particular occasion for the great actor had been at his favourite tipple. The brandy took such effect that as he prepared to take the pound of Antonio's flesh he assaulted his own, nearly taking his thumb off—"In a second the stage was deluged with blood and the curtain had to be lowered while Shylock's wound was attended to."

In later years, when things might have been expected to improve, Dickens described Drury Lane as "A bear garden resounding with foul language, oaths, cat-calls, shrieks, yells, blasphemy, obscenity—a truly diabolical clamour."

Some of the high-spirited antics of Northampton audiences in later years did not escape the record and will be recounted from time to time. But the fact is that if the spectators of May, 1806, were uniformly genteel and orderly, they were exceptional—especially those in the "gods".

So much for the "genteel audience".

What then of the play? I do not propose in this book to moralise over-much on the quality and texture of plays but something must be said about *The Castle Spectre*. A Member of Parliament was its author but in fact its text had many fathers. Matthew Gregory ("Monk") Lewis (1775–1818), the Member for Hindon, had stolen from many sources. As a diplomat he had the opportunity to plunder abroad as well as at home. Not that he was alone in this, in days long before copyright and author's privilege were established. *The Castle Spectre* is typical of plays of that era in being an amalgam of a number of other plays and characters. Juliet's nurse was the source of one character; another was based on Sheridan's *Father Paul*; one scene is from Horace Walpole's *The Castle of Otranto*, and another from Schillers's *The Robber*. Lewis got his nickname from his "shamelessly voluptuous" novel, *The Romance of The Monk*, published in 1795 which resulted in a demand by the Society for the Suppression of Vice for him to be prosecuted. He had followed its sensational and gory pattern with *The Castle Spectre*, which was produced at Drury Lane in 1797.

The play was set in the Castle of Conway and its dramatis personae included Earl Osmond, Usurper of the Castle; Father Philip, an Honest Fryar; Kenric, creature of Osmond; Reginald, supposedly murdered by his brother but in fact incarcerated for sixteen years in a deep dungeon.

One act was set in the Castle Armoury from a tower of which Percy leaps into the river. Another scene was the Oratory where Angela, the heroine, sees the spectre, her murdered mother . . . "her white and flowing garments spotted with blood; her veil is thrown back and discovers a pale and melancholy countenance; her eyes are lifted upwards, her arms extended towards heaven and a large wound appears upon her bosom . . . the spectre waves her hand, bidding farewell, instantly the organ's swell is heard; a full chorus of female voices chant 'Jubilate'; a blaze of light flashes through the oratory and the folding doors close with a loud noise, Angela falls motionless to the floor . . ."

It was like a Hammer Films production.

Yet it had merits. Four negro slaves appeared in it serving as castle guards, and Lewis allowed one of them, Hassan, to be his mouthpiece against slavery; "My heart once was gentle; once was good; but sorrows have broken it, insults have made it hard. I have been dragged from my native land; from a wife who was everything to me, to whom I was everything. Twenty years have elapsed since these Christians tore me away . . . was I not free and am I not a slave?" In later years Ira Aldridge, the African Roscius, made a great impression as Hassan.

But whatever its merits, *The Castle Spectre* was an enormous success. It was one of the hits of the day. When it was performed at Warwick, for instance, in 1799 by a company from the Theatre Royal, Cheltenham, the playbill announced : "Nearly £100,000 has this play drawn to the Treasury of the Drury Lane Theatre and still continues to fill the immense space of that magnificent building every night it is performed. 'The Castle Spectre' evinces greater strength of imagination than has been displayed since the days of our Immortal Shakespeare."

Lewis appears to have been a betting man, offering a wager to Sheridan with the stake as "all the money that the Castle Spectre has brought to the box office". Sheridan said that he could not afford so much "but I'll bet you all it's worth".

The play which set a vogue in castles, prisoners in them, bleeding ghosts, and general blood, thunder and lightning crops up for many years in the repertoire of the period I am covering. Yet mention it today or refer to its Parliamentary author, even to people well up in drama, is normally to meet with blankness. To such a degree has the vast majority of the drama of this period vanished into limbo—virtually without trace. Shakespeare and Sheridan apart, scarcely one of the authors then being performed survives today.

Shakespeare came first to the new theatre on Thursday, June 12, 1806, when *Romeo and Juliet* shared the bill with *The Hunter of The Alps*. Other titles of the inaugural season were *The Stranger*, *The Follies of a Day*, *The Sultan*, *The Honey-Moon*, *Love Laughs at Locksmiths*, *The Prior Claim*,

The Soldier's Daughter, The Purse, The Sleeping Beauty or Harlequin in Northampton (a pantomimical sketch) and *Who Wants a Guinea?*

After his customary round of the Lincoln Circuit, Robertson was back in 1807 to announce on April 25 that he would open the theatre for his usual season of six weeks on Wednesday, May 6, and that his programme would include the "new grand dramatic romance of 'The Forty Thieves', with new dresses, scenery and appropriate decorations."

Who Wants a Guinea? was presented on the opening night when the cast included Mr. Robson from the Theatre Royal, Bath ("his first appearance here these three yars"), Mr. J. Brown, from the Theatre Royal, Liverpool, and Miss Jackson from the Theatre Royal, York.

On May 23 Mrs. Bouverie, of Delapre Abbey, desired *The Provok'd Husband or A Journey to London* which had been a regular favourite in Northampton for many years, and others to "bespeak" performances were the Mayor and Corporation, Col. Delaval, Mrs. Hanbury, Lord Althorp (*The Wonder: A Woman Keeps a Secret*, another perennial), and the Officers and Corps of Northampton and Castle Ashby Volunteer Infantry.

The Northampton Theatre had its own spot of excitement during the second season. On June 1, 1807, "a great disturbance occurred which at its outset gave the audience reason to expect that it would terminate seriously". Apparently an officer of a regiment stationed in the town refused to take his hat off while "God Save the King" was being sung. "Many of the Household Cavalry being in the house they proceeded with drawn swords to attack him and succeeded in getting him out. Several ladies in the boxes fainted, some were dragged from the pit into the boxes and the greatest confusion appeared throughout the theatre." It is said that the incident formed the material for an episode in an American novel.

On the surface, at least, Northampton was intensely patriotic. On the monarch's birthday a contingent of the troops quartered in the town or the local volunteers would form up on the Market Square and fire off three vollies in salute, the bells would ring and the prominent citizens would dine at one of the leading inns.

After only two seasons in the new theatre Thomas Shaftoe Robertson dropped Northampton from his circuit. In some later instances one can find reasons for a manager giving up the theatre. The bad business being done is sometimes revealed in advertisements or editorial reports, sometimes in letters or books. In her diary, covering the later years of the Lincoln Company, Thomas Shaftoe Robertson's widow was very frank about the parlous state of its affairs. But there are no clues as to why Robertson left the town in 1807, after changing the pattern of his tours to fit Northampton in annually instead of every two years, as at the former theatre. Perhaps the alteration upset his pattern of movement. Perhaps the "handsome rent" he paid at Northampton was not matched by the takings.

He gave no hint of his departure. Indeed, on June 20, 1807, his end-of-season advertisement stated: "Mr. Robertson returns his most grateful acknowledgments to the town and vicinity of Northampton and begs to add that on every occasion it will be his pride and study to merit and preserve that kind patronage which he has for many years experienced and for which he shall ever retain the sincerest gratitude and respect."

Whatever the causes, on October 31, a small advertisement in the Mercury announced that a new tenant was required: "New Theatre, Northampton. This elegant little THEATRE to be Lett to a respectable manager of a provincial theatre for the present season or on lease for a short term of years. Enquire of Mr. Abbey, Solicitor, Northampton."

In between the Lincoln Company's season and the appearance of the advertisement the theatre was opened in July for one of the Nelsonian entertainments which were to continue almost throughout the life of the theatre. This was "a moving panorama of the funeral honours, both by land and water, observed to commemorate our late gallant hero Lord Viscount Nelson. This splendid spectacle must fill every heart with respect for a man whose brilliant services obtained him the love of his Sovereign and the adoration of his country." The Mercury said that the panorama included the funeral car drawn by six led horses with its canopy and rich appendages, accompanied by grand marches, dirges, the Dead March from Saul, and other solemn music as in the original procession, and concluding with a "grand and brilliant display of pyrotechny or artificial fireworks without smoke or gunpowder upon the German plan as brought forward by Professor Robertson in Paris and exhibited upwards of 100 nights at the Lyceum in the Strand with unbounded approbation".

Thrown in as an extra was a demonstration of hydraulic experiments— "an egg will be made to ascend and descend by a small jet of water, without breaking" and "the two great elementary powers of fire and water will be blended together without one extinguishing the other".

Altogether, summed up the Mercury, "It was the best exhibition we remember to have seen in Northampton." Even more revealing was the comment that "the immense crowd far exceeded anything we have ever witnessed at the presentation of the most favourite play".

A new manager was soon forthcoming for the theatre. In December, 1807, Mr. Mudie, proprietor of the Theatre Royal, Windsor, "now performing there", was announced to be planning a season in Northampton the following February. As well as promising to open in "very superior style", ornamenting the theatre with new decorations and new scenery, Mudie declared that he would "raise the roof" of the two-year-old theatre. "Raising the roof" is, of course, every manager's aim but Mudie did it literally—raising the roof of the gallery. For the alterations and decorations he engaged Mr. Merrick and his assistant from Drury Lane.

So much work had to be done, in fact, that the opening night had to be postponed a few days. When Kotzebue's comedy *The Stranger* and the farce *Raising The Wind* were presented on the opening night of the season of His Majesty's Servants of the Theatre Royal, Windsor, it appears to have been an even more impressive occasion than the night when the theatre opened for the first time. Mr. Mudie had got Stephen Kemble, a member of the famous theatrical family, to write a special address which was read by Mrs. Mudie and which has survived:

"The season of suspension being past
And our dramatic corps arrived at last
I am sent forward ere the curtain draws
To beg you'll greet our strangers with applause
Our little bark we launch with rigging new
A staunch commander and an active crew
Prepared alike the taste of all to hit
Our deck the gallery and our steerage, Pit
And cabin'd boxes neatly we prepare
To court the custom of the British Fair
Give but your smiles, your bounteous presence give
'For those who live to please must please to live.'
And may I ask those critics who are skilled in
Architecture how they like our building?
Tho' hurried on perhaps, with too much haste
Our artists hope they have displayed some taste;
And you'll acknowledge they have given proof
At least of judgment—for they have raised the roof
By classic rule the gallery should be high
For Gods should sit enthroned in the sky
The colours blended thus with grace and ease
Give the soft harmony that's sure to please
Here may the tragic muse essay her art
And fair Thalia magic bliss impart
While we their agents with our best endeavours
Still strive to merit your applause and favour
And should success our humble efforts crown
Should we pass muster 'fore the general town
While your applause new ardour will excite
Our task of duty will be sweet delight
Till our Inspectors (soon we may deserve this)
Report the Corps completely Fit for Service
Then let these walls with cheerful chorus ring
Of Rule Britannia and God Save the King."

Tickets were to be had and places taken in the boxes of Mr. Phillips at the box office every day from eleven to three o'clock, "but no places can be kept without tickets are had when the places are taken. Tickets for the season may be had. Terms known by applying at the Box Office. Servants, who are to keep places, to be at the box door by six."

Other pieces presented during the season included *Venice Preserved*, *Time's a Tell-Tale* (by H. Siddons and "now performing at Drury Lane with the greatest marks of applause"), *Adrian and Orrila*, *The Beaux Stratagem*, *Ella Rosenberg*, *High Life Below Stairs*, *Isabella* and *No Song No Supper*.

A number of evenings, as was customary, were devoted to benefit nights for various members of the company, including in this case Mr. Fitzwilliam, box office treasurer, and Mr. Phillips, treasurer. Benefits were a means of augmenting their small salaries which probably ranged from 15s. to a guinea a week. Out of this sum all sorts of things had to be provided by the player. In his *Fifty Years of Green Room Gossip*, the actor Walter Donaldson (1793–1877) wrote that the famous manager Thomas Wilson Manly ". . . made it a rule never to engage married couples or old people. This was politic as the walking on the circuit in one year amounted to 500 miles. Coaching in those days was no trifling matter and salaries being on the lowest scale actors were obliged to walk. The means afforded by the manager did not allow of much indulgence either in eating or drinking. The salaries were one guinea weekly and for this miserable stipend the actor had to find boots, shoes, buckles, silk stockings, hats, feathers, swords, canes, wigs, modern dress, long hose, gloves, military costume; and those that unfortunately possessed vocal ability were obliged to furnish the part of their songs for the orchestra. The actor that could sing was in request for glees and choruses and was even compelled to sing the songs of other characters when certain performers were incompetent." Thus the strolling player might have to sing for someone else's supper as well as his own.

But on the night of his own benefit he would be doing his utmost in his own interest. There were various types of benefit and the subject is covered comprehensively in *The Benefit System in the British Theatre*, written by the late Sir St. Vincent Troubridge and published by the Society for Theatre Research. One point he makes is that the benefit could in certain circumstances be a mixed blessing. If the actor had to pay the night's expenses in return for the night's takings, with a poor house he might actually be out of pocket. Preparing for a benefit usually meant going round touting for the sale of tickets. Even the most respectable country actor had to go cap-in-hand, soliciting support.

Some of the performances were "bespeaks" when prominent people or organisations lent their names and patronage to the evening, taking a block of seats for the privilege of choosing the plays. On Wednesday, February 24, 1808, *The Soldier's Daughter* was by desire of Col. Vandeleur and the Officers of the 19th Light Dragoons. The choices of Mrs. Strickland, of Brixworth Hall, on Monday, March 7, were *The Honeymoon* and *The Turnpike Gate*. Mrs. Bouverie, of Delapre Abbey (now the home of Northamptonshire Record Office and Northamptonshire Record Society) selected *She Stoops to Conquer* and *We Fly By Night* for Wednesday, March 16. The following Friday an unnamed play and farce were by desire of the proprietors of the theatre.

The night the Mayor went along to give civic encouragement was during the short engagement of a tight-rope artist named Richer "whose exhibition of manly ability in London, Paris, Madrid, and Lisbon has decidedly established him as the first rope dancer in Europe". He varied his act by "the introduction of numerous extraordinary feats and points of effect peculiar to himself, including specimens of hornpipe, elastic, fanciful, gavotte, bizarre, retrograde and lofty style, with and without the balance pole, particularly the favourite waltz, accompanied by himself on the tambourine, being a most astonishing display of attitude and activity which every summer has drawn the most crowded houses at Astley's, The Circus and in the first provincial theatres in the U.K., with the most distinguished applause." On two nights he drew such crowds that "numbers were obliged to return from the door, not being able to obtain admission".

For Richer's first night the principal play was *The Gamester* by Mrs. Centlivre, who owed her dramatic career to the fact that her first husband was killed in a duel, after which she became an actor and authoress. It was only after several non-successes that she wrote *The Gamester*, a typical moralising melodrama, in which the heroine promised to marry a man if he would give up gambling. She shocked him into reforming by dressing as a man and so outwitting him that she won from him her own picture. Her second husband, whom she met while performing at Windsor, was chief cook to Queen Anne and George I. The part of the woman who wore man's clothes was played by Mrs. Mudie, it being "the last night she can perform for some time". We can guess at the reason for her temporary retirement, remembering the description by a "gentleman" quoted by York comedian Joseph Yarrow describing meeting a company of strolling players on the road :

> *"From Hereford the jovial crew departed*
> *Kings walked on foot and princesses were carted*
> *In pure compassion to the maiden queen*
> *That wanted but a month of lying-in*
> *Thus on a heap lay piled; there the brandy bottle*
> *Here the child . . ."*

Mr. Mudie brought with him not only his wife but also, for three nights, his sister Miss Mudie. She was one of the child stars who plagued the stage at that time. The early nineteenth century saw a fair number of "young marvels" strutting the British boards, forerunners of the child film-stars of the 1930s, such as Shirley Temple and Jackie Coogan. "Actors" and "actresses" of tender years have always tended to be a pain in the neck for the adult Thespian. Trying to gain the audience's attention and favour while there is a child in view is almost as lost a cause as trying to compete with an attractive animal on stage. But at least the modern youngsters did stick to child parts whereas those of the former era would actually take a man's or woman's part—even Hamlet or Macbeth—ridiculous though this might appear and indeed was.

One of the precocious youngsters of 175 years ago was billed as "Master Carey, the Pupil of Nature". In this guise he did not cause a sensation but later he was to gain success as an adult, as Edmund Kean, and was to appear in Northampton as a top star.

Others were nine-day wonders and these included the most remarkable and successful member of the school of youth, Master Betty West, known as "The Young Roscius" and hailed, with obvious extravagance, as the natural successor to David Garrick, possibly the greatest actor of all time. To the best of my knowledge Master Betty never appeared at Northampton (though his son did in the 1840s) but a word or two about this young chap would not be out of place as it fills in the background to other remarkable young chaps (and girls) who did visit the town.

The thirteen-year-old "Young Roscius" came to the rescue in 1804 when Richard Brinsley Sheridan was facing seemingly insoluble problems in his lesseeship of the Drury Lane theatre. Sheridan was a stranger character than many in plays. Despite the talents which made him almost the only memorable dramatist of his time he said he hated the drama, regarding it merely as a means to an end—the end being his political career. His dramatic activities paid for his strutting on the real life stage of politics. He had no greater respect for Master Betty than for a performing animal but the young talent served his purpose by attracting more people to the theatre than the leading actress of the day, Sarah Siddons. A few years later Sheridan came to a problem he could not solve when, in February, 1809, the Drury Lane theatre was burned down. Watching the fire that put an end to his aspirations Sheridan is reputed to have had a bottle in his hand and to have spoken a line which might have come from one of his plays: "Cannot a man take a glass by his own fireside?"

But to return to the Northampton stage and Miss Mudie. She was announced as having appeared at the Theatres Royal Dublin, Belfast, Birmingham, Liverpool, Cheltenham, York, Windsor and most of the provincial theatres in the United Kingdom. For the first of her three nights at Northampton, on Monday, March 21, she appeared as Young Norval in the tragedy of *Douglas*. This was one of the roles in which Master Betty had drawn capacity audiences to Drury Lane and in his admirable new history of that theatre Brian Dobbs makes the following point: "Possibly Giles Playfair is correct in reading something sexual into the universal ardour. His playing of Young Norval was said not to leave a dry eye in the house; perhaps it left not a dry seat either."

The downfall of Miss Mudie at Covent Garden in November, 1805, had derived from the basic ludicrousness of children taking adult roles. Allegedly aged eight she was small even for those years—it is possible she was indeed a midget and not a child at all—and in *The Country Girl* she was cast as a wife and moreover had as a fellow player Miss Louisa Brunton (later Countess of Craven) whom an unwise director had allowed to wear on her head a plume of ostrich feathers, making a total height of seven feet. The audience howled down the performance until Miss Mudie was replaced by someone more credible.

Or as Mrs. Mathews, wife of actor Charles Mathews, put it in her Memoirs: "... the Miss Mudies and the other little monstrosities of transient interest strained public wonder until its eye-strings almost cracked and asked for rest and refreshment. The baby-bubble, blown too wide, naturally broke and dispersed itself into thin air. Miss Mudie's brief appearance in London acted as a mirror to the public—it reflected their folly and showed them the fallacy of turning national theatres into baby-houses."

But at Northampton in 1808 the Mercury referred to "the astonishing abilities of this child. For her the house was crowded with as fashionable an audience as we remember to have seen during the season."

Was "Miss Mudie" indeed a child? Mrs. Mathews quotes John Kemble on this point: "One evening when the age of Miss Mudie was questioned, she having an antiquated looking face, a green room wag observed that if she really was the child she was said to be he must confess that he never saw so young a body with so old a head. At which Mr. Kemble in his solemn and measured tone of jesting replied : 'Child sir—Pooh Pooh—why sir, when I was a very young actor in the York Company that little creature kept an inn at Tadcaster and had a large family of children.' "

Mrs. Mathews comments that after the Covent Garden fiasco Miss Mudie went into the provinces "where her puny constitution and efforts perished rapidly from coldness and died a natural death from neglect". The little Miss did in fact die the following August. No age is given in the death report, which said she died "after a lingering illness".

The actress Mrs. Jordan (1762–1816) who bore ten children to the Duke of Clarence, later William IV, summed up the professional protest against the young idea in acting : "Oh for the days of Herod!"

Although Mrs. Mudie was out of action as far as acting was concerned she still had a benefit on the last night of the season, Friday, April 29, 1808, when the new play *The World* and the farce *Matrimony* were staged. After the farce she addressed the audience, as she had done on the opening night. Thus hers was the first and last Mudie voice to be heard in Northampton for this was the company's first and last season.

Straight from Northampton we find Mudie respectfully informing the nobility, gentry and public in general of Banbury that he had fitted up the old theatre there in a superior style of elegance and was about to start a season. The company interrupted this engagement to play at Windsor during the Ascot Race Week but on the way back to Banbury the coach in which a number of the players were travelling had an accident at Oxford and some were injured. Mr. M'Gibbon had a wheel go over one of his legs and was left in Oxford "in a most dangerous state"; Mrs. Whaley was severely bruised; and Mrs. Mudie herself was injured but evidently recovered for in September it was announced that she was engaged for the coming season at Drury Lane. How Mudie managed to cope with the situation and whether his Banbury operations were brought to a halt I have failed to discover.

The practice of breaking into a season at one town to perform during a race week elsewhere was not uncommon. The nature of the disaster is also a reminder that road accidents did not suddenly begin with the invention of the internal combustion engine. In fact the accident rate during the era of the stage coach, gig, wagon, cart and saddle appears to have been quite high. The very first issue of the Northampton Mercury on May 2, 1720, mentioned fatalities, though not local, "by the kick of a horse" and "the wheel of a wagon". In reading a century-and-a-half of issues of the paper from 1720 to 1887, as basic research for this book, I came across innumerable instances of runaway horses, broken axles, stage coaches and other vehicles going over the parapets of bridges, even one of a man riding on top of a stage coach into an inn yard, forgetting that the archway had been lowered, with dreadful results. On the penal side you could be prosecuted for "driving furiously", "being asleep in charge of a wagon going along", or, in later years, neglect or cruelty to your horse.

The Windsor Theatre which Mudie managed was an interesting one in that though insignificant, it held the Royal Patent, because the monarch attended it. Indeed, in his *Theatric Tourist* in 1805, Winston wrote of it : "Is a Theatre Royal : which can scarcely be said to enjoy a regular season, as it greatly depends upon the time of His Majesty's residence, who is almost its only support . . . on the left is a private house which serves His Majesty for an avenue, whenever he honours the theatre with his presence. It is recorded in the Playhouse Companion for 1764 that Mrs. Centlivre, the dramatist, whose name at that time was Carrol, performed in this town the part of Alexander the Great, in 1706. Mr. Joseph Centlivre, one of Queen Anne's cooks, fell in love with and married her."

Mrs. Centilivre did not perform in the theatre in the High Street of which Mudie was manager as this had been erected only in August, 1793, but in a barn theatre "in a dirty farmyard, nearly a mile from town at the bottom of Pescod Street".

The new theatre was managed by a Mr. Thornton who was "of the opinion that six bad nights per week are better than three middling ones and consequently works his actors" and who was still in office when the book was written, but with a new partner, a Mr. Davenport. When Mudie took over does not appear to be on the record.

The High Street theatre was replaced by a new one in Thames Street costing £6,000 in 1815. In 1908 this was destroyed by fire but rebuilt two years later.

In June, 1808, the Northampton theatre had been taken for one night by Mr. Bannister, of Drury Lane, for *Bannister's Budget or An Actor's Ways and Means.*

On the last day of the year another "To Lett" advertisement appeared for the theatre. It seems likely that both Mr. Robertson and Mr. Mudie had found their seasons unprofitable in the first three years of the theatre's life.

Perhaps the most distinguished audience which ever attended the theatre was that for a concert on October 11, 1809, during Northampton's Grand Musical Festival of which the musical director was Mr. Barrett, for many years organist of All Saints Church. There were five earls—Euston, Northampton, Pomfret, Spencer and Upper Ossory; two M.P.s, the Rt. Hon. Spencer Perceval and the Hon. Edward Bouverie (both to die within three years, the former by assassination); Sir William Wake, Sir George Robinson, Sir William Langham, Sir Richard de Capell Brook, Sir William Dolben, and Sir Edward Dryden. In the daytime *Messiah* was given at All Saints and in the evening the concert took place in a theatre in which pit and boxes had been "laid together" and tickets were 10s. 6d. and 5s.

The theatre was "superbly illuminated with wax" and was "considerably enlarged" for this musical occasion. How this was achieved is not clear but one feature was a "new and commodious entrance". Such was the pressure that ladies and gentlemen were "obliged to take seats in the orchestra".

After Robertson from Lincoln and Mudie from Windsor came Simms— "from the Theatres Royal, Birmingham and Manchester" as he billed himself. In my mind's eye he will always be billed as "Unlucky Simms" for anything he was connected with seems to have had a fair chance of going wrong. His seasons started late, his company went on strike, his messengers missed their stage coaches—J. Simms had a great talent for putting his foot in it.

I first traced him at the New Theatre, Warwick, between September and November, 1802, with "Their Majesties' Servants from the Theatre Royal, Cheltenham." The New Theatre was probably the one in Theatre Street, conveniently near the Race Ground with which its activities were often connected. There had been racing at Warwick since 1707 when Lord Brooke gave £5 to his chamberlain to make a horse race. Regular meetings began four years later.

Mr. Watson was the manager of the 1802 company which included as guests Mrs. Carleton, of the Theatres Brighton and Margate, Mr. Blissett, of the Theatre Royal, Bath, and the before-mentioned tight rope artist Richer, who turns out to be Watson's brother-in-law. Here Richer was billed as having performed "last year at the grand fete at Windsor Castle, with general applause of Their Majesties, the Royal Family and all the nobility". It was probably in Watson's company that Simms first struck up an acquaintanceship with Richer, whom he was to engage for his own company twelve years later. Closing at Warwick on Thursday, November 4, 1802, Simms moved on to Manchester, where he made his debut as Stephen Harrowby in *The Poor Gentleman* and remained for the rest of the season.

I next "picked him up" at Bedford immediately prior to his first season at Northampton. A Bedford playbill shows him appearing at the Theatre, St. Lloyd's, on Friday, November 10, 1809, with a company including Messrs. Browne, Frost, Howitt, Williams, Tuxford, Wartnaby, Mr. and Mrs. Comerford, Mrs. Hudson, Miss Hudson, Mrs. Campbell, Miss Walcott and Miss Wood. Simms was presumably the manager, although this is not stated. Several of the Bedford company moved with him to Northampton where his first night was on Monday, December 4, 1809. He charged 3s. 6d. for his boxes (second price 2s.), pit 2s. (1s.) and gallery 1s. Tickets could be obtained from him at Mr. Hickman's, The Parade, on the north side of the Market Square.

Whether Simms' accident-proneness was due to over-optimism in some cases, bad relations with his players in others, or sheer bad management it is difficult to say at this distance in time. But he certainly had more than his share of mishaps.

During his first season at Northampton, he fell out with his leading tragedian, Mr. Browne. On Browne joining the company Simms promised to find costumes for him. When Simms cast him as Macbeth, Browne therefore asked for his costume but was told that there wasn't one. "The manager gave his reasons which, not proving satisfactory, Browne discharged himself." The wrangle appears to have gone on in the theatre with the audience present for after Simms had asked to be allowed to read the part the audience pleaded with Browne not to let them down. He agreed. What costume he adopted is not on record.

Two months later a dispute was not so happily resolved and the management had to "respectfully inform the public that the celebrated play of *The Traveller* advertised to be performed on Thursday, March 8, cannot be brought forward this season in consequence of the company having unlawfully withdrawn their services at a moment's notice; for which and other circumstances a legal inquiry will speedily be instituted".

In March, 1811, Simms' season at Northampton did not start on time and he went into a long rigmarole to explain why not. "J. Simms, impressed with the highest sense of the respect due to the Ladies and Gentlemen of Northampton, its vicinity, and the public in general feels himself called upon to offer every apology in his power for the disappointment occasioned from the theatre not being opened on Monday last, March 4, agreeably to advertisement; a circumstance of which he did not know until the Wednesday following and which arose from one of the performers commissioned with necessary instructions being disappointed of a place in the coach and could not leave Sheffield on Friday morning, March 1, having taking leave of J.S. with that intent the night previous. He further begs leave to inform the public that though the Sheffield theatre did not close until the 4th instant yet every performer announced in the two bills was in town in sufficient time with the exception of Mr. Curson and the gentleman who was instructed with a direction for Mr. Benwell to study the part which Mr. Curson was to have played. Relying on the kind consideration and liberality of the public, J.S. hopes this unforeseen event will be the only cause for soliciting their indulgence during the season."

Announcing the special attractions for the season Simms said that some would be brought forward "as soon as the new scenery can arrive from Sheffield". A man with Simms' facility for misfortune seems to have tempted fate with his timings for two seasons in places so far apart.

The French explorer Perouse was the central figure depicted in the "serious pantomime" entitled La Perouse and Simms' advertisement was at pains to list every eye-taking aspect of the scenery and every gripping turn of the plot. "Moonlight, sea, storm and shipwreck. Perouse is seen swimming to shore and afterwards climbing rocks; side wings of wild rocks covered with snow; chimpanzee's cave, etc.; a chest of Perouse's stores is thrown on to the shore by the waves; a large black bear which is shot on the stage; a mountainous part of the island covered with snow; a marine grotto or cavern naturally ornamented with icicles and shells; extensive view of the country, frozen lake; Perouse breaks the ice with his gun and obtains fresh water; during scene a great white bear enters which is shot by Perouse; stupendous rock covered with snow : Perouse's hut, practical drawbridge, skins of wild animals etc.; scene the last, Perouse tied to a rock about to be burnt alive by the savages but is preserved by the fortunate arrival of Madame Perouse, her son, and a party of English sailors who by chance have landed here."

Fancy giving the plot away in this manner! And how this mammoth spectacular was presented on the minuscule stage of the Northampton theatre it is hard to imagine. At all events it was claimed to be so expensive to stage that nothing under full price could be taken. The performance was under the patronage of Mrs. Bouverie, of Delapre Abbey.

Simms' run of bad luck appears to have attached itself to the theatre which he built and opened at Leamington on Tuesday, October 26, 1813. Previous performances had been at the Crown Hotel. Almost needless to say, Simms did not manage to get the place fully completed on time. It was without plaster (so as to be free from damp, he explained) and ornamental paintings and other decorations, all of which were deferred until after the end of the season. It must have been a rather bare shell, therefore, in which *The Earl of Warwick* was performed on the opening night. A song called "The Ballad of Lilla of Leamington" had been composed by Bisset, that remarkable figure in Leamington history, and was sung by Mr. Povey. However unfinished the interior may have been, the outside of the theatre was quite pleasing as a surviving drawing shows. (*Page 139.*)

In a brief and chequered career the Leamington theatre was visited by many great actors and actresses—Charles Mathews, Robert Elliston, Edmund Kean, Miss Foote—but in 1833, after a life of a mere twenty years, it was sold to Mr. Ind who converted it to liquor vaults.

Even with his star guest, tightrope man Richer, Simms was unlucky in November, 1814, at Northampton. It was explained that owing to an alteration of the programme at Covent Garden Richer had to leave Northampton early and could not appear for all the performances for which he was billed.

During Simms' era some of the dozens of performances at the theatre of *The Wonder; A Woman Keeps a Secret* took place and at the presentation in February, 1810, there was a little extra. A "gentleman of the town" had written a special St. Valentine epilogue which was spoken by Miss Hudson in the character of Volante. Its advice on flattering the female is as relevant today as 160 years ago :

> *"The frailties which o'er womankind prevail*
> *Have been the theme of many a comic tale*
> *But see among the gods (pointing to the gallery) our Johnny sits*
> *Searching his head and puzzling sore his wits*
> *Alas! Poor soul his study's brown and dull*
> *See how he bites his nails and pats his scull*
> *What is't his soul's thus striving to design*
> *Humph—I have it—Wednesday's Valentine*
> *His study, sirs, has made him melancholy*
> *To think how he should praise his dearest Molly*
> *Now John, a secret, listen and attend*
> *Nor slight the counsel of a knowing friend*
> *Say that she breath's more fragrant than the rose*
> *And praise her coral lip, and high arched nose*
> *If when she stirs she limps at each advance*
> *Tell her she walks as though she'd learned to dance*
> *If her eyes resemble two dull balls of lead*
> *Or two boil'd gooseberries peering from her head*
> *Tell her their splendid beams have charmed your heart*
> *Though black as coal her skin in every part*
> *Tell her she's fair, nor think yourself a sinner*

Flatter her well—and you'll be sure to win her
And when obtained, thy kindness further show
And tell her all that she perchance may know
Then will the trade of secrets stand reversed
And thine, dear John, can never be rehearsed."

Secrets of a more serious nature were confided by another visitor to the theatre, Joseph Lancaster, pioneer in new methods of education. Such as how to teach 1,000 children as easily as twenty! In November, 1810, Lancaster gave two demonstration-lectures, one at the theatre, the other at the George Hotel. His scheme for educating poor children was under the patronage of the King, Queen, Prince of Wales and Royal Family and certainly had some remarkable features. He set out to explain "how one master may govern and teach 1,000 children with as much facility as twenty, in half the usual time and at one-third the common expense. The Principle of Order, the method whereby one book will serve for 500 or 1,000 children and the manner in which 500 children may spell at the same instant of time."

Mr. Lancaster sounds like an educational crackpot, a quack equivalent in the sphere of learning of the many "doctors" and "professors" who visited the town or advertised in the Mercury with sure cures—like the "surgeon", Mr. Gent, of Fenny Stratford, who offered a cure for cancer, "extirpating the dreadful disease without an operation". In fact, though Lancaster's claims were undoubtedly extravagant, his ideas were soundly-based and gained wide acceptance.

There is no detailed account of his night at the theatre but it was no doubt similar to the lecture at the George, of which there is a report. "By the aid of paintings and with a number of boys procured for the occasion in this place, Mr. Lancaster clearly and satisfactorily exhibited the principles of his plan which appears peculiarly calculated to produce habits of attention and application from the change of employment of both mind and body and the relaxation it constantly affords the scholar. Nothing of harshness or severity is comprised in the discipline, nevertheless it is strict and uniform and always adapted to the age and capacity of its objects. It appears evident that a few years of the early period of childhood subjected to the regulations of this system will induce those habits of regularity, obedience and industry that would afford the fairest prospect of the future good conduct of its subjects in society." It was stated that a school on Lancasterian principles was already in being in New York and that others were contemplated in Boston and other U.S. cities.

The Northampton audiences seem to have been entirely captivated and a subscription fund was immediately set up for the purpose of establishing a Lancasterian School in Northampton. Robert Abbey gave two guineas and so did George Baker, the county historian. A £50 subscription came from the Earl of Northampton. The following year it was announced that as a suitable building could not be found a site would instead be acquired and new premises built. A site was found in Derngate and the school opened on Monday, April 13, 1812, "for children of all persuasions, but none admitted under four years of age". It later became the British School when Lancaster's sympathisers founded the British and Foreign School Society. In 1846 it moved to Campbell Square, subsequently changing its guise and coming under State control in 1878. It finally closed in 1964; half the premises have been demolished and the rest serve at the time of writing for various offices, including motor taxation.

In August, 1811, Mr. Hathaway brought his show of wax figures to the town, not to the theatre but to the Black Boy Hotel, Wood Hill. It included figures of the British Royal Family and the unfortunate Royal Family of France along with many other kings and emperors, living and dead. For your shilling you could also see that perennial favourite the Funeral of Nelson. In November that year the Nelsonian obsequies were in town yet again, presented by the man with the hydraulic experiments of 1809. As an extra item this time he filled a balloon and sent it up, with its passenger car, over the pit. It was a replica model of one in which Mr. Sadler, the English aeronaut, had ascended at Birmingham in September.

Simms took his company to some sort of fit-up theatre at Thrapston, Northants, in April, 1813. The only evidence of this visit turned up in 1972 in a sack of wastepaper about to be burned. An antique collector had bought the contents of a house, cataloguing the valuable items and then telling his assistant to "Put the rubbish in those sacks". Making a final check he noticed a sharp corner sticking out of one of the sacks and investigated. It turned out to be a framed playbill. *(Page 38.)*

Another theatrical night at Thrapston is recalled in a parish magazine: ". . . it was the exciting evening of the theatricals. Post chaises and saddle horses loomed up through the night through the dimness of the streets. Then they arrived with clipping hooves and rumble of iron shod wheels on to the cobbled Market Hill. The brightly lighted entrance of the theatre cast the gay gowns and Sunday suits into strong relief. For these people had come to see the once in a decade evening on the brightly lighted stage."

Daventry was another small Northamptonshire town in which Simms operated. The location of the "superior and improved accommodation" in which he gave a season in 1810 is not clear. There is a record of dramatic performances at Daventry as far back as April, 1770, when Messrs. Kennedy and Booth's Company of Comedians from Warwick appeared at the Moot Hall (a forerunner of the present building). In the last year of the eighteenth century the company from the Theatre Royal, Cheltenham, was at Daventry, as a single playbill among the collection kept in the ancient coffre-fort at the present Moot Hall testifies. In June, 1793, Mr. Beynon's Nottingham and Derby Company appeared at the Theatre, Daventry, one performance being "by desire of the gentlemen of the Sheaf Bowling Green".

In 1803 the theatre was in a barn. We know this because the barn was burned to the ground in February that year, as follows: "Providentially none of the performers were come to dress nor any of the audience assembled. About five o'clock Mr. Richards, the manager, went into the ladies' dressing room previous to opening the doors and found it in flames, a hot coal having dropped upon the mat and communicated to the canvas which lined the walls of the building, which, being a thatched barn, the whole was soon in a conflagration. The building and the carpenter's property, who erected the stage, boxes, etc, were insured and also the theatrical apparatus but, it is imagined, not to the value destroyed." An adjacent barn belonging to a Mr. Whaddon was also lost. From the reference to the carpenter constructing the stage, this was clearly a fit-up.

In 1806 Mr. Harper, of the Theatre Royal, Richmond, wrote for permission to perform at Daventry and also to build a theatre there. His letter, now in Northamptonshire Record Office, presented his respects to the Mayor and asked leave to perform in a temporary theatre for the present season and "upon his being favour'd with their approbation he would be happy to build or take shares in a regular one ... as Daventry has been some years without a theatrical amusement". Two letters of recommendation supported the application. One was from Mr. Maunsel, a magistrate at Cosgrove, on the Northants-Bucks border, who said Harper had conducted himself with propriety at Cosgrove and brought a respectable company. The second was from an old schoolfriend (of the Mayor, presumably, Benjamin Palmer, to whom it was addressed), Jno. Malpas, of Stony Stratford, and said there had not been a more respectable company in Stratford.

In January, 1815, Simms announced that he was fitting up a theatre in the premises of Mr. Mollady, hatter, High Street, Daventry, and would open on Wednesday, January 25. Once again he was late starting, "the theatre not being ready". Edmund Mollady, who also operated at Nuneaton, had removed to these "extensive premises" in the High Street from the Market Hill in 1811, his new place having previously been used by a carrier. When Simms did get started, his first piece was *The Earl of Warwick*.

Just as the Daventry run ended, an important event in the transport history of Northampton was taking place—the opening of the canal arm linking the town with the Grand Junction Canal at nearby Blisworth. As the Mercury noted : "This gives a water communication to all parts of the kingdom. There were great multitudes to witness the first arrivals of boats, several laden with various kinds of merchandise manufactured in Ireland, Liverpool, Manchester, Yorkshire, Lancashire, Cheshire, Staffordshire, Derbyshire, Warwickshire, London, Bristol etc. and upwards of twenty with coals. From the greater facilities thus afforded the inhabitants of this place may reasonably expect considerable advantage." There were great celebrations with the firing of cannon, ringing of bells, etc. but the day was marred by two accidents when a gun burst and a man's thigh was fractured and a boy had a finger torn off going through one of the locks. A fortnight later an enterprising Northampton coal merchant succeeded in getting coal-laden canal boats along the River Nene to Wellingborough. The ten miles took ten hours.

During the Daventry season there was a performance by desire of the young ladies of Mrs. Bagnell's and Miss Houghton's School. The following night, Tuesday, February 28, attention was drawn to the "advantage of moonlight for those who may wish to come from the country". No doubt this was a reference to the dangers of travel on dark nights. Thieves and highwaymen might relieve one of the finery in which one was attired for the rare night out. The previous year Simms himself was a victim of a robbery during his season at Northampton, and at the October, 1814, Sessions, James Wilson was convicted of stealing £28 in bank and cash notes, Simms' property, from a dressing room at the Northampton theatre. For this crime, which today would earn no greater penalty than a conditional discharge (i.e. no penalty at all) Wilson was transported for seven years.

I refer elsewhere to the harsh penalties of this era for the criminal and indeed, one did not need even to be a criminal to be in danger of apprehension. That gipsies were fair game is clear from an advertisement sponsored by the Harlestone Association for Prosecuting Robbers, Thieves, etc. The police system was by no means what it is now (though even today a large proportion of crime goes unpunished) and in those pre-Peeler days if you wanted to catch someone who had stolen your cattle, sheep or horses, set fire to your hay-rick, or burgled your home or stolen from your dressing room, the most effective course was to be a member of one of these associations dedicated to detection and punishment and offering cash rewards to the public to look out for criminals and gipsies, and also for criminals to inform on their accomplices.

The gipsy was on the same unsure footing as the actor—wandering abroad without visible means of support or a trade—and as such guilty of misdemeanour. The advertisement read : "The Harlestone Association for Prosecuting Thieves, Robbers etc. earnestly recommend all persons resident in the County of Northampton and elsewhere to exert themselves to prevent the wandering and encampment of *GIPSIES* and *VAGABONDS* : which may be effected by calling the Constables in their respective parishes to do their duty. By the Vagrant Act all persons pretending to be gipsies or wandering in the habit or form of Egyptians; all persons wandering abroad and lodging in barns, out-houses or the open air, not giving a good account of themselves; and all persons wandering abroad and begging— are declared to be rogues and vagabonds."

"The Constable or any other person (without a warrant) is authorised to apprehend any of the above offenders and to convey him, her or them before a Justice of the Peace to be punished according to the Law. The Justices may order the High Constable to pay such Constable or other person a reward of ten shillings for every offender so apprehended, and if any Constable shall refuse to convey such offenders to some Justice he is liable to forfeit ten shilling to the poor."

The notice was signed Richard Buswell, Treasurer and Solicitor, who also signed the notices of the annual general meetings at the Sign of the Fox and Hounds, Harlestone, each March, when the members could see the bloodhounds kept by the association in training.

In April the following year William Gibbins was sentenced at Northampton Quarter Sessions for stealing a greatcoat—seven years transportation. Someone appears to have been inspired to action by the notice of the Harlestone Association for at the following Quarter Sessions three persons were sentenced as being rogues and vagabonds. Elizabeth Clitherhoe was transported for seven years (this seems to have been a good round term, and if you returned within the time you were likely to be hanged); William West was sent to sea; and Thomas Rowley was given one month in the House of Correction. An odd mixture of penalties! That same month Thomas Boyson was executed at Northampton for sheep-stealing.

A by-then rare punishment was imposed during the Simms era at the theatre. In March, 1811, John Butlin provided the public with some free entertainment as a result of attempting to rape a child aged under ten. He was put into a pillory specially erected on the Market Square. "The novelty of the scene attracted a vast concourse of people but the fineness of the weather and consequent cleanliness of the streets was greatly in favour of the culprit as his assailants were in consequence deprived of a supply of the missiles most used at such exhibitions; eggs, however, appeared pretty plentiful as they were thrown from all quarters the greater part of the time." (Could we afford eggs today to throw at a miscreant?)

Returning to our main theme of paid entertainment, a pertinent question to ask is: what was the standard of acting of such provincial companies as that of Simms'? The art of dramatic criticism was not far advanced in the provinces and such notices as did appear were as much concerned with flattering the audiences as evaluating the players. Such reports as there were consisted largely of what the twentieth-century journalist would dismiss as "jam label" compliments.

Perhaps more significant is the one-word condemnation by one of the London professionals who came down from the heights of the Lane and the Garden to perform a couple of nights at Northampton in September, 1815. To his extended and detailed Memoirs we owe many invaluable insights into theatrical life in the first three decades of the nineteenth century.

The star visitor was Charles Mathews. The name probably means little or nothing to many of my readers outside the somewhat narrow circles of those British folk who are deeply interested in the theatre and its history. In case that sounds a little pompous let me say straightaway that I had never heard of Mathews until I began researching this book. Now, through the medium of his letters to his wife and to her interpretation and amplification of them, the way of life of the actor of 150 years ago comes vividly to life.

It was in a letter from Northampton written on Tuesday, September 19, 1815, that Charles Mathews gives us his five-letter word description of Mr. Simms' Company. "... from Warwick Castle Mr. Hall took the third of a chaise with Mr. Simpson and myself on towards Derby, highly delighted at meeting with such post-chaise companions. On Sunday we had a charming journey to this place (Northampton). I last night played Buskin, Cypher and Somno, the house crammed—hold fifty and we had fifty-six and a clear half and expect as good tonight." [The roles were: Buskin in *Killing No Murder*, a farce by Theodore Hook, 1809, created by Mathews in the first performance at the Haymarket Theatre, London, July 1, 1809; Dick

Cypher, in the musical farce *Hit Or Miss* by J. Pocock, 1810; and Somno, in *The Sleepwalker or Which Is the Lady?* by W. C. Oulton, 1812.]

This presumably means that the "house full" takings of the theatre were reckoned to be £50; that the admissions on this night totalled £56; and that Mathews had a clear half of this, i.e. £28. *(Page38.)*

He went on : "At present, therefore, all is propitious and it had need to be for the misery I endured at rehearsal yesterday and last night. Oh! Such *PUMPS*! Tonight I do the entertainment—such velvet after acting with them! Tomorrow Coventry."

Mathews' next letter was from Stone, in Staffordshire, six days later. "We have just arrived after a delightful drive from Birmingham, 40 miles on our road to Manchester where I am going to give my entertainment on Monday. Our mode of travelling is most delightful; and we have not had one shower since we started from London. I have fagged very hard; have played already six nights and shall play six nights again next week.

"Was on stage at Northampton at half-past eleven o'clock on Tuesday; up at half-past five, Wednesday; went thirty-five miles to Coventry and played that night. Found on my arrival a hall empty : not a seat, not a chandelier—no musicians—NO NOTHING : and at a quarter before five I had not a prospect of being able to open. I went through every street of Coventry—to the Mayor, to an Alderman, to carpenters, to fiddlers. You can have no notion of my temper, my coolness, my perseverance : Simpson was astonished—hobbler as I am, I knocked him up : he could not follow me. At half-past seven I had a very elegant audience, all seated on about 30 long forms dragged from a church; sixty candles in two chandeliers, dragged from the town hall, a raised stage, three music stands and three bad fiddlers who could not play 'God Save the King' between them. It was magic and all went off well."

After Birmingham Mathews was to go on to Sheffield, Derby and Leicester before returning home to London. By then he had travelled nearly 500 miles. With Derby and Leicester (two nights there) to go he had already cleared £225.

And his five-letter summing up on Simms and Co. was *PUMPS*.

The Spencers of Althorp were prominent over the years among those who patronised or bespoke performances at the Northampton theatre. One such evening of noble attendance was Monday, November 20, 1815, when Lady Althorp selected the comedy *Education* and the "new, laughable farce" of *Love, Law and Physic*. The audience were assured that "Fires are constantly kept in the pit passages which completely air the boxes all round and render them warm and comfortable". The present Earl Spencer tells me that among his vast library and collection of historical documents are a number of special programmes, printed on satin, for the nights patronised by his forebears.

Right in the middle of the Simms reign of eight years there pops up quite unexpectedly and unexplained a further and final Northampton season by the Lincoln Company of Mr. Thomas Shaftoe Robertson. Whether there was a move to entice him back or whether it was merely a case of filling in a few weeks unexpectedly vacant, there is no clue, but

The FAIR, and LAST NIGHT.

THEATRE, NORTHAMPTON.

This present FRIDAY, SEPTEMBER 19th, 1817,

Will be presented, the admired Comedy of

THE WAY
To get Married.

Tangent	Mr. J. G. RAYMOND
Captain Faulkner	Mr. HORTON
Toby Allspice	Mr. CROSS
Caustic	Mr. SIMMS
M·Queery	Mr. MURPHY
Jeffery	Mr. BUTLER
Dashall	Mr. RAYMOND
Shopman	Mr. NEWTON
Servant	Master IVERS
Ned	Mr. COPPIN
Julia Faulkner	Miss SIMMS
Clementina Allspice	Mrs. BUTLER
Lady Sorrell	Mrs. JAMES

END OF THE PLAY,

A Comic Song by Mr. Butler,

And a COMIC SONG by Mr. RAYMOND.

To which will be added, the favourite Farce of

PAST TEN o'CLOCK
AND A RAINY NIGHT.

Charles Wildfire. Mr. J. G. RAYMOND .... Sir Peter Punctual, Mr. BUTLER
Old Snaps, Mr. MURPHY .. Young Snaps. Mr. NEWTON
Harry Punctual, Mr. HORTON .... Bantam, Mr. RAYMOND ... Waiter, Master IVERS
Dozey, Mr. SIMMS .. Sam Squib, Mr. CROSS
Lucy, Miss SIMMS
Nancy, Mrs. BUTLER .... Silence, Mrs. JAMES

Tickets and Places for the Boxes to be had of Mr. ABEL, on the Parade; and at the PRINTERS'.
Boxes, 3s. 6d.—Pit, 2s.—Gallery, 1s.   To begin at SEVEN o'Clock.

Freeman, Printer and Bookseller, Northampton.

NORTHAMPTON, 1817—right at the end of the Simms regime. (*British Museum and Northampton Public Library*) on May 9, 1812, he was back to announce in the Mercury "with the utmost respect" that he would have the honour of opening the theatre for a season of six weeks.

One of the bespeak performances was of *The Royal Oak or King Charles Preserved* which had a local interest because Charles II gave 1,000 tons of oak towards the rebuilding of All Saints Church, Northampton, following the Dreadful Fire of Northampton in 1675 when most of the town was burned down. The monarch's statue stands in place of honour above the portico of the church. This evening was by desire of Peter Denys Esq., High Sheriff of Northamptonshire, and thereby there is a link with another local statue. Within a few days of his night at the theatre Mr. Denys took the chair at a meeting at the County Hall to pass a resolution of condolence to the Prince Regent on the assassination on May 11 of Spencer Perceval, Prime Minister and Chancellor of the Exchequer and M.P. for Northampton, which took place within the precincts of the House. Mr. Robert Abbey, secretary of the theatre proprietors, was a member of the committee formed to collect subscriptions for a monument to be placed in All Saints Church. Today the statue stands in the Town (or District) Council Chamber at Northampton, a memorial to a man who is noted in the history books mainly for the violent manner of his death.

The Lincoln Company's other productions during this last season included several Shakespeare plays, *Macbeth, Cymbeline, As You Like It,* which was for Civic Night, and *The Merchant of Venice* which was by desire of the proprietors of the theatre. The final performance of the company at Northampton was of *The Sons of Erin or Modern Sentiment* written by Mrs. Lefanu, sister of Richard Brinsley Sheridan, then performing at the Theatre Royal, Lyceum, "with the most unbounded applause". That was on Friday, June 19, 1812, and marked the end of the Robertson Company's links with the town though many years later, as will emerge, a celebrated play by a Robertson was performed at the theatre by another Robertson company.

Northampton being a shoe town, it may be a suitable moment to re-tell a shoe story concerning the Lincoln Company. It appears in the memoirs of a member of the Robertson clan who was made a Dame for her services to the drama—Dame Madge Kendal. She recalls that life could be hard for the stroller. On one thirty-miles "stroll" with the company, her father, William Robertson (nephew of Thomas Shaftoe Robertson), Mr. Chippendale and Mr. Henry Compton were to walk together but one of them had only one shoe. "Under these circumstances there was only one thing to be done and to the credit of the profession they did it. They stuck by each other, as they always do, always have done and I hope always will do— and took it in turns to walk with a single shoe."

Compton became a leading actor and was the father of Edward Compton whose company opened the Theatre Royal and Opera House, Guildhall Road, Northampton, in 1884, when it supplanted the Marefair house. His real name was Mackenzie and this is why his literary descendant was "Compton Mackenzie". Born in Huntingdon, Compton made his first appearance with the Lincoln Company at Spalding.

In September, 1816, Simms brought to the town the man who was to succeed him as lessee, the great Robert William Elliston, "from the Theatre Royal, Drury Lane", which theatre Elliston was also soon to control. His guest appearance at Northampton with Simms included *Three and the Deuce*, *Of Age Tomorrow*, and *The Liar*.

In 1817 Simms fades away from the Northampton scene, putting in an appearance only for the September Races Week and Fair Night.

What happened to Unlucky Simms? In December that year he turns up at the Warwick Theatre in a company including Francis Raymond, another future lessee of the Northampton theatre, and Mrs. Raymond. A playbill of Thursday, January 1, 1818, carries this preamble : "Several gentlemen having kindly expressed a wish to use their endeavours to make a good night in consideration of the loss that has been sustained from the great failure of the theatrical season . . ." Simms had come unstuck again.

And after that? There was a Mr. Simms who operated in the 1820s as a booking agent for actors throughout the country. He made his headquarters in the Harp Tavern, Russell Street, Drury Lane. Whether he was the same man I do not know. But it seems likely. For this Simms sent the afore-mentioned Henry Compton from London to Leicester to take up an acting post with his old friend Francis Raymond. Having no money Compton walked the ninety-six miles between Friday and Monday. But by the time he got there the manager had given the job to someone else . . .

Scene Two

KING OF THE STAGE

On Monday, April 27, 1818, the comedy of *The Strolling Gentleman* was performed "by desire of the Worshipful the Mayor" and that month saw the start of the Northampton management of a man who has himself been termed "The Strolling Gentleman of the English Stage"—Robert William Elliston, who had made a guest appearance eighteen months earlier with the Simms Company.

Born in 1774 and therefore aged forty-four at the time he took over the Northampton theatre Elliston billed himself as "late principal performer at the Theatre Royal, Drury Lane", of which he was also shortly to become the lessee. It was he who had spoken the prologue written by Lord Byron when the Drury Lane Theatre was opened on October 10, 1812, the previous one having been burned down in February, 1809. That night he played Hamlet in the new house which seated no fewer than 3,060. The farce which followed was prophetic, *The Devil to Pay*. The Byron prologue included these lines :

> *"In one dread night our city saw and sighed*
> *Bowed to the dust the Drama's tower of pride*
> *In one short hour beheld the blazing fane*
> *Apollo sink and Shakespeare cease to reign."*

Elliston was a true "character", somewhat in the Ustinov mould. Certainly the following anecdote from George Raymond's Life of Elliston gains in quality if one imagines Ustinov in the role of the manager.

A country actor who called on Elliston seeking a job was of ungainly appearance but something in his manner tickled Elliston and he decided to have a bit of fun with him, while resolving to have nothing to do with him as an actor. After he had listed his many provincial engagements, the man was halted by Elliston : "Ay now, sir, I recollect you well—you played a kangaroo."

The man protested that he had never played a kangaroo but Elliston insisted : "You do yourself an injustice. Your versatility is great and your parts have been numerous but you cannot have forgotten the kangaroo."

"Forgotten, Mr. Elliston?" said the actor, beginning to take the bait.

"Norwich was the place . . . you have played at Norwich?"

For the Benefit of Mr. BOWES,
(TREASURER.)

THEATRE, NORTHAMPTON.

On THURSDAY Evening, MAY 14th, 1818,

Will be performed, the admired Play of

THE
STRANGER

OR,

Misanthropy and Repentance.

The Stranger, Mr. BURTON
Count Wintersen, Mr. ELLIOTT .... Baron Steinfort, Mr. BURKE
Solomon, Mr. THOMPSON .... Peter, Mr. KEELEY
Tobias, Mr. MAXWELL .. Francis, Mr. SHIELD
Count's Son, Miss THOMPSON .. Stranger's Son, Master THOMPSON

Mrs. Haller, Mrs. PITT
Countess Wintersen, Miss NELSON
Charlotte, Mrs. THOMPSON .... Annette, Mrs. MAXWELL

END OF THE PLAY,

A SONG BY MR. MAXWELL.

To which will be added, the Farce of

THE
POOR SOLDIER

Captain Fitzroy, Mr. BURKE
Patrick, Mr. MAXWELL — Dermot, Mr. M'KEON
Father Luke, Mr SHIELD
Bagatelle, Mr. ELLIOTT — Pot Boy, Master BROWN
Derby, Mr. THOMPSON

Norah, Mrs. MAXWELL — Kathleen, Mrs. THOMPSON

BOXES. 3s. 6d. — PIT, 2s — GALLERY, 1s.

Tickets and Places for the Boxes to be had of Mr. ABEL, Parade; and of Mr.
FREEMAN, Printer, Sheep-Street.

Doors opened at Six, and to begin at Seven o'Clock.

Freeman, Printer, Northampton

NORTHAMPTON, 1818—during the first season with Robert William Elliston as lessee.
(*British Museum and Northampton Public Library*)

"Yes, sir, many times. I remember about the period of Waterloo we got up 'The Death of Captain Cook' . . ."

"Ah, I knew you had played a kangaroo. Striking things always make an impression with me and I remember your kangaroo as though it were yesterday. Let's see," continued Elliston, jumping up and making a grotesque twist of the body. "It was somewhat after this manner that you did it . . . no, no, not quite like that either. I can't exactly make the movement . . ."

"Hold, hold," cried the Rural Thespian, leaping to the middle of the room and throwing himself into a bizarre attitude balancing on one leg, "the kangaroo advances in this manner."

"Ay ay, I knew you had played a kangaroo," exclaimed Elliston, *"and when I get up an Australian spectacle I'll send for you!"*

Elliston seems to have taken on the Northampton theatre in quite casual manner. He came in April, 1818, for a few nights but then decided to take the lease for three years. In his advertisement he said that the theatre was found in a "very dismantled state" but promised to bring it up to par. "Fires having been kept in every part of the theatre some days previous to the opening the visitants on the first night found it completely warm. Patent Liverpool burners are used on the stage and to the side wings and the audience part of the house is lighted with wax."

The previously mentioned Mayoral night included *The Strolling Gentleman*, *Wild Oats*, a song "Nobody Coming to Marry Me" by Miss Thompson in the character of an old maid, and the melodrama, *The Broken Sword*, with a "grand view of the Pyrenees and a vineyard, the garden of the chateau belonging to the baron, also the mountainous path and torrent."

In *The Heir at Law* Elliston appeared as Dr. Pangloss while the well-known London actor Mr. Brunton was Dick Dowlas and Mrs. Pitt was Cicely Homespun—many names of characters in those days were "spun" so as to label the part.

Mr. Elliston's first season ran from April to May and the company was back in September for the Race Week, announcing "The scenery has been newly painted; a new drop scene has been prepared; the house entirely decorated; the chandeliers are brilliantly ornamented"— the only reference to the house possessing chandeliers. The star attraction was not an actor but "Il Diavolo Antonio" who performed on the "corde volante", presumably a trapeze artist whose tour de force came on his benefit night on Saturday, September 12, in between George Colman's play, *The Mountaineers* and the petite comic drama of *Sylvester Daggerwood or The Dunstable Actor* when he was announced to "while in full swing play the trumpet, accompanying the band in the overture to Lodoiska and conclude in an evolution as rapid as a windmill can turn, surrounded by fireworks imitative of the Three Royal Feathers". For this bumper bundle of entertainment the box price was 4s.

In October the company were back for three further nights when they staged "a new comic pantomime in which the greatest variety of tricks will be produced, *Harlequin Horner or Jewels Newly Set*, with Signior Paulo, from Drury Lane as the Clown".

An accident occurred on the stage during the first night performance of *The Spoiled Child* for the benefit of Miss Hart, who played the part of Little Pickle. The actor who played Old Pickle dragged his child with too much vigour and broke her left arm. A doctor who was in the audience attended to her.

One must not overstress the importance of Northampton in Elliston's theatrical gallery. Brian Dobbs said that Elliston, "The Great Lessee", "had fingers in more pies than Simple Simon. He took over innumerable small theatres, opened a subscription library and in his early days broke his rounds of gambling, drinking and fornication only to give a series of lectures on morality during Lent."

Birmingham was one of the places where he had operated. Becoming manager in 1813 he was at first allowed to open only three nights a week because the proprietors thought there was insufficient support for more performances. By the following season they were congratulating him on profits of £1,200, which he had obtained by sensational tactics—acrobats, equestrians and weight-lifters. During the Birmingham season immediately prior to his September, 1818, appearances at Northampton, he had struck a bad patch, however. One of the morning newspapers reported that his theatrical speculation at Birmingham had proved unfortunate and quoted the figures for some nights when guarantees had to be paid to star guests— Mrs. C. Kemble takings £39 18s. (guarantee £50); Mrs. de Camp £32 19s. 6d. (£40); Miss Clara Fisher £45 3s. 6d. (£100); Miss Kelly £45 0s. 6d. (£90); Mr. M'Cready £95 (£100).

The following March, of 1819, a new piece of apparatus was used at a Northampton event which seems to have been regarded as a form of public entertainment. It was the "New Drop", designed to snap the necks of criminals instead of their being pushed off a cart at the end of a rope and left to strangle to death.

The New Drop was at the County Gaol, Angel Lane, and before it came into use executions took place in a close near Northampton Racecourse, then known as Northampton Heath, the last men hanged there being James Cobbett and George Wilkins on March 27, 1818, their crime being the uttering of forged notes. Following the custom they had been driven from the gaol in a mourning coach with the chance of a last drink at the Bantam Cock public house on Abington Square, which lay on the route.

The first hangings at the new site were of five men sentenced for house-breaking in the village of Preston Deanery. William Minards, William George, Benjamin Panther, Edward Porter and John Taffs died simultaneously, watched by an enormous crowd, many of whom had travelled several miles.

The usual mealy-mouthed phrases accompanied the announcement of the executions: "Since their condemnation the unhappy men have conducted themselves with great propriety, respectively acknowledging the justice of their sentence, at the same time evincing a disposition to repent of their manifold and aggravated crimes and to die in peace with all mankind. At the place of execution their behaviour was very suitable to persons in their unhappy situation. Soon after 12 o'clock they were launched into eternity; and after hanging the usual time, their bodies were taken down and those of Minards, Panther and Taffs were delivered to their friends for interment; and those of George and Porter were buried in St. Giles's Churchyard."

There was not, however, universal acquiescence in this legalised ritual of butchery. The same month at Bedford Shire Hall, for instance, a meeting was held to petition for revision of the criminal statutes "to prevent comparatively small offences from being visited with the same awful sentences". In their own effective way juries were rebelling. "Though sworn to give true verdicts according to evidence, they yet feel so great a repugnance to convict capitally for minor offences that out of 19,748 indictments on capital charges only 9,510 verdicts of guilty were found." Even the judges were accomplices—"The learned and humane judges of the land, feeling as we presume the extreme severity of such statutes have during the late years uniformly reprieved a very great majority of capital convicts insomuch that out of the above 9,510 only 327 were left to suffer that irremediable punishment." The Bedford meeting was convened by the Mayor, John Cooke. The mood was changing and a whole wave of reform was to come.

In October, 1819, the Northampton theatre again served as a concert room for events organised by Mr. Barrett, organist of All Saints Church. Tickets were 10s. 6d. or, if taken along with a ball afterwards at the George Hotel Assembly Rooms, 18s. This was as much as many actors earned in a week. The most famous tenor of the day, Braham, sang at the concerts.

Just previously Elliston sent a company to appear for only four nights, including Mr. de Camp, Mr. M'Keon, Mr. Keely, Mr. Elliott, Mrs. Pearce, Miss Cook and Mrs. Austin.

In November a five week season was played by the "Inimitable Theatre of Arts, from Spring Gardens, London". This appears to have been an art display with "mechanical and beautiful pictures representative of various parts of the world, including a voyage to the North Pole, the garden and palace of the Thuilleries, the Cape of Good Hope, the City of Naples, a wonderful representation of a storm at sea, songs, tales, rope dancing and a Lecture on Heads".

The first two months of 1820 found Northampton joining in the mourning for two Royal deaths—in January of the Duke of Kent (father of Queen Victoria) and in February of his father, George III. In April the town hailed the new monarch with the ringing of church bells and firing of volleys on the Market Square by Northampton Volunteer Cavalry and the County Militia.

In May the theatre was taken for one night by Mr. Horn of the Theatre Royal, Drury Lane, and Mr. J. Russell, of the Covent Garden and Haymarket theatres. Later they paid a second visit.

Whether Elliston was too busy with his many other commitments or disenchanted with his experiences at Northampton we do not know but his company again came for only four nights of the Race Week that year, in August. Whatever his oversight at Northampton lacked in quantity, he made up for in quality the following month when he brought Edmund Kean to the town, the actor of whom it was said by Coleridge that to see him act was like reading Shakespeare by lightning.

Shortly before this visit Kean and Elliston had been contenders for the lesseeship of Drury Lane. Elliston had won and was about to start on the spectacular reign which was to lead him to the bankruptcy court. For the "Lane" he had to pay £10,000 a year rent; what he paid for the Northampton theatre is not on record but judging by his casual approach it could not have been much.

Kean was on the eve of the trip to America during which he nearly provoked a riot at Boston by refusing to play to a small house. At Northampton on Monday, September 18, 1820, he appeared in *Richard III* and the following night in *The Merchant of Venice*. It was his performance of Shylock which had made him an overnight success at his first appearance at Drury Lane on January 26, 1814. Neither appearance received a mention in the local paper! It is only from the prior advertisement that we know that the theatre was "as at the music meetings, superbly illuminated, the gallery seats covered". From Northampton Kean moved on to Leamington on the Wednesday (*Richard III*), Coventry on Thursday (*Richard III*) and Friday (*The Merchant of Venice*) and back to Leamington on the Saturday for another "Merchant". Elliston played in the afterpieces.

For some personal witness on this great pair, Kean and Elliston, we fortunately have available the memoirs of Francis Courtney Wemyss who himself played under the Elliston banner at Northampton in 1821.

In his fascinating *Life of an Actor and Manager* Wemyss wrote : "How shall I attempt to describe the 'star' of the British stage, the man who without a single friend overcame obstacles almost insurmountable; and by one bold effort swept away the cold and polished school of Kemble from the stage, astonishing the English metropolis by his bold and natural conception of character... he moved like a comet."

Kean did not even know his parentage. Wemyss's background was very different. Losing his parents early in life he was raised by an uncle who ran a large weaving business in the Dundee district and at only fifteen young Wemyss was superintending operations in Courtney and Sons, employing two-thirds of the population of Kirkaldy, Dysart, East and West Wemyss, Perth, Dundee, Forfar, Arbroath, Brechin, Montrose and Aberdeen. The taste of the silver spoon thus jammed into his mouth did not, however, suit the lad and he ran away in classic style to "go on the stage". His first encounter was unfortunate. Joining a strolling manager named Moss at Falkirk his stomach heaved on being introduced to the company at first rehearsal. "Oh what a check for proud ambition ! The 'theatre', the object of my hope and desire, was a barn fitted up in the rudest style; but I consoled myself with the knowledge that John Kemble had acted in a barn. But when the ladies and gentlemen assembled to rehearse, Falstaff's ragged regiment in apparel were princes to them—with the solitary exception of the manager there was not a single decently dressed individual... my courage failed; I resolved not to make one of their number."

There was some ground, therefore, to his uncle's pleadings to young Wemyss to give up all idea of the stage—"the lowest dregs of humanity, a ruinous and disgraceful career". The would-be actor persisted, however, and it was perhaps as a reaction to his sight of the "ragged regiment" that he set out to gain a reputation as one of the best-dressed actors. His subsequent career included a pleasant spell with Robertson and his Lincoln Company and now we find him joining up with another of the Northampton line of managers, Elliston.

Wemyss was in joint management at Plymouth when he first heard from Robert William—"I received an offer from no less a personage than Mr. Robert Elliston, the Napoleon of the drama, of whom it has been justly said that if thrown overboard in rags from one side of a ship would appear before his tormentor could turn round upon the other side dressed as a gentleman, ready to begin the world again; who as the manager of a minor theatre held the town a captive, daily infringing the rights of the Royal theatre with impunity and who, as the lessee of a patented theatre, forthwith brought civil actions against the minor theatres for infringing his rights."

With this call from on high in his ears Wemyss handed over his rights in theatres at Plymouth, Dock, Liskeard, Bodmin, Penzance, Truro and Falmouth to his colleague, named Dawson, and set off to London. When he got there he found that the elusive Elliston was not offering quite as good a prospect in the capital as he had promised and the outcome was that Wemyss took on as a member of Elliston's country theatres, at Coventry, Leamington Spa, Northampton etc. The "etcetera" places are not entirely clear but seem to have included visits to Warwick, Birmingham, and "Weadon" (presumably Weedon, Northants, though by no means certain). Wemyss refers to these travels of 1821 as constituting a "delightful summer".

During the season at Leamington, each Wednesday night was played at Coventry, the manager providing a vehicle known at Leamington as a "pleasure car", into which six players were crammed. It was during one of these visits that a reminder came of the uncertain standing of the actor in the eyes of the law. In theory, at least, he was still liable to be cast in the role of a "vagabond" and imprisoned at the whim of a magistrate.

The dispute at Coventry was a question of interpretation. Elliston had permission to open for sixty nights, which he took to mean a total of sixty nights but which the Bench conceived to be sixty nights continuously.

Wemyss described the incident with relish : "Everyone acquainted with English theatricals is aware that by law actors and actresses playing without a licence are liable to be apprehended as sturdy vagrants and vagabonds and as such committed to the House of Correction. Some squabbling having taken place between Mr. Elliston and the magistrates of Coventry in which the latter felt themselves to be insulted by the dignified patentee of the Theatre Royal, Drury Lane, they resolved upon avenging their wrongs upon the unconscious actors. On our arrival from Leamington while dressing for the play of *Venice Preserved* a gentleman with a red collar and cuffs to his coat, usually known as a police officer, walked into the room and informed us in the most pleasant manner that we were his prisoners : that none of us must leave the building until the return of Mr. Penley, the manager, who was forthwith summoned before the Mayor."

When Penley returned an hour and a half later Wemyss and his fellow actors were disappointed to hear that the matter had been settled. "Had we been committed to prison, as threatened, it would have created a sensation in our profession throughout the country and in all probability would have made the fortune of the more than one of our community who, whatever might have been the opinion of the public as to their merits as players, were universally respected for their deportment off the stage." Evidently Wemyss visualised sensational billings such as "See the Actors who were sent to Prison at Coventry!" As it was, the performance merely started late, at half-past nine and, the news having got round, to a larger house than would otherwise have been the case.

And so the company were later than usual, making their way back to Leamington in their pleasure cars. And the good folk of Kenilworth were disturbed from their slumbers even later than usual, probably at half past two instead of the usual one o'clock in the morning, as the actors sang their customary "God Save the King" in full chorus as they passed through— "in honour, as we were pleased to say, of the revels of the Earl of Leicester to Queen Elizabeth".

Mention of the National Anthem leads naturally to a performance at Northampton which was said to be the most spectacular in the history of the Marefair theatre—nothing less than a Royal Coronation, the grand flourish with which the Great Lessee parted from the town.

Initially Elliston had wanted to assert the rights of his Drury Lane Company as "His Majesty's (patented) Servants" but when authority would not grant them an ancestral place in the actual Coronation he resolved to present as near a facsimile of it as possible in his theatre. The King himself gave the Royal stamp of approval by attending a performance to see the stage George IV strutting about in the person of Robert William. In fact Elliston, who was given to flights of fancy at times, got so carried away that he stepped into the footlights for one of the impromptu addresses for which he was celebrated, to address "My People..."

Having reaped a golden harvest in London Elliston decided to cash in provincially and the first call was at Northampton. He himself was too busy reigning at Drury Lane to visit Marefair but even without him his "correct facsimile of the gorgeous and impressive ceremony of the Coronation" played to overflowing houses. The Mercury rated it "the most splendid representation ever witnessed in this or any provincial theatre—the beauty and correctness of the scenery, the splendour and magnificence of the robes and regalia and the various ceremonies were faithfully delineated, with the imposing effect of the 'Champion in Real Armour' on a beautiful charger, richly plumed and caparisoned, exciting the admiration of crowded houses".

Wemyss, who appeared as Lord Castlereagh, in the full Order of the Garter, tells us that the provincial production was in the hands of Mr. Lee, formerly stage manager of the Adelphi Theatre. Mr. S. Penley played the King and Mr. Montague Penley was Prince Leopold who, like Wemyss, was in full Garter outfit and could not make the quick changes required of the rest of the cast who each had six roles to cope with as the procession carried on its way, taking three quarters of an hour to do so.

The make-believe Castlereagh contrasts the reception afforded at Northampton with that at Coventry, which followed : "In Northampton everything passed off with great eclat and is remembered by those who witnessed it as the most delightful theatrical representation ever seen. The champion and the procession accompanying the King into the body of the cathedral, passing through the very centre of the audience, had a magical and grand appearance. From Northampton we proceeded to Coventry, decidedly at that time one of the most radical towns in England. Here the actors had to endure the groans and hisses of the audience, as the representatives of those persons politically offensive to the spectators. The ceremony was a scene of tumult, each character being received with tumultuous applause or with hisses, cat-calls or other deafening noise. I, as Lord Castlereagh, was the first obnoxious person who made his appearance. From the moment I placed my foot upon the stage, until the last page supporting my train disappeared, it was one cry of 'Shame, Shame'', 'Off, Off', 'Queen, Queen', 'Who sold his country?', 'Ha', 'Off', 'Go Along' mingled with hisses and groans. This ceremony usually occupied two minutes. The Duke of York followed me and the change from hissing and hooting to applauding and huzzaing was wonderful."

Next to incur the displeasure of the audience were the Attorney-General and the Judges. The appearance of the King himself was the signal for a trial of strength between those who favoured him and those who did not. "Here the row generally terminated in a fight between His Majesty's loyal subjects and the admirers of the Queen which lasted until the scene changed to the banqueting hall. This was repeated on every representation and when the last night arrived I felt relieved from the most disagreeable task I ever had imposed upon me during my professional career."

In case the reader is mystified by the reference to the Queen I should perhaps recall that their Majesties were separated and the Queen drove up to Westminster Abbey but was refused admission to the Coronation.

After thus being sent to Coventry Wemyss returned to Northampton to complete the season and it was then that he received an offer to appear in the United States. At first he turned it down but subsequently accepted an engagement with Areen and Wood at the Philadelphia Theatre for three years at 6 guineas a week "with the accustomed benefits and advantages" to commence on December 1, 1822, with the opening of the new theatre. To fill in the time he took a six weeks engagement with Mr. Smith, of the Theatre Royal, Windsor, who was in fact briefly one of Elliston's successors at Northampton. (Another was a Mr. Warwick, but about him I could find precisely nothing.)

Crossing the Atlantic was a more daunting enterprise than it is today, of course, and the agent who booked Wemyss told him that it was a difficult matter to persuade an actor to make the trip—he said that he could "scarcely calculate upon my departure until he saw me on board".

The erstwhile Lord Castlereagh liked what he found in the States, despite being told on arrival in New York that the yellow fever was raging there and he should not go ashore. Judds Hotel in Philadelphia found particular favour with him : "There was something of the bustle of the hotel which pleased me, the rush to the dinner table on the sound of the bell, the rapidity with which the ample provisions disappeared really amused me."

He did not, on the other hand, like the chandelier in the new Chestnut Theatre—"This mode of lighting exposed to view that very portion which should be kept as much as possible in the shade and which has contributed more to the downfall of the drama than all the other causes; I allude to the third tier of boxes where licentiousness prevails in its worst form."

As a result of Wemyss's emigration a Coronation was staged in Republican surroundings. The representations at Drury Lane, Northampton and Coventry had their counterparts in the Walnut Theatre, Philadelphia, in August, 1838. Remembering Elliston's success with George IV, Wemyss did a repeat with Queen Victoria. "In face of remonstrance from all quarters I produced a pageant of the Coronation of Queen Victoria. I followed as nearly as I could recollect the arrangements of Elliston's grand spectacle, refreshing my memory from the London newspapers which were filled with accounts of the Coronation of Britain's youthful Queen."

Oddly enough the ex-colonials liked what they saw. This flaunting of Royal ceremonial was a success. "It taught the audience once more the road to the Walnut Street theatre which they appeared to have forgotten." An exception was an actress in the cast, a Mrs. Bannister who "so far forgot her position to the manager and the audience that she hissed the last verse of 'God Save The Queen' for four nights."

Wemyss, who at times managed the Chestnut Street and Walnut Street and Arch Street theatres in Philadelphia, the Holiday Street and Front Street theatres in Baltimore, and the Pittsburgh Theatre, would never hear England assailed without defending it; but "no inducement could prevail upon me to take up my abode in my native country".

Wemyss and Elliston had more than the "Coronation" in common. As a result of their theatrical endeavours both went bankrupt. Despite phenomenal initial successes things turned sour for Wemyss in the United States and in March, 1841, he had to apply for the relief of the insolvency laws.

"My large establishment was completely broken up. Philadelphia, Baltimore and Pittsburgh theatres all passed from my hands. My property was disposed of under the Sheriff's hammer at a time when real estate would scarcely be taken as a gift, ruining me without aiding my creditors. A theatrical wardrobe the most extensive in the United States which 10,000 dollars would not replace sold for 136 dollars. The Pennsylvania Theatre which cost me 15,000 dollars exclusive of the mortgage of 5,000 dollars, sold, subject to the same mortgage, for 62 dollars. The month of April, 1841, found me without one cent, crushed, heartbroken and degraded in my own estimation. I have never been the same man since."

And Elliston? As Brian Dobbs has pungently written in his Drury Lane history : "The advent of Elliston brings us to a 60-year period when Drury Lane management was as hazardous an occupation as tightrope walking. At times it looked like an apprenticeship preparatory to the bankruptcy court." In 1826 he became £500 in arrears in rent and despite having spent £22,000 on altering the interior, was pressed into bankruptcy.

Thus both the "King" and "Castlereagh" went bust . . .

INTERLUDE

in Act the First

*RECITATIONS on the subjects of Air, Gas & Wax
with a few well-chosen words on Good Causes*

*UP & AWAY
    An Account of Aerial Adventures*

*GAS
    Some Illuminating Remarks*

*WAX
    The Celebrated Madame Tussaud*

*GOOD CAUSES
    Some Touches of Benevolence*

GRAHAM & PICKERING were to have been "Accompanied by a Lady". In fact she went up alone and had to escape through an attic window. See Page 78. (*Northampton and County Independent*)

UP & AWAY

An Account of Aerial Adventures

In the age of the aeroplane and space travel it is difficult to conceive how powerful an effect the sight of a man disappearing into the sky must have had on the citizenry of the late eighteenth and early nineteenth centuries. The age of witchcraft was not far behind.

The dare-devil ascents below a bag of gas were not only a means of bold adventure, but of making money. They were part of Georgian show-biz. Customers given a promise of performance were not always happy when it failed to mature. When a Mr. Harper announced an ascent by balloon at Birmingham in 1785 but was thwarted at the first attempt by a defect in the materials for forming the gas, the angry crowd threw stones and the Riot Act had to be read. Later Harper did get up and away and used a speaking trumpet to ask a person on the ground how far away he was from Birmingham. "About 40 miles, Master," came the answer, "but you are going the wrong road!"

The drawing power of ascent into the atmosphere was exploited in Northampton as elsewhere.

In January, 1812, there was the comparatively minor spectacle of sending up an unmanned balloon. "Precisely at one o'clock it will be set off (from the Market Hill) for a view of which the small subscription of one shilling each is requested to remunerate the proprietor for the expenses and total loss of the balloon." Filling it was to commence at 11 and the shillings would be collected during the process.

Three years later a balloon was sent up from Mr. Comfield's premises in the Horsemarket from which a "car and parachute" were detached in mid-air two miles from the point of departure and "descended in a most uniform and satisfactory manner".

When Charles Mathews visited Northampton in August, 1821, at the close of the Elliston period, it was announced that he would have the honour to attempt a description of his travels in *AIR, EARTH* and *WATER*. In this the great comedian was guilty of misrepresentation. He had dearly wanted to go up in a balloon and had a contract signed to do so with Mr. Arnold, manager of the London Vauxhall Gardens, but Mrs. Mathews had strictly forbidden her husband to take the risk. When he withdrew he had to pay a heavy penalty for breaking the contract. Mathews was due to appear at the Theatre Royal, English Opera House, at the time, in the Strand, and the crafty manager exploited the event as if it had happened.

When a manned ascent was at last planned in Northampton it was in the year 1828 and an officer from Weedon Barracks was so keen to accompany Mr. Green, aeronaut, that he paid a fare. Alas! he was to be disappointed.

The flight was to be from the town's gasworks, near the theatre. Owing to damage the balloon had deteriorated on the road from a previous ascent at Exeter, including exposure to the rain; "on being unpacked it was in so great heat that had it been confined a few days longer, spontaneous combustion must have ensued". As it was inflated by hydrogen it soon became apparent that much of the varnish had decomposed resulting in the escape of a large quantity of the gas. "In this emergency Captain Ryan, who was to have accompanied Mr. Green, was informed, to his extreme disappointment, mortification and chagrin, that it was utterly impossible. When all was ready, however, the gallant captain jumped into the car which was immediately detached from the balloon by cutting the ropes, Mr. Green at the same time getting upon the hoop above the car. The gallant captain quickly succeeded in getting astride the hoop also from which he was forcibly removed by several individuals connected with Mr. Green, who immediately ascended at the imminent risk of his life, without car, grappling iron or any other instrument to assist in his descent."

Come down safely he did, however, in a field at nearby Dallington, to the west of the town. He had collected £100 in admission money from spectators and promised to do a further ascent free of charge.

Later that year there was an even more exciting balloon incident, this time right in the heart of the town. Messrs Graham and Pickering chose the central Market Square (or Market Hill as it was often called) as their point of departure. Again there was an escape of gas which meant that only a lightweight person could be carried. Mrs. Graham bravely volunteered.

First the balloon had been inflated at the gas works and en route to the Square it had already knocked off several chimney pots. On its launch the craft moved south-east but did not rise fast enough and got stuck at the height of Widow Ager's attic window, at the south-east corner of the square.

"Every voice was hushed and the busy hum which a few moments before had ascended from the assembled throng was succeeded by a death-like and solemn pause. The fair aeronaut appeared to be the only one who did not participate in the general alarm for she continued with the most entire self-possession to make preparations for a retreat from her perilous situation and all this amidst a volley of bricks and mortar that were detached from a chimney which the stupendous aerostatic machine was all the time most majestically belabouring. At length the gallant Amazon, amidst the joyous plaudits of the assembled multitude, safely effected her escape through the garret window of Mrs. Ager."

The balloon eventually disentangled itself and sped away and was at first thought to be lost. It came down at Tansor, near Oundle, where some of the villagers thought it signified the end of the world. One good wife sank on her knees : "The prophecies are fulfilled. The end of the world is at hand and Noah's Ark is in view."

In August, 1830, the balloon went up at a Tory rally in Newland, just north of the Market Square. Four hundred women sat down to tea in a paddock where the huge Grosvenor Centre is now, in 1974, replacing streets of early Victorian property. Sixty feet round, the balloon bore the message "Victory of Sir R. H. Gunning, the Pride of Northampton".

Another variation was for a parachute to be released with a rabbit as passenger. One of these was presumably the first astonished parachutist to drop in on the Northamptonshire countryside!

Mr. Gyngell, whose firework, tight-rope and other entertainments were given at Northampton over many years, introduced a balloon into the programme for his visit in December, 1838. "For the gratification of the public a large Montgolfier balloon will ascend from the front of the theatre at a quarter past seven, to which will be attached a brilliant light which will change to blue, green, purple and crimson and, at a considerable height, will discharge an innumerable quantity of variegated stars which will completely illumine the atmosphere."

The first account of the activities of one of the pyrotechnists (as they were called) comes in 1788 when a Mr. Hengler gave his show on the Market Hill (i.e. Market Square). At a first performance the collection had not come up to his expectations so he advertised his hope that "the respectable householders on the Market Hill will indulge him with the favour of collecting the same evening in their houses". Evidently the houses around the Square provided a grandstand. Mr. Hengler, who described himself as an artist in fireworks and professor of natural history from High Germany, appears to have suffered from the activities of unofficial collectors and therefore requested that the public "will not give anything to any person unless they have a tin box and a transparent lanthorn".

But the most notable of the artists in pyrotechny was the aforesaid Gyngell who would sometimes, after a show on the Square, take his audience with him down Gold Street to the theatre. More than once his son took part there. Master Gyngell would "make a flight from the back of the gallery through a chromatic fire cloud and showers of sparks". It is perhaps surprising that the theatre did not join the many which went up in flames!

No such disaster did occur. But tragedy did attend one of the Gyngell displays on the Square. This was after he had performed his piece de resistance of walking up a tight-rope from a waggon in the centre of the Square to the attic window of the Queen's Arms public house. He had done this "daring ascent up an inclined plane of fiery rope" more than once and completed the two-way trip successfully again in 1845. It was afterwards that the accident occurred.

To set off one of his rockets he stood it against the wrist-thick rope. As he lit the fuse some boys larking about jarred the rope and the rocket fell and shot off like a bullet among the spectators. It hit a woman named Elizabeth Smith in the face and she fell as if pole-axed. Mrs. Smith, who was a widow with two children, died in Northampton General Infirmary a few days later.

At the inquest the jury suggested he used a staple to support his rockets in future and Mr. Gyngell said the melancholy accident had suggested to him a means of firing out of a tube.

GAS

Some Illuminating Remarks

> *"Those eyes*
> *Like lamps whose wasting oil is spent*
> *Wax dim"*

Mortimer's remarks in *Henry VI* make an admirable introduction to a subject I have not touched upon before, apart from a casual reference to the theatre's possessing chandeliers.

It is the most trite remark to say that nothing is more taken for granted today than light, heat, washing power, radio sound and television picture at the touch of a switch.* In harking back to the old days one must remember that if a threatre manager wanted to warm the pit he had to light a fire of some sort in it; and that if he wanted to light stage or auditorium he had to light some candles.

In the pre-gas age a vital member of the theatre staff was the snuff boy among whose duties was attention to smoking candles during the performance. The action on stage might have reached its most crucial, most tragic, most breath-poising point. But if a candle began to smoke, on would come the snuff boy to deal with it. Small wonder that he might get an ironic cheer. If the boy was on the nod, an actor or actress might interrupt his part to deal with the offending tallow. For it was the tallow candle which caused the problem. When wax was substituted the nuisance was reduced. The wax variety could be left burning for hours without attention.

Expense on candles, of whatever variety, was quite an item on the theatrical budget and often an actor's part-payment at the end of an engagement would be to have the unexpired portion of the candles!

Time for a little more Shakespeare, this time some Gaunt words from *Richard III* :

> *"My oil dried lamp and time bewasted light*
> *Shall be extinct with age and endless night*
> *My inch of taper will be burnt and done."*

The first building in Northampton to be lit by gas was the Marefair theatre. There, on Monday, June 7, 1824, Mr. Bradley, engineer of the Northampton Gas Company, gave a demonstration. Although this was something of a public relations exercise to convince the public that the new-fangled illumination was not an invention of the devil and likely to lead to explosions, it was also sufficient of an entertainment for the private enterprise promoters of the new system to be able to charge for admission. Box tickets were 3s. 6d., pit 2s. and gallery 1s.

* This was written before the 1974 Power Crisis!

The evening was reported in considerable detail in the Mercury along with the lighting of the streets of the town by gas two days later. "Jets of flame issued forth from ten thousand apertures. The flood of radiance which poured forth upon us from a variety of burners clearly evinced the excellence and purity of the gas. Its effect upon the eye is rather grateful than distressing. From the fullness of the attendance and the number of lights exhibited the heat was, of course, considerable but not the least odour of gas was perceived and we are much mistaken if the same quantity of light could have been produced by candles or oil without most oppressive and disgusting exhalations from those materials." Gas lighting, in the commercial sense, had been born in the world of theatre. As early as 1788 some sort of inflammable gas had been used by a German chemist named Diller in a display of "Philosophical fireworks" at the English Opera House, later called the Lyceum. Sixteen years later another German, F. A. Winser, hired the same theatre from Madame Tussaud for a demonstration of lighting by coal gas generated in a retort on the stage. This had many of the aspects of a theatrical performance for Winser spoke little English and merely carried on the experiment whilst a lecture about it in English was read by an assistant stationed in the orchestra pit. Circulating among the audience were boys who distributed handbills about the new miracle and seeking capital for a new Gas Light and Heat Company. As regards raising the wind—which I suppose is the direct object of nearly all theatrical performances—it was most successful. Subscriptions totalled £50,000.

Winser was later responsible for the first demonstration of gas street lighting, outside his home in The Mall, London, and in 1809 Pall Mall was lit by gas—the first public street lighting of its kind in the world.

In 1817 both the stage and auditorium of the Lyceum were lit by gas. Meantime in 1796 limelight had been invented by Drummond but it was more than half-a-century before the innovation reached the theatre.

WAX

The Celebrated Madame Tussaud

It was thus in a gas-lit Northampton theatre, the month after Mr. Bradley's demonstration, that the house received its most famous visitor of all. Names of many of the leading actors and actresses who trod the Northampton boards are today known only to theatre historians but the luminosity of Madame Tussaud is even more bright today than when she brought her "Collection of Composition Figures" to Northampton in July, 1824.

She seems to have taken the town by storm. For thirty-one years the little old lady who had, with her uncle, Dr. Curtius, moulded the head of almost every distinguished victim of the guillotine, toured the United Kingdom, exhibiting in assembly rooms, town halls and theatres. Her sons, Joseph and Francis, took silhouettes and played from 7.30 to 10 p.m. in the orchestra which accompanied the show. For three weeks Madame Tussaud staged her display in the theatre, although she preferred assembly rooms. She explained in an advertisement that she had chosen the theatre "because the Town Hall is not sufficiently large". The Town Hall she rejected—and her comment is a reflection of how tiny it must have been, to be smaller than the theatre—was the one at the corner of Abington Street and Wood Hill, which served the town until the present one was opened in 1864.

There had been wax figure shows in Northampton before, such as the one at Balaam's Coffee House in May, 1793, of a "Grand Cabinet of Figures". These predecessors were dismissed by the Mercury when it reviewed the Tussaud exhibition : "Wax figures, from the inferior specimens which have been exhibited, produce generally a most unpleasant effect from the disagreeable hue of the countenance but it has been reserved for Madame Tussaud to bring this pleasing art to perfection. Upon first entrance the mind is absolutely bewildered with the magic effect of the numerous figures dressed in the most appropriate and splendid costumes." Madame Tussaud's own figure was said to have produced many ludicrous errors, "being mistaken for a living person and from its being placed in the centre of the room".

For this special occasion the theatre pit was boarded over and with the stage "formed one of the largest rooms in Northampton". It was set out to represent the throne room of the Carlton Palace with two Coronation groups on show, one of George IV (which Elliston had staged three years earlier) and the other of Bonaparte. Many of the figures on show at Northampton in 1824 can still be seen 150 years later at the Madame Tussaud premises in London, the moulds having been kept.

The townsfolk also had the chance to see a forerunner of the "Chamber of Horrors", referred to then as "a separate exhibition" and seen in an adjoining room. It included Robespierre, taken immediately after his execution and Marat, after his assassination; both are still on show today. There was a model of the guillotine and the actual shirt worn by Henry IV when he was stabbed. An Egyptian mummy was another exhibit.

No catalogue appears to have survived of the Northampton stay but there is one of the visit to Bath during the first three months of that year. Madame Tussaud had moved on from there via Cirencester and Oxford and had also recently exhibited in Manchester, Liverpool, Birmingham and Bristol. Three years earlier she had survived a shipwreck when trying to move her exhibits from Liverpool to Dublin for the State Visit of George IV.

GOOD CAUSES

Some Touches of Benevolence

Over the years a large number of good causes were aided by performances at the Northampton theatres.

At the earlier theatre Mr. Beynon's Company had given a night's takings in November, 1793, to "the laudable purpose of purchasing warm clothing for the use of British Troops on Foreign Service who in a cold climate are fighting for the protection of our laws and constitutions" i.e. for the British Army in Flanders under the command of the Duke of York. Earlier still Kemble had given nights for the poor debtors in the Town Gaol.

Thomas Shaftoe Robertson was very proud of his effort to assist the Patriotic Fund at Lloyds. In a letter to Mr. Winston from Newark in 1803 he fairly preened himself: "I have lately received the appelation of the Patriotic Manager from the circumstance of giving the entire receipts of one night's performance in each town of my circuit for one twelve month to the Patriotic Fund at Lloyds . . . in the postscript are the receipts that I have sent (the expenses of the night being paid by myself) Lloyds in the towns that I have been in since my offer and I hope by the end of the year the sum will do credit to my circuit." Sums listed were : Spalding, August 23, £29 2s. 6d.; Lincoln, September 24, £29 11s.; and Newark, November 19, £33 15s. At Northampton the performance for this cause took place on Monday, May 7, 1804, during the Lincoln Company's final season at the old theatre, when the plays were *Love Laughs at Locksmiths* and *As You Like It*.

In April, 1808, the Mudie Company gave a performance for the benefit of the Northampton General Infirmary. The entire receipts, without any deduction were to be given but as a result of bad weather they amounted only to £12 14s. Mudie assured the public he would do the same each season but as he did not come again this did not arise.

The Poor Soldier was the highly appropriate choice when Simms gave a night's receipts in April, 1811, "for the benefit of our countrymen prisoners-of-war". The takings were £28. The Mercury commented : "The sufferings of our brave fellows who have so often fought the battles of their country and whose captivity reflects no honour on France, many of them being unjustly detained while great numbers were shipwrecked on the shores of a cruel and tyrannical foe." A local gentleman also had his say, in poetry, when his "Eulogy on Britain" was spoken during the evening, including :

> *"Let us, like Britons, act a British part*
> *And strive to cheer each suffering captive's heart . . ."*

The starving Irish were the "good cause" on Monday, June 24, 1822, when Northamptonshire Philharmonic Society held a concert at the theatre "for the benefit of the distressed peasantry of our sister kingdom". It occurs to me that the use of such a phrase in this year of grace 1974 might well induce the planting of a bomb in the theatre where the charitable musicians were to appear. In the "sister kingdom" it was reported that "the wretched people are dropping down dead in numbers from sheer starvation; pestilence is rapidly and frighteningly extending its ravages amongst them; and those still existing and unsmitten by disease are, in the certainty of speedily perishing, preparing themselves for death by partaking of the last sacred offices of their religion".

The Philharmonic Society had previously performed at the old Town Hall, at the corner of Abington Street and Wood Hill, but had moved because of the inadequate accommodation there.

Announcing the Irish benefit the Mercury stated: "The distresses of our unhappy and extremely afflicted fellow subjects in Ireland appear to interest every description of persons in every variety of circumstance. Not only the devotions of the pulpit, undoubtedly the most legitimate quarter, but the declamation of the stage, the gaiety of the ballroom, the success of the turf and the cardtable, all are contributing to this great cause of national commiseration and charity . . . the Northamptonshire Philharmonic Society, only in a state of infancy and labouring under consequent difficulty, have set apart a night for the benefit of the poor peasantry of Ireland."

There could not have been a very large attendance for this "miscellanenous concert of the most favourite songs, duets, glees, choruses and overtures" raised only £7 0s. 4d. But the local Irish Fund proper topped £1,250 including £18 4s. collected by the Rev. Vere Isham in Lamport and Faxton, the latter being a village which has since almost completely vanished and which now has a population of nil.

Scene Three

STRATFORD &
SIMPSON, Etc.

During the half-century preceding the opening in 1879 of what is usually regarded as the first Shakespeare Theatre at Stratford-upon-Avon, the fact that drama in general and Shakespearean works in particular were kept alive in his native town owes more to the aggregate efforts of five managers of the Northampton theatre than to anything or anyone else.

The five were Francis Raymond (at Northampton from 1824 to 1830), Mercer Hampson Simpson (1835–8), Henry Jackman (1839–52) and Charles Jackman and Frederick Morgan, partners at Northampton (1852–61). Later their individual contributions will be examined.

In fact there was an earlier link between Northampton and Stratford for they also shared a theatre manager in the late eighteenth century. A bill of June 24, 1795, has Mr. Beynon and his Nottingham and Derby Company appearing at the "New Theatre", Stratford, in the comedy *Wheel of Fortune* and the farce *The Farmhouse*. The Beynon company also appeared at Northampton at about this time. This Stratford "New Theatre" was presumably one of the barn theatres which served the town before the first permanent structure was erected in 1827.

Testimony about this era comes from the great comedian Charles Mathews (1776–1835) who was a prime but unsuccessful mover in efforts to get a permanent theatre built. He paid the first of a number of visits to Stratford in December, 1814, and describes the "theatre" in a letter quoted in the Memoirs published by his wife in 1838, three years after his death. He complained that the manager had taken him in.

"I finished performing here tonight (December 24, 1814). Ha! Taken in completely. But I would not have missed my visit here altogether had it been twice as bad. I thought of course that there was a theatre here. When I came, behold, it was a barn! A miserable barn! However, Bannister, Incledon, Dowton, Mrs. Bartsey and others had acted here and all for the honour of Shakespeare. I am just going off to Warwick in a chaise, eight miles, to perform tonight and return afterwards here, to take the mail to Shrewsbury in the morning. Since Garrick and the Jubilee we actors are held in high esteem here (at Stratford) and I received an invitation to dine with the Mayor and Corporation at the Town Hall."

Mathews had similar misgivings about nearby Leamington. "When I saw the handful of houses that compose the town I felt that Mr. Ling had hoaxed me and much did I regret that I was advertised. No musician could I get far or near till seven o'clock when one wretched country dance fiddler arrived from a distance of five miles. I soon found that he could not play a note." So Mathews began his performance with an apology, stating that he had written to request that all the musicians in the town might be engaged. "Ladies and gentleman", he announced, "strictly all that are to be found are now in the orchestra : HE is all. I hope, however, that the defects of the singer may be compensated by the ability of the musician and vice-versa." When they came to the first song the fiddler "in vain attempted to scratch a note or two and then was literally not heard during the whole evening except between the acts, when, to rescue his fame, he boldly struck up a country dance which he rasped away to the no small amusement of the audience".

It was at the suggestion of Charles Mathews that a meeting of the inhabitants of Stratford took place in the Town Hall on December 19, 1820, to consider the best mode of erecting "in the form of a theatre" a national monument to Shakespeare. The actor promised to exert what influence he possessed with men of rank and talent. In future years, he declared, it would be the proudest boast of any person's life to say, when passing by the building, "Ay, I had a hand in that" (overtones of Henry V?).

Mathews was appointed president and treasurer of the committee and a committee of management was formed in London, under his direction. He set about the business with a will and got the support of the King; his vice-presidents included the Duke of Bedford, the Duke of Devonshire and Earl Spencer. But the majority were willing to contribute only if the memorial was to be in London and not in the birthplace. At length Mathews gave up.

Oddly enough, what the great Mathews failed to do was achieved by a few locals, with the co-operation of Francis Raymond. But for his enthusiasm and vigour it is quite possible that what really was Shakespear's first theatre at Stratford would never have been built in Chapel Lane, on part of New Place gardens.

There are two more oddities. A very great deal has been written about the Shakespeare Memorial Theatre opened in 1879 and burned down in 1929 and its successor opened in 1932 (apart from the opposite number Shakespeare theatres in Stratford, Ontario, and Stratford, Connectitcut) but except for a few paragraphs in Victoria County History and the Memorial Theatre book by Day and Trewin virtually nothing has been written about the first Shakespeare Theatre at Stratford-upon-Avon which lasted from 1827 to 1872.

Equally, a great deal has been written about the first Shakespeare Festival organised by David Garrick in 1769 when "rain stopped play" in his plans to stage a pageant of Shakespearean characters. But little or nothing is heard of the Festival of April, 1827, at which the corner stone of the first theatre was laid and to which Francis Raymond took his company from Northampton for a pageant of Shakespearean characters which *DID* take place.

Francis Raymond is a fairly obscure figure whose birth and death dates I have not managed to trace (though I have found the approximate date of the bankruptcy to which his theatrical ventures led him). At Stratford, Raymond's name first turns up in a cast list of 1818. He can also be found in companies in many other towns, assuming it is the same "Mr. Raymond". When he began operating at Northampton in February, 1824, the advertisements were in the name of his father-in-law, a Mr. Nicholson, who announced that Raymond had secured the theatre for him for three years. There was the customary re-painting etc. with two new drop scenes by Mr. J. W. Gill, of Northampton, and Mr. Phillips, of Covent Garden. Mr. Nicholson boldly proclaimed that the changes he was making "will warrant its being called a New Theatre". Operations began on Wednesday, February 25, with the opera *Rob Roy*.

Francis Raymond's collection of theatres also included Leicester and Uxbridge. At Leicester in September, 1826, he announced an entirely new company and a new gold curtain. This was the theatre erected in 1800 and due to be pulled down in 1836. In 1827 at Leicester Mr. and Mrs. Raymond were the only professionals in a last-night performance of *Wild Oats*, the other characters being played by local amateurs.

It is early in Raymond's time at Northampton that we are afforded a single intimation that the theatre was showing a dividend for its owners. On Friday, March 26, 1824, a general meeting of the proprietors was held at the George Hotel, when a payment of £3 per share could be claimed by producing one's title. The announcement was signed by George Abbey, secretary to the proprietors. Robert Abbey, moving spirit behind the theatre's construction, had died on Sunday, November 16, 1823, at the age of sixty-nine. He had lived just long enough to see the formation in Northamptonshire of a Law Society. At the same meeting place where the theatre project had emerged, the George Hotel, Robert Sherard, Under-Sheriff, was in the chair when it was resolved to form the new organisation because "the existing laws whereby the duties and privileges of attorneys and solicitors are regulated so far from protecting regular practitioners subject them to much injury and discredit, by the sufferance of irregular and unqualified persons".

Like so many testators, and although he was a lawyer and should have known better, Robert Abbey had deferred making his will until he felt the shadow of death beginning to fall upon him. Only ten weeks before his decease did he sign the testament willing the bulk of his considerable estate —"messuages, cottages, closes, lands, tenements, heraditments and real estate"—to his widow Anne who was to live to a great age and almost outlive their son George. To George, Robert Abbey left all his law books and papers, while the daughter Charlotte was to make her choice among his medals and coins "not current".

Law books and papers were, in effect, not all that George inherited for he got his father's old jobs as secretary of the theatre, and secretary to the Old Stratford Turnpike Trust and, no doubt in deference to his father's memory, he was elected Coroner. This election took place at a County Court, on the proposal of Mr. T. S. W. Samwell, seconded by Mr. W. T. Smyth. George acknowledged the favour in a newspaper advertisement which was every bit as humble and obsequious as that of a theatre manager :

"To the Nobility, Gentry, Clergy and others, Freeholders of the County of Northampton : My Lords and Gentlemen, permit me to return my warmest acknowledgments for the honour you have this day conferred upon me by electing me one of the Coroners for this county and also for the extraordinary exertions which have been made for me by professional and other friends, during a time of domestic affliction. I have the honour to be, my Lords and Gentlemen, Your Very Obedient and Humble Servant, George Abbey."

Robert Abbey was buried in All Saints Churchyard where George was to follow him to the same grave twenty-three years later. Their names can still be found on the same tombstone there, though probably not much longer as it has been relegated to use as a paving stone.

To return to Francis Raymond and Stratford. In 1826 he took the Henley Street barn theatre, which was among four operating in the 1820s, the others being a converted barn at Moor Town's End, the Corporation Tithe Barn, and Scowton's Theatre in Rother Market Lane.

A bill during Raymond's 1826 season in Henley Street described the house as "fitted up in the neatest and most commodious style possible" and claimed that "no money has or will be spared in producing the performances in a way equal to any theatre out of London, which he is enabled to effect from his immediate connection with the Metropolitan and Leicester, Northampton and other theatres." But the true facts about the limitations of the theatre emerge in a delightful apologia spoken by Mr. Serle at the performance there on Friday, August 18, of *The Merchant of Venice* :

> *"Mine host the manager his welcome sends*
> *To you his guests, his patrons and his friends*
> *And in his ancient hospitable way*
> *He requests me, his orator, to say*
> *The fare this night he offers is the best*
> *Tho' humble given heartily—the rest*
> *He leaves to your indulgence—and indeed*
> *Of your indulgence there may be some need*
> *If not for the entertainment, for the place*
> *In which we serve it up, and through your grace*
> *Our walls, I fear we shall all agree*
> *This is scarce worthy Shakespeare's fame to be*
> *Yet if you think so from what you behold*
> *I could behind a far worse tale unfold*
> *Our long trained Portia when the prompt bell rings*
> *Can scarcely scramble round the narrow wings*
> *Bassanio here and Romeo must prove*
> *Being forc'd to climb a ladder to his love*
> *With Gratanio his inveterate scorner*
> *The rich jew Shylock is rammed into a corner*
> *And while you wonder at some long delay*
> *The Prompter's squeezing out of Jessie's way*
> *To let her pass he most gallantly pinches*

Six feet circumference to as many inches
T'will not always be thus; another year
And we a handsome theatre may rear
Box ladies need no longer fear for satins
Pit ones in winter may come in without pattens
The gallery to see and hear be able
The stage be larger than a dining table
While polite ears against its mirth to warn
The place no longer shall be called a Barn
Why should we build a tomb for him who gives
Light to the world? Yet yet his spirit lives
Does it not breathe, move, speak, in all his lays
A temple for the living let us raise
And fondly fancy on that hallowed ground
Where once he sung, his soul yet hovers round
And again his ancient song inspires
And each rapt spirit charming soothes or fires
Let us idolaters of Shakespeare's fame
Rear this a monument to his great name
There his own writings best shall speak his praise
His epilogue his own immortal plays."

The dream came true. April the following year found Francis Raymond interrupting his Northampton season so that his company could take part in the Festival organised by the Shakespeare Club, which had been founded three years earlier with the holding of such celebrations as one of its principal aims. The intention was to hold a three-day event every third year. In 1827 the Bard's Birthday, April 23, fell on a Monday and soon after six o'clock that morning the inhabitants were serenaded by various bands of instrumental performers parading through the town and later by the ringing of bells and firing of cannon. Stage coaches to the town were crowded and vehicles of every description were requisitioned in Birmingham, Warwick, Leamington and other towns and villages to convey the vast numbers anxious to see what was going on.

At eleven o'clock fifty constables helped to marshal the procession and pageant, including the committee wearing sashes and with the club banner, Shakespearean characters depicted by Raymond's company, augmented by amateurs, there being insufficient professionals to portray all the kings, queens, witches, and ghosts. Heading the procession, preceded by the Royal Standard of England were a full military band playing "Warwickshire Lads and Lasses" and in it were St. George in armour on horseback bearing the ancient sword of the Corporation Armour dating from the time of Edward III and members of the Union Jack Club, wearing medals struck especially for the occasion. In contrast with Garrick's unfortunate wash-out the event was a great success.

After a service at the church containing the tomb of the Bard, the entourage moved on to the site of the new theatre which was partly erected. There the Mayor, assisted by the Corporation, laid a corner stone.

Then it was time for dinner, a grand dinner. Over the entrance to the hall where it was consumed was a transparency representing the sun shining through the clouds (shades of Garrick?) and a portrait of Shakespeare. The demand for tickets had been greater than there was room for. A member of Raymond's company had his own moment of glory during the proceedings when he sang "We Shall Never See His Like Again", adding an extra verse he had composed in the inspiring surroundings of the Bard's house that morning :

"What nation ever yet produced
What we can boast of here;
That truly great immortal Bard
Our country's pride—Shakespeare!
With high delight
At this day's sight
We'll one and all maintain
His glory due
Yet ever new
For we shall never see his like again!"

For their return to Northampton the Raymond company had a memorable send-off. They were escorted by the Shakespeare Committee walking in procession before a coach drawn by six horses ridden by postillions "in full Shakespearian colours" and a large crowd. Back in Northampton they included in their programme "a selection from the concert so much approved of at the late Stratford-upon-Avon Jubilee".

For the first night on resumption they had as guest artist Miss Maria Foote who probably drew an audience as much out of curiosity to see the actress who had won £3,000 two years before from a Mr. Hayne in a celebrated breach-of-promise action, as for her talents. Maria, who was to set the town talking even more when she became Countess of Harrington in 1831, was seen in one of her most popular roles, as Maria Darlington in *A Rowland for an Oliver* and sang "a number of her peculiar dancing songs, together with many popular ballads". For her three nights the box price was 4s. and there was no half-price.

The 1827 Northampton Spring season ended on May 21, after what the Mercury said "may be termed a successful campaign". The company came back for the September Race Week.

In December that year they returned to Stratford to open the new theatre, the first Shakespearean Theatre, with *As You Like It* on Wednesday, December 12. On the second night the plays were *The Wonder! A Woman Keeps a Secret* and *The Rival Valets* when the bill stated : "F. Raymond (manager) begs leave to inform the Nobility, Gentry and the Public in general of Stratford-upon-Avon and its vicinity that the theatre being fully completed and carefully aired commenced its first season on Wednesday and trusts that the excellent company he has provided and his arrangements altogether will give general satisfaction and procure him that support which to merit will be his constant endeavour. Doors to open at six, the performance to commence at seven o'clock. Boxes 3s. 6d., Pit 2s., Gallery 1s. Half price 9 o'clock, Boxes 2s., Pit 1s. Tickets for the season, not transferable, £2 2s. Places to be taken at Mr. Ward's Library, High Street. As the demand for places is very great, it will be esteemed a particular favour if parties taking seats will also take tickets at the same time, that Ladies and Gentlemen may be accommodated as far as possible. Performances on Friday and Saturday, and Monday, Tuesday, Thursday and Friday next week. No admission whatever behind the scenes." The bill spelt the name of the house as the "Shakespearian Theatre".

In addition to Raymond and his wife the company on this historic occasion included Messrs Mordaunt, Saunders, Gill, Brooks, Reynolds, Scriven, Gannon, Rignold, Scrimshaw and Simpson (another member of the Stratford quintet of Northampton managers), Mrs. Saunders, Miss Morton, Miss Mordaunt, Miss Redman, and Master Rignold.

Whereas £1,500 had been needed to get the Northampton theatre project into being in 1806, a mere £800 sufficed at Stratford—there were thirty-two shares of £25 each. The 365 square yards of land required give a good idea of the size of the theatre, of which a photograph survives *(Page 33.)* As the land was only 4s. a square yard, the cheque required for it was £73 which had been duly paid on February 23, 1827. On April 3, 1827, the committee agreed to a request from the Shakespeare Club that they might be allowed to lay a corner stone (as related) on April 23, the first day of the Festival, and by August such details as the portico, six copperspouts and stone coping, and in November as wings, carpenter's gallery, drop scene roller and green curtain were being sorted out.

The terms Raymond offered as manager appeared to ensure the financial success of the venture for at least seven years. That was the term he agreed, at £50 per annum, for using the house three months in the year, leaving it free for other uses the remaining nine months. To show his own confidence Raymond also took shares himself. With such a lease in their hands it looked as though the backers could sit back and allow the coffers to fill automatically. Not only could they bask in Bard-reflected glory but make a dividend too.

At first things did go well between Raymond and his fellow-shareholders. In January, 1828, during the first season, they resolved to bespeak a performance of *The Belles Stratagem* and *Raising the Wind* as acknowledgment of the fact that the manager had given a night's takings to the Stratford Dispensary. Their patronage of a piece with the title *Raising the Wind* was tempting fate, as will emerge.

Back in Northampton, the 1828 season commenced in March, a black month in theatrical history. A company were in rehearsal at the Brunswick Theatre in London's Well Street when the house literally came down. A cracking noise was heard from the roof and it fell in with a crash, killing over twenty people. The calamity was thought to be due to the weight of the iron roof being too much on walls too "green" and insufficiently cemented.

At Northampton Francis Raymond was as ambitious as ever, bringing down Mrs. Waylett from the Theatre Royal, Haymarket, in April, and Madame Vestris for the Race Week in September. For the Madame, who

THEATRE, NORTHAMPTON.

By Desire and under the Immediate Patronage of the Worshipful

The Mayor & Corporation.

On **WEDNESDAY, APRIL** 16th, 1828,

WILL BE PERFORMED THE EXCELLENT COMEDY CALLED

Such Things are;

Or, The Benevolent Briton.

Lord Flint, Mr. BROOKS.—Sir Luke Tremor, Mr. SIMPSON.
Mr. Twineall, Mr. RAYMOND.—Mr. Haswell, Mr. BOND.—Mr. Meanwell, Mr. WATKINS.
The Sultan, Mr. SAUNDERS.—Zedan, Mr. REYNOLDS.—Keeper of the Prisons, Mr. FRASER.
Servant, Mr. RIGNOLD.—Messenger, Mr. FORD.—Elvirus, Mr. ALEXANDER.
Prisoner, Mr. SCRIMSHAW.—Guards, Prisoners, &c.
Lady Tremor, Mrs. SAUNDERS.—Amelia, Miss MORTON.—Female Prisoner, Miss MORDAUNT.

END OF THE PLAY,

" The King, God bless him," by Mr. FORD.
Comic Song—" London Newspapers"—by Mr. GILL.
Comic Song, "The Chapter of Accidents," Mr. BROOKS.

THE WHOLE TO CONCLUDE WITH AN ENTIRE NEW NAUTICAL DRAMA, CALLED THE

Pilot;

Or, A TALE of the SEA.

The Pilot, Mr. ALEXANDER.—Long Tom Coffin, with the Hornpipe, Mr. Raymond.
Kate Plowden, Miss MORDAUNT.
The rest of the Characters as before.
In the course of the Piece the following entire new Scenery, &c. as represented in London:—
A ROCKY SHORE, with distant View of Frigate and Schooner, Boat, &c.
INTERIOR OF COLONEL HOWARD'S HOUSE.
Another Chamber in ditto, with Storm seen through the Window.
The Storm Glee.
FORE AND AFT VIEW OF THE

Schooner Ariel,

Manned and Rigged, at the time she is attempting to claw off a lee shore, and to pass the bight of a shoal.
To give effect to which, the Whole Stage is converted into Moving Water,—And a two-mast Vessel of
adequate size has been constructed, at a considerable expense, in order to give the liveliest effect to a

Storm at Sea,

In which is depicted the heaving of the lead—the breakers on her lee bow—tacking—breakers dead
a-head—letting fly her jib and mainsail—luff and run, hard a weather the helm—ease off the sheets,
and square away—she's safe—the wind abates—the storm ceases—and safely the
PILOT WEATHERS THE STORM.
Gun Deck of the Frigate.
Exterior of Col. Howard's House, with Guard House, and distant View of the Sea.

MOONLIGHT MARINE VIEW.

Rocky Pass bordered by the Sea—Combat of Tom and the Americans—Cabin of the Ariel—a Man
overboard—Tom Coffin rescued from the Waves—Main Deck of the Enemy's Frigate
boarded by the Cutter of the Ariel, and

TRIUMPH of the BRITISH FLAG.

At the End of the Performance,

" GOD SAVE THE KING,"

Will be Sung by the WHOLE OF THE COMPANY.

An Engagement has been formed with Mrs. WAYLETT, of the THEATRE ROYAL,
HAYMARKET, for a few Evenings, and of whose first Appearance due Notice will
be given.

Doors open at Six, and commence at Seven. Half-price at Half-past Eight.
Tickets and Places for the Boxes to be had at The MERCURY PRINTING OFFICE, Parade; and at
Mr. FREEMAN's, Bookseller, Market Square.

To-morrow (THURSDAY) Evening, by Desire and under the Immediate Patronage of JOHN
HARVEY THURSBY, Jun. Esq. the excellent Comedy of "LAUGH WHEN YOU CAN," with
other entertainments.

Birdsall & Son, Printers, Parade, Northampton.

NORTHAMPTON, 1828—during the tenure of
Francis Raymond. (*British Museum and Northampton
Public Library*)

Theatre, N. thampton.

For the BENEFIT of

Mast. Burke

And positively the Last Night of his acting here.

Mr. RAYMOND respectfully begs of his Friends and the Patrons of the
Drama, that they will not neglect this
The ONLY OPPORTUNITY
(Which in all probability will be for a great length of time), afforded them, of witnessing the extraordinary Talents of this RARA AVIS. He assures the Public
with the firmest conviction that their judgment will bear out his, that, of the many
ROSCII who have claimed the distinction of precocity and versatility, NO ONE
has ever attained that pitch of excellence which is universally decreed to Mast.
BURKE:—and that as his appearance forms an Æra in Theatrical History,
it would argue a want of taste in any one to neglect the opportunity thus offered of
judging for himself.

On **SATURDAY** Evening, March 27th, 1830,
The Evening's Amusements will commence with the Drama (by J. T. Allingham,
Esq. of the Inner Temple), called,

The Weathercock

Or Every Point in the Compass.

Tristram Fickle...........................Master BURKE!
Counsellor Bother'em.......................Master BURKE!!
Mr. Tag-Rag and Bob-Tail Fickle (an Actor of promise);..Master BURKE!!!
Doctor Cataplasm...........................Master BURKE!!!!
Captain Cut-and-Come-Again ....Master BURKE!!!!!
David Daisy (a Gardener) ....Master BURKE!!!!!!
Broadbrim (one of the Faithful) ....Master BURKE!!!!!!!
Mr. Mustachio Navarino.....................Master BURKE!!!!!!!!
Old Fickle, Mr. REYNOLDS....Counsellor Briefwit, Mr. GILL...Gardener, Mr. TALBOT
Barber, Mr. GIFFORD....Sexer, Mr. GRANBY
Variella, Mrs. RAYMOND..................Ready, Mrs. GRANBY

After which, the excellent laughable Afterpiece of, The

Irish Tutor;

Or, NEW LIGHTS.

Thady O'Rouke, alias Dr. O'Toole (with a new Song)
Master BURKE,
As acted by him in London 90 nights, with shouts of laughter and immense approbation.
Doctor Flail. Mr. SIMPSON...Charles, Mr. TALBOT...Beadle, Mr. GRANBY
Countryman, Mr. GIFFORD...Tillwell Mr. REYNOLDS...Fiddler, Mr. BIDDOLES
Mary, Mrs. RAYMOND....Rosa, Miss NEWMAN

During the Evening,

Master BURKE

Will lead the Overture to *Guy Mannering*, and the
celebrated Concerto of *Du Beriot*.

A Song by Mr. Gill, and a Song by Mr. Granby.

To conclude with the far-famed Piece, written expressly for Master Burke, and performed by him
in London upwards of 200 Nights, called, The

March of Intellect

In which Mast. BURKE will assume and sustain
Six different Characters! viz.

Master Socrates Camelion (youth of parts) ....Master BURKE!
Mr. Terence O'Leary, from Kilkarney ....Master BURKE!!
Signor Sordini, from Italy, with an Air curie on the Violin Master BURKE!!!
Bluster Bubble, Esq. (from the Moon) ....Master BURKE!!!!
Jack Rattline from the Terrific Gun Brig, with a Hornpipe Master BURKE!!!!!
Napoleon Bonaparte (from Elysium) ....Master BURKE!!!!!!

Mr. Camelion, late Colournan of Tooley-Street, Mr. SIMPSON
Frederick Multiplex, Usher of his Father's Academy at Ramsgate, Mr. WRIGHT
Miss Cerulia Leggit, an antiquated Blue-Stocking, Mrs. GRANBY
Penelope Camelion. her Niece, Miss NEWMAN

Tickets and Places for the Boxes to be had of Mr. FREEMAN, Bookseller, &c.
Market-Square.

FREEMAN, PRINTER, MARKET-SQUARE, NORTHAMPTON.

NORTHAMPTON, 1830—a visit by Mast
Burke, one of the "young geniuses" of the 19
century stage. (*British Museum and Northamp
Public Library*)

was to marry Charles Mathews Junior, the box prices went up to 4s. 6d. and even the gallery was 1s. 6d. The Mercury reported : "The fascinating actress has been received with that applause and enthusiasm which we trust will induce her to repeat her visit. She was well supported by the regular performers of the establishment in addition to whom our manager's brother, from Covent Garden, has been acting with high credit to himself and gratification to the public."

Deserted by and divorced from Armand Vestris, ballet master at the Kings Theatre, whom she had married at sixteen, Madame Vestris was now thirty-one. In another ten years she was to marry again, this time Charles Mathews the younger. The extravagance of the "Queen of Burlesque" was to land him twice in the bankruptcy court.

But despite the star attractions he had brought to the town, Raymond was not making the theatre pay. He was unusually frank in his advertisement of the following year : "Though he last year experienced a most unproductive season and sustained a heavy loss yet he feels in no way disheartened, convinced that a considerable county town like Northampton possessing (among various other things) the advantages afforded it through a well conducted theatre (and he flatters himself that he has endeavoured to make it so) must, knowing it has a property to support which affords almost the only general amusement, be eventually successful."

Pieces presented that season included *Guy Mannering or The Gipsy's Prophecy*, *The Haunted Inn or The Corporal and the Captain* and *Catharine and Petruchio or The Taming of The Shrew*. The last-named is a reminder that during the first half of the nineteenth century many of Shakespeare's works appeared in other guises, partly as a ruse to get round the law restricting legitimate plays. As Allardyce Nicoll notes in his *A History of English Drama* the minor theatres "discovered that Shakespeare had in him the stuff of which excellent 'burlettas' and melodramas are made ... as a burletta 'Antony and Cleopatra' appeared at the Surrey in 1810. 'The Battle of Bosworth Field,' in 1827, is simply 'Richard III'. 'Julius Caesar' became a melodrama at the East London in 1818 while at the Royalty in 1812 appeared a burletta of 'King Lear and His Three Daughters'. A melodrama, 'The Life and Death of King Richard II or Wat Tyler and Jack Straw' (1834) was indebted partly to Shakespeare, while 'Romeo and Juliet' was a melodrama at the Surrey in 1813. Another melodrama called 'The Royal Dane' (Surrey, 1827) is only 'Hamlet' adapted. These pieces were obviously successful as is directly attested by the extraordinary number of Shakespearian burlesques and travesties which this age produced." He also mentions "King Leer"(!) and "King Lear and His Daughters Queer" (!!)

Raymond was as good as his word. He was not downhearted but brought to Northampton Miss Love and the returning Miss Foote, for whom it was said that it might be a last visit—"During the past four years Miss Foote has travelled upwards of 18,000 miles and fulfilled more than 300 different engagements in England, Ireland, Scotland and France and it is now her intention to relax if not totally to retire from such incessant and very great exertions, therefore this will probably be the last time she will have the honour of appearing in Northampton."

On this last acting engagement she was cast as Lady Teazle in *The School for Scandal*, Beatrice in *Much Ado About Nothing*, Arinette in a farce called *The Little Jockey*, Douna Olivia in *A Bold Stroke for a Husband* and Moggy M'Gilpin in the musical afterpiece *The Highland Reel*.

To travel 18,000 miles in four years in those days was, of course, much more of a feat of endurance than it would be today. Roads were either not what they are or did not exist at all. One of the roads now leading from Northampton towards Bedford, as far as Cold Brayfield, had only just been constructed as a turnpike (i.e. pay-as-you-go to the lessees of the road) and was reported to be proving "a great accommodation to the public".

In September that year of 1829 the corpse of the Earl of Harrington passed in funeral procession through Northampton on its way to Elvaston, Derbyshire. In 1831 Miss Foote was to retire from the stage to become the next Countess of Harrington and as such she was a member of the audience on her next visit to the Northampton theatre in 1835.

The craze for young stars reasserted itself in November when W. R. Grossmith was billed as "The Young Roscius of the Age, unrivalled hero of the stage who is not yet 10 years old". This pre-teenager had received high praise from the Sheffield Mercury : "He took upon himself the difficult task of personating characters the very Antipodes of each other in age, feeling and assumed and changed them with a rapidity truly astonishing. His representation of Shylock was above all praise." The nine-year-old Jew, who also undertook Richard III, appeared in "a little moveable theatre, a very ingenious contrivance, the size of the proscenium being of such proportions to Master Grossmith's height as to make him appear a full grown person".

The puffing advertisement gives some rare details about the actual numbers of the audience, not only at Northampton, but at other theatres played by the young genius. "He is to appear again, induced from the kind reception on Monday last from a highly delighted auditory (above 360 in number)." He also appeared at the Town Hall, Wellingborough; the Saracen's Head, Newport Pagnell; the Leicester theatre; and at Coventry, Banbury and Reading. His largest house on the present tour was stated to be at Sheffield (840) and the smallest at Mansfield (136).

In Northampton he did not stay at any back-street lodgings, as some of the adult actors visiting the town did, but at the ancient Peacock Inn on the Market Square where, it was announced, "Families in the country may secure places by sending the number required".

In 1830 Francis Raymond was a moving spirit in the second Shakespeare Festival at Stratford for which he engaged Charles Kean, son of Edmund, and his misfortunes seem to have increased with the Festival. The story of his downfall may be traced in the minute books and accounts of the Stratford theatre.

As none of the records books of the Northampton theatre appear to have survived we do not know what rents were paid by the various managers or what their other expenses were, except that Raymond is stated in 1827 to have paid his actors from £1 to £1. 10s. per week. Accounts do exist for some other theatres of which Northampton managers had charge at various times and there is no reason to doubt that the finances would have been similar. In 1828 a year's rent of the Stratford theatre cost Francis Raymond £60. It was the only year he managed to pay in full. In 1829 he paid three instalments of £20, £10, and £13, leaving £17 owing. Their rent bill unpaid, the Stratford proprietors grew disenchanted with Raymond and put that fact on record in the theatre minute book on June 15, 1830 : "Mr. Raymond having neglected paying the balance of the rent due April 23, 1830, resolved that the committee feel themselves and the rest of the proprietors neglected by Mr. Raymond, he having on the recent Jubilee been supported by them and other inhabitants of Stratford in the best manner possible. The secretary having laid Mr. Raymond's letter of 15th instant before the committee they hereby request him that he is hereby authorised to obtain the said rents of Mr. Raymond in the best manner he may be able."

Unfortunately Mr. Raymond's letter of the 15th instant does not appear to have survived. It would have been interesting to hear what excuses he offered.

On April 12, 1831, the committee finally decided that Raymond's lease should be declared invalid and resolved to advertise the theatre to let in Bell's Life in London, the Avis Gazeteer, and the Warwickshire Advertiser, the county newspaper launched in 1806. When Mr. Watson of Birmingham wrote in response they decided on what we would now term a cut-price offer—£20 for three months of one year but 12 guineas (60 guineas altogether) if taken for five years.

Two years later, in June, 1832, the committee were even more alarmed and aggrieved to receive a further communication from their old friend to say that he intended to take the benefit of the Insolvent Act. "The committee feel surprised at his having done so, they supposing from his letter that his debt was compounded." The thought of not merely having to wait for their money but instead losing part or all of it in bankruptcy proceedings gave them the shivers and stirred them to action. "We feel it requisite that Raymond should be seen on the subject and that Mr. Ashwin be deputed to wait upon him on their behalf in London and that he be allowed £3 towards expenses." A journey to London being the expedition that it was; and £3 being quite a sizeable sum; both these facts reflect the concern of the committee at their so promising relationship with Raymond turning sour.

The Stratford theatre will crop up again in our recital of the fortunes of the Northampton theatre, through the managership of Mercer Hampson Simpson, who was in the Raymond Company. Then through old Henry Jackman : the Jackman Company's half-century of strolling forms our Second Act but here I will merely mention that its first season at Stratford appears to have been in 1838; that playing at Stratford was not its only connection, in that one of its leading members became a Stratford Town Councillor and inn-keeper; that one of Jackman's daughters was married at Stratford; that the son-in-law thus acquired teamed up with Charles Jackman after Old Henry's death and carried on the company until a "final and farewell" season at Stratford in 1862; and that Charles Jackman himself became the first librarian of the Shakespeare Birthplace Trust and a subscriber to the 1879 Memorial Theatre.

Meantime, suffice it to say that post-Raymond the house was let seasonally and that the lessee in 1837 was C. W. Elliston, a son of the Great Lessee, Robert William Elliston.

When George IV died on Saturday, June 26, 1830 (Saturday was the favourite day for the demise of monarchs) his brother William IV was proclaimed in quintuplicate in Northampton by the Mayor, John Birdsall. During a procession from the Old Town Hall, Abington Street, preceded by the Corporation Band to the Market Square, along the Drapery and George Row, the first citizen proclaimed the new King five times. For good measure there was a county proclamation by the High Sheriff, Richard Pack.

The Coronation of September, 1831, was marked by the ringing of church bells, music in the streets, rockets, squibs, crackers and other fireworks—and by the breaking of the windows of some prominent citizens who had failed to illuminate their premises.

This was a time of great changes in many directions, an age of Reform.

In October, 1832, the Marquess of Northampton accepted the presidency of the Northampton Mechanics Institute, the setting up of which was an early sign that the working man was beginning to find his feet and to consider asserting himself. The previous month the liberal-minded Marquess had surprised many of his contemporaries by telling his tenants that they were free to exercise their right of franchise as their consciences dictated and that he would not try to influence their votes. To some this was heresy —"This manly and honest statement", said the Mercury, "has excited the anger of some persons who conceive that landlords ought to influence their tenants on the grounds that if they do not, someone else will".

It did occur to the Reformers to give more liberty to the stage which could do so much to forward their cause. In 1832 a Bill to end the Patent monopoly was passed by the Commons but rejected by the Lords. Reform here had to wait until the Theatre Regulation Act of 1843 and even then it was to have effects which were not wholly to the good.

The same qualification applied to The Drink, an earlier candidate for "freedom". So keen were the Reformers to give everyone the unfettered right to do as he chose that they, as one writer has said, launched the nation on a flood tide of beer. This particular reform is of special interest to Northamptonshire because the then Lord Althorp, of Althorp, Northants, son of Earl Spencer, was one of the leading apologists for the Beer Bill of 1830. He succeeded its principal sponsor, Goulburn, as Chancellor of the Exchequer.

Why, it was asked, should the trade of beer-selling be subject to the whim of a bench of magistrates who might ruin a man by withdrawing his licence, when their motives might be spite, prejudice, corruption or caprice? It was petty tyranny.

So Goulburn, Chancellor of the Exchequer in the Duke of Wellington's ministry, decided to repeal the tax on beer and cider and throw the retail trade completely open. Another of his motives was to halt the increase in spirit drinking, which had doubled between 1807 and 1827. Attempts to restrict the new beer-shops to off-sales only were defeated by large majorities in both Houses. The result of the Act was that to set up a beer-only public house all you had to do was to pay two guineas for the licence—as easy as getting a dog licence. The magistrates no longer had any say.

The result? Sydney Smith wrote : "Everyone is drunk. Those who are not singing are sprawling." Another writer : "So instant and dramatic a transformation as occurred in October, 1830, has seldom been effected by an Act of Parliament. The very day on which the statute came into operation a perfect swarm of what, for some inexplicable reason, were called 'Tom and Jerry' shops were opened in every town and village." A Justice of the Peace said that "one could scarcely put a foot down without meeting a public house—they were found in all directions".

The surfeit of drinking dens was blamed for disaffection and disorder which occurred in 1831. One form this took in Northamptonshire was rick-firing. In Northampton itself, the shoemakers in the staple trade might spend three days a week in heavy drinking. In the county capital the law helped to create a street consisting almost wholly of public houses or hotels —Bridge Street, of which more later.

It is said that Wellington regarded the Beer Act as a greater victory than any of his military ones.

What was spent on booze could not be spent on drama. The more money that went over the bars of the town the less could find its way into the pocket of the mnager of the theatre.

Many of the older roads of Northamptonshire are so full of twists and turns (the Watling Street being the great exception) that it has often been said that they must have been laid out by men who were drunk. This is one thing for which the Beer Act cannot be blamed, for most of the routes came into being long before it was passed. (The period since the 1939–45 War has seen a great deal of straightening out, by a vigorous policy of improvement in the highways.)

At this period of change the Mercury commented how well placed Northampton was in the road network. "We think ourselves called upon to remind our readers of the extensive accommodation which Northampton affords beyond any other great towns in the United Kingdom. For instance a turnpike road to London through Newport Pagnell and Stony Stratford; to Towcester, Buckingham, Banbury and Oxford; to Daventry and Warwick; to Rugby, Coventry and Birmingham; to Lutterworth and Hinckley; to Harborough and Leicester; to Kettering and Stamford; to Wellingborough, Thrapston and Oundle and Peterborough and Cambridge; and lastly, the new road to Bedford."

All of which was of especial interest to theatre folk who were the most itinerant of people. Both to the managers and stars who could afford conveyance and to the lower orders who had still to stroll.

Taking advantage of the new Bedford road, a coach service began to operate from Bedford to Birmingham, calling at the Tinker Inn, Turvey;

George Hotel, Northampton; Wheat Sheaf, Daventry; Craven Arms, Southam; Royal Hotel, Leamington; Warwick Arms, Warwick; and finishing at the Nelson Hotel, Birmingham, which it reached in time to connect with the northern coaches.

About this time the vexed question of Northampton getting on to the railway system came into discussion. Some of the landowners whose property or land was adjacent to or on the proposed route from London to Birmingham got together to oppose the project. Sir William Wake, of Courteenhall, Northants, took the chair at one meeting at the White Horse, Towcester. Opposition came too from the trustees of the Hardingstone–Old Stratford Turnpike Trust who decided to petition both Houses of Parliament because the proposed railway would cut across their road.

Others wanted the railway to be built—and the nearer to Northampton the better, preferably through the town. At a public meeting at the Town Hall Mr. Charles Whitworth, a banker whose son was to be a proprietor of the theatre, bemoaned that the suggested "road" (railroad) would not approach nearer than four miles from the town and that travellers coming from the east of the county would pass through the town without stopping; if it could be brought nearer they would call at the Northampton inns, leaving their horses and gigs to catch the railway.

In November, 1832, the directors of the London and Birmingham Railway came to an arrangement with two noblemen whose opposition had led to the rejection of the Bill in the previous session of Parliament and the scheme proceeded.

The coming of the railways was, of course, revolutionary in many directions and it had a great effect on the provincial theatre. For one thing it increased the mobility of companies; for another it increased the mobility of their audiences, particularly important as regards the middle and upper classes whose patronage was so important.

Yet another sphere in which great changes were taking place was that of the penal code. When Thomas Swannell was hanged at Northampton in March, 1830, for the rape of Ann Swannell, aged under ten, at Cosgrove, it was the first execution in the town for four years. When Thomas Gee, of Guilsborough, was hanged in Northampton in 1834 for setting fire to a stack of wheat, there was not to be another neck-stretching ceremony for eighteen years.

Gee, by the way, died a particularly painful death. At the last moment he made an effort of movement so that his neck was not dislocated by the drop and he hung strangling for twenty minutes. "Very large crowds expressed their disapprobation of the awful spectacle," reported the Mercury. Their distaste did not, however, prevent a number of women who were suffering from enlargement of the neck going up on to the scaffold to rub the affected part with the hand of the executed man, following a superstition that this would effect a cure. "We had supposed that the notion of the efficacy of this ignorant practice had long since been exploded or at least that the practice had been prohibited by the proper authorities," said the newspaper which reported that the body had been cut down for delivery to friends, for burial at Guilsborough the same evening.

In June, 1830, Earl Spencer had presented to the House of Lords a petition from the Wesleyan Methodist inhabitants of Croydon, praying against the death penalty for forgery, adding that he was strongly inclined to agree with it.

These happenings in the field of Reform and change have been taken together for convenience. To take up the story of Northampton's theatre we must turn back the years to February, 1831.

On the fifth of that month we find that Francis Raymond's era had come to an end and that "This elegant theatre" was again to be let to a "respectable manager of a provincial company for the present season or on lease for a short term of years".

There were no dramatics to accompany the Spring Races but the advertisement had caught an eye and the following July Mr. Stuart brought the Bath Company to Northampton, under the management of Mr. Hamilton. They consisted of Mr. Milton, Mr. Connor, Mr. Owen, Mr. Young and Miss Stuart, all of the Theatre Royal, Bath; Mr. Mason, Theatre Royal, Covent Garden; Mr. Barrett and Mr. Beckwith, Theatre Royal, Liverpool; Mr. Spencer, Theatre Royal, Dover; Mr. Green and Mr. Cooke, Theatre Royal, Southampton; Miss Millard, Theatre Royal, Dublin; Miss Penley, Theatre Royal, Newcastle upon Tyne; and Miss Green, Theatre Royal, Birmingham. There is also a rare reference to the musical department, always the most unsaluted members of an establishment; only two were listed, Mr. Pittman, leader, and Mr. A. Taylor, flute. Presumably their numbers were swelled by local recruitment.

The improvements made at the theatre were boasted of with traditional aplomb. A new green curtain, proscenium and act drop ("a most spirited and classical design") had been hung and the seats of the pit covered. In addition there is an intriguing reference to the peripheral facilities: "A cloakroom has been fitted up for the accommodation of ladies and a female attendant provided to wait upon them." Whether the cloakroom was only for the ladies to hang their cloaks in is not clear. References to the sanitary provisions of the theatre are lacking. Certainly, in view of the marathon length of the performances, some conveniences must surely have been provided.

The collection of Northampton playbills at the British Museum, of which xerox copies have recently been acquired by Northampton Public Library, is prolific in the 1830s and includes details not found in the newspaper reports. Indeed there is far more day-to-day information than can be included here but of 1831, where the collection appears to be complete for every performance, we must note the appearance early in August of M. Gouffee, the "celebrated man monkey who runs up the proscenium and then commences his wonderful race round the front of the boxes and gallery", and in September of "An Actor of Colour, known throughout America by the appelation of African Roscius".

The actor whose name they did not trouble to record and who was himself sometimes treated as a "man monkey", so powerful was colour prejudice in those days, was Ira Aldridge, who had made a great impression as Othello at the Royal Theatre, London, in 1826, and who appeared in

Theatre, Northampton.

THE Ladies and Gentlemen of NORTHAMPTON and its vicinity are most respectfully informed, that the Theatre, will open at the Assizes, for a limited Season, under a new management, having undergone the most complete repair, and with a Company of first rate provincial celebrity. The Management being resolved upon sparing no cost, in catering for the amusement of the public, have likewise at a great expence, engaged

Mr. Adams,

Of the Theatre-Royal, Drury-Lane,

By whom, every scene has been designed and painted, entirely new for the occasion. They therefore throw themselves upon the liberality of the public, and solicit their patronage and support to the establishment, which will in every instance be conducted with the most unremitting endeavours to afford satisfaction to those, who may be pleased to honour them with their presence.

On MONDAY the 11th Day of JULY, 1831,

Will be performed, Shakespeare's celebrated Comedy of THE

Merchant
OF
Venice;
Or, The Inexorable JEW.

The Duke of Venice .... Mr. YOUNG, of the Theatre-Royal, Bath
Antonio, the Merchant .... Mr. GREEN, of the Theatre-Royal, Southampton
Bassanio .... Mr. MASON, of the Theatre-Royal, Covent-Garden
Gratiano .... Mr. MILLTON, of the Theatre-Royal, Bath
Lorenzo .... Mr. BECKWITH, of the Theatre-Royal, Liverpool
Launcelot .... Mr. BARRATT, of the Theatre-Royal, Newcastle
Solanio .... Mr. OWEN, of the Theatre-Royal, Bath
Salarino .... Mr. CONNOR, of the Theatre-Royal, Bath
Old Gobbo .... Mr. COOK, of the Theatre-Royal, Southampton
Tubal .... Mr. SPENCER, of the Theatre-Royal, Dover
And Shylock, the Jew .... Mr. STUART, of the Theatre-Royal, Bath

Jessica .... Miss STUART, of the Theatre-Royal, Bath
Nerissa .... Miss MILLARD, of the Theatre Royal, Southampton
And Portia .... Miss PENLEY, of the Theatre-Royal, Newcastle

At the end of the First Act will be exhibited, The

New Act Drop,
Designed and painted by Mr. Adams.

In the course of the Evening,

The following Songs:===

" Lo! Here the gentle Lark."
" Tell me, my Heart." } .... Miss STUART
" Bid me discourse." }

" The Rose of Love,"
" The Death of Nelson," } Mr. BECKWITH.
Duet with Miss Stuart, " Love flutters ever," }
A COMIC SONG .... Mr. BARRATT.

To conclude with Kenny's Laughable Farce, in two Acts, called,

Raising the Wind;
Or, Out at Elbows.

Jeremy Diddler, Mr. MASON
Plainwould, Mr. BECKWITH ...... Sam, Mr. BARRATT
Old Plainway, Mr. COOK .. Richard, Mr. SPENCER
Waiter, Mr. YOUNG .. John, Mr. OWEN
Peggy Plainway, Miss MILLARD
And Miss Laurelia Durable, Mrs. PEARCE, of the Theatre-Royal, Dublin,
her first appearance in Northampton for many seasons.

In addition to other improvements, a New Green Curtain and Proscenium have been hung, and the seats of the Pit covered.
☞ A Cloak Room fitted up for the accommodation of Ladies, and a female attendant provided to wait upon them.
Doors opened at Seven o'Clock, and to commence at Half-past.
Tickets and Places for the Boxes, may be obtained at Mr. FREEMAN's, Printer and Bookseller, Market-square.
Boxes, 3s. 6d.—Pit, 2s.—Gallery, 1s.—Half-price at Nine o'Clock.
In Rehearsal, and shortly to be produced, the last new Pieces, of " The Wreck Ashore," and " The Brigand," as performing in London, to crowded houses, with great applause.

Acting Manager, Mr. STUART.

FREEMAN, PRINTER, MARKET-SQUARE, NORTHAMPTON.

NORTHAMPTON, 1831—the one-season visit of the Bath Company. (*British Museum and Northampton Public Library*)

Theatre, Northampton.

By Desire and under the immediate Patronage of
Sir R. H.
Gunning
BART.

On THURSDAY EVENING, Sept. 26th, 1833,

Will be performed, Sheridan's much-admired Comedy of THE

RIVALS

Sir Anthony Absolute, Mr. SCOTT
Captain Absolute, Mr. MOSS .. Sir Lucius O'Trigger, Mr. JOHNSON
Faulkner, Mr. BARRY .. David, Mr. FORBES .. Acres, Mr. SHEPHERD
Fag, Mr. MONTAGU WATKINS .. Coachman, Mr. JONES
Miss Lydia Languish, Miss GLIDDON .. Miss Julia Melville, Mrs. MONTAGU WATKINS
Mrs. Malaprop, Mrs. FREDERICK .... Lucy, Miss HOPE

END OF THE PLAY,

" LO! HERE THE GENTLE LARK!"
AND
" THE MINSTREL HARP,"
Accompanied by herself on the HARP ...... by Miss HOPE.

After which, the Comic Interlude, called,

Three Weeks after
MARRIAGE.

Sir Charles Racket, Mr. SHEPHERD
Drugget, Mr. BARRY .. Woodley, Mr. MONTAGU WATKINS
Lady Racket, Miss GLIDDON .. Mrs. Drugget, Mrs. FREDERICK .. Nancy, Mrs. SHEPHERD

AN ENTIRE NEW COMIC SONG,
By Mr. SCOTT.

" The SEA," by Mr. WATKINS

To conclude with the Musical Farce of THE

TURNPIKE
GATE.

Joe Standfast, Mr. JOHNSON .. Henry Blunt, Mr. MONTAGU WATKINS
Sir Edward Dashaway, Mr. BARRY .. Bob Maythorn, Mr. FORBES
Crack, Mr. SCOTT
Smart, Mr. SHEPHERD .. Frisk, Mr. WILTON
Mary, Miss K. GLIDDON .. Peggy, Miss HOPE .. Hostess, Mrs. FREDERICK

In the course of the Evening will be exhibited,

A NEW SCENE,
Representing a View of
HORTON HALL,
The seat of this Night's Patron.

Doors opened at Six and to commence at Seven o'Clock precisely.
Boxes, 3s. 6d.—Pit, 2s.—Gallery, 1s.
Half price at NINE o'Clock.
Boxes, 2s. ...... Pit, 1s. ...... Gallery, 6d.

NORTHAMPTON, 1833—note the new scene representing a view of the home of the principal patron. (*British Museum and Northampton Public Library*)

the role at Northampton. The "Actor of Colour" appeared again at Northampton in 1846 and later scored remarkable success on the Continent.

The Bath company played only one season. Mr. Stuart, the acting manager, suffered an illness for part of the stay but recovered in time to appear as Mercutio on August 10. One of the plays during the season was *The Castle Spectre* which had been given on the very first night in 1806.

In December, 1831, the Mercury found itself facing competition, in the form of the Northampton Herald. Some local Tory interests did not like the Reforms taking place and were not enamoured by the support which the Mercury lent for further changes. Not everyone approved the ending of hanging for many offences, the attack on Rotten Boroughs (and similar electoral chicanery) and other acts of revolution. So in order to counter the activities of the 111-year-old Mercury, the Northampton Herald was launched.

The new newspaper managed to bring most human activities into the political sphere and even its reports on the theatre could be blue-tinged.

In 1832, with Messrs. Parry and Hamilton as managers, there was a performance patronised by Sir Robert Gunning, Bart., of Horton Hall. This is how the Herald reported the evening : "Long before the time of opening the doors were besieged by a vast body of respectable townspeople, anxious to be present on such an occasion. The theatre in every part was crowded to an overflow and many were unable to gain admission at all. Sir Robert Gunning, Charles Ross, Esq., our popular candidate, and several members of the family were present and were loudly and enthusiastically cheered. On the falling of the curtain after the first scene three times three cheers were given for Mr. Ross and Miss Gunning, the female part of the audience waving their handkerchiefs. The reception by so large a body of all classes of the people, from the magistrates to the honest and industrious operatives, must have been exceedingly gratifying to the large party of friends who had accompanied Sir Robert from Horton Hall. Such an enthusiastic display of respect and attachment has never been equalled." [Ross was M.P. for Northampton from 1832–7.]

As an afterthought, the Herald added that the performances were equally good, though admitting "We were present only for a short period and are unable to speak of them particularly."

Other performances during the season were under the patronage of the Earl of Euston (*Laugh When You Can*), the Masonic Lodge of Northampton (*Laugh When You Can* and *Damp Beds*), Mr. W. I. Watson Samwell (*The Somnambulist or The White Phantom* and a new comic pantomime, *The Witch of the Adamantine Caves or Harlequin at Northampton* plus a firework display by Mr. Wood "whose exhibition of the art has been the theme of admiration throughout the kingdom"), W. R. Cartwright, Esq. (*The Youthful Queen* and *Turning the Tables*), this being for the benefit of Mr. Parry and the last night of the season, Monday, September 24. Cartwright, added the Herald with fervour, was "the highly popular candidate for the southern division of this county".

A member of the Parry and Hamilton Company was next in the line of managers—Mr. Scott, who announced that he would open a season on

Monday, August 26, 1833, with the hope that he would enjoy "a continuation of the patronage and support which has so liberally been bestowed upon his predecessors". Judging by the personal testimony of Francis Raymond and the short stays of Stuart and Parry and Hamilton this was mere euphemism. Equally he would had to have been a true magician to justify his claim to have turned the theatre into "one of the most magnificent in appearance and convenient for accommodation in the United Kingdom".

In fact, he was even unable to meet his opening date. On August 17 the Mercury reported that he was "now in London selecting a company and, we are informed, has already procured the services of many very talented performers". But some he had selected failed to turn up on time and the first night had to be postponed two days. Nevertheless, according to the Herald, there was an "overflowing house" for *Rob Roy* and *A Rowland for an Oliver*.

For a patronage night on Monday, September 9, for George Payne and the members of Sulby, Newport and Northampton Cricket Clubs the choice was Morton's popular domestic comedy *Speed the Plough* (the play mentioning Mrs. Grundy) and a specially painted scene was exhibited showing a perspective view of George Payne's home, Sulby Hall, on the Northamptonshire border with Leicestershire. *(Page 40.)*

About this Northamptonshire character a separate book could be written. His colourful life encompassed a drama as exciting as many a stage plot. As a betting man, he must have been the biggest "mug" in history. Sometimes he would back nearly every horse in a race and still not manage to find the winner. In 1824, he lost £33,000 on one horse. His father, also George Payne, Sheriff of Leicester in 1805, had been killed in a duel. Until five o'clock on the morning of September 4, 1810, he was playing cards in White's Club, London, then excusing himself to keep an appointment. An hour later he was fatally injured in a pistol duel on Wimbledon Common. A married man with three other children besides George junior, Payne had been having an affair with a Miss Clarke, of Newcastle, a close friend of his wife and a frequent visitor to Sulby. It was Miss Clarke's brother who had challenged the sullier of his sister's honour to the duel. It was an unequal contest for as the pair took their places Payne whispered to his second that he would not return Clarke's fire!

In the case of the Paynes, truth was indeed stranger than fiction. What George Payne junior saw on the stage of the Northampton theatre that night could not compare with the extravagances of his own life.

The grandfather, banker Mr. Rene Payne, had been rolling in money and left it to his sons John (who won the Derby with Azor in 1817) and George, who was due to inherit Sulby Hall and a £14,000-a-year rent roll the year after the fatal duel, at the age of twenty-seven. His eldest son, our George, was six at the time but succeeded immediately to Sulby and by the time he reached his majority the income had increased to £17,000. He also inherited £300,000 in ready money, which was the sort he liked. He seems to have set out to spend it as fast as possible. His coming-of-age party was fabulous.

At Oxford, where he said his only college was the Mitre Hotel, he was sent down, his chief distinction in that district being a reputation as one of the pluckiest riders across the country from Chipping Norton to Bicester. Later he became Master of the Pytchley Hunt. To quote an obituary : "He was not less popular as a youngster among the battered voluptuaries of George IV's court than he continued to be during the last half-dozen years of his life with the Prince and Princess of Wales and with their children." The Prince of Wales—the future Edward VII—was at Payne's funeral in 1878 when he was buried in a paddock in full hunting dress.

And Sulby? As a result of Payne's profligacy he had to sell the house to Lady Elizabeth and the Hon. Frederick Villiers. During the 1914–18 War it became a V.A.D. Hospital. Later it was again lived in, by Major Guy Paget and a rich American; then used for a school; finally, after standing derelict for several years, it was pulled down. Built in 1795 by Sir John Soans, architect of the Bank of England, it was one of a number of mansions which used to grace the Northamptonshire countryside but for which the present generation sadly failed to find a use.

Competition for the Scott Company's 1833 season arrived in mid-September in the shape of Batty's Equestrian Establishment from the Royal Amphitheatre, Liverpool, which had appeared before the Royal Family in the Isle of Wight two months previously and which now revealed its splendours in the yard of Northampton's Bull Inn, "brilliantly illuminated with gas". However, they did not stay long and meanwhile at the theatre the Mayor and Corporation patronised *The Busy Body* with *The Irish Tutor* and *The Happiest Days of My Life* while our old Tory friend Sir Robert Gunning drove in from Horton to see *The Rivals* and hear Mayseder's Grand Terna, with variations for violin by Mr. Phillips with orchestral accompaniment.

On Mondays, September 30, and October 7, Scott brought back to the town Charles Mathews to give his "Fourth Volume, Comic Annual" and the visit is recalled in the memoirs of that great but now fading comedian. It was on the stage at Northampton that Mathews had his gout-ravaged foot attended to by his servant without the audience knowing what was going on! Mathews was suffering acutely, a fact of which the audience were not aware. The Mercury knew part of the story and explained that the "slight observable confusion" was attributed by many to forgetfulness but that Mathews was in pain and "the admirable manner in which he went through the evening's performances was not a little surprising".

What the Mercury did not know was that at one period during the play Mathews was having medical attention. From Exeter, where he paid a call later on this tour, he explained : "To-day I can put my foot on the ground without pain. I forgot when I wrote to you yesterday that you were not at Northampton. What I alluded to was Willson polticing my foot under the table in the middle of the first act. He did so again last night. The trap is a capital thing for such a purpose. How the audience would have been astonished had they known it!"

From Northampton, Mathews went on to Banbury and also visited his old school friend, the Rev. Thomas Speidel, at Crick Rectory, Northamptonshire. I believe he was travelling on this occasion in his "special machine which takes me, Crisp, Mr. Moss, pianist, Master Willson (theatrical servant), bed, dresses etc".

In April, 1835, the actor was back at Crick and was also a guest of Sir Charles Knightley, of Fawsley Manor, also in the county. To Speidel he wrote : "I can never forget your unwearied affectionate attention to me, they are engraved on my heart. You have saved my life, if it be but for a short time." It was indeed to be but for a short time. Mathews died at Plymouth on June 28, 1835. Speidel outlived his old friend by only a few months. Of Mathews the Sunday Times said : "He was on the stage what Hogarth was on canvas—a moral satirist; he did not imitate, he conceived and created characters, each one of which was recognised as a specimen of its class."

In between Mathews' two evenings at Northampton in 1833 the unusual presentation of a scene in a play called *Jonathan Bradford* drew favourable comment. "The complicated and unique scene at the end of the first act produced an excellent effect. The novelty of exhibiting at one view the exterior and interior of Jonathan Bradford's house, the action and development of the piece going on at the same time was not lost upon a very respectable and numerous audience."

The Scott season concluded about the end of October. During 1834 there are several references to another troupe of actors operating in the county and in neighbouring Rutland. Mr. Abbott's Company of Comedians played successively at Uppingham, Oakham, Kettering and Wellingborough.

Meantime the Spring Race Week entertainment at Northampton was by one man, Ching Lau Lauro, who offered for five nights "cabalisticks, ventriloquism, imitation of the feathered creation, corpuscular feats, and a musical miscellany". Charging from 2s. in the boxes to 6d. in the gallery, he described himself as the "Paganini of all naturists".

In May the original Paganini, the great violinist, appeared at the George Hotel, Northampton, charging 7s. 6d. The previous year he had met his match, financially, in the City of Lincoln. "The fiddling professor advertised his prices to be boxes, 7s. 6d., pit 5s. and gallery 2s. 6d. but the Lincolnites determined that they would pay no such money and hinted to the prince of fiddlers that they would submit to no imposition though they were willing to give him the full reward of his talents which they estimated at the following rates : boxes 4s., pit 3s. and gallery 1s. 6d. The hint was taken and the prices accepted and Paganini had a crowded house and smiling faces . . . at the conclusion he came forward and played another tune."

At Northampton Paganini had two vocalists supporting him and appears to have got his seven-and-sixpences without demur, this

> *"pale magician of the bow*
> *With his mournful look,*
> *Dreary and gaunt; hanging his pallid face*
> *Twixt his dark flowing locks"*

with his violin "glorifying, laughing, lamenting". As he appeared there was general surprise at his slight figure of infirm step, as if suffering from extreme weakness; he seemed to take but little notice of the audience.

Scott was back for a second season at the end of August, with Mr. Cathcart, of the Victoria Theatre, and Mrs. Cowle as leads. Also among the company were Mr. Southey, brother of the Poet Laureate, Robert Southey; Mr. Maddox; and Mr. Clement White "vocalist, with whom Northampton audiences are already acquainted". The Races with which the season was linked were not very successful and neither was the Race Ball at the George Hotel.

Whether or not things were now going to their satisfaction is not clear but the following March the proprietors of the theatre called a general meeting to discuss important changes. The relevant advertisement was as follows: "A general meeting of the proprietors of this theatre will be held at the George Hotel, in this town, on Friday, March 6, 1835, at 11 in the forenoon to consider and determine upon the propriety of requesting the representatives of the surviving trustees, named in a certain lease to the Master and Co-Brethren of the House and Hospital of St. John Baptist in the said town of Northampton; to the intent that a new lease may be granted by the said Master and Co-Brethren to three other proprietors then to be nominated." The notice was signed by George Abbey, secretary to the proprietors.

This is the first historical intimation of the owners of the site and property (subject to the lease) being St. John's Hospital, a charity dating from the reign of King Stephen when it was founded by William de St. Clere, Archdeacon of Northampton, probably in 1138.

It still survives today but in a revised form. Indeed, a re-revised form, as will presently emerge. At first it had been converted into an ecclesiastical sinecure, the Mastership being held by a non-resident stranger whose only occupation in regard to it was receiving the greater portion of its revenues. Records show that in 1535 it had possessed lands in Slipton, Stoke juxta Owndell, Rusheden, Wenlingborughe, Whyshton, Harroden, Walgrave, Hannyngton, Oldthroppe, Wotton, Cortnall, Harwell, Abyngton, Kyslyngbury, Gayton, Tyffeld, Blesworthe, Northampton, Thynden, Quinton, and Hangyng Houghton. [Slipton, Stoke Doyle, Rushden, Wellingborough, Whiston, Harrowden, Walgrave, Hannington, Althorp, Wootton, Courteenhall, Hartwell, Abington, Kislingbury, Gayton, Tiffield, Blisworth, Northampton, Finedon, Quinton, and Hanging Houghton.]

Over the years the clergymen who had been appointed Master by the Bishop of Lincoln (before the Reformation the County of Northampton used to be in the Lincoln Diocese) looked upon the job as a "perk", making a good thing out of it. The most blatant piece of nepotism and graft was when the then Bishop of Lincoln gave the Mastership to his son, the Rev. Richard Pretyman, Rector of Stony Middleton, Oxon, who was also a Canon of the Lincoln Cathedral. Instead of increasing the rents of the various properties and lands and finding a charitable use for the money, beyond the small cost of keeping the prescribed handful of men and women in the old "hospice" at Northampton, Master Pretyman left the rents as they were but levied large sums, known as "fines", for the renewal of leases, which sums he pocketed.

This un-Christian piece of chicanery was to be challenged by the Attorney-General in the Court of Chancery and in 1842 a decree was made to prevent further disintegration of the properties. Pretyman died in 1866 and there was then a gap until the Rev. N. T. Hughes, of St. Edmund's, Northampton, became an upright Master. A few years later still a proper new scheme was drawn up with a respectable body of local trustees, which was in due course to dispose of the Marefair premises to the town council for road-widening purposes, as will also emerge.

But to get back to the meeting of the theatre proprietors in March, 1835. On Friday, June 8, 1973, it appeared that I had come to a blank wall in the path of my researches in this direction. There were records and minute books neither of the theatre proprietors, nor of St. John's Hospital. The riddle of identifying the trio of new proprietors—if indeed the decision had been taken to re-assign the lease—appeared impossible to solve.

That I did find out who they were was due to the fact that the next day my wife sought my help for an article she was writing on the windmills of the county (there used to be 144 of them, but that is neither here nor there in this regard, except to say that mills figured in many a play plot and title). Grudgingly I tore myself away from my theatriana and accompanied her to Northamptonshire Record Office to investigate some windmilliana. The first bundle of papers we got out was about the famous milling family of Whitworth. At least it was that name which led us to the three documents in the bundle. Among the three documents was one that had nothing to do with milling but contained the names of the three new proprietors of the theatre in 1835! The trio were revealed as Henry Billington Whitworth, Charles Markham, and our old friend, George Abbey.

Whitworth was a banker whose home and premises were in what is now the George Row Club, which bought the property after his death for £6,000, moving from rooms in the Corn Exchange. His name is perpetuated in the adjacent Whitworth Chambers and in three Northampton street names—Henry Street, Billington Street and Whitworth Road (in which I was born, but that is quite irrelevant!). The site of the club is said at one time to have been that of that of a monastery associated with All Saints Church and later of the old Northampton Hospital.

Whitworth was quite a character though not greatly beloved. Money was the focal point of his life and he was the central figure of a novel *Ready-Money Mortiboy* written, partly in Northampton, by Walter Besant and James Rice, based largely on the facts of his life. Mortiboy's sister died and left him £25,000 unencumbered except that he had to provide a memorial window to her in St. Giles Church. After her funeral old Ready Money was discovered prowling around the church to seek out which was the smallest window—"The will said nothing about size!"

Until his death in 1877 Henry Billington Whitworth was Borough Treasurer, for which the annual payment was £25 and those who knew him nodded knowingly and said that he would not have taken on the job at that money unless there had been some other perks. During the nineteenth century there was a certain amount of irregularity in municipal affairs and on one occasion £1,000 was paid from town funds towards the election expenses of Sir Robert Gunning. In 1877 the office of Borough Treasurer was replaced, perhaps significantly, by that of Borough Accountant and the man who got the job was Whitworth's former chief clerk Samuel Hull, who was also a character in the novel. Presumably he knew all the ropes!

A poorer man is said to have once begged Whitworth to tell him the secret of making money. "I'll tell you for a guinea," said the banker. The money changed hands, then the recipe: "I never spend a shilling until I have made half-a-crown."

The recipe appeared to work for when H.B.W., then of Dallington Hall, died he left approaching £180,000.

The name of Charles Markham led me to a little bundle of diaries at the Record Office. Markham, who was born in December, 1778, son of John Markham, Attorney, had been Clerk of the Peace for the County since 1823.

I searched the diaries, for 1822, 1828, 1830, 1831, 1838 and 1842, to see what they might reveal of his theatrical activities. They could not tell me much about any of his activities for the entries were few and brief and mainly concerned with legal matters. The earliest reference of interest was of June 3, 1822: "At Abbey's 2s." Judging from the ambience of other entries this may have meant a visit to George or Robert Abbey and the loss of 2s. at cards. March 10, 1828, found him paying out (or winning?) another 2s. at Abbey's. There follow five entries of "Play" each showing payments of 2s. On September 9, the insertion is quite plain: "At theatre. Mad. Vestris 4s. 6d." Evidently he was in the boxes for the visit by the great actress during the regime of Francis Raymond.

Markham's 1830 diary is trade-marked "The Regent or Royal Tablet of Memory". For 1831 and 1838 he switched to "Peacock's Polite Repository or Pocket Companion" and like the diaries of today it provided a great deal of information, useful in the contemporary sense, interesting in retrospection.

About taxes, for instance. If Mr. Markham had any servant-men (which he certainly did) he could check up in the Repository whether he was paying the correct amount to the Exchequer. The Master was to pay yearly for one servant £1 4s.; for two £1 11s. each; for nine £3 1s. each. Soaking the rich indeed! While on the subject of servants, the pocket book warned of the existence on the Statute Book of an Act of 1791 whereby persons giving false characters for servants were liable to a penalty of £20.

The surprising principle, for those days, of heavier taxes for the richest men, or at least those who kept the most splendid establishments applied also to horses. The man who kept one horse used for riding or drawing a carriage paid annually £1 8s. 9d. but from the owner of two, more than double was extracted—£4 14s. 6d. And so on up the scale. For three it was £7 16s. 9d., for four £11, while for twenty it was £66—over £3 each. Racehorses were £3 10s. each.

Windows were taxed. For eight the charge was 16s. 6d.; for nine a guinea; for ten £1 8s.; if you had a mansion with 180 windows the tax was £46 11s. 3d. with eighteenpence for every additional one. So that here the sliding scale was in reverse. But there was a size limit, in that a window measuring more than 11 ft. by 4 ft. 6 ins. was charged as two (unless it had been made before April 5, 1785). Shops and warehouses were exempt. Theatres were not mentioned, but they are normally, by definition, not rich in windows.

Hair powder also attracted the attention of the Chancellor, which must have affected the acting fraternity. Every person who wore hair powder was to pay £1 3s. 6d. annually but no person was to pay for more than two unmarried daughters.

As now, there was a canine tax. Greyhounds were £1 a year. For other breeds the payments was 14s. where more than one were kept. And one-dog owners? "Every person who shall inhabit any dwelling house assessed to any of the duties on inhabited houses or on windows or lights and shall keep one dog and no more to pay 8s." Farmers with farms of less than £100 in value and shepherds were exempt.

Armorial bearings were taxed. "Any person keeping a coach or other carriage and using or wearing an armorial bearing to pay annually £2 8s." Almost needless to state, the coach itself, like the motor-car of today, did not escape. "For every coach, chariot, landeau, chaise, caravan, etc. with four wheels" there was an ascending scale—£6 for one, £13 for two, £21 for three and so on up to nine and upwards, £81 13s. 6d.

How many bureaucrats were needed to go round to see whether a house-holder had installed any new windows, count the chariots and tot up the man-servants, it is hard to say. Nor is it clear how it would work out for a rich actor-manager with bogus armorial bearings, living when not on tour in a country farmhouse with seventy-three good windows and three broken and two Labradors and a sheepdog; with a company of actors who worked on the farm when not strolling and also served at table on every other Wednesday; who liked to powder his own hair and had three unmarried daughters who rode around in two wheeled dog carts I cannot work out.

But it all shows what nonsense a tax system automatically creates, in whatever age it is operated.

The diary also noted that the abolition of the death penalty for forgery and many other crimes had been effected by an Act passed on July 17, 1837. This must have greatly affected the professional life of Charles Markham.

The final diary, for 1842, has a number of theatrical entries. June 4, Fitzgerald, an actor £1 (a gift to a needy Thespian?). August 29, the theatre, Miss Higgins (and others—names illegible). August 29, theatre, a party 12s. September 2, theatre, a party, 12s.

Generally speaking it would appear that Charles Markham patronised his own theatre only on Race Nights or other special occasions. Unless the entries are incomplete, he was not a "regular".

It was thus under a new proprietorship that a new manager took over in August, 1835. Not for the first time it was a man who had played under the banner of a previous manager—M. H. Simpson. He had appeared under the now-fallen standard of Francis Raymond at Leicester and Stratford and probably at Northampton too.

Other places where I have come across a Simpson—presumably the same one—are Abingdon (1823 with Mr. Hannan, manager of the Chelmsford and Andover theatres), Walsall (1824), Leamington (1826), and in 1831 at Stamford (March), Nottingham (July) and Retford (December). His real name was in fact Mercer Hampson, the Simpson being a stage addition.

He is the Mercer Hampson Simpson Senior who joined Mr. Munro in the management of the Birmingham Theatre in 1837 and who became sole lessee of that house on Boxing Day, 1843. In 1837 Simpson and Munro (manager of the New Leicester Theatre built following the demolition of the old one in March, 1836) figured in a joint season at Northampton and the following year the company was advertised as being "selected from the Theatre Royal, Birmingham".

As Francis Raymond had done, Simpson made a considerable effort to establish the Northampton theatre on a good basis, bringing down a number of leading players from London and being ready to innovate to attract custom. He began to excellent houses.

Plays of his first season included *The Vampire*, *Tom and Jerry*, *Scapegrace*, *The Beggar of Brussels*, *Turning the Tables*, *The Murdered Maid* and *The Manager in Distress*, the last-named being a novelty piece with actors speaking their lines from seats in the audience, Simpson himself playing the part of the "countryman in the gallery".

In his *Memoirs of the Colman Family*, written in 1841, Richard Brinsley Peake refers to *The Manager in Distress* as one of the few pieces of note produced at the Haymarket, London, during 1770. Written by George Colman senior it had the "manager" on stage apologising for the non-arrival of some of his players and certain members of the audience joining in to discuss what is to be done. The "audience members" are in fact actors, the whole thing starting off as a leg-pull. In the gallery is the "countryman", played in this case by the real manager.

The device of putting actors off-stage led to further experiments of a similar nature but it was not new. Ben Jonson was fond of making performers impersonate audience and bringing them on to the stage to criticise a new play during its performance.

However, some of the audience do not always realise when they are having their legs pulled. On more than one occasion duller members of the audience, on hearing of the manager's distress, made their way to the box office to ask for their money back.

Nor is it always safe to hoax an audience. On January 14, 1749, it was announced that a magician would put himself into a quart bottle at the Haymarket Theatre, London. The obvious hoax attracted an immense audience who avenged themselves for their credibility by demolishing the interior of the theatre! It was thought that the affair originated in a bet.

Patronage nights during the first Simpson season at Northampton were by the Odd Fellows Club, Sir R. H. Gunning, George Payne and members of the Northampton and Sulby cricket clubs. One Saturday there was a performance "in consequence of the Cheese Fair".

A Mr. Warren caused a sensation with an act of a type later seen in the music hall, shooting with a rifle at apples perched on the head of his son and on the head of Miss Rees, a member of the company.

Taking his leave when the season closed on Wednesday, November 11, Simpson specially requested any tradesman or inhabitant to whom he owed money to take or send their bills to his wife before mid-day on Saturday, November 21, as she was then to leave the town. He announced that he would be back the following year.

Simpson was another Northampton manager who operated at Stratford-upon-Avon. His first managerial visit there was in 1834 when instead of a lump sum for the season he paid a weekly rent of £5, from February 19 to April 7 and then £1 5s. for a single night on April 18. When a Mr. Fitzgibbons wrote to the theatre committee asking to rent the theatre in August, 1834, he was told that "Mr. Simpson has the refuse of the theatre to play next Spring". The accounts section of the Stratford records show a second and final season for Simpson from the end of November, 1835, to early in January, 1836.

Following it, Simpson appears to have fallen foul of the Stratford theatre owners in respect of some gas apparatus he had installed at the theatre. A minute of February 8, 1836, states : "Mr. Thomas Gill, having by the order of Mr. Simpson, put a quantity of gas fittings into the theatre and being unable to obtain any part of the cost from Mr. Simpson, agreed that Mr. Gill be considered a creditor for £10 18s. 6d. upon the books of the theatre, the whole of the fittings being the absolute property of the share-holders. Mr. Gill agrees that if he ever obtains from Mr. Simpson more than £5 he will pay it to the shareholders."

If Simpson ever did pay up it was not recorded in the books. But as far as the general fortunes of the theatre are concerned the books reflect clearly that things were not going anywhere near as well as had been hoped when a theatre was planned in the birthplace of the Bard. At the same meeting at which the gas fittings were discussed the thoughts of the committee turned to dissolution : "If at any future period it should be found expedient to dispose of the theatre it is ordered that four-fifths in value shall constitute a majority."

A couple of months later, Mr. Leyton, of the Shakespeare Hotel, who had sold part of his land for the theatre to be built, applied to store empty casks and crates under its stage—and was accepted at a fee of £2 a year. There must have been quite a heady atmosphere on stage as the lingering alcoholic odours filtered up through the "boards".

The year 1837 brought more indications that things had not got any more rosy. Mr. Elliston, one of the sons of the Great Lessee, was told that if he did not pay the 8 gns. due from the previous year's rent he would not be allowed into the theatre. And the value for fire insurance was cut from £800 to £500, a sure sign that money was tight.

In January, 1838, Simpson ran a twelve-night season at Northampton at reduced prices—2s. 6d., for boxes (second price 1s. 6d.), 1s. for the pit and a mere "tanner" for the gallery.

In February that year he produced a real novelty : for two nights the theatre was turned into a ballroom. Announcing a "Grand Masquerade

Theatre, Northampton.

Second Race Night

By Desire and under the immediate Patronage of His Grace the

DUKE OF

BUCCLEUCH,

C. ROSS & R. V. SMITH, Esqs.

STEWARDS of the RACES.

On *FRIDAY Evening, AUGUST 28th, 1835,*

Will be performed, a Comedy in five acts, entitled,

A CURE

FOR THE

Heart Ache

Ellen, Miss REES   ..   Miss Vortex, Mrs. BROOKS
Jessy, Mrs. SIMPSON   ....   Mary, Mrs. ROGERS
Sir Hubert Stanley, Mr. MILLS .... Charles Stanley, Mr. RIGNOLD
Vortex, Mr. PALMER .... Young Rapid, Mr. HUTCHINGS .... Old Rapid, Mr. SIMPSON
Frank Oatland, Mr. WRIGHT .... Bronze, Mr. T. LEE
Landlord, Mr. ROGERS

END OF THE PLAY,

DANCING by Mrs. ROGERS.
A COMIC SONG by Mr. SIMPSON.
A SONG by Mr. HUTCHINGS.
A DANCE by Mr. RIGNOLD,
And a Comic Song by Mr. T. LEE.

The whole to conclude with (second time here) THE

BEGGAR of

BRUSSELS,

Or the Convict and the Deserter.

Albertine, Mrs. SIMPSON .... Catherine, Mrs. BROOKS
Colonel Florestine, Mr. MILLS ...... Dubois, Mr. PALMER ...... Julius, Mr. ROGERS
Francesco (*The Beggar of Brussels*), Mr. SIMPSON .. Mulver, Mr. RIGNOLD
Felix, Mr. HENDERSON .... Peter, Mr. WRIGHT

Doors opened at a Quarter before Seven o'Clock, and to commence at Half-past.
Boxes, 3s. 6d. .. Pit, 2s. .. Gallery, 1s.
Family Ticket to admit Four, 12s.   ....   Ditto to admit Three, 10s.
Children admitted at Second Price from the commencement.
Second Price at Nine o'Clock.
Boxes, 2s. .. Pit, 1s. .. **No half-price to Gallery on the Race Nights.**
Season Tickets, not transferable, admissable every Night except Benefits, £1 1s.
Nights of Playing next week, Monday, Wednesday, and Friday.
Tickets and Places for the Boxes to be had of Mr. FREEMAN, Market-Square.

FREEMAN, PRINTER, MARKET-SQUARE, NORTHAMPTON.

Unrivalled Attraction!

THEATRE, NORTHAMPTON.

On WEDNESDAY EVENING, OCT. 28th, 1835,

FOR THE BENEFIT OF

Mr. T. LEE,

The Performance to commence with the Drama entitled

FRANKENSTEIN

OR THE

Man and the Monster.

Emmeline..Mrs. BROOKS   Lisetta..Miss FORBES   Rosania..Mrs. OWEN
Frankenstein..Mr. HENDERSON   ....Mr. T. LEE   Prince..Mr. RIGNOLD
Ritzberg..Mr. PALMER   Quadro..Mr. MILLS   Strutt..Mr. ROGERS
Julio..Miss REES.

Mr. ROBERTS,

Having in the most handsome manner offered his services, will Sing in the course of the Evening,

"THE BAY OF BISCAY,"

AND

"JERRY BLOSSOM."

After which the laughable Farce of

More Blunders

THAN ONE.

Louisa.. Miss FORBES   Susan..Mrs. BROOKS   Letty..Mrs. ROGERS
Old Melbourn..Mr. PALMER   Young Melbourn..Mr. HENDERSON
Larry Hoolagan..Mr. T. LEE   Bailiff..Mr. ROGERS   Trap..Mr. MILLS

Song---"Oysters, Sir," by Miss Rees.
By Desire, the Comic Song of
"All round my Hat," in character by Mr. T. LEE,
accompanied by his favourite Jerusalem Pony.

The Evening's Entertainment to conclude with

CLARI,

THE

MAID OF MILAN.

Clari..Mrs. BROOKS............Vespina..Miss FORBES..........Ninetta..Miss REES
Fadalma..Mrs. OWEN....................Wife of Peregrino..Mrs ROGERS
Duke Vivaldi..Mr. PALMER............Rolamo..Mr. HENDERSON
Jocoso..Mr. RIGNOLD....................Nicolo..Mr ROGERS
Geronio..Mr. WILSON................Nimpedo..Mr. T. LEE

The Doors will be opened at Half-past Six o'Clock, to commence at Seven precisely.
BOXES, 3s.; PIT, 2s.; GALLERY, 1s.
Children admitted at Second Price from the Commencement.
Second Price to commence at A QUARTER BEFORE NINE o'Clock.
Boxes, 1s. 6d.; Pit, 1s.; Gallery, 6d.
Ladies and Family Parties are respectfully informed that the performances will conclude this evening before
Eleven o'clock.
Tickets and Places for the Boxes to be had of Mr. FREEMAN, Market-square; and of Mr. T. LEE, at Mr.
Gisson's, Horsemarket.

Stage Manager, Mr. HENDERSON.

C. S. Atkins, Herald Office, Northampton.]

NORTHAMPTON, 1835—the Duke of Buccleuch was a patron of a performance (left) early in the Simpson regime. "Frankenstein or The Man and the Monster" (right) was an "unrivalled attraction." (*British Museum and Northampton Public Library*) and Fancy Dress Ball" Simpson said the pit would be boarded over and the theatre ornamented and decorated in the most graceful style. "Refreshments will be served of the very best description and the respectability and comfort of the visitors will be attended to with Mr. Simpson's greatest care and attention." Tickets, at 4s. for the boxes and 1s. 6d. for the gallery, could be had of Mr. Simpson at his lodgings in Commercial Street and no one would be admitted except by presenting a ticket personally to Mr. Simpson at the door of the theatre. A further announcement said that the house would be lit with variegated lamps and that the festivities of the dance would be interspersed with songs, recitations and the unique performance of Adolphe Eugene Raussbure. The band had been considerably augmented and would perform the "most approved compositions". Dresses, masks and dominoes could also be obtained from Mr. Simpson. Thus he was also cashing in on the use of his wardrobe. Carriages were to set down with the horses' heads towards the West Bridge.

Following the event the Mercury reported that there had been a crowded house but that parties who went as spectators outnumbered those who took part but "there was nothing very surprising in this considering that nothing of the kind had ever before been attempted in the town and that many might have been unprepared for the perfect decorum and respectability which characterised the whole of the arrangements."

The top "name" brought to the town by Simpson was that of Sheridan Knowles, Irish-born playwright and leading figure in the dramatic world of the 1830s, though today he is completely forgotten. Knowles was the author of a popular play called *The Hunchback* and in this appeared at Northampton his pupil and future wife Miss Elphinstone. He also wrote *William Tell, Virginius* and *The Wife.*

"Natural" acting was still very far in the future but by comparison with the flamboyant styles then current, Knowles' acting was most restrained. The Mercury indulged for once in a little serious dramatic criticism : "As an actor Knowles has not been as generally appreciated as he deserves. A notion seems to exist that there is a radical distinction between creative and mimetic genius. Beyond doubt the latter does not include the former but the assumed unfitness of the poet to personate his own creations is to us a mystery. The case of Shakespeare can scarcely be cited against us with effect. The extent of Shakespeare's literary labours could have left him with but little time for the duties of an actor. It is, besides, by no means certain that his acting, so far as it went, was not of high merit. We know little of his stage history . . . had he never dazzled the world with the blaze of his genius as a writer he would probably have won their homage as an actor."

Getting down to cases the paper said : "With the conventionalities which so freely compromise the whole trading stock of the actor Knowles has nothing to do. He acts on the stage as you feel he would act, under the same circumstances, in real life. We are not too sure that this is the best way to draw the best houses—it may be too 'caviare for the generale' for that—but we are sure that it is the perfection of acting." Knowles, in the opinion of the Mercury, was not surpassed by any living actor.

In later life, Knowles did a Sheridan, by spurning his old love of the drama. Unlike Sheridan, the cause in his case was not an addiction to politics but a turning to religion. He became a Nonconformist preacher and detested the stage as much as he once cherished it. It is said that he continued to draw the monetary rewards of his writings, in the form of royalties, only under protest!

Despite his considerable efforts Simpson does not appear to have been financially successful at Northampton. There are many references to business not coming up to expectations.

One night when he was assured of a good house was when he appeared as "Brother" Simpson for a night in January, 1838, under the patronage, as the Herald reported, of "a great number of that excellent fraternity the Freemasons and their families and altogether an excellent and highly respectable house". The pieces chosen were appropriate—*Simpson and Co.*, *My Neighbour's Wife* and a domestic sketch entitled *The Freemasons* given by Miss M. Pincott and Brother Simpson which "excited universal admiration and applause" plus the perennial favourite farce, *A Rowland for an Oliver*.

Links between the Masonic order and the stage date back at least two centuries. At Norwich in 1740 the brethren were desired to be at Brother Lindsey's by five o'clock precisely to go "cloathed as Masons in procession to the theatre" where boxes had been prepared. There was a special prologue by Brother Pearson, Masonic songs, a dance by Brother Hind and an epilogue recited by Sister Pearson (!?)

When that great managerial character Jemmy Whitely took his benefit in August, 1766, at the Nottingham Theatre he had built six years before he recited a Mason's prologue in the character of a Master Mason and sang several Masonic songs between the acts. A century later in that city Mrs. J. F. Saville was to receive great favours from the Masonic fraternity, in deference no doubt, to her late husband.

The Craft comes in for favourable mention in Volume Two of the *Random Records* of George Colman the Younger, dramatist and later Examiner (i.e. Censor) of Plays. He had been granted the Freedom of the City of New Aberdeen and noted that he could now therefore return there and set up a shop whenever he pleased. "A further gain, too—which I had forgot but the word Freedom put me in mind of it—was my initiation into the craft of Free-Masonry—that Grand Arcanum which is confided to thousands all over the world and has therefore become, as Lingo would call it, 'a secret pro bono publico'. It appears that I valued the honours of the New-Town Lodge above those of the Old-Town University; for I was proud of being raised to the rank of a Master Mason; but when King's College complimented me with the offer of a Master of Arts degree I declined it."

The next Dramatic Mason (that is, Mason to my knowledge, of course) I came across in my researches was caught in the act of organising dancing on Shakespeare's bowling green at Stratford-upon-Avon.

After his final season at Northampton in the autumn of 1838, of which the Masonic evening formed part, Simpson appears to have concentrated his attention on the Birmingham Theatre Royal. There he was succeeded by his son, also Mercer Hampson Simpson, and the consecutive tenure of the father and son ran to fifty-four years. Father retired on December 16, 1864, and died on March 2, 1877, aged seventy-six, at Brighton. The son retired in 1891 and died on August 12, 1902. Between them the two Mercer Hampson Simpsons made the Birmingham theatre nationally known.

Simpson's long and successful stay at the Birmingham theatre was in contrast to the experience of most of his predecessors since the place opened in 1774. In sixty-odd years it had experienced two fires (1792 and 1820) and seen several of its managers either in gaol or being pursued to put them there, for debt. M'Cready senior had done well. But in 1822 Bunn owed the owners nearly £500 at the end of his tenure and had to sell off his scenery and dramatic library. Richard Brunton, of Plymouth, lost money and offered the committee of owners 3s. 6d. in the pound. In 1828 came Mr. Lewis from the Liverpool Theatre who intended to stay three years but had to withdraw after two. Watson, of Cheltenham, was imprisoned in Warwick Gaol for debt. In 1833 came the brief stay of a man named Fraser who engaged Paganini for three nights and absconded with the profits on the third. Fitzgibbon and Wightman who took the theatre in partnership had their largest audience when Wightman's creditors turned up to make trouble. In his history of the theatre, John E. Cunningham tells us that Wightman was seen outside the theatre only on Sundays as the Sheriff could not arrest him on the day of rest. Also from Liverpool came Mr. Armistead and when he went to gaol and his case came up at Warwick Assizes he was released only on condition of abandoning all claim to the theatre.

Things changed for the better, financially at least, with the arrival in April, 1838, of Monro (or Munro) as manager and Simpson as stage manager (and partner?).

How did Simpson succeed at Birmingham where so many others had failed and at a period when the provincial theatre was in a generally parlous condition? Cunningham explains that it was achieved by suiting the tune to the listener. "Ten years show a lamentable change. In 1846 the manager could boast of elephants, horses and camels on the stage but scarcely a good play throughout the year. Spectacle ruled, with domestic drama close to it. Perhaps twice during the year the Royal audience were shown how drama should be presented."

One significant introduction by Simpson was that of Christmas panto-mimes in 1840–1. The son introduced the stock company to Birmingham in 1849, when Northampton had many years to run under the circuit actor-manager system.

Of the long Simpson era at Birmingham there is a remarkable and unique survival—a superb collection of play-books from the former theatre library. Used by generations of actors they date back, indeed, before Simpson's management but he was evidently responsible for gathering them and keeping them together. The majority of them carry his specially printed label. Libraries like these were part of the regular working material of every stock company. Old plays from the seventeenth and eighteenth century drifted on with surprising vitality as Percy Hinton recalled in a *Theatre*

Notebook article, with due changes made for time and fashion. Being in such long and regular use the copies are dog-eared, thumbed, marked, altered and some bear signs of being in a fire.

The bulk of this collection is now in the Birmingham Reference Library and was not available at the time I wished to inspect it, because the library was moving to more commodious premises. Other parts of the collection are at the Victoria and Albert Museum and in the possession of Mr. Hinton.

An actor who was employed by Simpson at Birmingham describes him as "a testy man". In his *Random Recollections of an Old Actor* Fred Belton also says that Simpson "always looked sharply after the pounds, shillings and pence".

Mercer Simpson junior, incidentally, was educated at Edgbaston Proprietary School and intended by his father to cut loose from the family's drama links. He was to be a dentist and it was his own decision to abandon this line and follow in his father's footsteps.

As Simpson Senior left Northampton for Birmingham and greater glories the first train was running from Euston, London, to that city. Despite the efforts made by some far-sighted Northamptonians, Northampton was off the line, the nearest point being at Blisworth where the station was a mere wooden shed with a tremendous flight of wooden steps up the embankment to the track. The first train was on September 17, 1838, and a fortnight later a railway mail service began from Northampton, a mail cart taking the post to Blisworth.

A Mercury leader said it was notorious that it had been promised that Blisworth would be a first-class station and Roade a second-class one. This had been reversed so that all trains stopped at Roade (a little further from Northampton) but few at Blisworth.

What was the reason for this? Six months earlier two large meetings had been held in the town, one of leading inhabitants of the borough the other of gentlemen associated with the gentry and nobility in the neighbourhood, to represent to the directors of the London and Birmingham Railway the extreme importance of having a first-class station at Blisworth. The directors replied that they found the road from Blisworth to Northampton very indifferent and there was no chance of any efforts being made speedily to improve it. Though it was rumoured that there were plans to lower Hunsbury Hill and erect an inn within a short distance of the station. Later Blisworth Hotel was erected. Today, of course, the station is closed. A county which once had dozens of railway stations today has only five—at Northampton, Kettering, Wellingborough, Long Buckby and Kings Sutton.

The effect which the introduction of railways was to have on the provincial people of the world of theatre was great indeed but could not yet be guessed at.

Meanwhile some consequences of the coming of the railroad were immediate. One of the rail policemen employed at Roade was killed when he mistook on which lane a train was approaching. In the Barbican, London, 100 horses, the property of Mr. Chaplin "the extensive coach proprietor" were sold. They had been used to draw the Portsmouth, Southampton and

Exeter coaches. "During the last six months," reported the Mercury, "at least 1,000 horses have been sold, the greater part being from the great northern road to Birmingham, Manchester and Liverpool".

A new age, indeed, was dawning. Queen Victoria had come to the throne in 1837. In Northampton the old Windmill Inn on the Market Square was renamed in her honour, the Queen's Arms. There I had many a drink with characters from the entertainment world of our time, people like Ted Lune and Des O'Connor. But that's quite another story.

ACT
THE
SECOND

OLD HENRY'S HOUSE

*... being an account of Respectable Old Henry Jack-
man and his Company, which mostly amounted to
his family so that in "Macbeth" two of the witches
might be the ambitious Henry Hartley and his mother-
in-law. Telling how Old Henry quit the stage and
this life simultaneously at the old age of 66 and was
laid to rest in Northampton. How a son and son-in-
law became partners to carry on with the show. But
how eventually the company itself expired.*

THE FIRST Jackman Playbill I have traced is of a season at St. Albans in 1818. The original has been lost and this is taken from a reproduction in "Herts Countryside." See Page 124.

Scene One

ALL IN THE FAMILY

Miss Joan Wake, founder of Northamptonshire Record Society and its moving spirit for several decades (despite the fact that she had but twenty-two birthdays*), got to know a thing or two about the habits of solicitors during the years she was cajoling them, along with owners of county houses etc., to let the society have their old documents.

In an article in the Northampton and County Independent in 1971, following the society's golden jubilee, Miss Wake passed on her findings about the men of law : "I made over the years a great study of the habits of solicitors. The deeds of their clients were kept in tin boxes in a strong room in the basement. Other papers no longer wanted were taken upstairs to the attic."

One of the attics penetrated by this determined lady—equally as single-minded and heroic a figure as any member of her ancient family called Hereward—was that of Messrs. Burton and Snell at Daventry, Northants.

"After much persuasion I was allowed to go up to the attic where I found the whole floor two or three feet deep in a promiscuous heap of documents—two centuries of them I should say—smothered in dirt and dust—but preserved from damp by broken window panes which ensured a circulation of air.

"It was like an archaeological dig. I summoned two hefty lads to help me put the lot into sacks but two of us developed sore throats from the dust and had to break off work for a day or two. At the end of the week we took a lorry load of sacks to the Record Rooms at Northampton. I found in them the history of the local administration of the area from the early eighteenth century—Parliamentary election papers, inclosure records, early railway documents, records of societies for the prosecution of felons, manorial records, etc., etc., etc., even a medieval charter or two among the rest."

It is from the depths of one or more of those seventy-six sackfuls of promiscuous documents that we hear the voice from the grave of the next manager of the Northampton Theatre, Henry Jackman. For among the papers were letters from him and from members of his company on tour at some of the two dozen theatres the Jackman players visited in an overall lifetime of some fifty-seven years.

* Her birthday was on February 29. Miss Wake died, aged 89, as this book went to press.

Henry Jackman corresponded in a businesslike manner with a Daventry solicitor named Gery, in connection with the company's appearances at Daventry. Furthermore two members of the Jackman Company were on a friendly basis with the solicitor and their letters contained not merely matters of business but also family news, comments on the state of the stage, in some cases their innermost thoughts, hopes, aspirations, disappointments, and in one letter there are also some confidences about a difference of opinion with the manager who was also father-in-law.

When I began researching the Northampton Theatre, Marefair, in June, 1972, Jackman was just another surname. I had not even realised that it was a Jackman playbill which had been reproduced on page 13 of my previous book, *Death of a Theatre*, history of the New Theatre, Northampton (1912–60). That bill turns out to be especially significant, as it is of the very first season by the company at Northampton, at the start of a twenty-year tenure. Oddly enough, when I asked around, scarcely anyone appeared to have even heard of Jackman's troupe, despite its long life and the wide area over which it "strolled".

The list to date is as follows and is probably incomplete:

ABINGDON	MARKET HARBOROUGH
AYLESBURY	NEWPORT PAGNELL
BANBURY	NORTHAMPTON
BARNET	READING
BEDFORD	ST. ALBANS
BICESTER	STONY STRATFORD
BUCKINGHAM	STRATFORD-UPON-AVON
DAVENTRY	UXBRIDGE
EVESHAM	WALLINGFORD
HIGHGATE	WARWICK
LEAMINGTON	WELLINGBOROUGH
LEIGHTON BUZZARD	WOBURN
LUDLOW	WOODSTOCK

Apart from a few articles in county magazines virtually nothing had been written about Henry Jackman and his brood. I use that expression advisedly because the company was for many years very much a family affair. As many as nine of the fourteen or so members might be relations of the manager. As members of the brood reached sufficient years—it could be as few as six—they would as a matter of course begin to take parts or perhaps become a musician or back-stage helper. They were chosen for roles not for their talent, but because they were Jackmans or had married Jackmans. As regards the daughters, of whom there were six, if they married, the bridegroom was almost certain to be an actor who had joined the company, seeking a living but also finding a wife. And the wedding ceremony would take place wherever the company happened to be at the time the knot was to be tied.

John Henry (Harry) Fenton joined the company in the mid-1820s. At St. John's Church, Bedford, on November 5, 1829, he married Henry Jackman's eldest daughter Eliza, during the season which had begun early in September. Sister Caroline was a witness at the marriage, along with Old Henry and Henry Junior. Later Henry Hartley, born on the last day of 1812 at Chipping Norton, Oxon, son of Robert and Ann Hartley, joined the company and Caroline was herself his bride at Wellingborough on August 16, 1836, with Old Henry and another daughter, Sophia, as witnesses. Sophia was the only daughter destined to remain a spinster. At some date in between these marriages, but before 1834, when a son was born, George Partleton, musician, actor, and dancer, joined the Jackman ranks and in due course married Frances Jackman, who was named after her mother.

Just as their marriages took place wherever the company happened to be, so too had the nine Jackman children been born on tour, possibly, like some celebrities of the stage, in the wings. The actual birthplace of the oldest child, Eliza, has so far eluded me. I say "so far" because I have so got to "know" the Jackmans that I feel I owe this entirely unsung company a book on their own and if means present themselves I hope to bring one out at greater length than this chapter, and with information I have yet to find. A probable title is "Old Henry's Houses". As Eliza was the oldest, her birth must have been before 1809, as will be seen.

Several of the others I have managed to track down. Henry Junior, oldest of the sons, was born at Barking and baptised there on the first day of 1812. Which would seem to suggest that the company were playing at Barking at the time. Unfortunately, nothing in the way of a playbill or newspaper account has yet come to light to confirm this. If you have a framed Barking playbill of Christmas Eve, 1811, hanging on the wall do please let me know. Then this omission can be rectified in the later book. At the same time you may care to send me a fiver subscription as advance payment for a copy of the book. If it fails to come out your money would be returned—the same money-back guarantee which was given to the trusting patrons of this book, which happily did not have to be implemented.

For the moment, however, that is all we know about Henry Junior's entry into the world. The church records are not very informative. As the helpful Vicar of Barking, Canon J. W. Roxborough, told me in December, 1972 : "Unfortunately the new law about registers being kept in printed books and with full details only came into force in June, 1812." Even in the case of some births after this date there are problems, either through the lack of detail or the lack of records, or not knowing in which town to look.

Caroline, the second daughter, was born at Romford in 1809–10, which is why her older sister's birth presumably pre-dates 1809. The information comes from the 1851 Census which found her at Stratford-upon-Avon as Mrs. Hartley, mother of five.

That Stratford census recorded the presence at Stratford of another Jackman daughter, Sophia. Like the rest she had known the heady atmosphere of the footlights but had forsaken it for the heady atmosphere of the taproom—she was a barmaid. All this we will come to in due course. The immediate point is that the Census gives her birthplace as another Stratford —Stony Stratford—and her age as thirty-five. It is very likely that this was during a season in this town on the border of Buckinghamshire and

9—TU * *

Northamptonshire and it is possible she was born there in 1815–16. Possible, but not certain, because even in the very serious and honesty-demanding context of an official census ladies do tend to underestimate their ages. That same census found the Jackman Company at Northampton and Mrs. Jackman is caught by the researcher in the act of making a mis-statement : she said she was sixty, when in fact she was sixty-seven. Even Old Henry, her husband, lopped five years off his true age of sixty-five.

Charles Jackman, the second son, came into the world at Ampthill, Bedfordshire, where the register gives his father's occupation as "strolling player". The date was February 23, 1819. Once again, it seems likely that the company were performing in this market town but there are no records to confirm this. They might have been on their way to or from Bedford or Woburn.

Harriet Jackman figured, like Charles, in the Northampton census of 1851, but as Harriet Morgan. By then, as we shall see, another actor who had joined the company had married a Jackman daughter. She gave her age as twenty-five (suggesting that she was born in 1825–6) and the place of her birth merely as London.

Louisa's birth cannot be confirmed either. The same census found her still unmarried and with the company at Northampton, when she gave her age as twenty-three and the birthplace as Luton. This gives 1826–7 and this is during a period for which the registers at Luton have disappeared.

About some other members of the company I have drawn a complete blank, so far. In the cast lists of the early 1840s a Master Jackman appears and he may well be the Mr. F. Jackman who crops up in 1845. Just where he fits in is not clear. He does not appear in Old Henry's will, although this does not prove anything as only the children are named therein, along with their mother. A Master Jackman of 1840 would be too young to be a child of Old Henry and his wife. Charles Jackman never married and it is not certain whether Henry Junior did or not.

That same will of the 1850s affords another possibility, for it provided me with a mystery figure (and, of course, every book should have a mystery figure) in the person of George Jackman. He is listed after Henry and Charles and was therefore presumably the youngest son. He appears nowhere else, so whether he was with the company as a supernumerary who would not get his name on the playbills or whether he was the odd man out in the family who revolted against the tradition of the stage is a question which is so far unanswered.

However, this chapter is getting very unruly. And therefore unrespectable. And though he played in un-royal theatres, that is something which Old Henry would not have tolerated. I can almost hear him raising protest from the tomb which is not 100 yards from where I am writing these lines. If there was one thing that Henry Jackman was, it was Respectable. With a capital R. The term crops up time and time again. "The respectability of our old friend Mr. Jackman . . ." and so forth, is read in the Press reports as though Respectability was the highest term of praise, more adulatory than qualities like proficiency, talent, or inspiration.

Jackman's letters, such as survive, show him to be extremely businesslike and orderly. He would never put an Epilogue before an Act. So order please! First things first, second things second, and so on until we reach the final curtain of the Jackmans.

The curtain went up on Henry Jackman's life in St. James, London, in 1786. His actual birthday has eluded me despite a special trip to London to establish it, by means of a long search and re-search through church registers deposited with the Westminster Public Libraries.

This was very frustrating. For it cheated me of the chance of confirming or disproving a very tempting theory that he was the son of a playwright who had pieces produced at the Theatre Royal, Drury Lane, in particular a very popular play called *All the World's A Stage*. What could be more appropriate, what more fitting a father could Old Henry be provided with than such a man?

The potential parent with whom I had hoped to fit him up was Isaac Jackman. Born in Dublin, the source of many Thespians as well as revolutionaries, Isaac practised as an attorney before moving to London where he wrote for the stage and had the comic opera *Milesian* produced at Drury Lane in March, 1777, and the farce *All The World's A Stage* the following month. From 1786 to 1795 he was one of two Irishmen who edited the Morning Post newspaper and landed the printers in several libel actions. Such a character would be thought to occupy a place of some distinction in the history of the descendant newspaper the Daily Telegraph. An inquiry to them yielded no information about their incautious editor.

After the failure to clinch an interesting theory—and after all Jackman is not a common name and dramatic Jackmans must be a limited field—by means of the faded two-centuries old writing in a church register, further information came to hand from Dublin Public Libraries which threw some doubt on the idea. First Dublin P.L. quoted the Dublin Magazine of August, 1855: "Isaac Jackman, born in Dublin, was the son of a clerk in the office of the Lord Mayor of that city, where he learned and practised for some years the profession of an attorney. He then came over to England, and endeavoured to improve his fortune by a marriage with a lady possessed of a comfortable annuity for life. She, however, died soon after, and the annuity dropped. Jackman then commenced dramatic writing."

With un-erring and un-Irish logic the Libraries pointed out that if Jackman began writing for the stage only after the death of his wife and beneficiary, and if his plays were on the stage by 1777, he could not have been the father of a son born in 1786. Unless, of course, he married again. But since receiving this comment I have found proof that Old Henry's mother was alive and acting in the 1820's. Another possibility, I suppose, is that Isaac was Old Henry's uncle...? At what age our worthy and respectable manager went on the stage we do not know but he was an actor-manager by the surprisingly early age of nineteen—in 1805. This is from the wording of his obituary in 1852—"for 47 years the respected manager of the principal provincial theatres in the counties of Bedfordshire, Buckinghamshire, Northamptonshire and Oxford."

About the early years of the company there is no information whatever beyond that which is suggested by the birthplaces of the children. The first playbill I have come across for the company is of 1818 and by then, if not already in 1805, he was, of course, married. So there is no playbill to reveal the maiden name of his wife, Frances. If she was not already an actress when she married the young manager, she soon became one. The only other information about her is that she came from Rotherham, Yorks (Northampton Census, 1851).

When I say that there is no information, this always means, of course, that I have not yet discovered anything. This book has been researched as a part-time occupation over a period of fifteen months and as this involved searching 150 years of a local newspaper time was limited in other directions, especially more distant ones.

A company such as Jackman's would normally consist of about fourteen —ten men and four women—but in fact his case was rather abnormal. It depended on how many daughters he had at the time and which of them had decided to marry! As many as nine of the company might be members of the family. This could indeed be termed "family entertainment". He might have to find a Shylock, a Portia, a Bassanio, a Gobbo, an Antonio, a Lorenzo, a Nerissa, all from his sons and daughters and their spouses.

There was a good deal of sensational drama in the Jackman playbills but there was also a fair ration of Shakespeare. Whether the audiences of that time appreciated the beauty of the verse of the Bard or were impressed only by his high drama, knifings, poisonings, sex-switch plots, added fun of the waistcoat variety etc. is it impossible to say for certain.

From the many sources I have consulted—playbills, newspaper articles, the "letters in the sacks", the few articles previously published about Jackman, the births, marriages and deaths announcements and certificates etc. I set out to build up a month-by-month itinerary of the movements of the company, from 1805, when it began, through to 1863, the year in which it probably ended, with a last season at Banbury.

In this "Jackman Diary" there are many gaps at present, the principal one being that I have been unable to find any playbills before 1818, when at St. Albans one finds them playing *Hamlet* and *Raymond and Agnes* on a January Saturday.

The Master Jackman who appeared in the role of a child would be Henry, then aged six. His name was to appear on few playbills as he became a musician in the orchestra and they were rarely in the limelight of publicity. There was a double hornpipe by Miss Jackman (Eliza, about eleven) and Miss C. Jackman (Caroline, about ten). Not yet old enough except for a possible "babe in arms" carry-on part or as a toddler was Sophia, aged two.

Thus Fanny Jackman had by this time had four of her children. A few months later she was to announce to her husband that another was on the way—Charles. But at St. Albans she appeared as Beatrice in *Raymond and Agnes*.

The lead in *Hamlet* was performed by Mr. Amhurst who was on the last night of his guest engagement. Henry Jackman was one of the gravediggers and the other was Tommy Styles with whom he shared a birthplace and year (London, 1786). Styles, who played at one time at the Theatre Royal, Glasgow, was to outlive his employer and soldier on with the company almost to the bitter end, by when he was seventy-seven. Others listed in this first playbill (the original has been lost, only a magazine reproduction surviving) were Messrs. Hunter, Henry, Forrester, Gilbert, Turner and Jones, Mrs. Henry, Mrs. Gilbert, and Miss Fisher.

Married couples were often employed on the ground that two could live as cheaply (and therefore he paid less than two) as one. According to an article by R. P. Mander, the Jackman Company were frequent visitors to St. Albans and used a number of theatres in buildings in the Dagnall Street area, probably including the old moot hall and the old market hall in Market Street on the site of one of the Eleanor Crosses.

Mr. Mander went on to say: "Jackman himself was probably an Irish man" (in another article Mr. Mander says he was probably an Irish Jew) ". . . it is highly probable that about 1850 old Jackman died and the family abandoned the circuit and confined their activities to playing at fairs."

If this was a guess at the date of Old Henry's death it was a fairly accurate one as he died in 1852. The company did not, however, abandon theatre proper and take to the fairgrounds. It is not impossible that they may have occasionally appeared at fairgrounds but I have no evidence of this.

After 1818 there is a gap until September, 1821, when an advertisement in the Northampton Mercury places the company at Buckingham: "The theatre being connected with the Swan and Castle Inn, every accommodation may be obtained by strangers who may honour it by their presence." The "theatre" here was in fact an assembly room, lofty and charming, over the coachhouse of this inn: it still survives as the "Cromwell Room". In December, 1790, performances had been given there by the Hounslow Company of Comedians, which normally operated only in Norfolk and Suffolk. Another "theatre" at Buckingham was a barn of stone on the London Road, just outside the town, which was pulled down in 1862, the stone being used to build a shop. After that the Town Hall was employed.

A playbill at the British Museum indicates that the 1821 season at Buckingham was still continuing on Tuesday, October 2, and shows that Jackman was printing his own playbills at that time, on a portable press. "From the Press of Jackman, Buckingham", states the imprint.

The principal entertainment that night is typical of the more sensational element in the company's productions. The title sets the tone: *The Murdered Maid or The Clock Struck Four*. But if it was sensational, life itself was in this instance to be blamed for it was based on fact, on "a late mysterious transaction in Warwickshire in the Spring of 1817, which excited one universal feeling of horror and indignation. Great was the regret of all, that a Person, whom there was too much reason to believe the perpetrator of this dreadful act, was suffered to escape condign punishment".

One wonders how Jackman and others may have stood with regard to the law of libel on such a publication, let alone stage depiction! Further details of this miscarriage of justice reveal that in the stage version "as the

MURDER MOST FOUL.

THEATRE, BUCKINGHAM.
THIS PRESENT TUESDAY Oct. 2nd. 1821.
Will be Acted for the First time in this Town, a Grand MeloDrama, Call'd THE

Murdered
MAID;
OR THE
CLOCK STRUCK FOUR!!!
As Performed in Paris & London, with the greatest Admiration & Applause.

4+↑§This Drama is founded on a late Mysterious transaction in Warwickshire, in the Spring of 1817, which excited one universal feeling of horror & indignation. great was the regret of all, that a Person, whom there was too much reason to believe the perpetrator of this dreadful act, was suffered to escape condign Punishment.---the purpose of the Drama, whose end is, says the immortal Poet,
"To shew Virtue her own feature,—Scorn her own image,
—And the very age and body of the time, his form and pressure."

From this plan, the Spectator may be able to extract a confirmation of that great moral lesson "that although vice may for a time triumph, a merciful but just God fails not to punish in this world, as well as in a future state, the perpetration of a crime of which of late years, we have so many dreadful instances to deplore."
The Scene of Action for many reasons, is laid near CHATEAU BROMEGE in NORMANDY,

Thornville[supposed to have murdered Marie]   Mr. GOUGH,
Lalol(Seneshal of Chateau Bromege]   Mr. BULLEN,
Coquen(a Solicitor)   Mr. JACKMAN,
Landlord Mr. ROWELL, Guillaume(Brother to Marie) Mr. TURNER,
Old Ashville[Grandfather to Marie]   Mr. DORMER,
Marie [the Murdered Maid]   Miss WALDON,
Anna(her Friend)   Mrs. CORNWALL,

ACT THE FIRST. A DARK FOREST,
THROUGH WHICH MARIE FLIES FROM THORNVILLE;
IN ACT THE SECOND.
THE MURDERED BODY OF MARIE IS DISCOVERED ON A SABLE
BIER, IN VIEW OF THORNVILLE,
IN ACT THE THIRD
THE AWFUL CLOCK STRIKES FOUR !!!

A Chorus of Spirits is heard in the Air; violent Thunder & Lightning; a Figure as of Air, thickening into a Substance, becomes gradually visible, it is Clad in angelic Beauty, the figure resembles Marie.---After an awful warning to the Libertine, the Clouds become dark & rolling, the CLOCK again strikes FOUR, the Spirit becomes Pale & Deathlike. Streams of Blood issue from her Bosom, as she disappears. Thornville sinks on the ground, uttering a dismal cry.
END OF THE PLAY A NEW COMIC SONG CALL'D
THE BEAUTIFUL BOY, BY MR. JACKMAN,
GRIMALDI'S DANCE, FROM HARLEQUIN, & MOTHER GOOSE,
BY MR. TURNER. & MASTER JACKMAN,
After which the Musical Interlude call'd

The Sailors' Return,
OR, WILLIAM & SALLY.
A FAVORITE SONG, By Mrs. CORNWALL,
TO CONCLUDE WITH THE POPULAR New Farce OF THE

Spectre Bridegroom.
OR, A GHOST IN SPITE OF HIMSELF!!!
Mr. Nicodemus Mr. GOUGH, Squire Aldwinkle Mr. BULLEN, Paul Mr DORMER,
Captain Vauntington Mr. TURNER, Dickory Mr. JACKMAN,
Georgiana Mrs CORNWALL, Lavinia Miss WALDON,

Nights of Performing Monday, Tuesday, Thursday, & Saturday.
Doors open at half past 6 and begin at 7 o' Clock.
. BOXES 3s.---PIT 2s.---GALLERY 1s.
Second price to commence at half past 8. Boxes 2s. Pit 1s.---No Second Price to the Gallery.
From the Press of H. Jackman, Buckingham.

NEW THEATRE, UXBRIDGE.
BY PARTICULAR DESIRE.
For the Benefit of
MR. BROOKS.
J. B. with every sentiment of respect begs leave to solicit that Patronage and Support, which will ever be his constant study to preserve.

On WEDNESDAY Evening, FEB 8th. 1826,
Will be Performed the Popular COMEDY of

King Charles
The Second,
Or the Merry Monarch.
King Charles—Mr. REED.   Rochester—Mr. RAYMOND.
Edward (the Page)——Mr. GROVES.   Servant—Mr. PERCY.
Captain Copp (Landlord of the Grand Admiral) Mr. BROOKS.
Lady Clara—Miss GRAY.   Mary (Copp's Niece)—Mrs. RAYMOND.

END OF THE PLAY,
An entirely new COMIC SONG, Called
"PAUL PRY," or "I hope I don't intrude."
BY MR. MATHEWS.
And (By Desire)
"The Countryman's Petition." by Mr. Brooks.

After which the Laughable INTERLUDE of The

RENDEZVOUS,
Or More Frightened than Hurt.
Quake—Mr. BROOKS.   Bolding—Mr. REED.   Charles—Mr. GROVES.
Simon—Mr. MATHEWS.   Smart—Mr. RAYMOND.
Lucretia—Miss GRAY.   Sophia—Mrs. RAYMOND.   Rose—Miss SKINNERD.

After which the celebrated COMIC DUET of
"POLLY HOPKINS."
By Mrs. RAYMOND and Mr. MATHEWS.
AND A NEW COMIC SONG CALLED
"The Uxbridge Genius."
BY Mr. BROOKS.
The whole to conclude with a FARCE (never acted here) called

LOVE
AMONG THE ROSES
Or, THE MASTER KEY.
Alderman Marygold—Mr. FORD WHITE.   Captain Gorgon—Mr. BROOKS.
Edward——Mr. GROVES.   Hollyhock (a drunken Gardener)—Mr. MATHEWS.
Sharpset—Mr. RAYMOND.
Rose—Mrs. RAYMOND.

BOXES, 3s.   PIT, 2s.   GALLERY, 1s.
HALF-PRICE TO COMMENCE AT HALF-PAST EIGHT.   No Half price to the Gallery.
Tickets to be had of Mr. BROOKS at Mr. HOLDEN'S, Feathers, and of Mr. COSIER, Printer.

COSIER, Printer, Uxbridge.

BUCKINGHAM, 1821—sensational fare on a playbill "from the press of H. Jackman, Buckingham. (*British Museum*)

UXBRIDGE, 1826—Uxbridge was among the Jackman Company calls but this bill is of another Northampton manager, Francis Raymond. (*British Museum*) clock strikes four her spirit becomes pale and deathlike. Streams of blood pour from her bosom as she disappears. Thornville sinks on the ground, uttering a dismal cry."

At the end of these pleasantries there was a new comic song by Mr. Jackman called "The Beautiful Boy" and then Grimaldi's dance from *Harlequin and Mother Goose* by Mr. Turner and Master Jackman (it would still be Henry—Charles would now be two). To complete a bumper bundle of entertainment—no one could complain of short measure in these days of 150 years ago—there were the comic interlude "The Sailor's Return or William and Sally", a favourite song by Mrs. Cornwall and the popular new farce *The Spectre Bridegroom*. A spirited evening, withal!

Other performers listed at Buckingham in 1821 include Messrs. Gough, Bullen, Rowell and Dormer and Miss Waldon. Later seasons revealed by playbills are in July, 1829; June, 1832; and June, 1837, when *The Miller and His Men*, with an interior view of the windmill at work, and *The Miller of Arpenaz or The Unnatural Brother* were presented.

The following year, or thereabouts, the company performed at Highgate and it is here that the only positive reference occurs to Mrs. Jackman Senior, Old Henry's mother. There is no clue as to her family but the fact that she was an actress shows that he was at least following in his mother's footsteps.

Newspaper advertisements, in the Northampton Mercury, announced seasons at Bedford in 1823 and 1825, at the time of the Races there.

A former Bedford theatre was in the George Inn (perhaps in the yard, though a contemporary theory of the 1970s tends to discount the use of the yards of inns suggesting rather assembly rooms there) and Jackman's theatre at Bedford was also associated with an inn. It was in a barn in the yard of the Hop Pole Inn, in Cauldwell Street. It was often called the Theatre, St. Mary's, being near the church of that name. There the company played quite regularly, usually every two years, between about 1820 and 1860. The theatre shell remained and was described by a celebrated Bedford journalist writing under the pen-name of Touchstone. His aim was to see whether it could not be restored as a small amateur theatre. "But it did not take us long to realise that it was too low in the roof, too dark, and too generally decayed for the purpose. I wondered how the Bedford audiences of Victorian days could have endured the dim lighting, the cramped quarters, the hard benches and the close atmosphere of the place and concluded that their enthusiasm must have been strong. When I looked at the old theatre it was hard to picture that it ever held an audience of more than 300, so squat, dark and mean did it look."

On at least one occasion the Bedford season was interrupted for the company to attend Warwick Races.

It was at Bedford that the famous comedian Henry Compton, then a raw recruit, joined the company. It was Jackman who told him that his forte should be low rather than light comedy and it was in this vein that he became the most celebrated comedian of his day. One of Compton's sons, Edward was to head the company which opened the Northampton Theatre Royal and Opera House, Guildhall Road, which succeeded the Marefair theatre in 1884. A granddaughter Fay was to become a famous and

Theatre, Wheat Sheaf Inn, Woburn.

FOR THE BENEFIT OF

Mr. & Mrs. *Masterman*

Who respectfully solicit the Public Patronage on the Present occasion.

On MONDAY Evening Jan. 9th. 1832.

Will be Performed the Popular NEW Petite COMEDY, Never Acted Here, of

SPRING AND
AUTUMN,

Or A BRIDE at FIFTY!

Sir Simon Slack,   Mr. MASTERMAN,   Mr. Rattle,   Mr. H. FENTON,
Major Osmond,   Mr. BAILEY,   John,   Mr. H. JACKMAN,
Mrs. General Dartmouth,   Mrs. MASTERMAN,
Mrs. Rattle,   Mrs. JACKMAN,   Clara,   Miss. C. JACKMAN,

A HORNPIPE, by Mr. PARTLETON,

A COMIC SONG, by Mr. H. FENTON,

After which the Laughable Piece, of

The Intrigue

Or, the HIGH BATH ROAD.

Capt. Rambleton,   Mr. H. FENTON,   Varnish,   Mr. BAILEY,
Tom,   Mr. MASTERMAN ------ Ellen,   Miss C. JACKMAN.

A Comic Duett, by Mr. and Mrs. FENTON,

To conclude with the Musical Farce, of

The Haunted
HOUSE.

Phantom,   Mr. H. Fenton,   Sir Joshua Greybeard,   Mr. Masterman,
Carlton,   Mr. Bailey,   Bluff,   Mr. Partleton,
Watchman,   Mr. Smith,   Mumps,   Mr. H. Jackman,
Emily,   Mrs. H. Fenton,   Corinna,   Miss C. Jackman,   Patty,   Mrs. Jackman,

Tickets may be had of Mr. Masterman. At the WHITE HORSE INN.

All Demands on the Theatre are requested to be sent in Immediately.
As the Performances will Finally terminate on WEDNESDAY NEXT.

Doors open at half past SIX and begin at SEVEN o' Clock.

BOXES 3s.   PIT 2s.   GALLERY 1s.

Second price at half past 8 o' Clock, BOXES 2s. PIT 1s.

WOBURN, 1832—the Jackman Company at The Wheat Sheaf Inn "Theatre" (*British Museum*)

THEATRE, BEDFORD.

By DESIRE, & Under the Patronage of

F. Polhill,
AND
H. STUART, Esqs.
MEMBERS
For the BOROUGH.

On MONDAY Evening, July, 31st. 1837,

Will be Performed the late R. B. Sheridan's, Fashionable COMEDY, of THE

RIVALS!

Sir Anthony Absolute, Mr. HAMBLETON, Capt. Absolute, Mr. H. FENTON,
Faulkland, Mr. T. W. HENDERSON, Bob Acres, Mr. JACKMAN,
Sir Lucious O' Trigger, Mr. HARTLEY, David, Mr. C. JACKMAN,
Fag, Mr. JONES, Coachman, Mr. CLINTON, John, Mr. PARTLETON,
Mrs. Malaprop,   Mrs. JACKMAN,
Lydia Languish, Mrs. H. FENTON, Julia, Miss EVERSUN,
Lucy,   Mrs. PARTLETON,

A COMIC SONG, by Mr. Hambleton,

A SCOTCH DANCE,

By Mr. PARTLETON. & Misses JACKMAN,

A Favourite Song, by Mrs. H. FENTON,

COMIC SONG.

LICENSED TO BE DRUNK ON THE PREMISES, MR. HARTLEY,

To conclude with the Farce, of

TURNING THE
TABLES!

Old Knibbs,   Mr. CLINTON,   Jack Humphries,   Mr. JACKMAN,
Edgar de Courcy, Mr. T. W. HENDERSON, Tom Thornton, Mr. HARTLEY,
Jeremiah Bumps,   Mr. H. FENTON,
Miss Sally Knibbs, Miss S. JACKMAN, Mrs. Humphries, Mrs. JACKMAN,
Patty Larkins,   Mrs. H. FENTON,

Tickets may be had of Mr. WEBB, & Mr. MERRY, in the High Street,
And Tickets for the Season, may be had of Mr. Jackman, in the Ampthil Road.

BOXES 3s.   PIT 2s.   GALLERY 1s.

Doors open at half past SIX, and begin at SEVEN o' clock Precisely.

Half price at half past 8 o' clock, Boxes 2s. Pit 1s.

BEDFORD, 1837— The local M.P.s patron this Jackman performance. (*British Museum*)

beloved actress and a grandson was to be Compton Mackenzie, the novelist. Mackenzie was Henry Compton's real surname. He was born at Huntingdon.

One Bedford newspaper account says that when not touring Jackman lived in a house at the end of St. John's, near Ampthill Street. Whether the closer link with Bedford which this suggests can be substantiated is doubtful. To me it seems that Old Henry and his company were always on the *move*.

Other Bedford seasons of which evidence exists are September, 1829, when Mrs. H. Jackman appeared in *The School for Scandal* on Monday, the 29th; and August, 1835, when the plays included *John Bull or An Englishman's Fireside.*

The lack of a local newspaper is a serious bar to finding out very much about a company's activities in a particular town. The survival of playbills has been a chance affair; some have been kept by individuals interested in the theatre, others by the theatres themselves (but this in surprisingly few cases), others by libraries and record offices, and quite a few come from the files of the printers who created them, these often being proofs returned, ticked with managerial approval, together with a note of the number required and when they were required, written on in ink.

As I have noted, the Northampton Mercury files go right back to No. 1, of Saturday, May 2, 1720, without a break. Though its coverage of theatrical matters, both editorially and by way of advertising, is patchy, the record it provides is invaluable. It has been my principal source of information and it would, indeed, have been impossible to write the book without it. A newspaper is uniquely transitory and durable.

Bedford did not have a paper of its own until 1837. Until then it was served, as was half the kingdom, by the Northampton paper. But obviously the Northampton Mercury could not serve this vast area in as parochial a detail as could a local paper. So as soon as the Bedford Mercury started up on April 1, 1837, the flow of information about Jackman at Bedford increases. The season that year began in July and ended on October 2. The Bedford Mercury reported that Collins' *Ode On The Passions* by Mr. Henderson, assisted by the Corps Dramatique, drew repeated bursts of applause—"We hope this will be repeated as we do not remember to have seen anything which has given so much general satisfaction for some time past." It added that Mrs. Partleton's benefit was the following Monday while on Thursday "that deserving fellow Harry Fenton takes his".

The circulation of the Bedford Mercury was a mere 460 copies at this time.

After forty years of activity the Theatre St. Mary's ceased operations. Some companies subsequently used the Corn Exchange but it was not ideal for seeing or hearing—problems it shared with Northampton Corn Exchange. Early in 1898 there were two proposals to build theatres in Bedford, one of which was to be an Opera House, a scheme backed by Charles Rider-Noble, manager of the Northampton and Brixton theatres; A. C. Palmer, the Northampton accountant; Dr. George Robinson; Mr. H. M. Burge, later headmaster of Winchester School and Bishop of Oxford; Dr. Archdale Sharpin and Mr. Carl Milberg St. Amory. Stress was laid in the prospectus on the fact that all performances would be of an educational value. This lofty-minded project did not mature, however, the opposing scheme for the Bedford County Theatre being successful, backed by the much more mundane and practically minded Mr. Graham Falcon, of the Theatre Royal, Canterbury.

Thus after the Hop Pole theatre of Jackman packed up Bedford went theatre-less for nearly four decades.

The County Hall at Aylesbury's collection of playbills amounts to one, which has the date torn off. It shows, however, that the theatre was at the Cock Inn where the performance was by desire of the members of the Benefit Society. *Macbeth* was the main choice, in which Henry Hartley found himself playing a witch, along with his mother-in-law, Mrs. Jackman! From the personnel of the company it appears that the bill is of the late 1830s.

But bills at the British Museum show that the Jackman connection at Aylesbury goes back at least as far as 1824. The theatre was then described as in Buckingham Road.

R. P. Mander, who says the Jackman visits to Aylesbury began about 1820, adds that there is a record of an earlier theatre in about 1790, associated with an inn. In 1805, the Wynne "Diaries" describe a visit by the family, of Aston Abbots, to a barn theatre in the town, when the leading actor was a man named Lacey, seven feet tall. Mander says that the Buckingham Road theatre was probably near the Black Boy inn while the New Theatre mentioned in playbills of a season from at least Thursday, October 2, to Wednesday, November 21, 1832, was "nearer the Market Place and may have been the Corn Hall, for it is known that dramatic performances were given there about 1840".

Getting back to the chronicle of the Jackman Company (it is indeed proving difficult to be orderly and respectable!) we have now reached a point where a list exists of the company's calls. It occurs in *Road to the Stage*, a book of advice to those wishing to go on to the stage, written in 1827. Presumably it was useful to a beginner to know which manager's door to knock on. Jackman, now in his early forties, is listed as having a tour consisting of only six towns—Aylesbury, Buckingham, Bedford, Woburn, Wallingford and Woodstock. The tally is clearly incomplete, but it is valuable in that it provides almost the only statement that the company visited Wallingford and Woodstock.

One of the omissions from the list is Abingdon where in March, 1827, the playbills carried the amusing injunction : "Gentlemen are requested not to bring Segars to the theatre." The imprint was : "From the press of H. Jackman, Abingdon."

The Abingdon cast lists include "Mrs. Jackman" and "Mrs. H. Jackman", of which there are two interpretations. The first is that old Mrs. Jackman (Old Henry's mother) was still alive and playing, the other being that the "Mrs. H. Jackman" referred to is the wife of Henry Junior. Had the younger Henry, who took roles occasionally but mostly confined himself to music, got married, and did he sit there, fiddling or keyboarding away, watching his wife act on stage? Any attempt to find the truth is frustrated or at least made difficult by the fact that this was before the days of civil registration of births, marriages and deaths. Finding the wedding of a strolling player is very much a hit-or-miss affair. The ceremony could have taken place anywhere on the circuit, or anywhere within easy reach. It is a very different kettle of fish from finding the church register entries for a family of settled habitat.

When the company played at Abingdon in September, 1830, another piece founded on fact, *The Red Barn*, was given; Henry Compton was among the company; and tickets could be had of Mr. Jackman, "nearly opposite the Lamb Inn". In December, 1834, tickets were available from "Mr. Rowles, builder, Ock Street".

Barnet crops up in the Jackman File in February, 1830, with a "Last Night" playbill of Tuesday, the 16th, which hangs framed in the town's museum. *The Miller and His Men* was teamed with *The Rendezvous* and *Of Age Tomorrow*. Singing a song in between was Mrs. H. Fenton (Eliza Jackman). Her husband Harry played Baron Frederick Willinghurst in *Of Age Tomorrow* in which another nobleman, Baron Piffleburg, was portrayed by Mr. Masterman. Tickets for the Barnet season could be had from "Mr. Woodhall, bricklayer, Hadley, and of Mr. King at the theatre".

In November, 1832, the Barnet theatre was managed by Mr. J. F. Savill (spelt thus on the bill but presumably Saville) when the location was given as the Old Assembly Rooms, High Street; and in 1834 by Mr. Moulton. The theatre was last used as such on March 20, 1835. Just how long the Jackmans appeared in Barnet is at the moment a question unanswered.

Most theatre licences granted by magistrates were subject to the manager being bound in a sum of money for the good conduct of the premises and there was often a proviso that a police officer should be present during the performances. In some cases this was honoured more by omission than observance.

At one of the Banbury theatres used by Jackman there were police reinforcements readily at hand in the event of riot for the place was actually over the police station in Church Lane, until the Town Hall was built in 1854.

An earlier theatre where Jackman appeared was in Butchers Row Shambles. When the new theatre was constructed in Church Lane the old one was converted into shops. After the police had moved out the lower floor in Church Lane was in turn put to retail use by a furnisher and in later years the shopkeeper could point to doors to the theatre boarded up in a sitting room and bedrooms, which used to lead to the dressing rooms. The Church Lane premises being found inadequate the stage was extended into Softwater Pump Yard, an alley behind the lane. A picture shows a gallery supported only by two iron posts, a mere two inches thick.

The Jackman playbill at Banbury Library is of January 18, 1832, and concerns this Church Lane theatre. It includes *She Stoops to Conquer*, with Messrs Partleton, Masterman, Smith, Wilson, H. Jackman, Laws (or Lows), Mr. and Mrs. H. Fenton, Miss Briton, Miss C. Jackman.

Further Banbury playbills are at the British Museum. The first is three days later than the above one and lists also Messrs H. Jackman, Brunton,

Gannon, Bond, Mrs. Masterman, and Master Jackman. The rest are Thursday, December 26, 1833; Tuesday December 22, 1835; Friday, March 30, 1838 (last night but three); Monday, January 24, 1842; Monday, February 19, 1844; Monday, January 31, 1848. In 1862–3 what was probably the company's very last season was played at Banbury.

Woburn had been on the company's rounds since about 1814. The evidence for this is in reiterated statements in the Mercury that the company had visited the town for so many years. More than one inn served as a theatre, some performances being at the Bedford Arms, others at the Wheatsheaf. A playbill of January, 1832, is of the latter and refers to a benefit night of Mr. Masterman, who was staying at yet another inn, the White Horse, where tickets could be got from him. This night, January 9, 1832, was two nights before the season's end. The bills made a custom of warning the customers "Last Night But Five", etc. Mr. Partleton was already a member of the company at this time.

Another theatre at Woburn was in the Abbey itself, home of the Dukes of Bedford. As in many stately homes, one of the diversions was taking part in amateur theatricals, with many a titled member of the family or guest in the cast. On January 15, 1839, for instance, in a performance at the Woburn Abbey Theatre of *Polly Honeycombe* Lord Edward Russell was Scribble, Lord Cosmo Russell was Ledger, and Lady Georgina Russell was Polly, while a guest role as a nurse went to the Marchioness of Abercorn.

On these bills the noble actor-manager would cock a snook at the playbill prose of the real-life stroller, as in this case : "Owing to the unprecedented demand for places there will be no second price" and "the manager has to throw himself upon the kindness of a liberal and discriminating public and to claim their indulgence for those Debutantes who have kindly consented to assist him in his present speculation which was undertaken at the shortest notice, merely from a feeling that whilst so many old established favourites were at hand the Woburn Abbey Christmas Charter should be kept up— and from a conviction of the truth of the old maxim that 'all work and no play makes Tom a dull boy'." The bill was headed "Woburn Abbey Theatre".

It is a probability that on at least one occasion the Jackman Company were invited along to entertain at the "big house". In the following extract from the Northampton Mercury of February 6, 1819, the company is not named but it is quite likely that it was Old Henry's : "The Duke and Duchess of Bedford honoured the performance of 'Speed the Plough' and 'Raising the Wind' with their presence a few evenings since at the Theatre, Woburn, and on Saturday the company performed before their Graces and a numerous and elegant audience at the Abbey, when the performances went off with great eclat. The company, it is said, remove from Woburn to Wellingborough."

In about 1828 Louisa Jackman was born at Luton and the brood was complete, apart possibly for the mystery man George.

Bicester, another Jackman port-of-call, yields little information about itself on the subject of theatre. One of the best-loved writers about the town must surely be Sid Hedges, local researcher of the 1930s. In *Bicester Wuz a*

Little Town, his 126th book, he wrote : "If you go into the cemetery from the churchyard a large stone building extends on the left hand side from the gate to the cemetery keeper's hut . . . if tradition is to be believed this was once the tithe barn of the town. A legend persists that it was once used as a theatre. It may be that "once upon a time Bicester folk flocked here to watch actors present morality plays and simple folk dramas. The recently built church hall, it is interesting to note, incorporates the old 'barn' using it for a stage; the old play tradition is thus renewed. Bicester's only other theatre was the Tun Room, disused after the closure of the brewery and hired by strolling players for a few seasons in the 1930's."

A search of the playbills at the British Museum reveals three Bicester playbills not of the 1930s but the 1830s, within a span of three years. They are all of the Jackman company. On Thursday, May 3, 1832, *Joan of Arc or The Maid of Orleans* was given by a company including Messrs. Gannon, Brunton, H. Fenton, Masterman, W. Masterman, Partleton, Jackman, and Miss C. Jackman, Miss Jackman, Miss Brunton and Miss S. Jackman. A bill for April 30 the same year stated that tickets could be had of Mr. Jackman, "near the Cross Keys". Wherever the theatre was, it had boxes at 3s. as well as pit and gallery at 2s. and 1s. On June 18, it was the benefit night of Mr. Partleton and to fetch in the Bicestrians he performed a "sailor's hornpipe in fetters".

Days of playing were Monday, Wednesday and Friday. The final play-bill is of Monday, September 22, 1834, when Mrs. Jackman played Mrs. Malaprop in *The Rivals* and Mrs. Partleton (the former Frances Jackman) is in the cast.

Uxbridge first figures in the records in 1832 when the Jackman Company appeared at the New Theatre, Windsor Street. There are several playbills at the British Museum from Monday, December 10, to Monday, January 7, 1833. Late in 1836 the company were at the "New Theatre, near the Treaty House", with a season from at least Thursday, December 29, 1836, to a last night of Monday, March 13. Sheridan Knowles, the playwright, and his pupil and future wife Miss Elphinstone were guest artists.

A reflection of the disfavour in which the stage was sometimes regarded in elevated circles is to be found in the minutes of a local girls' charity school in 1804 where the committee passed a resolution that if any girl belonging to the establishment should visit the Edmonton theatre she should be immediately expelled.

Jackman's Company are said to have been regular visitors to the town, possibly from their inception, Uxbridge being near the likely London origins of Jackman himself.

During 1837 *Othello* was performed at the request of the officer commanding and officers of the Royal West Middlesex Militia with the title role taken by "the same young gentleman who undertook the role last Monday". No doubt an amateur thought it great fun to mix with the strollers. A brass band was in attendance. Uxbridge had no proper theatre until the completion of the Theatre Royal in 1869, so the Jackmans never appeared in other than fit-up premises. The new theatre had been started in 1854 but the death of the intended lessee is stated to have held up its completion until December, 1868, when Mr. Walter Edwin, later to be associated with the Northampton theatre, finished it off.

One of the players at Uxbridge in earlier times was Henry Compton, either with a Mr. Raymond or Henry Jackman. R. P. Mander states, incidentally, that Jackman took over a number of theatres from a man named Raymond, though whether this is so and whether it was Francis Raymond I have not been able to confirm. Compton's memoirs also refer to his being with Jackman at Daventry in 1827.

Another "possible" to add to the list of the Jackman tour is Chipping Norton, Oxon, for it was there that George Henry Partleton, son of George Partleton and the former Frances Jackman, was baptised on March 21, 1834. The father's rank or profession was given as "stage player". We can only guess whether this was during a Jackman season there.

From the Banbury season of late 1835 and early 1836 comes documentary testimony to the fact that George Henry Partleton's father was more than just a "stage player". This is in the shape of a leaflet he had printed to spread the news that during the season he would run a "dancing academy" : "Mr. Partleton begs leave to announce to the Ladies and Gentleman of Banbury and its vicinity that he intends during his stay to give lessons in the above elegant accomplishment in all its branches viz. quadrilles, gallopades, waltzes etc., and most respectfully solicits the patronage of those ladies and gentlemen who may wish to profit by his instruction." The terms were 10s. a month, the lessons on Wednesdays and Fridays, at two in the afternoon for young ladies and gentlemen and at seven in the evening for adults. He also offered to teach the violin and tune and teach the piano.

Banbury, which was now approaching a population of 7,000, was growing at a much slower pace than Northampton. When the Northampton theatre had opened in 1806 in a township of 7,700, Banbury had around 4,250 townsfolk : by the time the Northampton theatre closed in 1884 there were 53,000 Northamptonians but only 12,000 Banburians.

Daventry and Market Harborough are the first two towns mentioned in the Jackman, Hartley and Partleton correspondence which emerged from the seventy-six sacks in the Daventry solicitor's attic.

In 1836 Henry Jackman had inquired about the new theatre being erected at Daventry, addressing himself to his solicitor contact there, the drama-loving Mr. Thomas Lewis Gery. Gery maintained a correspondence with George Partleton, who augmented his income also by selling music, violin strings, and with Henry Hartley, another of the Jackman son-in-laws.

From Market Harborough, Leicestershire, on May 31, 1836, we find Partleton writing to Gery : "Mr. J. says that he thinks that Daventry might answer once in two years and is willing to take the bilding if it is not to expensive but I think he would not take it for any term of years. I am very sorry to say the rumour it true. Bisness has been very bad. We play to £5 10s. (?) a night. My night was last evening there was 30s. in the house. We close next Monday but it is not settled where we go to."

To this letter, in which the misspellings are Partleton's not the printers, there was an apologetic postscript : "You must excuse this for I am now writing this in a tap room with plenty of cow jobbers. I have been so very bussey that I can not send the overture as I promised you must excuse any more at present for the carrier is waiting."

Evidently Gery had enclosed his earlier letter to Jackman with one to Partleton for on June 7, 1836, Jackman sent this to the solicitor: "I have just received your letter from Mr. Partleton. In reply I beg to state that I shall have great pleasure in taking Mr. Line's premises for a theatre if he will make the alterations you mention and I can gain the consent of the magistrates of Daventry to my coming without whose sanction I should not feel myself justified. I am inclined to think it would answer in 18 months and should not mind giving £25 per season."

Notice how anxious Old Henry was to preserve his respectability. No unlicensed performances for him!

By then the next move had been decided upon: "My company will remove from this place to Wellingborough in a day or two and if Mr. Lines entertains any serious thoughts on the subject and my running over to Daventry will forward his views in any way I shall be happy to do so on receiving a line to that effect," said Jackman who signed himself, "Remaining sir, your most obliged and obedient servant."

Judging by his reply, also found at Daventry, Gery was a cautious man. Why, incidentally, should the reply turn up at Daventry, from where it was sent? It is presumably a duplicate, written by a clerk in pen and ink (when was carbon paper invented?) before the letter was posted.

He wrote: "The theatre is not yet quite completed which is owing to the illness of some of the workmen but there are not more than three or four days work to finish. The building was commenced late last year and the walls became so completely saturated with wet that it is still very damp and I should think hardly fit to use although Mr. Line does his utmost to get it aired and rendered comfortable. You ask my opinion respecting a short season at Daventry in Whitsun week. Not having confidence in my opinion I have mentioned it to a few of my friends all of whom agree with me in thinking about the middle or end of August it would be more likely to succeed than at the time proposed, for two reasons. The first is that a number of persons would be afraid of going into a building which is so damp until it has had the heat of summer upon it. The second that the harvest is drawing to a close about the end of August. Until that is over you can look for little or no support from the surrounding villages.

"I have now given you my opinion as requested but I hope you will not be persuaded by me contrary to your own judgment," wrote Gery, who added that the then-Mayor of Daventry was a great supporter of the drama. This was Richard Wildgose and his name appears prominently on one of the playbills of the first season of this New Theatre, dated Friday, October 20, 1837, for *Love in a Village* and *Catharine and Petruchio*. This is among a small collection kept at Daventry Moot Hall, in a centuries-old coffre-fort, with nine locks to guard it. *(Page 138.)*

It being November, and in view of the newness of the building, Mr. Jackman respectfully informed his patrons that he had had a stove fixed in the pit where a fire was constantly kept: he trusted that the theatre would be found perfectly warm and comfortable.

These hopes were expressed on a bill announcing *Country Girl, Miss in Her Teens,* sword dance by Miss Jackman and the Dashing White Sergeant by Mrs. Fenton. The patron that night was Sir Charles Knightley, Bart., who had been responsible six years earlier for setting up the Northampton Herald. He lived at Fawsley Manor, not far from Daventry.

This Daventry theatre was in Cow Lane, the old name for New Street on the site later occupied by Stead and Simpson's shoe factory. Both Gery and Line were borough councillors. The theatre was to remain in use for one sort of function or another until at least 1871 when an assembly hall was built in New Street and Foundry Place at a cost of £1,400 and having stage, ante-rooms and vestibule. Today this is the Regal Cinema.

Henry Jackman's first visit to Stratford-upon-Avon, on business that is, was in 1838 and is duly reflected in the account and minute books of the theatre there—the one opened by Francis Morgan's company eleven years earlier. He paid £23 15s. for a five week season—about half the total receipts of the "Royal Shakespearean Theatre" that year.

Three Stratford playbills of June show that he had as guest artists Mr. Benson of the Theatre Royal, Drury Lane, and Vauxhall Gardens, who appeared in the key role of Henry Bertram in *Guy Mannering,* and Les Quatres Freres Hemmings, a team of acrobat brothers.

The last bill available, for Wednesday, June 27, was for the benefit of Mr. and Mrs. Hartley and was "the last night but two". The entertainment consisted of a new farce *The Rifle Brigade,* a new drama *Rory o'More,* and a new piece *Advice Gratis,* plus a hornpipe by Mr. Partleton and comic songs by Mrs. H. Fenton, Mr. Hartley and Mr. Hambleton. Tickets could be had of Mr. and Mrs. Hartley, College Street.

Company members included also Messrs. C. Jackman, Carleton, H. Fenton, Underdown and Clinton, Mrs. Partleton, Mrs. Jackman, Miss S. Jackman, Miss H. Jackman, and Master Jackman. It will be observed that the entire feminine strength were members of the family!

While the company were at Uxbridge in the early summer of 1839 a daughter was born to George and Frances Partleton.

A bill surviving from this season is for *The Ocean Child* described as a popular nautical melodrama and which included "the ceremony of christening the Ocean Child" and the following sequence :

"Mutiny of the Crew—Harry Helm condemned to WALK THE PLANK ! ! ! In the agonies of death he clings to a ring bolt in the ship's side, his hand is cut off by order of the captain and with a wild shriek he sinks into the ocean."

Also on the bill that night was "a laughable new piece never acted here call'd '*My Young Wife and Old Umbrella*' ". Then, after Mr. Hartley had sung "The Flag That Braved A Thousand Years" and other songs by Mrs. H. Fenton and Mr. Hambleton, came "Shakespeare's popular farce call'd '*Catharine and Petruchio or The Taming of the Shrew*' ". Tickets could be had at the theatre or at Mr. Cosier's, printer, High Street.

This brings us to when Northampton figured for the first time in the company itinerary, after it had been in existence for thirty-four years.

STRATFORD'S UNSUNG THEATRE—This was the first Shakespeare Theatre at Stratford-upon-Avon, a predecessor of the two well-known ones. In April, 1827, Francis Raymond took his Northampton Company to Stratford for the Festival at which a corner stone of the theatre was laid and in December that year returned to play the inaugural season. The theatre was demolished in 1872. See chapter on "Stratford & Simpson Etc.", Pages 85 to 115 and Pages 136, 179–80, 187–9 and 197 (*Shakespeare Birthplace Trust*)

NORTHAMPTON 1831—A season with Mr. Hamilton as manager. (*Osborne Robinson*)

NEW THEATRE
DAVENTRY.

BY DESIRE,
And Under the Patronage of the Worshipful

The Mayor,
Robert Wildgose, Esq

On FRIDAY Evening, Oct, 20th. 1837,

When Will be Presented Bickerstaff's COMIC OPERA, of

Love in a
VILLAGE!

WITH THE ORIGINAL POPULAR MUSIC.

Justice Woodcock, Mr. HAMBLETON, Young Meadows, Mr. HARTL
Hawthorn, Mr. H. FENTON, Eustice, Mr. T. W. HENDERSO
Sir William Meadows, Mr. CLINTON, Hodge, Mr. JACKMAN,
Carter, Mr. C. JACKMAN, Footman, Mr. FENTON,
Rosetta, Mrs. H. FENTON, Lucinda, Mrs. HARTLEY,
Mrs. Deborah Woodcock, Mrs. JACKMAN, Madge, Miss S. JACKMA

A COMIC SONG, by Mr. HARTLEY,
Dancing, by Mr. Partleton, & Miss S. Jackma
Laughing Trio, 'Vadasi via di qua,'
By Miss S JACKMAN, and Messrs HARTLEY, & HAMILTON.
A COMIC SONG, by Mr. HAMBLETON.
Comic Duett, 'When a Little Farm we keep,'
By Mr. and Mrs. H. FENTON.

To conclude with Shakespeare's, COMEDY, of

Catharine & Petruchio
Or, the TAMING of a SHREW!

Petruchio, Mr. T. W. HENDERSON,
Baptista, Mr. HAMBLETON, Grumio, Mr. H. FENTON,
Biond-llo, Mr. C. JACKMAN, Hortenchio, Mr. HARTLEY,
Pedro, Mr. CLINTON, Taylor, Mr. JACKMAN,
Music Master, Mr PARTLETON, Nathaniel, Mr. FENTON,
Catharine, Mrs. HARTLEY,
Bianch, Mrs. H. FENTON, Curtis, Mrs. JACKMAN, Visitors, &c.

Tickets may be had of Mr. H. Line, at the Theatre.
Season Tickets BOXES, £ 1. PIT, 15s.

BOXES 3s. PIT 2s. GALLERY 1s.
Doors open at half past SIX, and begin at SEVEN o' clock Precisely.
Half price at half past 8 o' clock, Boxes 2s. Pit 1s.

DAVENTRY 1837—A first season at the New Theatre by Henry Jackman's Company. See Pages 135–6. (*Daventry Town Council*)

CHARLES MARKHAM, Clerk of the Peace for Northamptonshire and a joint proprietor of the Marefair Theatre. See Pages 106–8 and 164. (*Northampton Public Library*)

THE LEAMINGTON THEATRE in Bath Street opened by J. Simms on October 26, 1813, during his Northampton tenancy. (*T. E. Dudley's "Complete History of Royal Leamington Spa"*)

THE HOUSE BEHIND THE LAMP-POST, in Abington Street, Northampton, was the home of Charles Markham. (*Northampton Public Library*)

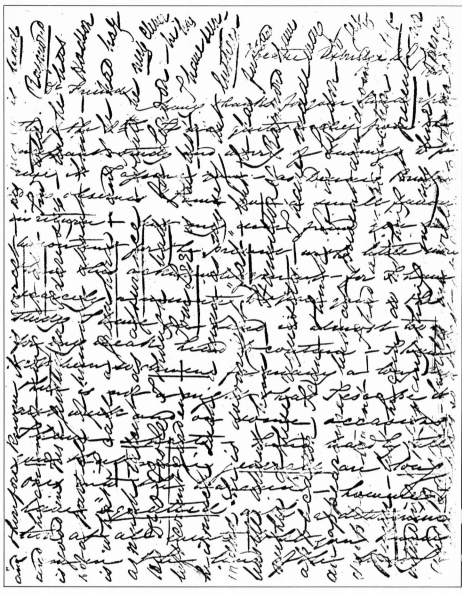

A SHEET OF THE CROSS-WRITTEN LETTER written by Henry Hartley, a member of the Henry Jackman Company, to Mr. T. L. Gery, a Daventry solicitor, from Uxbridge in 1843. This is one of the "letters in the sacks" discovered by Miss Joan Wake, opposite. See Pages 119 and 154–5. (*Northamptonshire Record Office*)

GUSTAVUS VAUGHAN BROOKE
who essayed Othello at Northampton
while inebriated and had to give up the
attempt. See Pages 233–5.

ON MAY 18, 1935, Miss Joan Wake helped to unload
76 sackfuls of documents she had retrieved from a
Daventry solicitor's attic. See Page 119 etc. (*Northampton
and County Independent*)

THEATRE, NORTHAMPTON.

Celebrated New Piece, The WHITE HORSE of the PEPPERS, And Nicholas Nickleby, at HALF PRICE.

This Evening MONDAY Sept. 2nd. 1839

Will be Presented the Popular New Comic DRAMA, never acted here, call'd THE

White Horse
Of the Peppers.

Colonel Chesham, Mr. H. FENTON. Major Hans Mansfelt, Mr. JACKMAN.
Gerald Pepper, Mr. HARTLEY, Darby Donague, Mr. CULLENFORD, Portreeve Mr. HAMBLETON,
Lawyer Dillon, Mr. ARMSTRONG, Rafferty, Mr. HOWARD JOHNSTON,
O' Shocknessy, Mr. C. JACKMAN, Looney, Mr. PARTLETON,
Phelim, Miss S. JACKMAN, Magdaline, Mrs. ARMSTRONG, Agatha, Mrs. H. FENTON,

NORTHAMPTON, 1839—part of a playbill from the Jackman
Company's first season at the Marefair Theatre. (*Northampton
Repertory Theatre*)

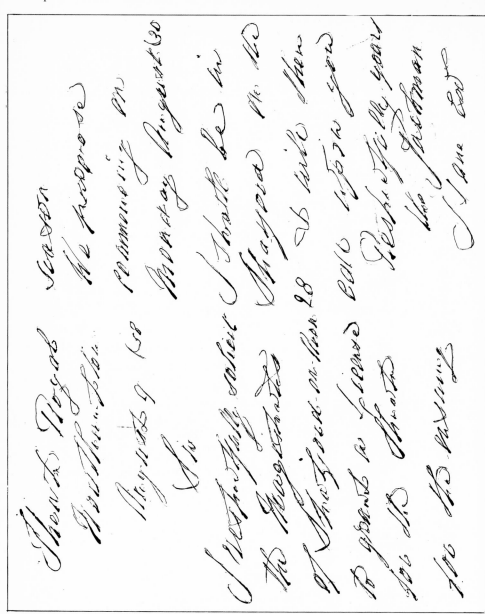

LETTER FROM CHARLES JACKMAN written from the Northampton Theatre to
Stratford-upon-Avon on August 9, 1858, applying for a licence for a season there. (*Shakespeare
Birthplace Trust*)

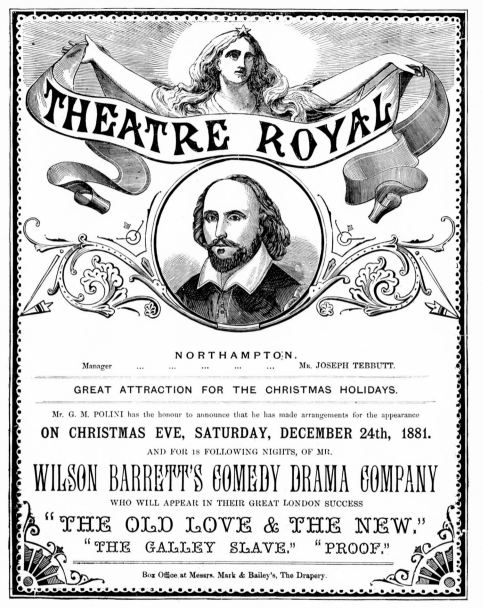

PROGRAMME COVER of the Marefair Theatre in 1881. The Wilson Barrett Company later appeared at the Theatre Royal and Opera House, Guildhall Road.

THE AUTHOR is standing here on the spot where Henry Jackman's coffin stood on October 3, 1852, in St. Katharine's Church, prior to burial in the churchyard. The stones in the foreground indicate the site of the altar. The church was demolished in 1950 and the area is now a Memorial Square—not to Henry Jackman but to the dead of the 1939–45 War. In the background is Northampton's recently-constructed Barclaycard Centre. See Pages 176–7. (*Photo by Bob Price*)

Scene Two

OUTLASTING THE LINCOLN

Tragedy appeared early on the personal "bill" for the Jackmans at Northampton, right at the start of their very first season. They must, indeed, have cursed the day they decided to play in the town.

Within a fortnight of their first appearance on Monday, August 19, 1839, Old Henry Jackman had lost one of his grandchildren—Helen, baby daughter of George and Frances Partleton. Infant deaths were by no means rare in those days but little Helen died not from an illness but from a medicine.

The baby girl had been born during the Uxbridge season the previous June. At Northampton her mother appears to have been on stage when the fatal dose was given on September 4. The child was in the lodgings in Wellington Street, in the care of Matilda Branston, described at the inquest as a servant to Mrs. Partleton. The little girl being restless, her mother had asked Matilda to fetch a pennyworth of "Infants' Cordial" from Mr. Harris, a druggist in Bridge Street. About a teaspoonful was given to the child, causing it to fall heavily asleep, so much like a coma that the servant girl grew concerned and took the baby to the drug shop to make sure that the correct medicine had been given. Mrs. Harris assured her it was. Back in the house the baby was put into the cradle and never woke up again.

A doctor who was called was met by an old woman outside the house and told that it was no use his going in, the child was dead. To his credit the doctor took no notice, went in and ordered the child to be placed in a warm bath. He inflated the lungs (was this a form of what we now know as the "kiss of life"?) but could not arouse the child from its torpor. At the inquest he gave his opinion that death was caused by poison of a sedative nature.

What was this "Infants' Cordial" which could kill as well as cure? There was a medicine called "Godfrey's Cordial" containing laudanum and Mr. Harris copied this with a mixture of his own. He just ladled it out, specifying no dosage. Harris gave evidence that he sold a gallon-and-a-half a week and had never before heard of any ill-effects. He said it was not prepared in the same way as Godfrey's Cordial but the effects were the same (!).

An expert witness, after testifying that he could not tell by tasting or smelling whether the mixture contained more laudanum than was usual,

11—TU * *

put forward his own startling opinion that the deaths of many infants were caused by the use of infant cordials. Had the druggist been careless with the proportions? The jury merely "commended to him the propriety of specifying the quantity to be used for the future" according to the age of the child to whom it was to be administered.

The Coroner at the inquest on the little girl was George Abbey, who was also secretary and part-proprietor of the theatre. One of the more pathetic pieces of paper among the mound I gathered while researching this book is little Helen's death certificate, with these brief magisterial words of obituary recorded on it: "Death through medicine incautiously administered."

For the company, with such a strong contingent of grandparents, aunts, uncles and cousins, as well as parents and brothers and perhaps sisters, this tragedy must have cast a heavy shadow over the first season.

The Jackman Company received a welcome from the Mercury which declared that it had "never seen anything on these boards approaching it in merit".

A guest player was Mr. H. Betty, son of W. H. Betty who had created such a great sensation at Drury Lane some thirty years before, as "the Young Roscius". He played Hamlet, among the cast of which the Mercury especially praised the Polonius of Mr. Cullenford. Other regular members of the company were Mr. and Mrs. H. Fenton, Mr. and Mrs. G. Partleton, Mr. Hambleton, Mr. Howard Johnston, Mr. C. Jackman, Miss S. Jackman, and Mr. and Mrs. Armstrong.

Shortly after the season ended the theatre was taken for an astronomical lecture. People seem to have been fascinated by the developing sciences and the occasion provided a rare indication of the numerical capacity of the house. "About 800 persons were present," said the Mercury, describing this as a crowded audience. The Mechanics Institute had made an arrangement with Mr. Keevil, the lecturer, for their members to be admitted and the following January the organisation sponsored a demonstration at the theatre by Mr. Bembridge, with his "grand hydro-oxygen microscope". This was followed up with four educational evenings on the Laws of Natural Chemistry, Chemistry of Atmosphere, Philosophy of Vegetation and Chemistry of Organised Matter, and Chemistry of Mineral Creation.

At this time the Penny Post was introduced, with variations. It was 1d. to nine o'clock; 2d. to ten o'clock; and 6d. after ten o'clock. These times applied to the mornings—the box was closed at half-past eight in the evening.

Jackman was back in town for the Spring season of 1840 with Mr. Rosslyn of the Theatre Royal, Bath, as a guest. In April there was a concert by the Cornopean Band, consisting of the "celebrated Hohlstein Family from Vienna, late of the Emperor of Austria's private band".

During the season beginning in August Jackman brought to the town the veteran singer Braham who, despite being nearly seventy, appeared in the juvenile lead in the popular *Guy Mannering*. The Mercury tried hard to be kind to the old stager: "Braham ventures to play the young lover, Henry Bertram in a theatre which, from its comparative smallness, affords but in trifling degree that aid to illusion which belongs to the misty atmosphere behind the footlights of a London stage." On the first night the audience was "wretchedly thin for Braham, although not particularly so for a Northampton house in general".

Two theatrical establishments appeared on Northampton Market Square when the Mop Fair, for the hiring of servants, took place in October. There was Scowton's Company, "under patronage of Her Majesty", and a penny show including "Jack Sheppard, Mix My Dolly Pals, Fake Away and a pantomime". The Mercury reported that the following day the latter had disappeared but "Scowton's Lot continue to dazzle the eyes and astonish the ears of the passers-by with the glories of glittering tinsel and stage muslins, shrieks of heroines and 'terrific combats' ". This was the theatre of the fairground, the lowest strata of all.

In the days of the British Raj, important Royal events almost invariably had some form of local celebration. It was a mark of respect to majesty to sit down and eat a vast meal at one of the local hotels—and they really were good trenchermen. Thus we find Christopher Markham, younger brother of Charles, in the chair at a dinner at the Angel Hotel, Bridge Street (proprietor T. Shaw) to mark the anniversary of the marriage of the Queen and Prince Albert and the birth of the Princess Royal. With one or two exceptions the entire assembly was Conservative. Tickets were 6s. 6d. including dessert. The starting time was four o'clock. The date, February 10, 1841.

I have mentioned already how fortunate it was that the letters in the attic came to light. There were only a dozen of them and it is in one way frustrating to think that there must have been hundreds which did not find their way upstairs in the Daventry solicitors' offices. On the other hand it may have been divine intervention for the amount of words found is almost exactly the amount that can be included in this book, with only small excisions, without the risk of boredom.

The next two letters are of 1841 and both are by George Partleton. The one he wrote from Leighton Buzzard on February 28, 1841, might have been written with an eye to posterity being quite Bradshaw-like, a positive route-card of the company's movements. "We leave here for Northampton in three weeks time and from thence to Aylesbury. Business was very good at Woburn considering the weather. I wish I could say the same for Leighton; they think of nothing here but drinking.

"Charles, Hartley, and Mr. and Mrs. Jackman have been to London from here. I should like to have gone with them if my pocket was not so low. George is going to play Tom Thumb for our benefit." Young George Henry Partleton was now aged seven. "Very well he sings the songs thou I say it that ought not to say it." The letter was written in the King's Arms, at Leighton, which may have been where the theatre was, though I know of no other evidence as to its location.

More family news given in the second letter, from Northampton at the end of March, provides evidence that George and Frances had "gone in for" another child immediately after their tragic loss of Helen in 1839— "The baby is very ill and Mrs. P. and Miss P. have got a bad could."

This March season was just one aspect of the entertainments and high jinks accompanying the Races. Recorded the Mercury : "Our town has had a week of extraordinary revelling, the concert" (in aid of the Lunatic Asylum, now St. Andrew's Hospital), "being about the most staid of the amusements. All the rest has been steeplechasing and racing and such uproarious doings. Never has the town been more unlike itself or more like a scene in pantomime. In addition to the principal performers and the main events every street has had its minor performers and under-plot. 'Shorts' and 'Codlins', monkeys, tumblers, dogs and grinders' lots, peripatetic pianos and prima donnas from Switzerland, were to be found at every turn. On Wednesday the outside of the George reminded us of some great contested election. There was a fair sprinkling of the nobility and officers from all parts of England, Ireland and Scotland and the town was thronged. The George Hotel had a bumper and had seventy beds engaged in the town. The Angel was full and most of the other inns had a fair complement."

The Market Square was an assembly point for steeplechase racing. "Gentlemen are not like professed steeple chase riders; they are very slow in coming to the scale and it was not without some trouble that they were all weighed in by half past two o'clock. At about three the different nags were paraded round the Market Square to gratify the ladies who occupied windows in the houses adjacent. The Market Hill was crowded and to add to the gay scene there were four-in-hands, barouches, and other elegant carriages. At the hour of half past three Mr. Waters gave the order to follow ME and away went the dense mass to the field of Mr. Merry's close to Abington Mill which was the place appointed for the start of the Grand Military Steeplechase." This was on the Wednesday of the Race Week; Thursday saw the Spring meeting on Northampton Racecourse.

July brought another "Young Roscius" to the stage of the Northampton theatre, in the person of Master Owen who recited "the most difficult scenes in 'Hamlet', 'The Revenge', 'Richard III' and 'Douglas' with an energy, justness of conception and accuracy which are not often found on provincial boards in old and practised actors and in one so young is really surprising".

Young Owen's mother sang songs and joined her son in some of the scenes but on the Monday night "she was prevented from appearing in consequence of the gross conduct of a couple of persons who, in a state of intoxication, forced their way upon the stage and broke open the door of her dressing room. The terror occasioned by this unmanly conduct threw her into alarming hysterics which continued for some time. She was hardly recovered for Wednesday night."

Attendance at Jackman's autumn season was "not particularly large, partaking of the depression which at this moment characterises assemblies of all kinds and for whatever purpose", despite the company being "strengthened from the Metropolis" and including Mr. H. Bedford, from the Theatre Royal, English Opera House.

From the various sources of information it has been possible to fill in the company's diary of movements for almost a full year. For 1842 there is a nearly comprehensive schedule of their strollings, in order from Banbury in January, to Uxbridge, Northampton, Aylesbury, Leamington, Newport

Pagnell, Buckingham, Northampton (again), Bedford, Woburn and back to Uxbridge in December.

The season at Banbury, where the company had appeared since at least 1827 (and almost certainly earlier), was from January 17 to February 7. From there on January 24, Henry Hartley sent his solicitor friend Gery at Daventry a playbill showing the names of new members of the company, commenting, "The new actors are useful and that is about all I can say for the present, indeed 'tis about all we want—will tell you more when able to judge better." As usual Hartley was busy, not learning parts this time, but painting the theatre. Business was "middling". He hoped that Gery would go over to Banbury to see him.

Things were better at the next port-of-call in 1842, Uxbridge, we learn from one of George Partleton's letters, written from Northampton on March 26. "Business was good at Uxbridge, therefore the newspapers spoke truth for once." At Northampton things went better still—"very good. I should have been glad to see you over here on the Race Day." In Partleton's opinion the company was also "very good" at this time.

In this letter Charles Jackman, younger son of Old Henry, comes in for his only mention—"Chas Jackman never touches the violin, tenor or bass— he as so much study." There was also the usual bit of business—"I have the tenor part of your quadrille at Aylesbury where we are going next."

Thus the first four months of the year had taken the company to Banbury, Uxbridge, Northampton and Aylesbury.

Aylesbury, indeed the entire county of Buckinghamshire, yields little confirmation of the evidence provided by these letters. The correspondence is the only proof of several of the company calls that year.

The Bucks County Record Office has but one playbill, of Aylesbury, and its value is lessened by having the date torn off it. The performances it announced were at the Cock Inn and were "by desire of the members of the Benefit Society". The main piece was *Macbeth* with Mr. Hartley as Hecate and two of his sisters-in-law, Mrs. H. Fenton and Miss Sophia Jackman, and mother-in-law, Mrs. Jackman, as the three witches. There were also *Quarter Day or A New Way to Pay Your Rent* and *Illustrious Stranger or Married and Buried*. Nights of playing were Monday, Wednesday, Thursday, Friday and Saturday but this week may have been exceptional, being the last of the season. As stated, the date had disappeared but from the membership of the company the year may be deduced as being 1838 or 1839.

During the Leamington season of 1842, Partleton wrote two letters to Gery, on May 12 and June 8, both mainly concerned with his sideline of selling music and books, the first "to inform you that there is some harp and piano music to be sold cheap; I also send you a list of strings" and the second with a further list of music "that is to be bought cheap" and a postscript that "Dr. Burn's 'Justice' in five volumes are to be sold for 5s. if you want them". No doubt the books would interest a solicitor.

It will have been observed that many of the company's calls were regular and fixed whereas others were fitted in, perhaps as an experiment and at short notice. If they paid off they might be added to the regular itinerary;

THEATRE, NORTHAMPTON.

For the BENEFIT of the MISSES

JACKMAN,
AND THE
LAST NIGHT
of PERFORMING.

On TUESDAY Evening, October 26th, 1841,

Will be acted, James Sheridan Knowles's celebrated Historical Play of

WILLIAM TELL.

Passing Scenes cannot fail to give a lively interest to the historical events recorded in this Play. Whilst there exists a patriot heart beating with generous love of Country; while love of offspring shall continue to be the predominant feeling in the breast of a parent; so long will every generous and noble passion be excited by the recollection of William Tell, the renowned deliverer of his Country,—

He, who with generous Peasants sat,   He winged the arrow sure as fate,
On Uri's Rock, in sage divan;   Which ascertain'd the rights of Man.

The Drama commences at the moment when Tell, bemoaning the fate of his unhappy Country, resolves to free it from the galling yoke of Austria. A singular act of oppression and cruelty on the part of the Usurper, determines him at once to strike the blow for liberty, and sends his son to warn the Patriots in the mountains. Here the boy encounters Gesler, and saves him from perishing in a dreadful storm. Inadvertently, Albert discloses his Father's Patriotic sentiments, but afterwards, aware of the danger he has exposed him to, refuses to tell his name, and is imprisoned. The Tyrant, entirely to subdue the spirit of the people, orders his Officers to place his

Cap on a Pole in the Market-place,

and commands that each person shall bow to it. Maddened at witnessing this degradation, Tell dashes to the earth and tramples on the badge of tyrannical insolence ; is taken before Gesler, he is confronted with his Son. Each, to save the other, deny their relationship, but on the boy being ordered to execution, the feelings of the Parent prevail, and the secret is known to Gesler, who ingenious in cruelty, offers them their liberty, but on conditions which place the Father in a most heart-rending situation. To save him, he yields, and

Shoots an Apple placed on his Son's Head
This event is followed by the
RISING OF THE PEOPLE.
DESTRUCTION OF THE TYRANT!!
The success of the Swiss, and Freedom of their Country.

AUSTRIANS.
Gesler (Governor of Waldstetten), Mr. NORMAN......Sarnem, Mr. PARTLETON
Lutold, Mr. C. JACKMAN......Rodolph, Mr. FISHER......Michael, Mr. H. R. CHESTER

SWISS.
William Tell (the Hero of Switzerland), Mr. HENDERSON....Albert (his son), Miss S. JACKMAN
Verner, Mr. HARTLEY .. Meichtal, Mr. STYLES .. Austrians, Peasantry, &c.—Emma, Mrs. HARTLEY

In the course of the Evening the celebrated Polish

PAGANINI,
ON ONE STRING,

Will appear and play several popular Airs, with variations,
Accompanied by the Band of the Theatre.

SINGING AND DANCING.
COMIC SONGS, by Messrs. Hartley and Styles.

After which (first time in this Theatre), an original Drama, in three Parts, written to illustrate some of the "Trials of Woman," and performed many successive nights at the London Theatres, called,

ISABELLE:
Or, WOMAN's LIFE!

Part 1st. The GIRL. Time 1794.
Opening Chorus, " Dance! dance ! be merry to-day"—The Village home—the Soldier's return—" Love's Young Dream"—Song, " Of all the Mountain Maidens"—the Mystery—the Quarrel—the Threat—the Reconciliation —the Farewell—Song and Chorus, " One look, perhaps the last."

Eugène Le Marc, Mr. T. W. HENDERSON ......Scipio, Mr. H. R. CHESTER
Andrew, a village Lad, Mr. HARTLEY .... Michael, Mr. STYLES........ Philippe, Mr. NORMAN
George, Master JACKMAN
Isabelle, Mrs. HARTLEY ....Sophie, Miss S. JACKMAN
Savoyards, the Misses JACKMAN, Mr. HENDERSON, &c. &c.

Part II. The WIFE. Time 1802.
Promotion—the General—the intended robbery—honor among thieves—an artist's studio—the model— " Sweep, soot O !"—cupboard love—how to raise the wind—the false step and its consequences.

General Le Marc, Mr. T. W. HENDERSON...Scipio, Mr. H. R. CHESTER..Coquin, Mr. C. JACKMAN
Epinoir, Mr. NORMAN .. Apollo Bejaset, Mr. JACKMAN .. Andrew, a Sweep, Mr. HARTLEY
Madame Le Marc, Mrs. HARTLEY.........Sophie, Miss S. JACKMAN......Marie, Miss H. JACKMAN
Cecile, Mrs. HENDERSON

Part III. The MOTHER. Time 1815.
Return to the mountain home—Rural life—the joys of matrimony—an old friend—jolly as sand boys—brandy versus brains—my uncle—the shark and the great coat—can't swallow it—don't you believe me?—" may the difference of opinion never lessen friendship"—down in the world—all unasked—unexpected reconvenr—the brigand's revenge—barn watch barn catch—fate of the guilty—the lost restored—guilt punished—and happy termination.

Monsieur Le Marc, Mr. T. W. HENDERSON ... Scipio, a Brigand, Mr. H. R. CHESTER
Vincent, Mrs. CHESTER........ Coquin and Epinoir (Ruffians), Mr. C. JACKMAN & Mr. NORMAN
Andrew, a Farmer, Mr. HARTLEY...........Apollo Bejaset, Mr. JACKMAN
Petit Matthew, Master PARTLETON ... Philippe, Mr. STYLES
Madame Isabelle, Mrs. HARTLEY....... Madame Sophie, Miss S. JACKMAN......Savoyards, &c. &c. &c.

Doors to be opened at Half-past Six ; the curtain to rise precisely at Seven o'Clock.
Boxes, 3s.—Pit, 2s.—Gallery, 1s.
Half Price at Half-past Eight.—Boxes, 2s.—Pit, 1s.—Gallery, 6d.
Tickets to be had of Mr. FREEMAN, Market-square, and of the Misses JACKMAN, in Horse-market.
The Manager once more returns thanks for the support the Theatre has been honored with, and, until the Spring Races, respectfully takes leave.

(Freeman, Printer, Market-square, Northampton.)

THEATRE ROYAL, NORTHAMPTON
Licensed pursuant to Act of Parliament, Lessee, Mr. H. JACKMAN, AUGUSTIN STREET
SECOND RACE NIGHT
UNDER THE DISTINGUISHED PATRONAGE OF
VISCOUNT CLIFDEN,
HONORABLE E. L. MOSTYN
AND
G. PAYNE, ESQ.
STEWARDS OF THE RACES.
Popular New Pieces—' ASMODEUS,' ' This House to be Sold,' and ' to Settle Accounts with your Laundress.'

This Evening, THURSDAY, MARCH 30, 1848,
When will be produced (first and only time in this Theatre) a New Drama, translated from " La Petit Diable," performed upwards of 100 nights at the principal Theatres in London and Paris, entitled

ASMODEUS,
THE LITTLE DEVIL.

Carlo, an Orphan and Wandering Minstrel, assuming the character of Asmodeus, or the Little Devil..Mad. PIEROTTI
Ferdinand, King of Spain . Mr. HARGRAVE......Antonio, Mr. F. MORGAN.
Frans Antonio, the Grand Inquisitor and Councilor to the King...Mr. NELSON.
Gil Vargas, his creature, Usher of the Black Rod, and Tutor of Don Rafael ......Mr. STYLES
Don Rafael D'Estrango, a Student of Theology, Pupil of Gil Vargas, and subsequently Captain of the Queen's Guard, Mr. C. JACKMAN,
Carlos...Mr. ALLEN,   Pages...Misses BROWN, and PIEROTTI.
Isabel, Queen of Spain.. Mrs HARGRAVE......Casilda, sister to Carlo, beloved by and in love with Don Rafael, Miss L. JACKMAN,
Ladies in Waiting, Inquisitors, Guards, Huntsmen, Attendants on the Court, &c. &c.

Programme of Scenery, Incidents, &c.
Act I.—The Castilian Arms—The Haunted Inn—The Tutor and his Pupil—The Sorcerer's Cell—The Troubled Conscience—The Shade—Music's Fascination—The Invocation—ASMODEUS ! ASMODEUS ! ! !—Mysterious and sudden Appearance of the Little Devil—The Compact—The Royal Hunt.
THE LUCKY LITTLE DEVIL!
Act II.—Splendid Apartment in the Royal Palace at Madrid—Unexpected promotion—The Little Devil—First Instalment of the compact—My Share ! Halves !—The King's Secret—The Incantation—The Spirit raised the ——Rafael accused of Sorcery—The Devil in a Hobble—Grand Inquisitor at fault—The Duel—The Little Devil bullet proof—The Devil a Usurer—A Match—The Compact demanded—Halves !—What half my wife ! I'll see you—My wife's my wife—Secret Revealed—A False Accusation—The Imprisonment and Release—More Promotion—The Caught—Virtue Triumphant—

THE DEVIL'S OWN LUCK. HAPPY DENOUEMENT!

A COMIC SONG, BY MR. MORGAN.
THE HIGHLAND FLING, BY MDLLE. CLARA GOODWIN.

After which the favourite Comedietta, of THE

Dead Shot.
Mr. Hector Timid... Mr. F. MORGAN.   Captain Cannon...Mr. STYLES.
Wiseman...Mr. HARGRAVE.   Frederick... Mr. NELSON.   Williams...Mr. ALLEN.
Louisa Lovetrick - Miss H. JACKMAN   Chatter, (her maid) Miss L. JACKMAN.

A COMIC SONG, BY MR. BARRY.

After which the laughable Farce, now acting nightly at the Theatre Royal, Adelphi, London, entitled

HOW TO SETTLE ACCOUNTS
WITH YOUR LAUNDRESS.
Wittington Widgets, (a West-end Tailor) Mr. C. JACKMAN
Jacob Brown (a Hair-dresser at the Opera) Mr. STYLES......Waiter, Mr. ALLEN.   Postman, Mr. ...
Barney Twill (Widget's Page and Light Porter) Mr. F. MORGAN.
Mademoiselle Cheri Bounce...... (an Opera Dancer)..... Mrs HARGRAVE.
Mary White (a young Laundress) Miss H. JACKMAN   Mary White's Boy, Miss H. JACKMAN
Mary White's young Man of Fashion, Miss H. JACKMAN

Comic Duet, " SISTER RUTH," Mr Morgan and Madame Pierotti
' THE CACHOUCA,' MDLLE. CLARA GOODWIN.

To conclude with a Dramatic Sketch by STIRLING COYNE, Esq. founded on the occasion of the late sale of Shakspeare's House, and now performing, with the greatest success, at the Theatre Royal, Adelphi, London, entitled—THE

HOUSE TO BE SOLD.
The Property of the late William Shakspeare,
ENQUIRE WITHIN!
With entire New Scenery, &c. &c. by Mr. WILLIAM BATTIE.
Chopkins (a Gent.)—Mr. C. JACKMAN.   Grimshaw—Mr. STYLES.   Tiffin—Mr. ALLEN.
William Shakspeare—Mr. HARGRAVE.
HAMLET ... Mr BATTIE.. HOMEO.... Mrs HARGRAVE.. OTHELLO.... Mr F. MORGAN.
Ghost of Hamlet's Father Mr JACKMAN SHYLOCK.... Mr STYLES Sir J. FALSTAFF... Mr F. MORGAN.
SLENDER.... Mdlle GOODWIN. MACBETH.... Mr NELSON. FRANCIS.... Mast. GEORGE
Lady MACBETH.. Mad. PIEROTTI. JULIET.... Miss L. JACKMAN. DESDEMONA.. Miss JACKMAN.
Dame QUICKLY.... Mrs ALLEN. ARIEL........ Miss H. JACKMAN.
Mrs Jarrat—Madame PIEROTTI.

In the course of the Piece the following Parodies :—
Song—'Ole Will sat at Covent Garden Gate.'   'Who is that knocking at the Door.'
SCENERY—The Exterior of Shakspeare's House at Stratford-upon-Avon.
The Interior of the Room where Shakspeare was Born :
GRAND ALLEGORICAL TABLEAU OF SHAKESPEARIAN CHARACTERS ! !

Tickets to be had of Mr. Freeman, Market Sq; & of Mr Burgess, Gold Street.
Boxes, 3s.   Pit 2s.   Gallery, 1s.
Half-price at Nine, Boxes, 1s. 6d ; Pit, 1s. ; Gallery, 6d.   Children under 12 years of age admitted Half-price, from the commencement.—Doors open at half-past Six, the Performance to commence at Seven o'clock precisely, and terminate at Eleven.

MUSICAL DIRECTOR, MR. JAMES TICEHURST.   ARTIST, MR. BATTIE.
SMOKING STRICTLY PROHIBITED.   Officers will be in attendance to preserve order.
The Theatre open every Evening.

NORTHAMPTON, 1841 and 1848, during the Jackman era, the latter the first year of "Royalty". (*British Museum and Northampton Public Library*)

if not, hail and farewell. The second Leamington letter, written towards the end of the season, reveals that a few days earlier the company did not know where they were going next—"It was not settled till Monday where we should go to next. We close here on Monday next and go to Newport Pagnell." This uncertainty must have added a certain zest to the strolling life, a break in the routine of familiar "theatres" and lodgings.

After arriving at Newport Pagnell, Partleton wrote again : "I left the music with Mr. W. Lines as we past through Daventry to here. We close next week and open at Buckingham next Monday week. The music comes to 6s. I should not have written for it had not business been so bad and so much owing." This was not the first time Partleton had pleaded poverty.

The letters of Henry Hartley reveal him to have been a warm-hearted likeable, sensitive but ambitious man. To say he was ambitious is not intended as a criticism. I suppose that of all the professions and occupations of this world the men and women who like to fret their hours upon the stage are among the most ambitious, at least in the early part of their careers. In Shakespeare, the spear-holder longs to mouth "Et tu Brute", even if he is doomed to die immediately thereafter; in Christie the walk-on butler would dearly like to be the detective; while today the respectable maid with only two lines to say sighs to be the prostitute with the nude scene. The only difference today is probably that whereas the most elevated ambition of yesteryear was to have one's name in lights outside Drury Lane the supreme desire today is to see it flashed in smaller letters across the million screens of domestic television, preferably in one's own series.

Henry Hartley simply lived for the day when he could talk a manager into giving him a chance in London. Whether his talents were insufficient, whether he was unlucky, whether the times were not propitious, we can only surmise, not having Henry Hartley here to give us an audition.

All the while he was trying to make contacts, pull strings, anything to get his chance. It was not only that he did not always hit it off with Old Henry Jackman, his father-in-law, that he longed to see the back of the Jackman Company and its eternal round of small theatres, audiences that were boisterous though often few in number and financial rewards that were small and sometimes uncertain. Moreover, if he did remain with the company, he probably thought he stood little chance of ever controlling it one day, the line of succession clearly being to the sons, Henry or Charles (in fact when Old Henry died a son-in-law did in fact become a partner, with Charles Jackman).

Henry Hartley and his wife had a rough time in the autumn of 1842. She was so ill that for some time she could not appear on the stage and even had to miss her own benefit night. This is clear from a letter he wrote to Gery from Bedford on September 6.

He harked back to the season at Leamington, presumably an experimental one, with special cause for regret at its failure. "A delightful place—spent my time very pleasantly there—had business been good it would have been a treat to have stayed two or three months." Bedford, on the other hand, was "dull".

He went on : "I am sure you think me a sad fellow for not obliging your request for writing to you while at Northampton—but I assure you this is the very first opportunity I have had of taking pen in hand, except in business for the last fortnight. I do not know that I ever worked harder —or that I was more harassed in my life—playing nearly every night— study" (the next words elude me) "for the stars and to crown all my wife was ill in bed nearly the whole of the time. I was up many nights with her and at the theatre rehearsing from 10 till 4 often—and in these circumstances you will, I am sure, forgive the seeming neglect." "The Mistress" was now "only the shadow of what she was".

Hartley, probably for reasons of envy, was never enamoured of the "stars" who appeared with the company and in this letter he summed up on the stellar guests at the Northampton August races season. "Miss P. Horton and Messrs. Allen and Stretton are very clever but did not draw much—business but middling all along—the races being so badly attended were in part the cause of this."

The Mercury report underlined this point about the Races. "The summer meeting was very miserable. We have seen more people at a donkey race. There is no disguising the fact that these races are going to the dogs. People were drawn to the courses to see one horse canter over. It was so completely a blank that the card-sellers got drunk out of sheer spite. They said they shouldn't come no more. Not even the stewards were present."

Following the week of drama at Northampton, Old Henry tried a week of opera which was highly praised by the Mercury, which singled out *La Sonnambula* for special commendation : "It is impossible, we heard some people say, when this piece was announced, to play it here. It wants space and scenic effects and accessories which it cannot have. We thought so too till we saw it and then we thought that the isolation of that perfect group— the complete subordination of all besides—was an advantage." Perhaps this artistic adulation helped to compensate Old Henry—for this was the week for which Miss Horton and Messrs. Allen and Stretton were specially engaged.

Concluding his letter from Bedford, right at the bottom of the sheet, Hartley, as usual, gave a reason why he could not write more—"Pray excuse this hasty scrawl—I have a part to study this evening."

From Bedford the company moved to Woburn and it was on the day they were about to open, November 1, 1842, that Hartley again unloaded his troubles to Gery.

"A month since, I began writing a letter to you but was called away and unable to finish it—since that time I have been terribly harassed both in mind and body and really could not sit down with any degree of happiness to give you an epistle. My poor wife has, I'm sorry to say, been a great sufferer—she had but just recovered from the illness I mentioned in my last when she again, I imagine, caught a severe cold which ended in inflam- mation of the eyes—for some days the total loss of one eye was threatened —this, of course, preyed much on the spirits added to which the doctors were obliged to apply the most severe remedies so that altogether I never saw her so ill before. She is now, I thank God, pretty well recovered and I trust with care will gradually regain her strength." One gains the impression that it was not the first time the former Caroline Jackman had been ill.

Apart from the worries about her health, there was the effect on business. Each actor or actress had a number of parts which he or she knew well and doubtless there was some hasty learning by another member of the company whenever there was an illness.

Hartley went on : "The inconvenience, too, in business was most annoying for Mrs. H. did not play for more than a fortnight—and then could do but little. This happening just at the end of the season when, owing to benefits, study and labour are great, was a loss to us into the bargain. We were obliged to do as we could—although Miss Harriet" (Jackman) "and Mrs. Myers were very industrious and did all they could to keep the loss of the lady from being felt." Despite these drawbacks, he reported that the end of the season was "pretty fair".

Surviving among the material from the Daventry attic is a small handbill for Mrs. Hartley's Bedford benefit, showing that it was on Wednesday, October 19, and included Douglas Jerrold's *The Prisoner of War*, the interlude of *Married Bachelor*, the extravaganza *The Happy Man* and the fashionable burletta *The Loan of a Lover*. Tickets for this marathon evening of entertainment could be had at Messrs. Merry's and Mr. F. Thompson's High Street, and of Mrs. Hartley at Mr. J. Smith's, Cauldwell Street. Merry's were also the printers of the bill, which makes no reference to Mrs. Hartley's illness.

Hartley had harsh words for the Bedford theatre—"cold and with a bad approach to it"—and said there was talk of building a new one. "The good people of Bedford were particularly kind to the company, however, and the emotional Hartley left the town with much regret—"I could not help shedding a tear at parting." Now they were to open at Woburn—"This town is very small but the neighbourhood is good." The company was the same as at Bedford except that Miss Stanley and Mr. Loraine had left— "No loss is felt. They were both muffs. If concerts would constitute actors, they would be great."

Lords Edward, Cosmo, and Alexander Russell, sons of the Duke of Bedford, along with other local personalities went along to the theatre in the village from their home at Woburn Abbey to see *Married and Single*, *More Blunders than One* and *The Steeplechase* under the patronage of Woburn Cricket Club. A report added that the Jackman Company's first season at Woburn had been about twenty-eight years before, i.e. in 1814.

In 1842, at least, they were not the only company to visit Woburn for in July the Wheat Sheaf Inn had been host to "Lawrence's Theatre". They appear to have been of a lower order, however, for their prices were a mere 1s. for the boxes, 6d. pit and 3d. gallery. *The Bridal Bed of a Murderer*, the main fare on the playbill, indicates the style of their performances.

A couple of years earlier the same issue of the Mercury which, on Boxing Day, 1840, had carried an account of Jackman's Company being in a temporary theatre in the Bedford Arms Hotel, Woburn, reported that the "beautiful little theatre at Woburn Abbey was in use with Miss Adelaide Lister as 'Cinderella' supported by Lords Edward and Francis Russell and

Mr. Shelley, the spectators being equally distinguished and including the Countess of Charlemont, Lord and Lady Southampton, Lord Melbourne, Lord John Russell, Lady C. Stanhope, Mr. and Lady Agnes Byng, Lords E. Howard, C. Russell, E. and F. Russell etc."

On at least one occasion a company of strollers, probably Jackman's, were invited to perform in the "big house". That was in 1819, as already recorded.

From Woburn the next move in 1842 was to Uxbridge where the company usually played to good business. Hartley looked forward to visiting the place for other reasons, because it was so near London, where he longed to act. "I anticipate much pleasure in the change—shall be near London and can take an eighteenpenny ride on the train to see a play as often as convenient. As to an engagement in the Great Metropolis I am as far off the desired object as ever. I know not how to move in it. The new theatre in Oxford is now being opened, the responsible man being Mr. Turner. He is living near Bedford. I have met him in company often but was not aware of his connection until Saturday last. A friend has promised me to put in a word but I do not think 'tis of any use—the arrangements are, I believe, made. I wish I could get a chance—but at present see none and must therefore wait, patiently, I suppose."

Next he gave news of the company and some of its former members. "Mr. Jackman and family are all well. Fenton" (married to Eliza Jackman) "is in Swansea. Heard from him a few weeks ago. Cullenford is out at the Adelphi and now at Birmingham." He mentions again the poor season at Northampton— "The stars ought to have drawn more than they did. £15 or £16 was the most they got in."

In his closing lines Hartley gave the customary excuse for his rush in writing and the need to close, with "I must write to my brother at Chipping Norton on business". Then he added a postscript : "Mrs. Hartley is looking over my shoulder and declares you will need an interpreter."

In fact this letter, like most of the others, is not hard to decipher having survived ordeal by attic in very good style. But one of Hartley's letters did give me eyestrain, some passages eluding me altogether. The special difficulty was that it was "cross-written". After writing normally across the four pages, Hartley had more to say but no more paper to hand; he therefore turned the sheets sideways and proceeded to write from bottom to top, across the other writing! One page of it is reproduced so that readers of the book may try it for themselves. (Page 140.)

Never short of something to say, Hartley wrote his double-length letter from Uxbridge on January 20, 1843 (at least that is what I make out the date to be). "I have made every application I can think of in London but at present am doomed to disappointment. I had an introduction to Mr. Bunn but he can do nothing at present, not intending to play anything in my line; opera and ballet, I am told, are all the rage. Captain Polhill" (of Bedford) "interested himself with Bunn for me. I wrote to Webster but he has already engaged ——; should —— fail I should perhaps stand a chance but 'tis a 100 to one and I at times get vexed and I think I shall cut it and yet I feel confident that if I continue on the stage I shall ultimately gain my aim (?). I will not, however, at all relax but say on the contrary, I assure you, I study more than many."

Hartley gives news of other actors' movements and sets out some of his own very firm ideas on what would happen if he were in charge. "We have as yet had no 'stars' nor would I have any if I was at the head of affairs ... our company is not what I call a good one, you see I am candid with you, one or two muffs, the leading man a greenhorn ... Henderson has left us and gone into the Lincoln Circuit but I think he is again on the look-out, the sooner he cuts the stage the better, he is a respectable good-natured fellow but he will never be an actor ... Fenton is playing at Milford Haven ... Partleton lost his father last week, who has left a wife and seven children ... I have been to London nearly every week since I have been in this part of the country, have seen all the Irishmen in London ... and have I confess more confidence in my own ability since seeing the London markets."

With the letter he enclosed a couple of playbills so that his friend could see any changes in the company for himself. At the close Hartley begs pardon for the scrawl—"I fear you will be puzzled to make it out, but take the will for the deed."

By August, 1843, Hartley had been eight or nine long years with the company. He was now aged thirty and was beginning to feel that, dramatically speaking, life was passing him by. Instead of getting the Forties Feeling at forty, he had it a decade early. To his evidently close friend Gery he revealed his innermost thoughts in a letter written in Buckingham on August 27. It is indeed so confidential that one feels as if one is prying into private family matters in reading it. But the historian must not be too squeamish. So read on : "I have been bothered of late pretty much— must leave particulars till I see you—suffice for the present—manager DISPLEASETH me" (the manager was, of course, his father-in-law, so it it quite possible that Hartley could discuss these particular problems better with his friend than with his wife) "felt annoyed, truly to confess to you ill treated—gave notice to cut—had an offer from Bennett to go to Worcester this week—accepted it—manager confessed to temper not being as ought to hoped I should not leave him and finally asked me to write and cancel the arrangement with Bennett—after this—I could not do otherwise—have done so although the other does not like it and am now going to continue as before unless anything good should turn up—in London or provinces—for two years at expiration of which time I shall in all probability close theatrical career."

This may have sounded like a dramatic gesture but Hartley was quite in earnest. Almost exactly two years later he did "cut", leaving the company and announcing himself in the Warwick and Warwickshire Advertiser (founded 1806, now the Warwick Advertiser) as the new "mine host" of the Golden Lion Inn, Stratford-upon-Avon. He had not, however, said a final farewell to the stage, as we shall see.

It should be explained, by the way, that the dashes in transcribing the "cross-written letter" are by way of truncation partly caused by illegibility; the above letter, however, is as it was written. In moments of stress Mr.

Hartley tended to write as Mr. Jingle tended to speak, when addressing the Pickwickians.

The closing lines of his letter from Buckingham were to say that Northampton was the next town to be visited, when he hoped to see Gery. His traditional excuse gives an insight into his family life—"I have a letter to write to Aylesbury and shall be late for the post. My two youngest kids are foisted out at Aylesbury—they are well and happy, thank God. Hope to see them on Tuesday. Mrs. H. joins me in best wishes."

The two children to whom he refers are probably Henry and Sophia.

When Hartley thus left to become an innkeeper it meant not only the loss of a popular performer, and of Mrs. Hartley, but also a further change in the "family" character of the company. The Fentons had some years before decided to go their own way, meaning that there were one daughter (Eliza) and one son-in-law less. When Hartley left not only did it involve the departure of his wife (Caroline Jackman) but also led to the desertion of Sophia Jackman. Unmarried and due to remain a spinster until her death at Neithrop, Oxon, in November, 1887, she decided to cast her lot in with the Hartleys and worked in the Stratford-upon-Avon inn as a barmaid. This we know from the census of 1851, by which time, incidentally, Hartley had increased his brood to five. They were (ages as in 1851) Frances Ann, born at Northampton, aged 11; Henry Charles, born at Bicester, aged 9; Sophia Clara, born at Northampton, aged 7; James Carpenter, aged 4, and Harriet Louisa, 3, both born at Stratford-upon-Avon. Notice the strong allegiance to the family embodied in the naming of the children—Frances, Henry, Charles, Sophia, Harriet and Louisa are all names clearly taken from the Jackmans; equally, we may deduce that Ann, James, Carpenter, and Clare came from the Hartley side. But despite carrying Jackman names, this third generation of the family were not to follow in Old Henry Jackman's footsteps. Changing conditions, and their father's decision ensured that.

The pull of the stage proved too strong for Hartley, however, and by 1845, only the year after he left, he began making guest appearances with his old comrades, now receiving much better billing and playing only for two or three nights during a season. Probably it turned out to be an ideal compromise. He had the security of the licensed trade, the chance of being able to play more or less when he liked, and the joy of having his Masonic lodge meet at his own hotel at Stratford.

As the family element lessened in the Jackman Company it gradually came to be dominated by the rest. Not only outnumbered but dominated. The "strangers" were those at the top of the bill, the family members, apart from Hartley, tending to be mentioned almost apologetically, as also rans. In March, 1846, for instance, when Hartley was a guest player at Northampton ("first appearance these two years") the cast included Mr. Waldron, from the Theatre Royal, Drury Lane; Mr. W. Waldron, from the Olympic Theatre; Mr. Barry, from the Theatre Royal, Adelphi; Mr. Southgate, from the Surrey Theatre; Mr. Stanley, from the Theatre Royal, Manchester; and Miss Kezia Love, from the Theatre Royal, English Opera House.

Queen Victoria passed by the theatre in November, 1844. After alighting from the train at Weedon, on the Watling Street, she entered Northampton via St. James End, on the west. The Mercury commented that Northampton could not boast of its approaches and "St. James End, with its abrupt, narrow and dirty turn is one of the worst".

The Mayoral greeting was at West Bridge, the Royal route then leading up Black Lion Hill, Marefair, Gold Street to All Saints Church—and it was there that there was a fatal accident.

Stands had been erected at All Saints Church for 4,000 children but when 2,000 had taken positions there was trouble. The carpentry showed signs of collapsing and did in fact break several gravestones. A forty-five-year-old carpenter named George Mason who went to put a sawing tool under a plank to support it was killed. At the subsequent inquest, presided over by George Abbey, evidence was given that it was not safe to put uprights on gravestones!

However, the accident did not mar the splendour of the Royal occasion. There were no mishaps to the stands erected on Black Lion Hill, in Gold Street, Mercers Row and Abington Street.

Every house on the way was decorated from base to parapet with evergreens and there were banners galore.

The Queen was on her way to Burleigh for the christening of a daughter of the Marquess and Marchioness of Exeter and the Mayor of Northampton (Edward H. Barwell) was among the guests at Burleigh that night. On the way back to Weedon there were further ceremonies to mark the Royal passage, which was quite an historic event. There had not been a Royal visit to the town since Queen Elizabeth passed through in 1564. The Mercury's comment was that kings had not the "locomotive propensities of queens".

To commemorate the day a fund was launched to build a Royal Victoria Dispensary in Albion Place, Northampton.

In the year 1845 I have traced the Jackman Company at Woburn in February, Northampton in March and November, Aylesbury in April, Bicester and Stony Stratford in July (this is the only reference to their appearing in Stony Stratford), Warwick in September, Buckingham in October and Daventry in November.

Some of Jackman's ports-of-call have left little trace for his chronicler. Just a couple of newspaper sentences in the case of two of the seasons in 1845. In the Mercury of July 26 : "Mr. Jackman with his company has finished his season at Bicester. This week he commences at Stony Stratford." Bicester is represented otherwise only by the few playbills of the 1830s already mentioned. Of Stony Stratford this is the only reference, apart from Sophia Jackman having been born there, presumably during a season in about 1816.

This year of 1845, by the way, was the one in which Bicester was first lit by gas, which, though belated, was rated a great improvement over oil. The only subsequent reference to the theatrical activities at Bicester I have come across is in February, 1860, when the Northampton Mercury recorded that "Mr. Bruton has fitted up the old theatre at Bicester and is with his company amusing the playgoing public".

July of 1846 saw a Marefair show by the former manager Simpson, now firmly installed at Birmingham. To his old stamping ground he sent a troupe of thirty-six girl dancers aged 4 to 10, under the direction of Miss J. Ridgeway, with a concert party. Simpson described himself on the bills as lessee of the Theatres Royal, Birmingham, Liverpool etc. At Liverpool City Library are playbills between the end of 1845 and April, 1847, showing him as lessee of the theatre built in 1802 to replace the original one of 1772. The second theatre ceased operations in 1885 and subsequently became a cold store. It was demolished a few years ago. In 1849 Simpson's son introduced touring shows into the Birmingham theatre.

For the Jackman company the year of 1846 had begun in Banbury but on the 27th of that month Old Henry returned to Stratford-upon-Avon, eight years after his first and only previous season there. It was at a period when the proprietors of the Shakespeare Theatre were seriously thinking of giving up. Indeed they did not even call it a theatre now; two years earlier they had spent money on converting and repairing the building and it was now called the "New Royal Shakespearian Rooms".

For his 1846 season Old Henry paid £30. The account books show that he also snapped up an old scene for 30s. For gas used he paid £6 17s. During the time he was there a Mrs. Merridew gave a concert and used some of his coal to heat the place. To the proprietors she paid £2 2s. for the hall and to Old Henry they paid 1s. 6d. for coal used from his stock!

In 1849 Jackman came to an agreement for a three-year lease and on May 15 he handed over £15, "on account of half three years rent". Later he paid a further £15 so that half of three years rent was £30. It was therefore £20 per annum.

Returning to 1846, a feature of the year was a very lengthy season at Bedford, from the beginning of July to the end of October, with a short break to be at Warwick at the start of September for the Races. After Bedford came another long stint, at Daventry lasting into January, 1848.

Meantime Northampton received another visit from Ira Aldridge, "the African Roscius". Aldridge's name was not mentioned in the press, the Mercury being content with a reference to the fact that "An African of colour has been playing at our theatre this week under the appelation of the African Roscius. We saw him as Gambia in 'The Slave'. He will be a decided acquisition to the stage."

This was somewhat patronising, for Aldridge had been a decided acquisition to the stage for many years. He had appeared with success as Othello in London in 1826 and had played the role in Northampton fifteen years before. He was now forty-two and endured with dignity such slights as being called a buck nigger and having his name overlooked by provincial journalists. Earlier he had acted with a negro company in New York.

In April 28, 1851, Aldridge appeared at the Shakespeare Theatre with the Jackman Company. He married a white woman and last appeared in England in 1853. After that he spent most of his time on the Continent, perhaps his most unlikely activity being performing with a German company

THEATRE, NORTHAMPTON.

Popular New Drama, now acting in London, and founded on the late Glorious Military events, Entitled 'THE WAR IN INDIA,' Popular New Farce, of 'The WATER WITCHES,' never acted Here, and the laughable Farce, of the 'SMOKED MISER.'

On MONDAY Evening, April 20th 1846,

Will be presented a NEW and original Oriental DRAMA, of peculiar interest, at the present time, entitled

WAR with the SIKHS

OR,

BRITANS TRIUMPHS IN INDIA,

AND THE DEATH OF SIR ROBERT SALE.

General Sir Robert Sale, the Hero of Jallalabad, Mr. MORRIS. Captain Wilmington, his Aid de Camp, Mr. W. WALDRON. Teja Sing, Chief Sirdar in Chief of the Sikh Army, Mr. WHYTE. Mectab Singh, } Chiefs, {Mr. STANLEY, Muly, } Two Sikh Officers, {Mr. SOUTHGATE. Bahadus Singh, } {Mr. KIRK. Omah, } {Mr. DILLON. Corporal Jollyboy, of the 13th Foot, of the British Bull Dogs, Mr. BARRY. Kooli, an Indoo Boy, Miss L. JACKMAN. Obadiah Mumpkins, a Lecturer on the Horrors of War, but ultimately a Turncoat, Mr. JACKMAN.——Zarina, a Female Slave, Mother of Kooli, the Hindoo Boy, Miss H. JACKMAN. Gabbla, an attendant on the Officers Ladies, with Songs, Miss LOVE. Zetti, Mrs. SMITHSON.

In the course of the Evening the Following ENTERTAINMENTS,

By Desire, 'The DASHING WHITE SERJEANT,' 'WHY DON'T the MEN PROPOSE' AND 'WHEN THE DEW IS ON THE GRASS,' BY MISS KAZIA LOVE, A COMIC DANCE, BY MR. A. DILLON, Comic Songs, 'Follow your Nose,' & in the Character of Tilly Slowboy, 'Going out A Charing,' BY MR. BARRY. & A FANCY DANCE, by Miss SOUTHGATE,

A Laughable NEW FARCE, first time in this Theatre, called

THE WATER WITCHES!

WATER WITCHES.

Fanny Sparks, alias Charles Popkins, Miss H. JACKMAN. Caroline Dormer, alias Jeremiah Brown, Miss L. JACKMAN, Clara Courtney, alias Henry Smith. Miss LOVE. Polly Mittens, alias Dick Pullaway, Coxswain of the Water Witches, Mrs. SMYTHSON. Betsy Minglemax, Bar Woman at the 8 Bells, Mrs. JACKMAN.

MEMBERS OF THE FUNNY CLUB.

Tom Townsend, Mr. DILLON. Charles Chester, Mr. SOUTHGATE. Augustus Warton, Mr. W. WALDRON. Frank Harland, Mr. STANLEY. Joe Smith, a Regular Waterman and Coxwain of the Lady of the Lake, Mr. BARRY. Jack in the Water, Mr. KIRK. Waiter, Mr. F. JACKMAN. Cabin Boy, Mast. PARTLETON

To conclude with the very Laughable FARCE entitled THE

SMOKED MISER

OR, THE BENEFIT OF HANGING!!!

Captain Daring, Mr. W. WALDRON. Old Screw, Mr. KIRK. Nail, Mr. BARRY. Goliah Spiderlimb, Mr. JACKMAN, Giles Sowthistle, Mr. DILLON.——Anne, Miss H. JACKMAN. Sally Ceres, Miss L. JACKMAN.

Nights of Playing this week, MONDAY, WEDNESDAY, and FRIDAY.

BOXES, 2s. 6d. PIT, 1s. GALLERY, 6d. Half price to the Boxes only, at half past 8 o' Clock. Doors open at Half-past Six, and the Performance to commence at 7 o' clock. Tickets may be had of Mr. Freeman, Market Square.——No Smoking allowed.——Children in Arms not admitted.

in English while the remainder of the cast spoke German! Aldridge died
and was buried at Lodz, Poland, in August, 1867.

When the present Shakespeare Memorial Theatre was opened at Stratford
on April 23, 1932, by the Prince of Wales (afterwards Edward VIII), one
of the contributions to the building fund was by the negroes of the United
States. Recognition, among thirty-three seats named after the greatest
names of world drama, Irving, Terry, Kemble, Garrick etc, was a seat in
the fourth row of the stalls with a bronze plate inscribed "Ira Aldridge".
He was the first negro to play white roles.

The Jackman Company still had some years to go but in general the
circuits were running down. In 1846 the Lincoln Circuit was on its last legs.
What trials the Jackman Company had to endure during its remaining
sixteen years of existence are largely concealed behind the journalistic
euphemisms of the day; unfortunately no further letters have come to light
to give us more reliable information.

Among the reasons for the decline was the introduction of the railways
which meant that both companies and theatre-goers were more mobile.

What Old Henry thought of the new fangled monster, the steam locomotive, and whether he realised they were going to put an end to his way
of life, we can only speculate.

But certain it is that all business came to a stop in Wellingborough on
Monday, June 2, 1845, the day when the first train ran on the new line
from Northampton to Peterborough. The train consisted of fifteen first class
carriages. Each station en route was packed with spectators and all the
week the train was jammed with people travelling for the sheer novelty of
it. The change which its coming brought to the many little towns and
villages on the route along the River Nene Valley can scarcely be imagined
by the sophisticated traveller of today (which means almost all of us). No
longer was a thirty-eight-mile journey a major expedition.

Said the Mercury: "If people have ceased to question the advantage
of railways in the abstract still less do they have any doubt about the
absolute necessity of railways in the particular. They constitute the universal
rule of travelling nowadays. The town which has not one in its vicinity is
an exception—isolated, shut off from the world. Not only does it not keep
place with its contemporaries—it retrogrades." To which the national newspaper The Times added: "To be destitute of a railway is the present day
reproach to the locality." By now the country was, indeed, in the grip of
railway madness. To be able to buy shares in a railway was seen as the
instant road to riches.

The ironroad insanity was reflected in the columns of the Mercury,
which at the command of its advertisers, went railway-mad itself. Everything was sacrificed to accommodate the paid-for announcements of the
projects of the railway promoters, some of them sound, others hare-brained.
Despite the fact that special supplements were run to accommodate the
overflow, on at least one occasion the leading article itself was left out.
"The overwhelming influx of railway advertisements and others yesterday
morning—indeed more than we have been able to find room for—compels
us to omit our leading articles and many matters we had prepared for

insertion." Even an account of the funeral of Earl Spencer was cut short on September 27, 1845.

An issue a month later carried announcements of schemes for the following lines :

Buckingham and London and Birmingham.
Buckinghamshire and Oxford and Wolverton Junction.
Cambridge Extension of the Bedford Railway Co.
Direct London and Manchester.
Eastern Counties Extension and Cambridge and Worcester Direct.
Harwich Docks and Birmingham and Central England.
Leamington and Warwick.
Leicester and Bedford.
London and Birmingham Extensions and Northampton, Daventry, Leamington and Warwick.
London and Northampton Direct Atmospheric.
Lynn, Wisbeach, Peterborough, Midland Counties and Birmingham Junction.
Midland and Eastern Counties.
Northampton, Banbury and Cheltenham.
Northampton, Bedford and Cambridge.
Northampton and Leicester.
Northampton, Towcester and Banbury.
Peterborough and Buckinghamshire Junction.
Peterborough and Nottingham Junction.
Peterborough, Wisbech, Midland Counties and Birmingham Junction.
Rugby and Huntingdon Junction.
Rugby, Warwick and Worcester.
Rugby, Market Harborough and Cambridge.
South Midland (Mr. Hudson, the "Railway King" was chairman).
South Midland and Southampton Junction.
Stamford, Market Harborough and Rugby Junction.
Worcester, Warwick and Rugby.
Warwickshire and London.

In case you may be wondering exactly what an atmospheric railway was, I will quote from the advertisement : "The atmospheric principle is aimed at mainly making the line through part of the existing turnpike road, leaving the remainder of its width for use by the present road, and screening it from the railway to prevent the trains from frightening the horses. Should the company be able, as they expect, to transact all the business of the line with a single line of railway the railway will be made cheaper than any other line in the kingdom. The atmospheric idea is to avoid the inconvenience of smoke and noise." [A book on "Atmospheric Railways", subtitled "A Victorian Venture in Silent Speed", was written by Charles Hadfield in 1967.]

One scheme was to sell the Warwick and Birmingham and the Warwick and Napton canals in order to convert them to railways.

Christopher Markham, brother of Charles, wrote a letter to the Mercury in December, 1845, pointing out that there were at the time no fewer than thirty-five rail projects on hand in the county of Northamptonshire. The previous month he had "bespoken" a performance of *The Honeymoon* at the theatre, an occasion marked by the presence of "an audience such as rarely gladdens the eyes of the playgoer in these parts". The explanation? Mr. Markham had his friends, political as well as private, clustered about him—"It was a complete galaxy of Conservative beauty." This crowded house was said to have had a cheering effect on the performers who acted with a vigour and spirit they did not always display.

George Abbey showed his concern for rail progress by seconding a motion approving the scheme for a new line running through Northampton put forward by the South Midlands Company in November, 1846. The meeting was held at the George Hotel.

Abbey also had his finger in one of the railway pies, the Northampton, Lincoln and Hull Direct Railway Company which was to have a capital of £2m and proceed by way of Kettering, Uppingham, Oakham and Grantham to Lincoln. The scheme came unstuck, like many more, and in February, 1846, all persons having claims against the company were asked to send them in. Abbey, who was on the provisional committee, no doubt lost money in this speculation.

It was the railway that brought to the town its largest-ever attraction in August, 1847, in the ample person of Mrs. Armitage, all 445 lbs of her, with 72-inch bust and 85-inch hips. No railway carriage being large enough to admit her proportions, she arrived in a specially constructed horse carriage, fitted up for her needs. She came not to the theatre but to the newly-constructed Temperance Hall in Newland. People paid a shilling to see this woman-mountain among them being Countess Spencer, who made two trips as if she could not believe the evidence of her own eyes, and the Duchess of Bedford.

Bicester, one of Jackman's theatrical towns, had no fewer than seven railways projected—"For some time we have had a number of surveyors taking up their temporary abode in this town."

Some idea of the railway fever among the investing public may be gained from the fact that of 335 joint stock companies registered between November, 1844, and June, 1845, no fewer than 252 were railways.

By 1848 there was a tremendous recession in railway stock and, wise after the event, the Mercury commented: "As is often the case, the public have run from one extreme to the other. Three years ago it was persuaded that the traffic which railways could develop was unlimited. Now it is thought that there can be no limits to the diminution."

One of the local effects of railways on the entertainment scene was to draw train-loads of people the four miles to Blisworth Pleasure Gardens. Close by the new station at the connecting point to the main line Mr. T. Shaw, proprietor of the Angel Inn, Northampton, had seized the opportunity to use the feeder line to take customers to what would today be called an entertainment complex, which he set up. At Blisworth he laid out some very attractive gardens, much in contrast to the squalid back streets and courts which constituted most of the accommodation for the working folk of Northampton. They flocked to escape for a few hours, to pay their sixpences for the train ride, itself an adventure. Despite unfavourable weather 1,500, including 800 who bought tickets at Northampton, attended the opening on Whit Monday, 1848. Its popularity grew apace and the following year there were 3,000 people in the grounds. They danced with much spirit to Jones Quadrille Band on the lawn and when rain came adjourned into the hotel opposite the railway station.

"The large third-class refreshment room was cleared out, the band used a temporary orchestra and dancing continued. In the hotel the scene beggared description. Every room, passage and corner was occupied; sitting down was out of the question, yet still the same feeling of hilarity prevailed."

Meanwhile, one of the plays presented at Northampton by the Jackman Company was topically entitled *The Railway King*.

The most unlikely factor in the decline of provincial theatre was the 1843 Act itself. It had set out to enfranchise the stage but its effect was to give a death blow, delayed in some cases, to the circuits which had been the backbone of provincial theatre. With the ending of restrictions of the length of the season, stock companies could now stay in one place if they chose and could command support. In turn the new situation led to the growth of touring companies which in turn killed off the stock companies.

It must also be remembered that these were the "Hungry Forties", and though this is something of a misnomer, in September, 1842, a club had been formed at the Fish Inn, Northampton, and other places in the town for the purpose of buying by weekly subscription corn or flour to be converted into bread. In 1847 the Queen decreed a national Public Fast, "in consequence of the severe distress which exists in the United Kingdom". People were asked to close their shops and abstain from business. What good could result from this it is hard to see but in Northampton every shop was in fact closed except that of the Friends (Quakers). The streets "presented a remarkable quietude equally removed from the stir of business and life of holiday".

In selecting March 24, Her Victorian Majesty had picked upon the second day of the Races at Northampton, so, perhaps not exactly in the spirit of the national demonstration the authorities merely brought the fixture forward a day. There was a splendid meeting, according to the Mercury, but the theatre did not do well—" 'The Love Chase' was produced for the benefit of the Misses Jackman. The play was creditably got up to the best of the manager's circumscribed ability (and looking at the stinted patronage he has received we will just add that the marvel is that his powers are not even more restricted."

Soup kitchens set up in Northampton provided that commodity to the poor at a penny a quart or gratuitously, through tickets handed out by the charitably minded whose money made the kitchens possible. One of these was the M.P., the Rt. Hon. R. Vernon Smith, who gave £20. Others made regular subscriptions of a guinea a month. Within three months, in March, 1848, the funds were exhausted and a fresh appeal had to be made.

In such conditions the ultra-radical movement of Chartism took passing root and one of its leaders, Mr. Hollowell, told a meeting on the Market Square that Corn Law Repeal and Free Trade having failed it was time for the working class to take matters into their own hands. He was allowed to say this, however, without fear of being hanged, drawn and quartered, or even imprisoned, which might not have been the case a century before. So much more tolerant was the atmosphere that when it rained the Mayor gave permission for the Chartists to hold a second meeting in the Town Hall.

Meanwhile the toll of young lives went on for one reason or another, for want of medical knowledge, care and attention, or sufficient sustenance. One of the most spectacular local funerals in the area was at Buckingham where three young children from one family, the eldest aged 6, were borne to the grave by twelve young women.

There were some pathetic inquests for Coroners to preside over. Like the one at Northampton on a fifteen-week-old baby, Thomas Isaac Simpson, who had been given some Godfrey's Cordial. The father had refused to go to work at the low wages then offered and the mother had gone to her labours, leaving the child. The Coroner upbraided the father : "If you had had the least glimmering of sense you would have known that it was better to work for even half wages than to let your wife and family starve. There are hundreds in the town willing to work for such wages" (three shillings a day). The man replied that he would not work for that money and it was no good saying he would. The mother, a half-starved looking object, cried throughout the proceedings and then went home to cope with her eight remaining children.

The Coroner now was John Becke who had succeeded George Abbey also as secretary of the theatre. Ten months after acting as pall-bearer to Charles Markham, his fellow proprietor of the theatre, who was buried in the family vault at St. Giles Church, Abbey died on Friday, August 13, 1847, at his Gold Street home, aged 59. His mother Anne had died the previous February at her home at Wellingborough Grange, aged 90.

The solicitors who fancied themselves to succeed Abbey as Coroner showed little sense of decorum or taste in laying their claims. Even to the cash-and-carry mentalities of today their haste seems most undignified. Abbey had died only on Friday but the copy of the Mercury which appeared the very next day carried six advertisements touting for his job. Not only was George not buried but could scarcely have been cold before the legal gentlemen were writing out their appeals for consideration and bustling round to the newspaper offices with them.

The advertisements were in terms rather similar to those of theatrical managers trying to seduce the populace to their support. In this case it was a restricted audience, consisting of the freeholders.

William Flesher, of Abington Street, pointed out that he had been an Attorney in Northampton for twenty-one years. John Becke admitted that he was personally unknown to many of the electors "yet during a residence of some years amongst you I have been fortunate enough to obtain the friendship and goodwill of many persons of influence who have encouraged me to make my present application". Robert Hewitt, who had been an Attorney in Northampton for twenty-four years, pointed out that on a previous occasion he had "yielded his pretensions at the solicitations of the friends of Mr. Abbey and for the consideration that he was the older practitioner". Then there were Thomas Scriven and P. E. Hicks who had both acted as Mr. Abbey's deputy, and Mr. John Jeffery, of the Parade, Market Square.

The Coroner was elected at a meeting of the Town Council and one point of dissension was whether the new man ought to be not a lawyer but a medical man (perhaps one who could understand the niceties of the amount of laudanum that ought to be put into infants' cordial!) The doctor suggested was named Buxton but despite a good deal of support for him it was held that he had entered the field too late. In the event John Becke, who was a Liberal, received virtually unanimous support.

Meantime George Abbey had been buried in All Saints Churchyard which was then in a ghoulish state, as an inquiry of two years earlier had pointed out, when there were two rival schemes for setting up a general cemetery on the outskirts of the town. George Abbey, along with the music dealer Abel, had been among the leading backers of one of these schemes. The advertisement for their Northampton Cemetery Company pointed out the evils of interment in crowded places in the midst of thickly populated districts.

"Most of the burial places in Northampton are in the heart of the town and overcrowded to an excess that makes decent interment impossible. In the parish of All Saints containing a population of nearly 9,000 the want of space is such that in many cases corpse is piled upon corpse until scarcely the depth of 18 inches divides the living from the dead." In 1844 there was room at All Saints for only a dozen new graves. In St. Mary's (situated immediately south of Castle Hill Chapel) it was almost impossible to make a grave of eight feet deep without disturbing human remains. At the newer St. Katharine's, on the other hand, there was room for sixty or seventy new graves.

At All Saints the method of determining whether a plot was fit for more burials was for the sexton to take a pole or probe stick and press it into the ground. If no resistance was met, digging could commence.

The special need for more room resulted from the immense increase in population—from 10,000 in 1821 to about 25,000.

The solicitor for the Northampton Cemetery Company project was John Jeffery, one of the unsuccessful would-be Coroners. The rival Northampton General Cemetery Company, which did succeed, was solicited by John Becke, the elected Coroner. Between the opposing cemetery organisations I believe there was eventually a degree of compromise.

However, as this is not a history of interment of human remains, I will reiterate the point I was making some way back that the downfall of the provincial theatre was due to many causes including:

(1) the demand for better standards, reflecting changing public taste and awareness;

(2) the consequent introduction of the touring companies;

(3) the railways which made companies and audiences more mobile;

THEATRE, DAVENTRY

FOR THE BENEFIT OF

Mr. BARRY

GREAT ATTRACTION!!

The Orchestra will be greatly Augmented by several Gentlemen, who have on this occasion kindly given their Services

First appearance of Mr. T. Yateman,

WHO WILL SING SEVERAL POPULAR SONGS.

Three Pieces never Acted here, The Charcoal Burner.----Wandering Minstrel.----The Mummy.----New Comic Songs, Dances, &c.

The MUMMY, 3000 Years Old.

MR. BARRY, AS

On Friday Evening, January 8th, 1847,

Mr. BARRY begs most respectfully to announce to his Friends and the Public of Daventry and its Vicinity, that his Benefit will take place on the above Evening, and he trusts the Entertainment selected for their Amusement, will secure

---

THEATRE, DAVENTRY.

FOR THE

BENEFIT OF MR. ABEL,

AND HIS LAST APPEARANCE WITH HIS CELEBRATED DOG HECTOR.

On MONDAY Evening, May 29th. 1848.

Will be presented a NEW DRAMA, founded on an event occured in London, in 1747, and Dramatized for the purpose of shewing the high training of Mr. ABEL'S Dog HECTOR, replete with novel effects, and startling situations, entitled

FOOT PAD JOE,

INCIDENTS. &c.

The Residence of Mr. Westwood, at Charing Cross—Dog of the Abbey The Rivals—Dark and Gloomy Wood—
The Robber discovered by his fireside
Terrific Staggle,
Daniel Saved by
THE DOG.

Road near London—
Murderous Compact—
Entrance to Mr. Westwood's Apartment.

The ROBBER
The Stolen WILL.
Escape of Joe—Rose suspected—Tableaux.
Act 2. Room at the Abbey—Richard's Remorse—Insolent Footman
Duplicate Will, the Desk
**The DOG opens
THE DESK!!!**
Joe Cramp, the Murderer,

And takes from it the
Real Will—The Family
in distress—Cramp's Bed
Room over the Stable—
secret evidence—William's search—
Discovery of the
Murderer's Apparel.
Lonely Wood, Joe
Seized by the Dog
His Escape—Justice
Chamber—A Magistrate's
Duty—Rose Maylie's
Innocence proved—
£500 REWARD!!!
The Pursuit—Richard
and Joe in danger—the
Alarm—Escape of Joe
up the Ladder followed
by the DOG,—Death of
the MURDERERS by
THE DOG,

Mr. A. ABEL,

Mr. Westwood, Mr. STYLES. William Seymour, Mr. G. NELSON. Richard Harvey,
Mr. HARGRAVE, B. Daniel Daisy. Mr. F. MORGAN. Maghistus. Mr. R. HARGRAVE.
Rose Maylie, Mrs. HARGRAVE. Emma, Miss GOODWIN. Betty Butterup Miss L. JACKMAN.
The Dog of the Abbey, by the CELEBRATED DOG HECTOR.

DAVENTRY, 1848 (above) and 1847 (right) *(Left Daventry Town Council; right, Northamptonshire Record Office)*

(4) the Theatre Act of 1843 relaxing restrictions on the length of seasons;
(5) the period of the Hungry Forties which meant that some had not money for soup, let alone the spiritual food of the drama;

and pass on to a theatrical interment, that of the Lincoln Company, which had opened the Northampton Theatre forty-one years before.

Thus from many causes the Henry Jackmans of the theatre world were facing an onslaught of change whose effect on the circuits was to be as radical as that of television on the music halls almost exactly a century later. To parallel the title of my previous book, *Death of a Theatre*, this was to be the *Death of the Provincial Theatre*.

After about a century of strolling the Lincoln Company came to its end in 1847. I do not know the precise date but as Squadron Leader John Richards, of Oakham, is researching a history of the circuit the full story will no doubt be told in due course.

One interesting speculation is why the Lincoln Company perished in 1847, while the Jackman Company was able to carry on for another fifteen years. A cynic might say that it was because the manager of the "Lincoln", William Robertson, had so many children that he didn't know what to do. Robertson had no fewer than twenty-two, nearly three times as many as Henry Jackman had had. Even more remarkable than the actual number of the Robertson brood is the fact that the two of them who achieved great theatrical fame were the very first and the very last. The oldest, T. W. Robertson, born at Newark on January 29, 1829, was to write a play which was a turning point of theatre history, while the youngest, Madge Robertson, was to be made a Dame (Dame Madge Kendal) for her services to the stage.

There had been a fair share of trial and tribulation for Thomas Shaftoe Robertson, often referred to as "The Mogul", we learn from Dame Madge's memoirs. She was his great-niece. Old Tom, manager of the Lincoln Company when it opened the Northampton theatre, had soldiered on in the circuit until he died at one of its ports of call, Huntingdon, on the last day of August, 1831, "without one struggle or even a sigh", as his widow recorded in her diary.

After his death the company battled on for another sixteen years before fading away in a state of penury. At first the management was in the hands of Tom Robertson's widow, a remarkable lady as well as a fine actress. Her frank diary gives a fair picture of the state of things: "The theatre has been open four nights and the business bad. I fear I shall again lose a heavy sum and if so I think I shall sing 'Oundle Farewell!'" The song was not necessary for a few days later the tune was changed: "The great excitement of the week is over and within a few pounds of last year. Bad enough 'tis true but I am grateful even as it is. I have sent £20 to Boston, £20 to Newark, and £5 to Wisbech so there is £45 debt paid. God give me the means through his mercy to pay everyone and I will ask no more."

The old lady died the week before Christmas in 1855 at the age of eighty-seven so she was alive to see the end of the company. Her name appears on playbills at Peterborough for 1832 and 1838 but in due course the day-to-day running of the company passed to her nephew William and in 1834 it is William's reactions to a thin house which are recorded in the diary of William Charles Macready, the great tragedian who played with the Lincoln Company as a guest star at Louth, which was among the towns which diversified the company's movements, in an effort, no doubt, to revive their flagging fortunes.

On the first night of his engagement Macready was ready to go on stage when Robertson appeared with a face full of dismay, the diary of the tragedian recalls.

"He began to apologise and I guessed the remainder. 'Bad House?'

" 'Bad, sir! There's no one!'

" 'What, nobody at all?'

" 'Not a soul, sir, except the Warden's party in the boxes.'

" 'What the devil? Not one person in the pit or gallery?'—" 'Oh yes, there are one or two.'

" 'Are there five?'—" 'Oh yes, five.'

" 'Then go on : we have no right to give ourselves airs if the people do not choose to come and see us : go on at once!'

" 'Mr. Robertson was evidently astonished at what he thought my philosophy : being accustomed, as he said, to being blown up by his stars when the houses were bad.' "

This incident reminds me of the closing years of the life of the New Theatre, Abington Street, Northampton, leading up to its demise in 1958 and demolition in 1960. I saw a circus go through its entire routine for a dozen and Christopher Fry's *The Lady's Not for Burning* performed to a handful by a company including John Gielgud, Pamela Brown, Peter Bull, Richard Burton, Claire Bloom, Esme Percy, Harcourt Williams, Eliot Makeham and Nora Nicholson.

The trials of the fading Robertson management are well illustrated by a story related by Edward Stirling who wrote 200 plays and performed with various companies : "At Sheffield in 1846 my benefit was to be half the receipts of an evening. Mrs. Robertson kindly invited me one evening to tea in a family way. The repast over, Mr. Robertson quitted the room with all his children, leaving the baby, Mrs. R. and myself. She could talk as will be seen. She painted a mournful picture of bad business, expenses of a home, difficulty in paying actors and winding up with many compliments on my kindness of heart." In short, Stirling never did get his money. Asked to wait first one week and then another he finished up months later with an offer of knives and spoons in lieu!

And so, leaving the Lincolnites tottering, we return to Northampton where in the same year of 1847 one Press comment was that the theatre was built when the town was small "yet a full house is a sight seldom seen within the walls, with a population of three times the number".

After the Northampton Spring week the Jackman Company moved on to Buckingham and then to Wellingborough. In July they were back in Northampton for a very special occasion which must surely have altered the rule of poor support. This was not only the week of Assize but also of the staging in Northampton of the Royal Agricultural Show, then held in a different town each year.

The Assize Week was one of the factors determining a company's movements, though a minor one compared with fairs, races, market days etc. Many an audience included the judge, counsel and members of the grand jury, a body of well-heeled members of the community who screened cases before they went to trial, to determine whether there was a "true bill" to go before the court : if not the matter proceeded no farther. At Northampton there was a material parallel between the real-life drama of the Assize Court and the make-believe goings-on on the stage, not a quarter-of-a-mile away. The courts civil and criminal were divided only by a curtain of green baize.

But it was the Royal Agricultural Show on Northampton Racecourse which provided the special incentive for the extra Northampton appearance. It was, said the Mercury, the most exciting week Northampton had ever known.

"No belle at her first ball was ever more intensely anxious to look dazzlingly charming than our town to look handsome and gratified in the eyes of her neighbour, country." For months past the town had been in a state of excitement and preparation for what was to be the biggest R.A.S. to date. An area of nearly 20 acres of the Racecourse had been enclosed and covered in with a range of 37 sheds for cattle, sheep, implements etc. Each shed was 77 yards long. Adjacent was the huge tent of the Royal Horticultural Society.

The Monday morning, July 19, was hectic. "The first train from London imported a motley group of waiters upon extraordinary events. Never came such a corps of ambulatory arts. The musical especially. Double basses broke your shins at every second; harps thrust their 'sea-maiden' faces in your face; loud bassoons opened their huge mouth at you and doubling drums kicked their way towards the scene of action—all the miscellaneous apparatus of mirth and laughter jostled together and with grave business-like aspect pressed up Bridge Street" (at the lower end of which the town's railway station was then situated).

"A vast quantity of cattle also arrived—plethoric pigs and cream white darlings of sheep made their way to the Racecourse during the day."

A dinner was given to vast numbers in a pavilion in Waterloo, Derngate, to where the Corporation made a procession from the George Hotel, at three-thirty. When the affair ended at eight there was a tremendous rush to be on the train leaving Bridge Street at half past. "The train was crammed within and without. On top of the carriages were multitudes of people intent on self-immolation under the first arch or tunnel on the line. A vigorous onslaught of railway police was repulsed at the first charge by the determined outsiders among whom were several ladies but the arrival of reinforcements and the threat that the train would not leave while they remained gave victory to the constituted authority and the dislodged proceeded forthwith to attack the interior of the carriages (already as full as they could hold) and succeeded in many cases in establishing a position on the laps or feet of the indignant occupants."

Charles Dillon, of the London and Continental theatres, was the star guest with the Jackman Company, appearing in *Fabien the Black Doctor, Virginius, The Wonder! A Woman Keeps a Secret* and *The Lady of Lyons.* Henry Hartley was back again as a guest and there was the added and unusual attraction of the "Celebrated Female Ethiopian Serenaders, from the Queens Concert Rooms, London, with their far-famed negro melodies".

Competition for the shillings of the gentry and the pence of the working man was intense indeed that week. The Great Concert Hall, Newland, had the Distin Family performing on their "new and extraordinary instruments, the silver sax horns and sax tubas". They were presented by Mr. Klitz who kept a music and pianoforte warehouse on the Market Square and who introduced a special song for the agricultural occasion, "Hurrah for the Land, Mother Earth". At the Angel Assembly Room John Parry was "as amusingly comic as ever" and may well have been the former manager of the theatre. His concert was arranged by Mr. Abel, whose music shop had been on the Market Square since the 1790s and was to last until 1970. At the Mechanics' Institute were the Lantum Ethiopian Serenaders, from the Egyptian Hall, London, and a musical entertainment by Henry Phillips, from the Theatres Royal, Drury Lane and Covent Garden.

Another form of competition was presented by the Penny Theatres which from time to time, without permission in most cases, set up in the town. One such came to Northampton the following November and led to the appearance in court of the wife of the proprietor. Once again, despite the danger that this book may become an edited version of the Northampton Mercury, I feel that to attempt to interfere with the prose of the contemporary journalist would not be an improvement:

"The theatre originally erected its imposing front during the Mop Fair on the Market Square and being driven thence took refuge in the close at the bottom of Scarletwell Street. Its success there was prodigious; overflowing houses and rapturous applause testified how well the qualities of the corps dramatique met the taste of the district. Three performances took place in one night and Charles Smith, the police sergeant who, in the discharge of his duties had taken a box in the dress circle stated that there were at least 300 persons in the house at every performance and at least as many besieging the doors and ready to rush in as soon as the current piece was over. The pathetic nautical drama of 'Black Ey'd Susan' was a special favourite and Smith, being asked by the magistrates as to the character of the performance said it was very good, qualifying his commendation however by adding that you couldn't expect much for a penny. The magistrates informed the parties that they had rendered themselves liable to a penalty of £10 for every performance and unless the theatre was removed that day they would enforce the liability. Mr. Melville, who does the heavy business, sighed and cast his eyes below with a more natural expression than ever he had given to his performance of William. Mrs. Rayner, who at first pleaded that being in the condition of Norval's mother, she was not in travelling case, brightened up and promised to be off that afternoon having evidently looked for something more than a conditional penalty. The parties then left, making a melodramatic bow and going out of the box as if at the side scenes. The police were ordered to see that the promise was fulfilled and in the course of the day 'the cloud-capped towers and gorgeous palaces were packed up and then went each actor upon his ass."

The same procedure was adopted in July, 1849, when a celebrated booth theatre proprietor Jos. Wildman was brought before the Bench for opening a penny theatre in a booth in Barker's Meadow, adjoining Scarletwell Street, without having a licence. He was discharged on condition that he "got out of town".

The visits, official or unofficial, of such establishments to Northampton were blamed for some of the disorder in the streets which appears to have been a feature of town life and this led some Town Councillors to the conclusion that penal fees should be charged. The scale proposed by Mr. Stanton in August, 1848, was as follows :

For every drinking and dancing booth 5 gns. a day.
For every theatrical, wrestling or conjuring booth 3 gns.
For every vehicle containing any exhibition, works of nature etc. 10s.
For every small table for gaming 10s. per day.
For every booth not containing an exhibit, for every 40 square feet, 10s.
    per day and in proportion.

The object, explained Mr. Stanton, was not so much to tax the visitors but to stop them coming altogether. The fees were to apply on the Market Square, public streets and lanes of the town, but would not apply to any regular occupiers or to persons living within seven miles of the borough. The remainder, the objectives of his attack, were principally strangers who never spent a farthing in the borough more than they were obliged, yet who took a lot of money out of it.

Alderman Porter wanted to know what the young folk of the town would think if they approved this scale of charges. Mr. Jeffery wanted all the shows bundled off to the Racecourse, out of harm's way. It was agreed that the matter required some further consideration.

The disorders in town which the Stanton scale of fees was intended to mitigate was referred to in the Council debate and in various letters to the Press. Council member Mr. Kilpin said in the Council Chamber that in Gold Street (which led to the theatre) the conversation on Saturday nights was abominable beyond all description. One of the letters, published in September, 1847, stated : "Dissolute women and groups, nay swarms, of young persons obstruct or sweep the pavements in the leading streets; and so loud and loud are their conversations and remarks and so boisterous and vulgar is their behaviour that for prudent females to go forth at all is very unpleasant and to walk alone is dangerous; while the very quiet and some-times the sanctity of our dwellings are invaded by the oaths, curses, and indecencies which are uttered beneath our windows."

This was followed up by J. Dalton, of the Seminary of St. Felix, Leicester Road, Northampton, who said that he had been in town only a few months but that the state of morals among the youth of the town seemed to surpass that of every place he had resided in. He was an R.C. priest.

"Well does your correspondent remark that it is dangerous for any prudent woman to be in the streets after nine or ten o'clock . . . idle groups that congregate evening after evening in The Parade, along our walks, and indeed along most of the principal streets; the oaths and curses that resound in our ears and the indecencies committed I may not dwell on. We have abundance of churches, chapels, schools and zealous teachers and yet how little progress seems to be made in checking vice and immorality."

However orderly or disorderly the town may have been by way of manners or morals it appears to have been a pretty filthy place in the matter of cleanliness. A number of vicars and curates banded together to send a letter to the Press bemoaning the insanitary state of the town, especially in view of the chance of cholera coming again. "It is well known by past experience that dissolute and intemperate habits imbued in the want of cleanliness renders attacks of this frightful disease almost certainly fatal, while a careful regard to the cleanliness, both of the residence and locality tends materially to mitigate its malignancy." Landlords, they averred, should be made to pay more attention to the internal purity of the dwellings of the poor.

The shows came up for debate in the Town Council again in July, 1849, when there was a move to ban all shows from the Market Square and Wood Hill and to restrict them to the open space on the Mounts.

The Mayor (Joseph Wykes) was interested to know whether he had the power to permit shows or not, harking back to customs persisting from the days when the travelling company would send a man ahead to gain the approval of the Mayor and magistrates.

Most showmen applying for leave, he said, asserted that in other towns where they had shown it had been by permission of the Mayor and if it was the Mayoral privilege in other towns it should also be in Northampton. Some shows were unobjectionable, claimed the first citizen, and prevented many of the poorer classes from frequenting the public houses.

The attitude of some members showed how narrow-nosed they were. Mr. Kilpin said that such events brought together parties who could ill afford to spend anything. The principal visitors were children who thus acquired habits of idleness or vice. He knew of an instance (one can sense the quivering sense of indignation with which he related this one) in which a pauper sold a loaf provided by the Guardians to take her children to Penny Shows.

On the other hand Thomas Sharp was averse to interfering with the amusements of the common people. Mr. Marshall said there was no objection to military bands playing on the Market Square.

In the end a good old Northampton conclusion was reached. Next business was moved and passed. Which meant they had decided to do nothing. The scene now moves back from the streets to the theatre.

Enter : Frederick Morgan. He was to play a leading part in the fortunes of the Jackman Company and family. When he first figured on a Northampton playbill in March, 1848, he was described as "of the Theatre Royal, Manchester," but he cannot be traced there. When Morgan married Harriet Jackman at Stratford-upon-Avon on May 26, 1849, his father, James Morgan, was described as a comedian, so it was evidently a theatrical family. Frederick was born in London in about 1823 : this information comes from the Northampton Census returns of 1851.

There is little apart from the earlier letters to fill in the characteristics of members of the Jackman Company, unlike those of the Lincoln. No one seems to have mentioned any of them in books of theatrical memoirs.

Photographs as well as anecdotes are conspicuous by their absence. If Henry Hartley or Sophia Jackman ever called in the photographic studio which Mr. Whitlock opened in Mercers Row in Northampton Town Centre in February, 1844, not one of the pictures has turned up so far. Nor are there any likenesses of the company during performances.

The Whitlock studio, by the way, operated under licence from a patent by Mr. Beard. "In the space of five seconds on a bright day the object is reflected on to a metal plate with a fidelity which is absolutely startling. There is no more possibility of mistaking the likeness than there is of mistaking the reflection of an individual in a looking glass. Not the features merely, but the particular expression of the moment. The ghostly hue which characterised the portraits taken by Daguerrotype is altogether done away with." Whitlock, who also had establishments at Birmingham, Leamington and Coventry, charged a guinea for a picture in a case, colouring 2s. 6d. extra. He offered the licence for sub-letting in Wellingborough, Peterborough, Kettering, Daventry and other towns in the county.

At the time of Morgan's first appearance at Northampton, in March, 1848, there were others from Manchester, namely Mr. and Mrs. Hargrave. From the Theatre Royal, Brighton, came Mr. Ticehurst, musical director, and Mr. William Ticehurst and Mr. C. Osborne. There were also Mr. Barry, of Sheffield; Mr. and Mrs. Allen, of Birmingham; Miss Eliza Case, of Bristol; and Mr. Nelson, of Liverpool. The stars were Mr. and Mrs. Vandenhoff, of the Covent Garden and Haymarket theatres.

"*How to Settle Accounts with Your Laundress*" was one of the titles of that season, which was helped by a successful race meeting.

Novelty entertainments in Northampton during this period of the late 1840s included a Rock Band (!) and the Female American Serenaders.

The Rock Band appeared at the Mechanics Institute. Yes it was 1848, not 1958. The sound they produced was not the strumming of guitars mingled with the hooting of hot saxophones but exactly what the name implied—it was a *ROCK* band; the musicians of Messrs. Richardson played on instruments made of rock. The tone produced was "quite delicious" according to the Mercury. The explanation was that Mr. Richardson had been a quarry worker and had hit upon the idea, based on the sounds he had heard while at work, of hitting lumps of mineral rock not to break them but to produce a melody. Ranged in lengths, like a piano frame, no doubt, the rocks were hit with wooden mallets. In later years they returned with a new instrumentation as the Rock and Steel Band. The addition of the steel, which is not otherwise elaborated upon, was said to be most noticeable in Handel's Harmonious Blacksmith. The Richardson ensemble also called at Buckingham, Banbury, Brackley, Deddington, Derby, Daventry, Biggleswade, Ampthill, Kettering, Newport Pagnell, Olney, Uppingham, Oakham, Rugby, Towcester, Stony Stratford, Leighton

Buzzard, Olney, Stamford, Leicester, Market Harborough, Wellingborough, Stony Stratford and Oundle.

Two months after the Jackman visit, the "Celebrated Female American Serenaders" appeared at the theatre, playing banjos, tambourines, bones, castanets, triangle, bells etc. They came with top credentials, being said to have been praised in such influential journals as The Times, Morning Post, Evening Sun, Globe, Literary Gazette, Court Journal, Bell's Life in London, Dispatch, Lady's Newspaper, Musical World, United Service Gazette, Sunday Times, Pictorial Times, Douglas Jerrold's Weekly Newspaper, Bell's Messenger, Observer, Family Times, Satirist, Theatrical Journal, Post Magazine, The Curtain etc.

Which seems to prove one thing. The Victorians do not appear to have been short of reading matter.

Another unusual attraction at the theatre in November, 1851, was a Bloomer Display. The daring new feminine style was in fact the subject of three shows in Northampton that week, the others being at the New Hall and the Corn Exchange. The Herald was disgusted—"They were all, as they deserved to be, miserable failures. The New Hall ladies were pursued from Bedford for £3 which they had decamped without paying. At the close of the performance on Monday it was found that the money taker had decamped without paying for the use of the hall or the use of the piano."

Who now owned the Northampton theatre? I confess to some mystification on this point. The ownership of the site was vested in St. John's Hospital. Of the three proprietors when the question was last resolved George Abbey and Charles Markham were now dead. But there were still holders of the original shares : where they fitted in is not clear. That they did still exist is confirmed in a document I found when turning out some old papers in a spring-clean at the newspaper office where I work and came across a share transfer document dated May 28, 1851. Just where it came from I do not know : I can only assume that someone must have given it to me during my dozen years as gossip columnist of the Northampton Chronicle and Echo. It recorded the sale of four-sixtieths of the shares— the original funding was by sixty shares of £25 each—numbered 43–46, by The Most Honourable Charles Douglas, Marquess of Northampton and others, executors of the late the Most Honourable Marquess of Northampton deceased, to Mr. Nathaniel Wells Freeman.

Originally these shares would have cost £100. Now this fifteenth part of the equity changed hands for £24 19s. The new owner, Mr. Freeman, was a printer. The document states quite clearly that the theatre was a leasehold building.

Now it becomes necessary to explain the title of this book. It was in March, 1848, that the first reference occurred to the Northampton theatre as being "Royal". *(Page 150.)*

How does a theatre become "Royal"? To be properly "Royal" in the sense of the old Royal patents legitimising the very existence of the establishment was a rare honour. The two principal Patent theatres were, of course, the Theatre Royal, Drury Lane, and the Theatre Royal, Covent

Garden. There were a number of patents in the provinces including the Theatre Royal, Windsor, which gained the honour because of the Royal Patronage from Windsor Castle (the Windsor Theatre, it will be recalled, provided the Northampton theatre with its second manager, Mr. Mudie) and theatres at Bath and Norwich (1768), York and Hull (1769), Liverpool (1771), Manchester (1775), Chester (1777), Bristol and Newcastle (1778), and Birmingham.

At Birmingham it was only at the second attempt that the Royal Patent was secured. The first, in 1777, was unsuccessful, the necessary Parliamentary Bill not getting through. When the second attempt did succeed thirty years later an immediate outcome was that the manager, M'Cready, handed in his notice, not because he did not fancy managing a Royal house but because the committee controlling it tried to double the rent from £500 to £1,000 a year. Their ground for this was probably that the accolade meant that the theatre was no longer restricted to seasons of sixty days, the maximum which the magistrates were empowered to grant under the Act of 1788. This limitation had been ended by the Act of 1843.

But in the case of the Northampton theatre and the scores of other "theatres royal", there was no Act of Parliament or letter from His or Her Majesty giving permission. One day it was the Northampton Theatre : the next day it was the Northampton Theatre Royal. The extra word was just tacked on at will. If you wished your theatre to be associated with Royalty as well as Nobility and Gentry you simply included the magic word when writing out your next batch of copy for the newspaper or bill printer and that was it. In the case of Northampton the word magic is appropriate for a magician seems to have assisted in effecting the transformation.

I must admit that it surprised me a great deal when I came to realise how little the word "Royal" signified in this context, especially when it is remembered how jealously the right to use it is guarded in the case of "By Royal Appointment" in other spheres.

But such is the case. I asked the eminent theatre historian Sybil Rosenfeld for confirmation. "Strictly speaking the title was allowable only to those theatres which had secured a Royal Patent but in practice anyone seems to have used it with impunity," she explained.

The actress Fanny Kemble (1809-93) made a wry comment on the situation in a letter she wrote during a visit to Plymouth in 1845. "All the theatres where I act—indeed, as far as I can see, all the theatres throughout the country—are Theatres Royal : and with very good reason, for they are certainly all equally patronised by Royalty." That is to say, not at all! Fanny Kemble did, by the way, make an appearance at Northampton in October, 1854, but not at the "Royal" establishment : her evening of Shakespearean readings was given at the Corn Exchange.

The first "Theatre Royal" billing at Northampton appears to have been in 1848 but it was not consistently adopted after that, the "Royal" disappearing in '49 but reappearing when Mr. Jacobs, "Wizard of Wizards", waved his wand and achieved the change in his advertisement of February 23, 1850. Jacobs himself, who was subsequently to move on to Rugby and

Leamington after his two nights at Northampton, could claim some Royal associations. A bill for him at the Daventry Theatre in February, 1846, pointed out that he had appeared before Her Majesty and Prince Albert, their Majesties the King and Queen of the Belgians, and Her Royal Highness the late Princess Augusta, not to mention five Dukes, a Marquis and seven Earls.

It was thus after forty-two years' existence, and with another thirty-six years to go before the last performance, that the Northampton Theatre began to be a Theatre Royal. Why did I adopt the title "Theatre Un-Royal"? Perhaps Theatre Semi-Royal would have been more accurate but in choosing as I did I wanted to emphasise how truly un-royal it really was with its tinyness, bad ventilation etc. etc. (apart from a journalistic desire to think up a title which no one else appears to have used).

In deference to my old friend Henry Jackman I would have liked to have called the book "Old Henry's House" for it was his longer than it was anyone else's. But this might have given the casual customer the idea that it was a novel or advice on property conversion. Instead this title has been relegated to this part of the book.

Perhaps the most telling act of scorn against the un-royal theatre was one which had the Clochemerle touch. It happened in December, 1852, when the theatre was already "Royal". This did not prevent the Improvement Commissioners dropping a plan to put a urinal in Dychurch Lane and deciding instead to site it at the east side of the theatre. Mr. J. Jeffery observed that as it was proposed to put the object near a window litigation might be avoided if they consulted the trustees of the theatre first.

Whatever was said at the conference the urinal was in fact erected. We know this because of the protests about this "intolerable nuisance" in later years which led to its removal.

Now came the time for the final exit of Old Henry Jackman. He had been in declining health for some time but still carried on touring, virtually the only life he knew. One of the facts I needed to establish was where and when he died. It could have been anywhere within a fifty-mile radius of Northampton but it was somehow fitting to find that he died and was buried only 100 yards from the Town Centre office where I was doing a good deal of research about him.

His demise came on September 29, 1852, during the season at Northampton. The death certificate gives his lodgings address as merely Horsemarket, 100 yards from the theatre. From there he was taken just round the corner to St. Katharine's Church, which had been opened in 1839 to cope with the growing population of All Saints Parish. Today the church which was erected by the early Victorians to cope with too many people in the vicinity has been pulled down and the area grassed over as a war memorial. It was demolished by the Georgians of 1950 because of the decline both in the population of the town centre and in the habit of church-going which led to congregations of a mere half-dozen in the latter years. Many of the housing areas which were adjacent to it have been replaced by shops, offices and industrial premises.

Thus the site of the altar before which Old Henry's coffin stood before being taken out to be buried in the churchyard is now marked only by a small cairn of stones near the war memorial plaque.

Henry, who was sixty-six, was said on the death certificate to have died of "old age". His death was notified to the Registrar by his eldest son Henry, this being one of the few indications that he was still in existence. As I have mentioned, he was a musician and they rarely came in for mentions.

No plan of the grave sites appears to have been made when the memorials were taken away so we do not know precisely where the Old Boy sleeps along with his wife, brought to Northampton from Banbury five years later.

Today the lawn is a central oasis of quiet sward among redevelopment on a vast and largely obliterative scale. There is the Saxon Inn, just over the old churchyard wall, eight storeys high; there is the national centre of Barclaycard just over the other side of Horsemarket. Gold Street, where people made their way to the theatre, is shortly to be pedestrianised, the traffic banished. If Old Henry could have chosen his own grave, it could scarcely have been in a more peaceful or appropriate spot.

It remains in the middle of things, not like the great expanse of Northampton General Cemetery set up in Northampton's Billing Road as a commercial enterprise and abandoned by the company in 1959 when it ceased to pay a dividend because it was virtually full up. Today that cemetery is also virtually cleared, levelled and grassed but unlike St. Katharine's Churchyard, hardly anyone ever goes there.

Henry Junior was the oldest son and it might have been expected that he would take over. In fact the announcements a few weeks after the death of his father seem to suggest that he had done so, as a partner with brother Charles. The title was Messrs. H. and C. Jackman. But he was the quiet man of the orchestra and, perhaps following a family discussion, it was decided that Charles should run the company in partnership with his brother-in-law Frederick Morgan, the husband of Harriet Jackman.

So now the old firm had a new title. It was Jackman and Morgan.

In his will, made at Stratford-upon-Avon five months before his death, during the season there. Old Henry left his money in Bank of England $3\frac{1}{4}$ per cent annuities, his books and other printing, material interests in theatres etc. to his widow, with, upon her death, "the remainder to my sons Henry, Charles and George Jackman and to my daughters Eliza Fenton, Caroline Hartley, Frances Partleton, Sophia, Harriet and Louisa to be divided in equal parts."

There are two surprises in the will. Why did Old Henry use married names for three of his married daughters but not for the fourth (Harriet)? Perhaps this was an old will he had carried about for some time, since before her marriage during the Stratford season of 1849? The other, bigger surprise, is the reference to a third son George: nowhere else has he appeared during my researches. Whether he was the odd child out who did not choose to stay with the family, or whether he was another "tacit" member of the band we shall perhaps never know.

One of Old Henry's last seasons had been the final one by the company at Warwick. The advertisement in the Warwickshire Advertiser for September 4, 1852, was of the briefest possible nature: "Theatre, Warwick. Open

Race Week under management of Mr. Jackman. For Particulars see the bills of the day." And that was that. No editorial coverage, as there had been before, on this last visit to the town.

The previous year, 1851, an attempt had been made to clean up the atmosphere of Warwick, which degenerated considerably at the times of the race meetings. The magistrates ordered that no booths for the sale of intoxicants should be opened on the course on the Sunday preceding the races. "The immense amount of drunkenness which hitherto indulged these occasions was happily prevented. It is to be hoped that on future occasions a similar course will be pursued," said the newspaper, "so that the objections of many who condemn these annual gatherings on the grounds of their immorality may to some extent be swept away. The fact that an immense number of thieves and bad characters of the worst possible description congregate at the Races cannot be denied but it has ever been the same in this as in other countries and ever will remain so, so that however innocent the amusement afforded the public—the sharper the pickpocket and, we will add, the cut-throat too, are sure to present themselves and so dash with impurity that which otherwise would be a bright and clear stream of enjoyment."

The theatre tributary of this stream of enjoyment ended with the Jackman season of 1852 and shortly afterwards the theatre, in Theatre Street, was supplanted by a slaughterhouse.

The year Old Henry died saw an end to the performances of another public entertainer, in public, anyway. On Tuesday, March 16, 1852, the last public execution took place in Northampton. As it happened, it was of a woman, Elizabeth Pinckard who suffered "the extreme penalty" on a gallows outside the County Gaol in Angel Lane. She had murdered her mother-in-law for her husband's inheritance of insurance money when they were behind with the rent and threatened with eviction from their cottage.

There had been a strong rumour that the hanging was to take place the previous Friday and people flocked in from the countryside to see it, resulting in scenes of drunkenness and riot. On the actual day the large crowd consisted mostly of townsfolk and, said the Herald, "on no public occasion has our populace behaved with more propriety . . . a general feeling of awe pervaded the assembly and scores of persons were affected even to tears".

The actual public performance by the executioner was very brief. "All necessary preparations were made in the prison and everything on the drop being in readiness not more than two or three minutes elapsed from the appearance of the criminal before the sentence was completed."

As he was not implicated in the crime Elizabeth's husband, or rather widower, got the £1,000 due to him. But he already had the expectation mortgaged.

Not only was this the final public execution in Northampton; it was the first hanging in town since 1834.

Scene Three

JACKMAN & MORGAN

For the final years of the Jackman Saga we must therefore strike the flag bearing a single name and run up a new banner: "Jackman and Morgan". If things had gone differently it might have been Jackman and Hartley, or Jackman and Fenton, or even Jackman and Partleton, but that is idle speculation.

The new partners appear to have got on well together, the bachelor son and the son-in-law. If they had any disputations no sign of it appears in the records I have examined. Had there been, it would not have been surprising for these must have been anxious years, with heart-searching as to what policies should be adopted to stop the rot. In fact its gradual process was as inevitable as that of a cancer. Nothing the pair could have devised, permutated or improvised could have long postponed the end of the company. It was simply part of history, as inevitable as the disappearance of horses from the streets, or the appearance of television screens in the corner of every living room.

The December after Old Henry's death found the company on one of its visits to Wellingborough ("The company is the best that has visited this town") and this was followed, with possibly an intervening visit to Banbury, by a two-and-a-half month season at Stratford-upon-Avon. One of the early decisions of the management was to cultivate Stratford. Possibly the fact that Henry Hartley and his wife, along with Sophia Jackman, were there at the Golden Lion may have had something to do with it. It is quite likely that some of the company stayed at that hostelry and we can imagine Hartley holding court in his bar after the show, talking about the days when he was on the road, with barmaid Sophia perhaps chipping in occasionally. Certainly many a tale about Old Henry's mannerisms and oddities would come up for nostalgic recollection.

As a keen Freemason, Hartley was more respected in his new role as landlord of the Golden Lion Inn than in his days as a strolling player. It was especially appropriate that he should become "mine host" of this particular inn for the True Blue Shakespeare Club had been formed there. And the Bard of Avon Lodge of Freemasons, No. 1080, met there on the first Monday of each month.

Hartley now owned shares in the Shakespeare Theatre (or Rooms) and

Hartley being Hartley he was not content merely to be a capitalist in the enterprise. He appeared in many performances there and other places on the circuit and from his billing, especially at Stratford and Warwick, it is clear that he became a well-known and well-liked figure in the area.

He also entered public life, serving as a town councillor. A search of the records (which I have not had time to undertake and which is rather outside the compass of this particular book) would no doubt reveal some interesting facts about his political standpoint.

Theatrical and political engagements were not the only ones which Hartley allowed to drag him from his bar in the Golden Lion. In November, 1853, we find him among those enlivening the proceedings with a song when a Masonic Chapter connected with the Pomfret Lodge was inaugurated at Northampton. Six years later we find him singing "Freedom of Opinion" at the Mayoral Banquet, attended by 350, at the Angel Hotel, Northampton, when he had the honour of being taken note of in a speech by Mr. George Hunt, M.P., who said that Hartley's song had been so amusing that he had forgotten his speech! The Mayor who footed the bill for this banquet in 1859 was William Roberts.

As Jackman and Morgan returned to the Stratford Theatre in 1853 some further changes had been made; for most of the year it listened now to the arguments of lawyers, being used as a County Court. So that before they could appear the company had to foot the bill for some rather novel expenses "in fitting up the stage and restoring court, as per Mr. Gibbs bill". In 1853 it amounted to £5 6s. on top of the rent of £20. The County Court paid a rent of £50 so that by having both the stage and the law as tenants the proprietors found themselves in the black at last. The records show that Hartley received dividends as follows : 1852, £1 17s.; 1854, £2 2s. 4d.; 1856 £1 17s.; 1858, £1 1s. 2d. : and 1861, the year that he died £1 6s. 6d. In 1863 his executors drew £1 11s. 9d.

Having mentioned his death, perhaps I should polish off the story of Henry Hartley before getting back into sequence. Although only in his late forties he became gravely ill and had to give up the Golden Lion. It was in the hope of preserving his health that he instead became goods agent to the Great Western Railway. He also gave up public office. It was in vain however, and he died on June 30, 1861, at the age of forty-eight. Obituaries appeared not only in the local Press but in the Sunday Times as well. This paper described him as "a man of refined tastes in works of art and an honest and conscientious lover of his dramatic profession, in which, until lately, he occasionally assisted any local or other good work. He was a member of the Reunion Club and of other London and provincial literary and artistic societies, a town councillor and an indefatigable member of the Shakespeare Society."

And so, back into sequence. In fact there is not a great deal to say about the Jackson and Morgan years. They tried a number of experiments, a principal one being longer seasons, particularly at Stratford. It naturally follows that if they stayed longer in one place, they did not visit so many places. They tried new towns. At Stratford there is an application to open the theatre there sent on from the Theatre Royal, Ludlow, by Charles

Jackman. On at least one occasion they appeared at Reading. Bedford, Banbury and Northampton continued to figure in their itinerary. There are probably some towns they adopted which have so far eluded me. I should appreciate any information, to complete the more detailed history of the company which I hope to be able to produce (that is, of course, if you are reading this while I am still alive).

In 1853 the company did not turn up for the Northampton Spring Races and in their default a local music retailer named Klitz provided entertainment by the Collins Family at the Corn Exchange, along with several distinguished singers, including Mr. A. C. Rowland, Miss Louisa Pyne, and Mr. W. H. Harrison. On the second night there was such a crowded audience that they overflowed on to the orchestra platform.

June saw one of the many feats of marathon walking which occupied the newspaper columns from time to time. In six days Alfred Elston, of Northampton, aged eighteen, walked three hundred miles back and forth the ten miles or so to and from Northampton to Wellingborough, an especially notable feat, it was pointed out, on this "uneven and difficult road".

There was now no necessity to walk, even for actors, nor yet submit to the saddle or swaying stage coach. You could go by rail. In the sphere of amusement as opposed to business travel, you could take an excursion from Peterborough, Oundle, Thrapston, Higham Ferrers, Wellingborough and Northampton to Liverpool, Manchester, Chester, Bangor, Conway or Dublin. The return fare to Liverpool was £1 10s. first class or 18s. "enclosed carriage".

A new version of *Uncle Tom's Cabin* was a feature of the 1853 November season of Jackman and Morgan at Northampton.

A firework display on the Market Hill (or Square) by Mr. Gyngell in December had as its highspot a representation of Nelson's Column "40 ft. high, formed by 2,000 jets of fire".

At the Borough Sessions that month a boy named Atkins was described as "an assistant of Mr. Jackman" when he gave evidence against two men charged with stealing twelve pounds of beef. They got four years penal servitude.

In 1854 parking restrictions appear to have been re-introduced in the street leading down to the Northampton Theatre, Gold Street, which on market days was becoming impassable. During his Mayoralties of 1849–51 Francis Parker had introduced regulations that carriers' carts on the south side of the street should range themselves from Hogan's Soda Water Factory to the Crow and Horseshoe while those on the north side should commence at the Wheatsheaf and continue to the west end of the Goat and no further. This had crept into non-observance, there being no traffic wardens in those days. Chaos was the result. In later years Earl Spencer complained that he had not room to drive up the street. Soon no one will be able to drive freely there for the wheeled vehicle is about to be banned and the pedestrian reign supreme.

Witchcraft and sorcery was evidently among the interests of John Becke, secretary of the theatre, for he gave a talk on the subject at the Mechanics Institute in January, 1854.

Amusements of the rural populace at this period included shooting sparrows, which were regarded as pests and could also be made up into a pie. The seventh anniversary meeting of the Harpole Village Sparrow Club on Thursday, January 12, was, however, the last because a few ratepayers there had refused to contribute towards the funds. The first prize of 50s. went to Thomas Farmer for assassinating 1,815 sparrows (whether by shooting or netting is not stated); while Edward Scriven got 30s. for 1,561 and John Lovell 20s. for disposing of a few short of six hundred. In the seven years the Harpolians had accounted for 39,503 of our feathered friends.

The delicate approach was needed in the advertising for an exhibition which came to the Northampton theatre in March, 1854. It was of the Florentine Models which "supply in the most striking and popular form anatomical information to the thousands who are quite precluded from obtaining it so effectively by any other channel. The physiology of health is thus clearly demonstrated and knowledge of the cause of disease is half its cure. It may be that there are those who can desire neither entertainment nor instruction from such an exhibition and whilst extolling the marvellous wonder displayed in the human form divine would shrink from enquiry into the wondrous agencies by which we live, move and have our being. No man, however, shrinks from knowledge of himself."

There were separate sessions for the ladies and the gentlemen, the former being lectured by Mrs. Barker on Tuesday and Thursdays and the latter by Mr. Barker on Mondays, Wednesdays, Fridays and Saturdays. The extra provision for the males is curious in that the advertisement noted that "at Norwich, Bury, Ipswich etc. the days especially appropriated to ladies have been the most numerously attended". No doubt they were intrigued by the new anatomical figure which could be taken to pieces in eighty-six sections and the twelve other models "of special interest to the ladies". At Northampton the ladies were entreated to let no feelings of false delicacy prevent them from seeing the "chaste and celebrated Florentine models". There were in fact "immense numbers" of females present.

Something different to tickle the public's fancy the following month was a band without instruments—Hoffman's Organophonic Band in which the only organ used was the mouth; "It is difficult to persuade oneself that the solos and concerted pieces do not really proceed from wind, stringed, and even percussion instruments. The clashing of a cymbals is given with marvellous truth by a sneeze."

Elliott Galer, later to be lessee of the Leicester Theatre Royal, came to the town in an opera company in December, performing *Lucia di Lammermoor*, *Fra Diavolo* and *The Waterman*.

While it has not a direct bearing on the theatre I feel I must record, in face of all that is said and can be proved about Northamptonians not being progressive folk, that 1855 was the year in which the Mayor, Alderman and Councillors of Northampton petitioned Parliament to be allowed to spend money from the rates on education, pointing out that of 557 criminals arrested in 1854 there were 225 who could not read or write.

Perhaps equally dubious of eligibility is the fact that the same year a fire escape was demonstrated for the first time on the Market Square. I include it because the record says that "no little amusement was caused by the spectacle of the portly form of Charles Smith sliding safely down the escape from the topmost window of the Guildhall".

Letter-writing is surely a public form of amusement (though a very expensive indulgence at the time of writing these lines) so perhaps I may be permitted to chronicle that at this time receiving houses were established for the reception of letters at Mr. Mayger's, chemists, Regent Square; Mr. Foster's, draper, Wellingborough Road; and Mr. Wooding's, Bridge Street. Until then, it would appear, you had to walk to the Post Office in the Drapery to post your letters.

That would be where Old Henry had forwarded on his applications for licences to open in the towns he was next visiting. Some of these letters survive, both of his time and of the Jackman and Morgan partnership. It is in one of these that the clue lies to the fact that the company appeared at Ludlow. From there came an application to the Stratford magistrates on August 20, 1856: "I beg respectfully to solicit the Worshipful the Mayor and the Magistrates of Stratford-on-Avon to grant a licence to open the Stratford Theatre for the usual season commencing on Monday, September 8." On August 9, 1858, there is one written from the Theatre Royal, Northampton. Both are signed by Charles Jackman.

In his time Old Henry had successfully introduced an opera company and this was carried on. Links which had been forged with a company run by Louisa Pyne and Charles Harrison stayed firm. Later this pair were to reach the top of their profession and to be lessees of the Theatre Royal, Covent Garden for the eight seasons ending March, 1864. In March, 1856, the Covent Garden Theatre had been burned down following its being leased by Professor Anderson, "Wizard of the North", who had tried to make up for a bad pantomime season by holding a masquerade at the theatre, in the latter stages of which, in the early morning, the fire began.

In November, 1855, the Northampton theatre was "in court" again when a boy employed as a supernumerary was charged with robbing Henry Corri, of the operatic corps then performing, of a canvas bag and 18s. 6d. Another boy, named Brown, gave evidence that John Hall gave him a halfpenny to hold a cottage "wing" for him and then disappeared. He was apprehended at the Crow and Horseshoe Inn, over the road, drinking gin and port paid for from the proceeds of his crime. Two months' imprisonment.

On the stage the pieces included *The Bohemian Girl*, *The Swiss Cottage* (no doubt the one in which the boy deserted his post at the scenery), *La Figlia del Reggimento* and *The Beggar's Opera*.

That month saw Northampton's first Conservative Mayor for nineteen years—Christopher Markham, whose family had been prominent in town for 100 years and included the former theatre proprietor, Charles Markham.

The Jackman and Morgan Company continued to leave the town to Klitz in the Spring but in May, 1857, there was a week of opera, which seems to have been more popular than drama at this period.

In April, 1856, Thomas Lewis Gery, the man we know as the recipient of the letters of Henry Hartley and George Partleton, lost his wife Elizabeth Anne, at the age of thirty-one. Their home was at West Lodge, Daventry.

In November, 1857, Frances Jackman, Old Henry's widow died at Banbury where she appears to have lived in retirement, at the age of seventy-three. She was brought to Northampton and buried in the same grave as her husband, at St. Katharine's.

During the week of the funeral of his mother Charles Jackman himself appeared in court at Northampton. Not for any misdemeanour, I hasten to add—he appears to have been as uniformly respectable as his late father. He turned up before the magistrates to lay information against an unlicensed theatre which had set itself up in the Mayorhold and was drawing crowded houses at a penny a time. The attraction was the drama, *The Warlock of the Glen*. The magistrates assured Mr. Jackman that he need not trouble himself further—they would see that the squatters should be made to pack up and depart.

The day of the hearing was Thursday, November 12, two days before the funeral. Who was present at the obsequies? There is no record, despite the custom of those days of often listing those who turned up to pay their last respects. Whether Henry Hartley and family managed to get over from Stratford, we cannot tell. Were the Fentons there? In September and October Harry Fenton, the son-in-law, was playing at the Nottingham Theatre so perhaps business kept him away.

An obituary in the Theatrical Observer gives a rare flash-back to the earlier days of the company: "The name of Jackman is familiar to our younger readers and still more known to our advanced subscribers, as the manager of a compact and clever theatrical company which visited, some forty or more years since, Highgate, Uxbridge, Buckingham, Banbury, Stratford-upon-Avon, Leamington, Evesham, Northampton, Bedford, Daventry, etc etc.; many of which towns are still retained by the present director Mr. Charles Jackman. His late father, an excellent comedian, who preceded him in those and many other places, was, at the time of his decease, one of the two oldest managers surviving; the other being Mr. Edward Barnet, who is still living, retired, at Hyde. Mr. Jackman bore a remarkable character for probity and gentlemanly bearing, and left behind him a truly honourable name. He had a worthy partner and helpmate in the lady whose decease we now record; her endeavours assisted his prosperity, while her life fully tallied with and enhanced his own respectability.

"Mrs. Frances Jackman died at Banbury, Oxon., on Saturday the 7th inst., aged 73. Her loss is regretted by a wide circle of friends throughout the circuit wherein she and her late husband were so well-known and deeply mourned by her sorrowing children, to whom she had been an assiduous and exemplary parent. The writer of this humble tribute recollects her appearing 35 years ago, in the full vigour of her talent, at Highgate, in the comedy of 'The School for Scandal'. The cast included the names of Messrs. Jackman, Stoddart, Henry Heathcote, Styles etc., Mrs. Jackman senior, the grandmother of the present manager, Mr. Charles Jackman, Mrs. Frances Jackman (now recorded deceased), Mrs. Henry etc. etc."

This is the only fleeting reference to performances by the company at Highgate and Evesham. The latter town could provide me with no further information but as regards Highgate I was told at Haringey Reference

THEATRE, BANBURY.

The above Theatre will open under the Patronage of the
Stewards of the Ball at the Red Lion Hotel.
MR. JACKMAN

Has the honour of again calling the attention of the nobility, Gentry, and Public of BANBURY, and its Suburbs, to the opening of the Theatre. The Company is of acknowledged talent, and selected from the principal Provincial and Metropolitan Theatres.

Mr. W. WALDRON, *(From the Theatre Royal, Olympic, London.)*
MR. PRESCOTT, *(From the Theatre Royal, Manchester.)*
MR. BARRY, *(From the Queen's Theatre, London.)*
MR. KIRK, *(From the Theatre Royal, Windsor.)*
MR. ANDREWS, *(From the Theatre Royal, York.)*
MR. STANLEY, *(From the Theatre Royal, Birmingham.)*
MR. TANNETT, *(From the Theatre Royal, Portsmouth.)*
MR. SMYTHSON, *(From the Theatre Royal, Windsor.)*
MISS KAZIA LOVE, *(Vocalist of the English Opera House, London.)*
MRS. TANNETT, *From the Theatre Royal, Portsmouth.*
MRS. BARRY, *(Of the Theatre Royal, Manchester.)*
Mr. Jackman. Mr. P. Jackman. Mr. Partleton.
The Misses Jackman. Mrs. Partleton. Mrs. Partleton, &c. &c.

On Wednesday Evening, Jan. 14, 1846,
Will be performed (First time here), the Original Domestic Drama, in Two Acts, by E. FITZBALL, Esq., founded on CRABBE'S popular "TALES OF THE HALL," called—THE
MOMENTOUS
QUESTION

Now playing at the Theatre Royal, Lyceum, London.—In the course of the Drama, an attempt will be made to realize the subject of the popular Engraving from Miss S. Setchel's celebrated Picture of "THE MOMENTOUS QUESTION," (published by Mr. Boys, Golden Square,) expressly dedicated by Royal Command, to HER MOST GRACIOUS MAJESTY THE QUEEN.

"She saw him fetter'd, full of grief, alone, / Still as the dead; and he suppressed a groan / At her appearance, now she gaz'd for strength, / And the sad couple could converse at length."
"I ask thee, Robert, lowe, canst thou part, / With this poor hand when master of the heart? / Shall I be thine own maid or James's wife?"

James Greenfield, a Gamekeeper.. Mr. PRESCOTT   Robert Shelley, a Poacher.. Mr. W. WALDRON
Chalk, Landlord of the Lucky Horseshoe.. Mr. KIRK
Union Jack, the Scamp of the Village.. Mr. BARRY   Moletrap.. Mr. PARTLETON
Gamekeepers, Poachers, Smugglers, &c.
Rachel Ryland.. Miss H. JACKMAN   Fanny Dossett, Servant at the Hall.. Miss L. JACKMAN

Ballad---"Kate Kearney," by Miss KAZIA LOVE.
NEGRO MELODY. MR. TANNETT
Comic Song----"The Nice Young Man," by Mr. BARRY

After which, a laughable Interlude (First time in this Theatre) entitled
POLKAMANIA!

Mr. Dorrington, a Gentleman with no particular Mania..... Mr. KIRK
Adolphus Wharton, a Medical Student, with a mania for the patter of the day..... Mr. W. WALDRON
Jemmy, a Tiger, with a mania for the Stage........Mr. TANNETT
Laura Dorrington, a Young Lady with a mania for London Life, and the Polka...........Miss H. JACKMAN
THE POLKA, BY MR. W. WALDRON, MR. TANNETT, AND THE MISSES JACKMAN.

Favourite Ballad, by Miss LOVE.
THE CAPTAIN IS NOT A-MISS.
Or, The Female Soldiers!

General Stormwell....Mr. KIRK   Captain Daring.. Mr. W. WALDRON
John Stock, his Tiger.. Mr. TANNETT   Roland Tunley, Landlord of the Black Eagle.. Mr. JACKMAN
Halbert............Mr. SMYTHSON
Emily, Disguised as Captain Daring..........Miss H. JACKMAN
Fanny, Disguised as his Tiger.. Miss L. JACKMAN   Mary........Mrs. TANNETT

The Nights of playing this week will be WEDNESDAY, THURSDAY and SATURDAY.
Doors open at half-past Six, and the Performance to Commence at Seven o'clock.

BOXES, 3s.   PIT, 2s.   GALLERY, 1s.
Half-price at half-past Eight: Boxes, 1s. 6d. Pit, 1s. Gallery, 6d.

Tickets to be had of Mr. James Hill.—Tickets for the Season may also be had on moderate terms.—A great variety of New and Popular Pieces, now acting in London, will speedily be brought forward.

BARRETT, PRINTER, DAVENTRY.

ROYAL SHAKSPEAREAN THEATRE, STRATFORD-ON-AVON.
Lessees: Messrs. C. JACKMAN, and F. MORGAN.
LAST AND FAREWELL SEASON.
ENGAGEMENT FOR FIVE NIGHTS ONLY
OF THE DISTINGUISHED TRAGEDIAN,
MR. JAMES BENNETT.
PROGRAMME FOR MONDAY, TUESDAY, & WEDNESDAY
On MONDAY, OCTOBER the 6th., 1862,
Will be presented, Shakspeare's celebrated tragedy of
HAMLET!!

Hamlet, Prince of Denmark .... Mr. JAMES BENNETT.
Horatio Mr. C. HARRINGTON. Claudius, King of Denmark, (on this occasion) Mr. J. B. LAMBERT. Polonius Mr. F. MORGAN.
Laertes.....Mr. C. JACKMAN. Guildenstern...Mr. JONES. Osric.......Miss ADA DOWDING.
Bernardo.......Mr. BOE. Ghost of Hamlet's Father....Mr. JACKMAN. First Gravedigger...Mr. F. MORGAN.
Second Gravedigger....Mr. LOMAX. Rosencrantz....Miss GREY. Player King......Mr. M. DAMPIER.
Gertrude.....Mrs. F. MORGAN. Ophelia....Miss LOUISA WOULDS. Player Queen....Mrs. LOMAX.

COMIC SONG EACH EVENING BY MR. LOMAX.
To conclude with the Comic Farce of
VOWS AND VALENTINES
Carlos : ... Mr. C. JACKMAN. Lopez ... Mr. LOMAX. Sancho ... Mr. F. MORGAN.
Leonora ... Miss ADA DOWDING. Jacintha ... Miss LOUISA WOULDS.

On TUESDAY, OCTOBER the 7th.,
The Performance will commence with the Beautiful Play of THE
STRANGER!

Stranger .... Mr. JAMES BENNETT.
Baron Steinfort .... Mr. J. Lambert.
Count Winterson .... Mr. C. JACKMAN.
Peter .... Mr. C. HARRINGTON.
Solomon .... Mr. LOMAX. Tobias .... Mr. F. MORGAN.
Mrs. Haller...Mrs. F. MORGAN. Countess Winterson. Miss ADA DOWDING. Charlotte. M'ss LOUISA WOULDS. .... Mr. DAMPIER.

To conclude with a new comic farce, called
The YOUNG MAN from the COUNTRY.
Characters by Messrs. JACKMAN, HARRINGTON, LOMAX, F. MORGAN, Misses LOUISA WOULDS, & ADA DOWDING.

On WEDNESDAY, OCTOBER 8th., 1862,
Shakspeare's Tragedy of
OTHELLO!

Iago .... Mr. JAMES BENNETT.
Othello .... Mr. J. B. LAMBERT. Cassio ... Mr. C. JACKMAN. Ludovico .... Mr. M. DAMPIER.
Duke of Venice .... Mr. HILL. Montano .... Mr. C. HARRINGTON.
Brabantio ... Mr. LOMAX. Roderigo ... Mr. F. MORGAN. Gratiano ... Mr. JONES.
Desdemona ... Mrs. F. MORGAN. Emilia ... Miss J. LOMAX.

To conclude with the Laughable Farce of
DEEP AS A WELL !!!
SUPPORTED BY THE COMPANY.

☞ On Friday Oct. 10th, the performance will be for the Benefit of Mr. JAMES BENNETT, and last but one of his engagement.

Doors open at Seven, to commence precisely at half-past.
Boxes 2s. Pit 1s. Gallery 6d. Second price at Nine o'clock, Boxes 1s., Pit 6d. No half-price to the Gallery.
Tickets may be had of the MANAGERS, at the Libraries of Mr. MORGAN, Bookseller and Stationer, and of Mr. ADAMS, Bookseller.
Season Tickets, Boxes (transferable) £1, and Pit ditto 10s. Leader of the Orchestra, Mr. F. HAWTHORN.
J. MORGAN, PRINTER AND BOOKSELLER, "CHRONICLE" OFFICE, STRATFORD-ON-AVON.

BANBURY, 1846 the Jackman Company is listed. Note the manager's order for 400 copies, top right. (*Northamptonshire Record Office*).

STRATFORD, 1862—a "last and farewell season" for the theatre, but it wasn't. See Pages 187-9 and 197. (*Shakespeare Birthplace Trust*)

Library: "The date seems to be right for Larne's Theatre, Castle Yard, Highgate Village, an old barn in the grounds of Castle Inn, between Southwood Lane and North Road. This is long since gone but is known to have been used as a theatre between 1780 and 1820. We have one playbill only, for 1812, when the theatre seems to have been run by a Mr. Smollett. The place must have been very small."

In January, 1858, the Northampton theatre was yet again "in court" when three men who had stolen a silver watch from a man getting his tickets at the box office were given hard labour.

During the winter of 1859–60 Northampton acquired its first industrial theatre, as an act of enlightened management. At the Eagle Foundry of Messrs. Barwell, a large reading room had been fitted up with a stage, with proscenium, drop scene and orchestra and "here the workmen have got up comediettas, farces and musical entertainments".

The last Northampton performances of the long Jackman, and Jackman and Morgan, era came in February, 1861, after a period of twenty-one years. These must have been sad, nostalgic nights for those who had been with the company for the whole of the time, notably Charles Jackman himself. Northampton turned out to give them a memorable send-off; in contrast to the thin houses which had ensured their departure, when the time came for them to go the houses were packed.

First came a farewell benefit for Charles Jackman's sister, Harriet Morgan and her husband. The Herald reported that they were honoured with a bumper such as had seldom been seen in Northampton. "Every available space where a sight of the stage could be obtained was crammed and in addition the stage itself accommodated a considerable number of people who were packed into the wings, somewhat to the inconvenience of the performers." At the close of the performance, which included *The Wanderer of the Hills,* the comic burletta *An Object of Interest,* and the farce of *My Supper Party or 7s. A Head,* Frederick Morgan made a little speech which he concluded by wishing prosperity to the ancient town of Northampton.

Three days later a popular newcomer named J. H. Windley and his sister Miss Windley took their benefit. Windley, who was being given his first chance in leading roles, was a Leicester man who was to become lessee of that city's Theatre Royal in 1868. He also operated the Potteries Royal Theatre, Hanley, for several years including its final season before demolition in 1870, in which year he took over the Royal Pottery Music Hall and Theatre of Varieties in Church Street, Hanley. His brother Harry is listed as a member of the company. The Windley brothers also turn up in co-management at the Theatre Royal, Stamford, in March–April, 1870, in a bill including a team of Can-can dancers. This was fourteen months before the final performance at that theatre on Saturday, June 24, 1871, with a cast headed by Mrs. C. A. Clarke, wife of a later manager at Northampton.

Among the Stamford cast list of April, 1870, it is intriguing to spot the name of Charles Jackman and warming to imagine that it was a case of Windley remembering his old employer with gratitude. Eventually Windley had to give up the theatre through ill-health and become a journalist in Leicester.

To return to the Jackman and Morgan farewell at Northampton, plays in which J. H. Windley took leading roles were *The Castle Spectre*, evidently still popular, and another "shocker" *The Iron Chest* ("set partly in an ancient burying ground in which a hurricane suddenly bursts forth... thunderbolts and lightnings glare beneath the tombs"), *Hamlet*, *The Foundling of the Forest*, and *The Female Bluebeard*.

Next came benefits for Mr. and Mrs. Ridyard; Mr. Romia, leader of the orchestra; Mr. Styles and Mr. Lewis; and then came the very last night, for Charles Jackman himself.

The very last piece of the Jackman era was *Nicholas Nickleby and Poor Smike or Doings at Do-the-Boys Hall* and then it was the beneficiary's turn to say a few words. Charles Jackman said he could have wished the relationship between him and his listeners could have been continued, but it had been ordained otherwise.

Then everyone joined in "God Save the Queen" and it was all over.

From Northampton the company moved on to Banbury where a playbill of March 18 discovers them in *As You Like It* with a cast including Messrs. Lewis, Windley, Skene, Gay, Jackman, Chaplin, Hall, Styles, Roe, Ridyard, and Mrs. F. Morgan, Miss Ann Laurie, Miss Windley, Miss Hilton and Miss Ridyard. The tragedian Wybert Rousby was billed to appear as a guest on Thursday, March 21. Season tickets were £1 for the boxes and 10s. for the pit. The bills were printed by Cheney and Hitchcock.

The Banbury season continued until May and at the end of that month the company were at Reading's Theatre Royal playing to indifferent houses, partly because of competition from a circus.

I cannot yet be absolutely positive as to when the company disintegrated but can merely record where the last trace has been found: this is at Banbury where a short season commenced on Thursday, December 4, 1862, including *The Castle Spectre*, *Black Doctor* and *The Stranger*, by a company including J. H. Lambert, Lomax, Dampier, Mrs. Lomax, Misses Woulds and Dowsing and Wybert Rousby as guest artist. The Era said Mr. Lomax's songs were rather too broad for its liking.

On January 25, 1863, the same paper noted a performance of *The Miller and His Men* in which amateurs, workers from the Britannia Iron Works, appeared to good effect, aided by the Foundry Band. They reported that *Jane Shore*, *Macbeth*, *Pizaro* and *The Castle Spectre* had been played to "very thin houses". The Banbury season was "rapidly drawing to a close", said the paper, using unusual phraseology which was seemingly a funeral oration for the Jackman and Morgan Company. "Owing to the great depression of trade, business is worse this season than has even been known in Banbury."

Thus the curtain fell on the fifty-seven years of dramatic enactments of the company Old Henry, or rather Young Henry as he was then, had begun at the age of nineteen in 1805, the year of Trafalgar and the year before the Marefair Theatre opened.

The Banbury run followed a nostalgic season at Stratford for which the bills were headed "Final and Farewell Season". At first sight this had appeared to be the company's adieu, as if it was about to be disbanded, but this is not the explanation. It was the theatre itself for which it was intended to be the "Final and Farewell Season".

A famous Shakespearian scholar had taken it into his head to honour Stratford-upon-Avon by depriving the town of its only theatre! It was well-intentioned, the idea being to clear the site and restore the vicinity of Shakespeare's Birthplace to its original state. James Orchard Halliwell, of 11 Tregunter Road, West Brompton, had raised a good sum of money and was willing also to dip into his own pocket but the theatre proprietors proved too greedy. They asked for £1,100, which Halliwell regarded as extortionate. As a result the farewell sentiment proved to be superfluous. Though not immediately, other companies did bring the Stratford Theatre back to life again, until 1872 when Mr. Halliwell made a further approach and got the place for exactly half what he had been asked before (£550, equal to £15 a share). The last performance was in fact an appearance by Mr. and Mrs. Wybert Rousby as Hamlet and Ophelia on April 30, 1872.

Mr. Halliwell having achieved his object Stratford remained theatreless until the inauguration of the Shakespeare Memorial Theatre of 1879. In contrast with the 1827 house its story is well known, how it was burned down on March 6, 1926, and replaced by the present theatre on the banks of the Avon.

As far as Northampton is concerned, the unexpected reprieve of the earlier theatre deprived the town which had had the distinction of providing the company for the inauguration of being closely linked with the last company to perform there.

One day I hope to be able to chronicle more fully the story of the unknown theatre at Stratford and also to fill in the gaps in the Jackman and Jackman and Morgan stories. Meantime there is one interesting further link with Stratford which I am pleased to have uncovered. Charles Jackman settled in Bard-land in about 1870, living in Henley Street with his sister Sophia. In 1873 he became the first librarian of the Shakespeare Birthplace Trust and held that office until his death on June 3, 1879, at the age of sixty.

Who was then left of the former company and family, besides Sophia? Charles Jackman's will shows that George Partleton was dead by then but his widow Fanny was living in Banbury. Louisa, who reported her brother's death to the registrar, was now Mrs. Steer, of West Street, Stratford. It is extremely tempting to suppose that she married Edward STaunton— presumably a stage name, in that case—with whom she was a company member. The former Eliza Jackman and her husband Harry Fenton were at Nottingham while the former Harriet Jackman and her husband Frederick Morgan were at Southsea. I hope this book may catch the eye of some of their descendants and that if so, I may hear from them.

The Stratford press paid tribute to Charles Jackman's memory : "It was our painful duty last week to record the death of Mr. Charles Jackman who, during the past few years, acted as custodian of the library in connection with Shakespeare's birthplace. During his lifetime he was a warm and energetic supporter of the drama, and we think that his demise should not be allowed to pass without some notice" (a sentiment I share).

"During the early part of the last half-century the name of Jackman was inseparably associated with the dramatic art and it is to a branch of the family bearing that name that credit must be given for the popularising of the legitimate drama in the Midland counties of England. Gifted with histrionic and musical abilities of no common order, the Jackmans for many years identified themselves closely with the theatrical world, and in the different sections of the profession to which they devoted their talents, they earned no mean reputation.

"Charles Jackman was the son of Henry and Fanny Jackman. When still a youth he occupied a place as violinist in the orchestra of his father's theatre, but he soon relinquished the instrument for the stage, upon which he proved himself a very useful comedian. For many years he rendered his father valuable aid in his managerial duties, and on the death of the latter he assumed the business in conjunction with his brother-in-law Mr. Frederick Morgan. During old Mr. Jackman's management of the Royal Shakespearian Theatre at Stratford-on-Avon, the drama flourished in the birth town of the poet and had it not been for the enterprise of Charles Jackman, Stratford would probably have been almost destitute of any kind of entertainment about twenty-five years ago. As a man of business he was energetic and of high integrity, and in private life he earned the esteem and respect of all by his amiability of disposition and courteousness of manner."

Had not interest in the drama thus been kept alive at Stratford who knows but that support might not have been sufficient to build the subsequent "iced-cake" theatre of 1879, completed and opened on Shakespeare's Day, just three months before Charles Jackman's death?

He was, no doubt, in the audience on the first night on April 23, 1879, to see Helena Faucit and Barry Sullivan in *Much Ado About Nothing* which Sullivan also produced.

The list of subscribers to the theatre building fund included : Charles Jackman—one guinea. His real contribution is incalculable.

ACT
THE
THIRD

NO BUSINESS

...demonstrating that there is, indeed, No Business quite like Show Business. Other song titles also demonstrated in an INTERLUDE. A register of a multitude of managers, one of whom threw a bailiff out of the house. The new pattern of provincial theatre described and the plans for a new theatre outlined. And how the old theatre faded away, rather than died.

JOSEPH GURNEY, who was twice
Mayor of Northampton, was secretary
of the Marefair Theatre for many years.
What is now the Anglia Building Society
was founded in his house in Gold Street.
See Pages 207–210.

Scene One

MANAGERS GALORE

With the end of the Jackman and Morgan era on February 25, 1861, the theatre owners did not have to go far to find a new lessee. He came from just across the way, in the irrepressible personage of Mr. William Thomas, Mine Host of Thomas's Music Hall at the Crow and Horseshoe Inn.

Full of confidence that he could show those actor types how to run a theatre on profitable lines, Mr. Thomas announced his intentions in a quick-fire advertisement rather like those for his music hall which had for several years enlivened the columns of the Mercury and the Herald: "Theatre Royal, Lessee Mr. W. Thomas of the Music Hall, will open March 18 with new COMPANY, new SCENERY, new DRESSES, new MACHINERY, new DECORATIONS, new DRAMAS, new BALLETS, new FARCES, brilliant illuminations, a DOUBLE BAND is engaged. A grand comic pantomime is now in active preparation."

The Crow and Horseshoe had stood on the corner of Gold Street and Horseshoe Street (formerly Horseshoe Lane and before that Crow and Horseshoe Lane) for many years. It was one of the lesser inns, with a reputation that was not of the highest. But only lately had it entered the entertainment arena, setting out to divert at least some of those who might otherwise have patronised the drama on the other side of the street.

It appears likely that William Thomas originated music hall there. In December, 1855, while Jackman and Morgan's season was in progress at the theatre, Mr. Thomas announced that "The Music Hall, Crow and Horseshoe Inn, Gold Street, Proprietor W. Thomas" was open every evening with the following "talented artistes": Mr. and Mrs. Benjamin Williams, unrivalled duet and solo comic singers; Mr. Fred Brown, the pleasing tenor; and Mr. William Thomas, the admired ballad singer. Mr. F. Frances, at the pianoforte, represented the entire musical accompaniment.

From this small beginning with a piano and four artistes including himself Mr. Thomas, who was evidently a thrusting, energetic, brash, and brassy type of individual, moved onwards and upwards. Opening a new season in October the following year he announced that the hall was "enlarged and thoroughly ventilated" and that "no person would be admitted that is intoxicated or not decently attired". His musical staff remained in the singular, now Mr. F. Brown.

When the premises came up for sale in March, 1860, they were described

14—TU * *

as having "a splendid concert room elegantly fitted up with every convenience" as well as "two arched cellars, two sitting rooms, convenient bar, dining room, tap room, kitchen, scullery, five bedrooms, large yard, brewhouse, ginger ale manufactory, stabling for fifteen horses, coachhouse, large malting with granaries and lofts over, sheds and other outbuildings, with a gateway thereto from Horseshoe Street".

Whether the place was sold is not clear but Thomas remained as tenant and was a couple of months later advertising "Thomas's Original Music Hall" with Henesier's Black Opera Troupe; Miss Clayton, ballad vocalist; Mr. Harry Baker, Irish comic dancer and singer; Mr. Williams, tenor vocalist; Mr. Josh Brown, comic singer; and Yankee Redman, the modern Black Paganini. The musical department was trebled—two violins (Mr. J. Dickens and Mr. C. Henesier) and piano (Miss C. Lindsay).

We will not inquire into what a single lady was doing playing the piano in what was often described as a den of iniquity but pass on instead to a couple of weeks later when Thomas engaged "Castrona and Harrison and their Wonderful Company of Performing Dogs" and had added the cornet of Mr. Bailey to make the band a quartet. Later a trombone appeared. Seemingly the man from the Crow and Horseshoe, who also ran drinking booths at local race meetings and fairs, was doing quite nicely and felt confident enough to extend his empire to the theatre, parlous though times were in the dramatic sphere.

One of the innovations of his regime was an attempt to stop the habit of smoking in the theatre. On the re-opening night the stage manager, Mr. Harry Haines, announced that the objectionable practice would not be tolerated under any circumstances and that any parties violating the regulation would be turned out.

Thomas's advertisements continued to have the music hall touch. His pantomime *Little Red Riding Hood or The Wolf that Gobbled up Granny* was a glorious success, according to him. After his season proper ended on Saturday, May 11, he told the "nobility and gentry of Northampton and the surrounding district and the public in general" that he had arranged for them to have "the greatest treat in the world". The news, proclaimed on huge placards throughout the town, resolved itself into a visit by Mr. and Mrs. Charles Kean on Friday, June 14. The son of the great Edmund Kean was to appear for "positively one night only" though this did not prevent his coming back the following week.

The newspapers reported good houses for Kean and there is no reason to doubt them. But that was the end of Theatre Thomas. Whereas the previous Jackman (and Jackman and Morgan) era had endured over twenty-one years, Thomas's lasted just four months. His ambition was by no means snuffed out, however. In August, 1863, he knocked down the old concert room at the Crow and Horseshoe and had another built to his own design. It was said to have 500 jets of gas and to accommodate 800 people.

As far as the theatre was concerned this was the first of a series of fits and starts in the management. Thomas's immediate successor was a woman —the only woman to run the theatre.

"I come to canvass you, box gallery and pit
Who now around in awful judgment sit . . ."

These were the opening lines of a somewhat tedious inaugural address spoken by Mrs. J. F. Saville, of the Nottingham Theatre, in November, 1861. The prologue had been written by Henry Faucit Saville, at least partly for the occasion :

"Below this altered roof which you behold
A phoenix risen from the ashes of the old."

Not for the first time and by no means the last the theatre had been "transformed". The amount of paint, gilt, carpentry and "strenuous exertions" which went into it from time to time must have reached a phenomenal aggregate if the various managers, aided and abetted by the journalists of the day, are to be believed. Yet the "greatly improved house" of Manager A was in retrospect "that dirty old theatre of last year" when Manager B came along. It was a miracle, no less, how much the place could be "improved" yet how tawdry it could remain.

Mrs. Saville, who was born in 1811, was the widow of John Faucit Saville who had managed theatres at Nottingham over a period of about a decade until his death on the last day of 1855. Like H. M. Simpson's, J. F. Saville's name was partly adopted, his real name being John Faucit. A story of the broken marriage of his father lay behind the change of name. John Saville Faucit, the father, had a runaway marriage in 1805 with Harriet Diddier, daughter of Charles Diddier, manager of the Margate Theatre. The romance endured for many years and there were six children, according to Malcolm Morley's book *Margate and Its Theatres*. John Saville Faucit began a twenty-year term as manager of the Margate Theatre in 1820 (he ran the Kent Circuit) but when the season began in 1825 he was announced as John Faucit Saville. It was the same man but the manager and his wife had separated, she having become involved with one William Farren. She retained her name of Faucit and her husband's name switch was in protest against this. The four sons, including John junior, were brought up by their father as Faucit Savilles and the two daughters, Harriet and Helen, by their mother as Faucits. This, apparently, accounts for the many seemingly erroneous statements that John Faucit Saville and Helen Faucit were half-brother and -sister. In 1879, as Lady Helen Martin, the latter daughter was to star in the inaugural performance at the Stratford Memorial Theatre.

John Faucit Saville senior, who wrote six plays, all of which were performed in London, died in 1853, aged seventy. Two years later J. F. S. junior passed on at the early age of forty-eight, leaving his widow with an inheritance of heavy debts. These arose in some measure from the fact that the previous year he had bid £1,950 for the existing theatre at Nottingham, in St. Mary's Gate, when it seemed likely to become a lace factory or warehouse, a possibility which stuck in his gorge. He razed to the ground the "curious pile of buildings" of which it consisted and built a new Theatre Royal.

In a difficult period Saville did not manage to be successful. Unlike

Simpson at Birmingham he was a purist and set his face against a surfeit of novelty and spectacle, preferring to adhere to the true dramatic tradition as he saw it, even in face of empty benches. For a time he also managed at Leicester (1846–7), Derby, Chesterfield and Sheffield and his farewell speech at the last-named sums up the situation. It was his benefit night but the house was slender and he was frank : "In all probability this is the last time I shall appear before you. I present myself to thank all present for their kind attendance and to give some account of my stewardship. I cannot disguise the fact, nor do I wish to do so, that my management has been most unsatisfactory to you and most unprofitable to myself. Can Sheffield justly lay claim to the title of being a theatrical town ? Never in my twenty-one years experience have I experienced such exaction with so little sympathy towards manager or actor as I have witnessed in Sheffield."

Saville's theatres at Derby, Nottingham and later Sheffield were part of the remnants following the break-up in 1840 of the Nottingham and Derby Circuit with the death of Thomas Wilson Manly who had kept it intact much as he found it in 1799 when he first joined the circuit.

Mrs. Saville had a rough ride when she took over at Nottingham as a widow. A season's end speech which she made there was of a similarly tart character. While it was not the custom at that theatre, she explained, for management to make closing speeches, she felt bound to justify herself. Her chief target was the Press : "I have not had one word of encouragement or the slightest assistance from the Press. They have always been ready to find fault, never to praise." (Cries of "Shame !")

In support of Charles Kean, Mrs. Saville had appeared before Queen Victoria and Prince Albert at Windsor Castle in 1849. Kean played Hamlet. A few years later, in other surroundings Mrs. Saville herself played Hamlet —Women's Lib was already in being in the 1860s ! In 1849, also, she took part in a farewell tour of Macready, the great tragedian.

There were three Saville daughters, two of whom, Eliza and Kate, proved strong allies of their widowed mother in her theatrical enterprises. Kate first appeared in a leading role in London in 1859 and in November, 1862, while her mother's company was at Northampton, she was making a great impression at the Olympic Theatre.

While at Northampton Mrs. Saville continued with her more important commitments at Nottingham and stayed at the 1854 premises until they ceased to be a theatre proper, in 1865. Two years later, in partnership with her daughter Kate, she leased and managed Nottingham's new Theatre Royal for two years. By then her relationship with the town was of the happiest character and on her last-but-one night a crowded house applauded wildly as she was handed a subscription gift of a silver tea service bearing the family crest, with jewellery for her daughters. The presentation folder which accompanied the gifts is preserved in Nottingham Reference Library.

The 1854 theatre at Nottingham subsequently became the Alhambra Music Hall. In 1883 it closed its entertainment career and became a warehouse. Its activity in the new guise ended abruptly in 1941 when it was burned down during an air raid on the Lace City.

An early visitor during the Saville era at Northampton was Frederick

Morgan, Charles Jackman's partner, who paid a return visit to the town in December, 1862, when the Jackman-Morgan company was on the verge of disintegration. From September to November they had played a "final and farewell season" at the Shakespearean Theatre, Stratford-upon-Avon—final because the theatre was about to be pulled down by a Shakespeare scholar. In fact the demolition was to be delayed a decade as already related, but the players were not to know this and it must have been a season of nostalgia. They must in any case have sensed that their own dissolution could not be far off. In fact when Frederick Morgan re-joined them at Banbury, after his Northampton appearance, it was for what was indeed (as far as I have traced) their last season, beginning on Friday, December 4, 1862.

At Stratford on Friday, November 27, Morgan had taken his final benefit and had spoken a special farewell, of which the poetic style may be criticised but the relevance cannot be challenged:

> *". . . the fates decree*
> *This Thespian temple shall no longer be*
> *I grieve for this. In Stratford's pleasant town*
> *Whereon the poet's birth confers renown*
> *Shall 'the poor player' no longer 'fret his hour'?*
> *Shall Shakespeare from his native home be driven?*
> *No honour be to your prophet given?*
> *Rather let those who venerate the Bard*
> *Combine to save him from a fate so hard*
> *Since of* THIS *building we have heard the doom*
> *May a* NEW THEATRE *in the future 'loom'*
> *Wherein the drama, virtue's powerful organ*
> *May still be guided by* JACKMAN AND MORGAN.
> *Meanwhile with heartfelt thanks for favours shown*
> *To me and mine for thirteen years bygone*
> *I take my leave, hoping that Stratford trade*
> *May flourish—that the Jubilee may aid*
> *Its progress in prosperity—to you*
> *Once more I bid a grateful, kind adieu!"*

Could Sir Laurence have spoken better?

From the heady nostalgia of Stratford on Friday, Morgan stepped down to reality at Northampton the following Monday, Tuesday and Wednesday, so that in fact he missed the very last night at Stratford on the Monday, when Charles Jackman took his parting benefit. Morgan's old friends in the shoe town were delighted to see him and gave him a rousing welcome. Some of the more elevated ones, in the gods, showed their joy by kicking large lumps of wood off the front of the gallery and hurling these down on to the heads of those in the pit, along with lighted pieces of paper. Describing the scene the Mercury added : "Smoking too was carried on with impunity in all parts of the house and this although it is stated on the bills that smoking is strictly forbidden and that 'Police Officers will be in attendance to enforce decorum and order'."

Nor was this the full extent of the week's misfortunes at the theatre. On the Friday, with several members of the Town Council in the audience for a civic patronage night, the principal piece was not played at all—"owing to the alleged absence from some cause or other of one of the principal characters, and perhaps the less said of the evening's entertainment the better it will be for the credit of the management," said the Mercury.

In October, 1863, Mrs. Saville entrusted the management to Mr. Charles Wilstone who had been a member of her Nottingham Company. Mrs. Saville's last appearance on the stage was as the Queen of Denmark in *Hamlet* at Cork with Barry Sullivan in 1872 and she then went to live with her daughters at Station Road, Kettering, Northamptonshire, where she died on March 31, 1889. Kate Saville had also retired in 1872, on getting married; she died in 1922.

About Charles Wilstone I have discovered little but what I have found adds one more to the list of insolvent managers of the Northampton theatre. Unlike the others, Wilstone went bankrupt before his Northampton management. In June, 1860, he had taken on the Theatre Royal, Derby, but just a year later the Derby Mercury was reporting his appearance in the Nottingham Insolvency Court, describing him as "late lessee of the Derby Theatre".

Nine months after Wilstone took over at Northampton two more old friends turned up in the company—Louisa Jackman, youngest daughter of "Old Henry", and Edward Staunton, a fellow-member of the Jackman company. The pair, who were dubbed by the Mercury as "players of moderate pretensions", had probably left the Jackman troupe at the same time, having formed a romantic attachment. Indeed my theory is that Louisa had either already married Edward or would do so later on—but under what I take to be his real name of Steer. The man she married and later settled down with at Stratford-upon-Avon was named Edward Steer and the fact of the first two letters of the surnames being the same seems more than one can accept as a coincidence. During the 1864 season Edward Staunton played Hamlet for which the Mercury gave him this back-handed compliment : "He played with an ability which, we confess, surprised us." On this occasion the house was "crammed in every part". Northampton audiences of this period seem to have liked their Shakespeare, though whether for the beauty of his language or for the high drama and goriness of some of his scenes we can but speculate.

In the 1860s the phenomenon of "child stars" was still in being, together with another novelty. This time the theatre not only had a twelve-year-old boy in Richard III but adult women playing Hamlet and heaving sighs to each other as Romeo and Juliet! An 1862 Hamlet at Northampton was Miss Goddard, "the celebrated tragic actress"; that was in July. The following November the Juliet of Miss Emily Brandon was teamed with the Romeo of Miss Rosa Cooper. Four years later Miss Helen Clyde played Romeo to the Juliet of an amateur lady. The "London Sketches" column of the Mercury noted in 1864 that a Miss Marriott had been appearing at the Sadlers Wells Theatre, London, as Hamlet, commenting : "It has been said by critics that the part should always be played by a woman, Hamlet being more feminine than masculine in his nature. The worst of this new experiment is that we may now expect to be inundated with female Hamlets."

Aged twelve, Master Percy Roselle essayed not only Hamlet, but also Macbeth, and Richard Duke of Gloucester in *Richard III*. His sister, age not stated, was also in the company at the Marefair theatre in November, 1864.

Charles Wilstone and William Thomas were perhaps better friends than previous theatre managers had been with the proprietor of the Crow and Horseshoe and one night we actually find W. Thomas singing on the stage of the theatre.

At the latter end of Wilstone's management came the episode of the Inebriate Othello. I defer the telling of this cautionary tale to the Interlude on Drinking.

Each manager who came to Marefair was hailed by the ever-hopeful Press as the long-awaited saviour of the place, a dramatic messiah who would deliver it from artistic aridness, decorative despond, commercial creakiness.

Along in November, 1865, came Mr. Douglas Stewart, "favourably known as manager of a Birmingham theatre as well as theatres in other places". It was his intention "to considerably improve its appearance and to endeavour to make the theatre a more popular and respectable place of amusement than it has been of late years". His dramatic gambits were *The Mystery or The Idiot in the Ruined Mill, The Roadside Inn or The Two Murders, Spring Heeled Jack or The Mysteries of the Old Red Grange* and *The Vampire Lover or The Midnight Hour*.

In the early 1860s managers seemed to be competing to see who could think up the longest title for a pantomime. Mrs. Saville's entry had been *Harlequin Tom Thumb or Merlin The Magician and The Fairy in The Grotto of Silvershells*. Mr. Wilstone had capped this with *The Old Woman That Lived in a Shoe or Harlequin Charles II and the Fairies of Harlestone Firs*. Even more wordy was Mr. Stewart's *Ye Merry Maire of Northampton or Harlequin Sir Tristram Sylvana, Ye Fairy Spirit of Ye Nen and Ye Demon God of Ye Wine Cask*, which featured a character named Sir Gregorygroundsellbarrenlandhardup.

Despite high hopes and seeming good intentions Mr. Stewart had given up within three months and in March, 1866, yet another lessee was installed. Again hopes were elevated—"Mr. J. P. Chadwick and a new company have undertaken, we are glad to say, to resuscitate the Drama in this town, which the last mismanagement rendered almost moribund." Once more the newcomers had "already greatly improved the condition of the theatre". Yet again it had been redecorated and the boxes repapered.

Mr. Chadwick's wife joined Northampton Amateur Dramatic Club in a performance to mark the opening in March, 1866, of a new Town Hall and Corn Exchange in the small town of Towcester on the Roman Watling Street some eight miles from Northampton. The company, which also included Miss Emily Bell from the Northampton company and Miss Murray and Miss Clara Lee, both of the Theatre Royal, Nottingham, gave *The Illustrious Stranger or Married and Buried, A Regular Fix*, and the trial scene from *Merchant of Venice*. The performances were patronised by the Duke of Grafton, the Earl of Pomfret (who earlier took the chair at a public dejeuner) and Lord Southampton.

A fortnight later Lt.-Col. The Duke of Grafton gave his patronage at the Northampton theatre along with Major Earl Spencer and fellow officers of the 5th Northamptonshire Rifle Volunteer Corps for a "Grand Shakespearean Night". Shortly after that there was a "Grand Military Night" with Col. Lord Burghley, Major Lord Brownlow Cecil and Officers of the 48th Northamptonshire and Rutland Militia, together with the Band of the Regiment.

Once again it was made to sound very permanent and promising but by June Mr. Chadwick had packed his bags.

The month saw a new company under the management of Messrs. Richardson and Melrose and July brought the triple control of Messrs. Smythe, T. Paulton and H. Thompson, presenting Miss Kate Saville of the Theatre Royal, Haymarket, in *Miriam's Crime* and *The Wolf In Sheep's Clothing*.

Next in the procession was Mr. Henry Nicholson of Leicester who was granted a twelve-month licence in September, presenting initially Messrs. A. and C. Leclerq's and A. Wood's Dramatic, Burlesque and Comedy Company, which included Avonia Jones, the widow of Gustavus Vaughan Brooke, who figures in our "Drunk Scene" interlude.

In December, 1866, Mrs. Saville and one of her daughters returned to join forces with Northampton Amateur Dramatic Club in *Used Up* and *Box and Cox*, in both of which Mark Dorman, a former Mayor of Northampton, appeared.

As far as the management was concerned it was the old story repeated: Nicholson did not last out his year and by January Mr. Thomas could advertise that his music hall was "the only place of amusement open in town". His seeming success was reflected in the fact that his advertisements also included the name of a "managing director". He was Mr. Rosencrantz who had first appeared in the billing as the "North American Indian and greatest tambourinist in the world" (he could play ten tambourines at once). Now he was top executive.

Thomas had a rebuff, however, when he offered to give a free show to the children of Northampton Workhouse. In response to a letter from the Master asking how much it would cost to take the young inmates to the music hall he had said he would admit them free. The outing was vetoed by the Guardians who pointed out that it might make the children too anxious to visit such places of amusement when they entered upon "the more active duties of life". At the time there were in the Workhouse 259 inmates of whom 125 were children. Mr. Thomas did have a body of children at the music hall the following year but this time they were in the cast—a troupe of fifty boys and girls doing "military evolutions" in the 1868 New Year show.

Meanwhile at the theatre a London company brought by Mr. W. R. Waldron for the Spring Race Week of 1867 had only "limited audiences".

But there was life in the old theatre yet. It needed only the magic touch of a good manager and this was forthcoming from Mr. C. A. Clarke, "lessee and manager of Her Majesty's Theatre, Windsor, and several important theatres in the kingdom" who opened on Monday, January 27, 1868, with the tear-jerking *East Lynne* which came to be known as the pot-boiler of all time. The house presented "the novel spectacle" of being crammed in all parts. What particular magic Mr. Clarke had employed to achieve this the Mercury was at a loss to know, for the audience did not even appear to have come to enjoy the play . . . "the pressure of the crowd in the pit and gallery and the constant NOISE was so incessant that the greater part of the performance was a dumb show".

East Lynne was an adaptation from Mrs. Henry Wood's popular novel *The Heir of East Lynne.* Another piece that season was *Jessie The Machine Girl,* reflecting the interest in the Victorian equivalent of automation—the herding of people into factories, a move which was riotously resisted by the shoemakers of Northampton. Elsewhere the programme was much as before —*Kathleen Mavourneen, The Stranger, Macbeth, The Man in the Iron Mask, The Corsair, A Wife's Honour, The French Spy, Othello, Omadhaun* which the Clarkes had presented at Windsor before Queen Victoria, and *The Charity Boy.*

Mention of a charity boy puts me in mind of charity girls. A good deal of charitable work was carried on during the period covered by this book (which precedes, of course, the Welfare State) but it was usually on a very class-conscious basis—crumbs from the rich man's table. The wealthy subscribed to help the orphaned children of the poor but the way they did so, initially at least, was to regard them as a source of future servants. The young girls were put into Northamptonshire Servants Training Institution where they were instructed in the gentle arts of dressing milady in her boudoir or cleaning the pots and pans in the kitchen.

Signs of some change in this lofty attitude came when the organisation changed its name to the Northamptonshire Orphanage for Girls. On its behalf two concerts were given in Northampton's new Town Hall in 1867 with a very distinguished list of amateur performers including Sir Charles Isham of Lamport on the horn, cornet-a-piston, and drum; Lady Isham and several other Ishams; Lt.-Col. The Hon. C. H. Lindsay, M.P., and Macleod of Macleod. Despite the hon. line-up the hall was not full for either concert, although £60 was raised. The Mercury explained, "The Town Hall is of great capacity and will hold a larger number of people than it is easy to get together, on a Saturday especially. Saturday is the special day for business in Northampton and its claims, whatever his will, peremptorily forbid the tradesman to desert his post."

Leaving in April to go to Chesterfield Mr. Clarke announced that he would be back in September and when he duly returned for the winter season a female Hamlet cropped up again in the person of his wife. When it came to Romeo, however, she allowed him to wear the hose.

Biggest "name" during the Clarke period was that of Charles Mathews junior, whose father had played at Northampton half-a-century before.

In the middle of August, 1869, a month when it was usually closed, the theatre was unexpectedly the scene of a "grand concert and amateur performance for the benefit of Mr. Rosencrantz and family (late manager of Thomas's Music Hall) who has suddenly been thrown out of work by unforeseen circumstances".

The "unforeseen circumstances" which necessitated a public appeal for the North American Indian and unrivalled tambourine player were that Mr. Thomas, his employer, had gone bankrupt. At a hearing in London the following December, when he successfully applied for his discharge, Thomas said his failure was caused by illness, insufficient capital and badness of trade. Assets in his deficiency account of £908 included debts doubtful £18, debts bad £60. Property worth £250 had been given to his assignees, Phillips Bros, who were also his brewers and landlords. He said his outgoings for the past two years had been £200 a year. Evidently running a music hall in Northampton had been no more profitable than running a theatre usually was.

One last word before leaving Mr. William Thomas. He had appeared on his own stage in two guises—as a ballad singer and as a negro. If we turn on the pages of the music hall story a year or two it is intriguing to speculate whether he made a comeback there in March, 1872, as "Professor Thomas, clever swordsman, who severs a lemon with sword held in naked hand, divides an apple in handkerchief without cutting the handkerchief, and shoots an apple off the head of Madame Thomas, with an arrow".

When the music hall attached to the Crow and Horseshoe acquired a new proprietor in October, 1869, it got a new name as well. Mr. Robert Higgitt, who introduced himself as having for twenty-three years catered for the people of Coventry to their entire satisfaction, re-named the Thomas Music Hall, not Higgitt's Hippodrome, but the Alhambra.

One of his early attractions was "the Man Fish", pseudonym of a Mr. Jefferson who appeared in a tank containing two thousand gallons of water and performed a number of "marvels"—undressing under water, drinking under water, etc. He described himself as the champion swimmer of the world.

At about the same time Mr. Walter Edwin took over the Theatre Royal from Mr. Clarke and one of his first acts was to give a benefit performance for those who had suffered as a result of a fire at Messrs Barwell and Co's Foundry, the progressive local firm who had provided their workers with their own little theatre and reading room. Then, during a period when the theatre received little coverage we find the name of a manager called Walter Shelley, but in respect of an appearance not at the theatre but in the dock at the police court as we shall see later on, in our drunken divertissement. Higgitt also appeared in court about this time, as a key witness. A shoemaker customer was charged with assaulting the music hall proprietor, on being asked to leave. Higgitt told the Bench that men like the defendant constantly came to the Alhambra, drank the liquor of his customers, and if they complained, insulted them. "It is impossible for me to conduct the house respectably unless I have the support of the Bench." They gave it— six weeks' hard labour.

Over at the Alhambra, which had acquired a chairman to preside over its activities, Higgitt was getting the same idea as his predecessor. That if he had both entertainment houses he could gain on the swings what he might lose on the roundabouts : and vice versa. Higgitt's name as lessee of the theatre first appears in October, 1869, and soon he was boasting that his company was the best Northampton had seen for years. Gradually, however, the touring company was coming to the fore. Higgitt's bookings for the theatre during 1873 included Wybert Reeve and His Olympic Company formed specially to appear in Wilkie Collins' *The Woman in White*, dramatised from his own novel (as played at the Olympic Theatre, London, and for upwards of 200 nights in the provinces); the London Opera Company managed by Isadore de Solla; and the comedy company of Miss Foote, a grand-niece of the original Maria Foote, who became Countess of Harrington.

In March that year Higgitt booked the most spectacular pantomime the theatre had seen to date—*Blue Beard*, which had run for eight weeks at Leicester's Theatre Royal, of which the manager was John Windley, who had made his debut in leading roles at the Northampton theatre during the terminal season of the Jackman and Morgan Company in 1860–1. Even allowing for the tendency to flatter, the notices he then received indicated that he had made a real impact. His talent appears to have commanded attention.

Later he showed that he could be an able manager too, adapting himself to the changing conditions, perhaps, in a manner in which Jackman and Morgan were too tied to tradition to emulate. He managed theatres at Hanley, Stafford, and Lichfield and also took companies to Stamford Windley had remained with the Jackman Company at Banbury and subsequently at Reading until May, 1861. July that year found him in his home town of Leicester under the lesseeship of H. Powell. He also performed at Nottingham, among other places, before taking over the Leicester theatre in April, 1868, from George Owen.

A particularly interesting Windley playbill I found was at Stamford where, in April, 1870, the cast of Lytton's *Money* includes John Windley, his brother Harry, and Charles Jackman. One would like to think that Windley never forgot the debt he owed to Charles Jackman for giving him his first big chance and was repaying it in small kind by giving him this acting assignment. Another Stamford bill of June that year shows that Windley was among the many members of the profession who belonged to the Masonic fraternity. *Meg's Diversion* was performed on Friday, June 10, 1870, for the benefit of Brother John Windley, Menturia Lodge, No. 418, and patronised by the Freemasons Lodge of Merit, No. 466.

Charles Jackman also turns up at Stamford on Friday, May 7, 1869, in the cast of a one-night performance by Charles Mathews and on this occasion Mr. C. A. Clarke, another former Northampton manager, and his wife, were also in the cast.

After his attempt at running the theatre, Mr. Higgitt tried another double venture, taking over the Circus, a wooden building in Abington Square, but he was not successful there. He grew disenchanted with Northampton, as so many had before him, and decided to return to Coventry, though not immediately. An advertisement of October, 1873, stated that the Alhambra Music Hall and Tavern was to let. Applicants were to approach Mr. Higgitt or Phillips Brothers, the brewers.

When Mr. Higgitt finally left the town in March, 1874, the Alhambra came into the management of Mr. W. Roche, from Nottingham, where he ran another Alhambra (the former Theatre Royal). Three months later Roche lost his wife because of a piece of orange peel. While pregnant she slipped on it walking in the street near the Alhambra, Nottingham, at about the time her husband was taking up the Northampton management. Three weeks after the accident she gave birth but took a turn for the worse and died, aged thirty-four, leaving five children. Roche was to be the last proprietor of the Northampton Alhambra in its old guise as a drinking den.

Some of the plainest words on the fortunes of the theatre at this time came not from the century-and-a-half-old Mercury or the forty-year-old Herald, but from a new newspaper which made it a three-way competition. Soon after its launching by Thomas Arlidge on June 27, 1873, the Northampton Albion commented: "The Northampton people are not as a rule playgoers and usually the better the company that favours the town the less patronage they get. On Tuesday last the audience was very thin. Perhaps this might be partly due to the excursions that left the town but certainly the present party deserves much better patronage. If the house be filled it is not much." And a little later: "Every manager who is enterprising enough to bring a company to this theatre is certain to do it at his own personal loss and, of course, the better the company the greater the loss. Under these circumstances it is to be wondered at that the Drama patronises Northampton quite as much as that Northampton does not patronise the Drama."

Meanwhile the Theatre Royal had four more fleeting managers and/or lessees—Mr. S. Geary, in late 1873; Mr. E. Walton Browne, in 1874; Chevalier Byron, in late 1874; and Mr. J. P. McFadyen, in 1875. About Chevalier Byron a little more must be said since he provided what might be counted as the best farcical entertainment ever at the theatre. Though not intentionally.

In Walsall on October 4, 1874, Mr. William John Simpson bought a copy of the national weekly newspaper The Era. Being an out-of-work actor he turned to the advertisements for "the profession" where he read: "Wanted for the winter season commencing October 24 and ending April 5, 1875, a complete dramatic company. Also a good scenic artist and stage carpenter. Ladies to send cartes. Also a good clown for Christmas. Apply George Craythorpe, secretary, Theatre Royal, Northampton." He answered, stating his terms, and accepted the offer which came in reply of 7s. a week less, on condition he received a share of the benefit.

After making his way to Northampton and presenting himself at the theatre he was met by a page in uniform who looked blank when he asked for Mr. Craythorpe. "I don't know a Mr. Craythorpe, Sir. There is an old gentleman . . ." He was introduced to Chevalier Byron and was bemused to note that the letter which the old gentleman signed confirming his engagement was in the same handwriting as the letter from "George Craythorpe". Simpson was engaged as "first old man"; his wife was also set on as "first old woman".

The old gentleman, Chevalier Byron, alias George Craythorpe, had been promising great things for his new regime at the Marefair theatre. His advertisements were long and rambling as if expense was of no account. He was billed as the lessee, while his wife, Madame Byron Lenca, was said to be the manager. Mrs. Lenca (or Byron) was described as of La Scala, Milan, though whether she ever graced that stage or indeed, whether Byron was a Chevalier subsequent events left some doubt.

The Byrons were going to make the theatre a magnificent place. Outside they placed some sort of wooden castellation to give suitable dignity and inside they banished draughts. According to the Albion they even made the ladies' cloakroom "habitable". The advertisement was prodigal in its detail. For some years adverts of any sort had been the exception but now they appeared listing the entire company and even giving their initials or Christian names, an unusual extravagance. There were Miss Vittoria Clyde, Miss Ada Tisdale, Miss Maria Marshall, Miss Louisa Stanhope, Miss Fanny Harrison, Mr. Harry Volaire, Mr. E. H. Francis, Mr. D. H. Curtis, Mr. Jas. Wright, Mr. H. Travers, and Mr. T. G. Harcourt, as well as the Byrons and Simpsons and a man named Wylson. They were summed up as "a galaxy of talent".

When opening night came, however, they were not all present. Nor were the "extensive alterations" completed. The première had to be postponed five days, to Thursday, October 29. When it did take place it could not have been a great success for Byron himself took a garrulous advertisement to admit that "with a few exceptions, they were, I candidly admit, dire bad—not fit for a travelling booth. Immediately on seeing their performance I gave the stage manager, Mr. W. J. Simpson, orders to put up a notice which, in theatrical rules, must extend a fortnight. I then set to work to obtain fresh artistes." He announced that he would re-open on Friday, November 20, with a good company.

What Byron failed to mention was that he had not paid the old company. And when in due course he sacked the second company he did not pay them either. That some of them needed dismissing was his own fault for engaging them : at least two of the ladies so grandly heralded had never set foot on the stage before. At the same time, it is not surprising that given this type of cavalier treatment some of the raw Thespians assembled themselves into a riot and threw stones which broke the windows of the theatre.

Just how much of a fool Chevalier Byron was and how much of a rogue it is hard to determine at this distance. He was of American origin and maybe had the Yankee gift for "flannel". Whatever the shade of his character he secured for the theatre its most extensive coverage in its history, mainly in the police court column. Space precludes a full reproduction of the court hearings but they were far more entertaining than what Byron presented at the theatre.

First Simpson prosecuted him for operating the theatre without a licence. Byron had overlooked this formality. The play on the night specified on the charge sheet was *David Garrick or An Actor's Honour*. Simpson supported his case with evidence such as "He is no actor. I and Wylson are the only actors. I have been here seven weeks and had only two weeks money. There was a riot there. He brought a lot of ladies from London and did not pay them." Byron countered with accusations that Simpson had stolen some green baize, had been trying to do him all the injury he could, and, without permission, had given recitations and comic songs at the Cross Keys. Byron was fined but the day after that hearing he threw out of the theatre a bailiff sent to collect the evening's takings, because he had not paid the theatre rent. So again he was in court.

The Mercury summed up the Byron episode thus : "For some months past the play-going public has had the infliction of a company of artists (?) whose performances have been of a wretched character. At last the manager, finding that the people of Northampton were not to be duped and that playing to empty benches would not pay, departed."

These then, were some of the managers of the years 1861–75. A number of leading characters in the life of Northampton also took roles of one sort or another at the theatre. Among them were Mark Dorman and Joseph Gurney, who both occupied the Mayoral office, and Charles Bradlaugh, who represented the town in Parliament, after several times being thrown out of the House, on one occasion bodily.

Many Mayors had given their patronage to the theatre but in 1864 a Mayor actually performed on the stage, just after a Mayoralty which had seen the opening of the new Town Hall. Unlike previous gentlemen who had lent their services to the local stage, Mark Dorman did not rub shoulders with professional actors but appeared with what was probably Northampton's first properly organised amateur dramatic society.

Northampton Amateur Dramatic Club gave its inaugural performance at the theatre in December, 1864, with several leading personalities in the town in the casts of *The Illustrious Stranger* and *Bombastes Furioso*. Mr. Dorman appeared in both and a prologue spoken by Captain Landon, secretary of the club, said :

> *"Bowbell-Cockney who has crossed the line*
> *Who could so well his feelings act and share*
> *As a poor devil who has been the Mayor?"*

The house glittered in every respect, as it had not done for some time. To quote the Mercury : "For many years the drama has led, as everyone knows, a somewhat forlorn life. The theatre has not been fashionable, although that love of the dramatic element which seems part of our nature, has never ceased to manifest itself in a variety of half-shabby ways. For example people who shun the adaptations for dramatic representations offered by a regular stage, and the conveniences of boxes, pit and gallery, flock to witness pretty much the same kind of thing on a makeshift, miniature stage at the end of a long room under the title of 'Drawing Room Entertainments', 'Monopylogues' and ingenious avoidances of the legitimate name. But the tide seems beginning to turn . . . the drama seems likely to take its place among fashionable amusements."

On this particular night "half a century at least has elapsed since such a line of carriages was seen in Gold Street destined to draw up at the hitherto-deserted doors at the corner of Marefair. Within the sight was as unusual as without. The pit had been boarded over and chairs supplied the place of benches; the boxes had been newly papered and decorated; the front taste-fully decorated with white muslin; and the pillars wreathed with artificial flowers. The appearance of the house alone was well worth the price of the tickets." Carriages were to be ordered at a quarter to ten, to take up with the horses' heads towards Gold Street.

Mark Dorman, one of the stars of the evening, was the proprietor of Dorman's United Libraries which had access to the works of Mudie's Library and the London Library Company thus affording the borrower a choice of half-a-million books for a subscription of a guinea a year. Free public libraries were not yet common. Dorman had also jumped on the band-wagon of photography, with a photographic portrait gallery with "the best apparatus and first class operators". There was also a Dorman's Waiting Room for the free use of customers and library subscribers— "Visitors from the country will find every accommodation for reading, waiting, letter-writing etc."

When Mark Dorman died in December, 1876, his library etc. in the Drapery was sold to Mark and Bailey. The business is still there today as W. Mark and Co. (1935) Ltd., one of the patrons of this book.

A Northampton Member of Parliament who was one of the most contro-versial figures in the history of British Parliaments made an early appearance at the Northampton theatre, when he stepped uninvited on to the stage. A newspaperman recalled the incident in 1922 when the premises were being demolished : "Northampton then had a passion for public discussion between representatives of the Christian Evidence Society and the Freethinkers. It was at the theatre that this correspondent first heard Charles Bradlaugh. A Christian Evidence Society speaker had been lecturing when, at the close, questions or comments were invited a youthful looking man stepped from the stalls on to the stage and delivered a telling retort upon the speaker's remarks. That was Charles Bradlaugh who was better known as the Iconoclast and was regarded as the leader of the Secularists."

Later Bradlaugh made more formal appearances at the theatre, such as in September, 1865, when he took part in a discussion with the Rev. W. Woodman, under the chairmanship of Mr. J. P. Berry, on the subject of "Bible Creation : Scientific or Revelationary?" So keen was the interest that when the subject was not exhausted after many hours on the first night, the two protagonists agreed to continue the following night. There was again a crowded house, this time with Joseph Gurney in the chair.

Joseph Gurney was in fact the secretary of the theatre for many years as well as a commanding figure in local politics, despite being an odd man out. Born on April 15, 1814, in the Northamptonshire village of Watford in real "squire" country, he was a natural reformer. He belonged to the Northampton Reform and Political Union, an extreme body (in those days!) which did not approve the Reform Bill because it did not go far enough. Its members wanted the ballot and Gurney was the Northampton agent of the Ballot Society. He was a stronger Chartist than the Chartists; a greater Radical than the Radicals; an advanced Socialist in the best sense of the word—that is to say that he believed in "volunteer Socialism", not the dragooning of the State.

Just how and when he became secretary of the theatre I have not managed to establish. It seems odd that he should do so : it was not his usual "scene", though his own life was so over-full of dramatic incident that it could have provided the plots for half-a-dozen meaty plays. He was one of Northampton's great Victorians. As to when he took on the job of theatre secretary : by 1877 he had held the post for many years, because he said so when the Town Council discussed whether a circus on Campbell Square should pay rates. He said : "I have had a good deal to do with the theatre for many years and it is difficult sometimes to make that pay, yet it is rated rather heavily. We ought not to put competing things in the way without making them pay rates."

At Watford Gurney's father had kept one of those village shops where almost anything could be bought though he was nominally a grocer, draper and tailor. When Joseph was but six, father died, leaving him the youngest of a family of boys. Brought up by a tailor he worked in the county villages of Yelvertoft, Long Buckby and Braunston before setting up his own tailor's shop in Castle Street, Northampton, as W. and J. Gurney, tailors and habit makers, offering "unprecedentedly low prices". W. Gurney was his brother. Later the business moved to George Row as J. Gurney, the brother having died, and West of England suits were offered at £4 and £5. From that address he married his first wife in 1837, being the fifth bridegroom to be married at Northampton Register Office, set up in that year under the Act ordaining the civil registration of births, marriages and deaths, as a result of which Somerset House is such a treasure store of information for the historian.

Had it not been for his responsibilities to his widowed mother and others, it is said that Gurney would have thrown in his lot with Robert Owen's idealistic Hampshire Community. Instead he remained in Northampton to urge reforms in many spheres.

After many attempts he was elected to the Town Council in July, 1858, filling the West Ward seat left vacant by the death of Christopher Markham, a Conservative. For his first ten years on the Council, Gurney was a man apart, often unable to find a seconder for his resolutions, let alone sufficient support to get them approved. As late as 1868 he was the only Radical on the council and it was as a result of the celebrated deal with the Liberals that further headway was made.

In 1874 he was made an Alderman and the following year he became Mayor, being the first in the United Kingdom to affirm instead of taking the oath of office. His second Mayoralty of 1879 was also fated to be historic, in that it was a dead-heat in the voting between him and the Conservative nominee W. J. Peirce. Scenes of uproar at the intended public Mayor-Making in the Town Hall had driven the councillors upstairs to the Council Chamber where Gurney got the chain by the casting vote of the outgoing Mayor, Alderman William Dennis, who observed that though they might differ from him on religious matters they considered him a man of business who had risen from the lowest rank.

What is now the mighty Anglia Building Society was formed, as the Northampton Freehold Land Society, in Gurney's house in Gold Street (he had moved first to George Street and then to Gold Street, near the theatre). The first secretary, in 1848, was Mr. J. Dyer, then Master of the town's Lancasterian School. Gurney succeeded him in 1856 and continued as secretary and a director until 1889. Many people called it not the Freehold Land Society but simply "Gurney's Society". Even when he retired in 1889 the connection was not lost for he then became president, succeeding Labouchere, Liberal M.P. and colleague of Charles Bradlaugh. He remained president until his death.

Meantime, in 1865 he had left Gold Street, having lost his second wife several years before, to live in a newly-built house, Elysium Cottage, in the appropriately-named Freehold Street.

From 1871–7, its first six years, he was a member of Northampton School Board. In March, 1879, against his wishes ("I am getting older and already have more on my hands than I can comfortably attend to") he was elected to the new Northampton Grammar School Charity as he would "more nearly represent the class for whom the charity is intended".

Later that year his name appears in the list of eighteen directors of the People's Cafe Company which took over the lease of Mr. Perkins' former grocery shop in Gold Street to provide the town with its first "People's Cafe" —a sort of working men's club, without the stimulation of alcohol. Gurney was a temperate and a quiet man—angry only in the cause of reform.

When he addressed the annual dinner of Northampton Riveters and Finishers in 1877 he said that he had been one of the working class all his life and his sympathies had always been with the working man. This was no doubt true, but he appears to have made some money along the way for in 1886 he lent Mr. Samuel Smith Campion £1,000 on mortgage to help him pay for the Northampton Mercury into which Campion subsequently merged the Northamptonshire Guardian and Northampton Weekly Reporter, which he had founded in 1876 and 1881 respectively. No doubt it was all for "the cause". Also odd was Gurney's role as an income tax collector!

The events leading to Gurney's death were as pulsating as melodrama. After a spell of poor health he went on a recuperation holiday to Southport, with his housekeeper, Miss Waters. From here he took a steamer trip to Llandudno but was taken ill and unable to leave the ship at the North Wales resort. On the way back the ship ran into high seas and in trying to make the difficult entrance to port ran aground where it remained for some time, Gurney lying "more dead than alive" in a cabin. When the tide freed the vessel it did so only after nearly turning it turtle, so that the passengers shouted and screamed in fear. Even when the boat got back to Southport after midnight there was a further trial in store. The pier was unmanned, no one having thought of staying to tie up the overdue steamer. So the weary passengers had to wait another three hours. Gurney never got over this ordeal. Mind you, he was nearly eighty at the time.

What Joseph Gurney, upholder of the working man's right to his own freehold house and described in his day as the most advanced of Socialists, would think to the antics of some of the present-day Socialists, busily depriving thousands of their freeholds in whatever name (progress, improvement, etc) but largely in the interest of the property developer, one can but speculate.* My own view is that they must make him positively spin in his grave in the General Cemetery, Billing Road, Northampton, to which he was borne in February, 1893, without flowers or wreaths (by request), with no religious service, only a graveside address by his friend, Mr. J. M. Robertson, concluding with the words ". . . for the rest, silence. Farewell." Hundreds saw the last informal rites.

The time is perhaps overdue that I should return to my proper theme of the theatre and to the year 1875 when its proprietors formulated a plan to knock it down and rebuild on the same site (to which reference will be made later). Instead they dropped the idea and set about trying, for the umpteenth time, to improve the place. Half-a-dozen new scenes were painted by Mr. Maugham of the Princess Theatre, London, among them an Act Drop of a Swiss Lake scene which is today the only surviving item of the theatre's possessions. When the building was demolished this scene was retained by Latimer and Crick, corn merchants, who had been the final occupiers. They took it to their new premises in Horsemarket and when these in turn were demolished it was still preserved. The present unofficial "curators" are Mr. and Mrs. Norman Gibbs, of Hedgerows, Harlestone, who are among the patrons of this book. *(Page 227.)*

Another improvement effected was a negative one. The proprietors sent a memorial to the Town Council protesting against the "intolerable nuisance" of the urinal which had been erected adjoining the theatre. In a motion seconded by Mr. T. P. Dorman (a future owner of the Theatre Royal and Opera House, Guildhall Road) the Sanitary, Lighting and Cleansing Committee agreed to remove it and place an enlarged facility on Wood Hill, behind All Saints churchyard.

What was it like to be in the theatre on a Saturday night at this time? For a lively account of such a visit in 1875 we are indebted to the Northampton Albion. Only a few weeks before the paper was to reach its last issue the editor had the bright idea of publishing a bit of real live journalism, in contrast to the usual flannel about respectable audiences and spirited managers. We can be there, with eye and ear. Here is the account the reporter brought back :

"The gallery and pit were crowded and the boxes filled. The audience was not a select one; the gods, principally in working attire and sans soap and water, were jubilant as they pressed forward, leaning in perilous manner over the gallery railings and their comments on the performances were too loud to be agreeable; they also had a bad habit of pitching orange peel and other refuse into the pit. In fact a piece of lighted paper at one time came floating down from the regions above, much to the horror of nervous people; fortunately the audience generally exhibited no signs of nervousness; they came to the theatre to enjoy themselves, each in his own way and they were determined to do so at any risk.

"The pit contained a more ordered assemblage, so wedged in that it was almost impossible to move and consequently the occupants had to submit to the indignities heaped upon them from above. Ever and anon an excited

* Lest I be accused of political bias I should add that the party of property-owning democracy have been similarly occupied.

individual would rise up in protest but his protestations were inaudible above the din and whistling; he could only shake his fist, mutter vengeance and then return to his seat.

"The side boxes appeared to have been turned into a nursery for here infantile specimens of humanity were being danced, soothed and fed by many mothers. Of course, they sometimes objected, as babies do, to the whole proceedings when shouts came from the Gods to 'Keep that young 'un quiet can't yer?'

"The centre boxes had a motley throng—ladies who did not object between the acts to sip out of bottles and gentlemen gallant enough to fetch in cans of beer from some neighbouring public for their spouses. The private boxes also had some occupants as well but none of these would have come under our observation had not one of the ladies between the acts handed down a suspicious looking bottle from her private seat to someone in the pit and afterwards a parcel of solid refreshments to some individual."

Two brothers performing on a trapeze received approval in the form of a shower of coppers and oranges. The Albion expressed sympathy with those who had to perform on the stage in such conditions. They certainly needed it for on this occasion they were amateurs.

Quite apart from what shenanigans went on when you got to the theatre, there was the question of getting there. For most people the route lay down Gold Street and this could be fraught with embarrassment if not danger. There was no question of golden silence in this thoroughfare.

After one Gold Street couple had been savagely attacked a grocer named Perkins (it must have been the one whose premises were later to become the People's Cafe) appeared in court to ask for better protection for the residents. Other streets were quiet, he said, but when you got into Gold Street there was always a crowd of roughs and it was impossible to walk down it. The obscene language was also trying. A Mr. Watts corroborated. : the morality of Gold Street was low indeed, he claimed, and there was uproar and confusion. The situation was not improved in summer by the lack of street lighting, said Mr. Watts, at which the Chief Constable recalled a time when people leaving All Saints Church (at the top of the street) knocked their heads together, it was so dark.

With this picture in mind of the theatre-lovers of Northampton fighting their way down Gold Street through crowds of insulting hooligans to attend a performance they might not be able to hear when they got there, we will pass on to consider what alternative forms of amusement there were in Northampton to tempt them in other directions, to other houses of pleasure.

INTERLUDE

in Act the Third

Consisting of three songs

"THE MORE THE MERRIER" sung in concert by guest artistes from the Corn Exchange, Town Hall, Lecture Halls, Thomas's Music Hall etc.

"DON'T LET YOUR KNICKERS CATCH ON FIRE" by Miss Davis.

"THE BOOZIEST STREET IN BRITAIN" rendered by Mr. Gustavus Vaughan Brooke, who will be supported (if necessary) by fellow members of the company.

N.B. The audience are requested not to leave empty bottles under their seats.

THE CORN EXCHANGE was a competitor but had a cavernous echo.

"THE MORE THE MERRIER"

Music hall was by no means the only alternative place and form of entertainment which competed for the shillings and pence of what the Victorians called the "pleasure-loving section of the community". There were all sorts of new diversions and a variety of new premises.

All over the country new town halls, assembly rooms, corn exchanges, mechanics' institutes etc. had been built and in at least some cases the more spacious and comfortable accommodation they provided actually supplanted the theatres. At Peterborough the old theatre had been pulled down to make way for a Corn Exchange; in its turn the Corn Exchange was demolished and the site, next to the parish church, is now occupied by a controversial office block. In Daventry an assembly room was used for entertainments after the 1837 theatre opened by Jackman had been relegated to use as a lecture hall. At Bedford the Jackman theatre became disused, giving way to corn exchange and assembly room.

In Northampton a far-sighted reader of the Mercury had written to the paper in July, 1858, asking how long Northampton, a town of 30,000 people, must wait for a commodious or decent building for transaction of public business and holding of public meetings. He added that if the new hall were built upon proper acoustic principles "a fair income might accrue from musical and other events". Within six years the new Town Hall was built in St. Giles Square, a stone's throw from where the old Playhouse had been. It was opened in 1864 during the Mayoralty of Mark Dorman.

In choosing the site for the new Town Hall the council had considered several alternatives before settling on that of Dr. Robertson's house, in St. Giles Square. The nearby Black Boy in Wood Hill (where the Midland Bank now stands) was one possibility; another public house, the Goat in Gold Street, had also been considered for sacrifice on the altar of municipal advancement.

Pickering Phipps, the brewer councillor, wanted to see the Corn Exchange used instead and this was followed up by a letter-writer—"It could also be used as a courthouse," he pointed out. "An easy modification of the orchestra would accommodate the jury excellently well. The stands of the Corn Exchange occupiers could be put together and covered to form as good a table as ever counsel enfisted his argument upon." When the Town Hall had been built he tried to get permission to use its cellars for storing his liquid wares. It would help to pay the hall's expenses, he explained. His offer was not taken up.

After much wrangling, in traditional Northampton style, about design and costs (especially costs) as well as site, the Town Fathers had allowed the Town Hall to be constructed on a surprising scale of splendour and style (architect William Godwin), though even so it had to be extended in the early 1890s. Subject to the limitation of its not having a dramatic licence, a wide variety of entertainments were staged there, including organ recitals sponsored by the Town Council.

When Chas. H. Du-Val, having performed at the theatre, announced that he was moving to the Town Hall, the Herald commented that "this was certainly a more suitable place for him." In spite of the suitability the attendance there was no better and the Herald then said that "in the existing multiplicity of means of amusement it is perhaps hardly to be wondered at that some should lack extensive support."

When Henry Loraine was appearing at the theatre his threat to take legal action against Millie Howard in respect of her "serio-comic" concerts at the Town Hall, which he referred to as an unlicensed building, caused her to alter the content of her programme of operettinas.

Before leaving the Town Hall I cannot refrain from remarking that as I write in 1973 it may be considered ironic that not having lifted a finger to stop the New Theatre, Abington Street (built in 1912) from being replaced by a supermarket, the local authority has spent money brightening up the Victorian Town Hall for public entertainments, unless one sees the latter act as one of contrition. For though the act of re-furbishing the hall is splendid in itself, the place is not suitable for this purpose, having acoustics leaving almost as much to be desired as the building next discussed.

I refer to the Corn Exchange. Besides the Town Hall, the tiny theatre faced the competition of this vast building on the north-western corner of the Market Square. Its promoters had much more in mind than the marketing of corn. The prospectus of 1848 said that the building would be for public meetings, lectures and concerts on a large scale and would provide rooms for literary and other societies. "As the want of adequate accommodation in Northampton has long been observed it is believed that a considerable income may be realised from these sources." First the existing buildings had to be cleared from the site at a cost of £3,500; the actual construction cost was estimated to be £7,500 but this was in fact exceeded.

The large hall of the exchange was called the music hall, in the sense of a hall for music. It may be wondered, perhaps, why the Corn Exchange, pre-dating as it did the Town Hall, did not indeed meet the requirements of the town for a large auditorium etc. The answer is that it had some shortcomings. It was impossible to heat it adequately: at one stage they installed stoves, with the chimney pipes stuck out of the windows. It had an echo: words declaimed in it got lost as they wandered around the lofty reaches of the roof. Far from being too small, the place was too big. The lighting, too, was inadequate. In December, 1862, following a concert in December 1862, the Mercury complained: "The hall was not well filled. Something was lost by those present for unless the hall is well filled the resonance is intolerable. We must renew our protest against the obstinate folly of omitting footlights, thus presenting the performers as so many silhouettes. To be straining the eyes at a set of shadows jumbled up with rails and pianoforte legs is merely to distract the ear and weary the eye."

The Guardian suggested that a folding ceiling of canvas would solve the echo problem and that curtains dividing up the vast room would make it more available.

The promoters must have been short-sighted indeed to spend money building a place so enormous that it defeated their attempts to make it practicable. In the present century the problems were overcome and it became a cinema, where the first sound film show was given in the town. It is now the Odeon Cinema.

But to return to the age which concerns us at present, at the start of their week in Northampton in June, 1872, Miss Virginia Blackwood announced loftily that her company was obliged to appear at the theatre "in consequence of there being no scenery at the Corn Exchange". After taking a good benefit on Friday night Miss Blackwood did a flit with the leading man, leaving the company unable to perform properly on the Saturday night. Only two acts of the main piece were played and the farce was not even attempted. An irate audience set about dismantling the theatre fittings and considerable damage was done.

As had been promised, the Mechanics Institute occupied rooms at the Exchange and in October, 1872, it managed to acquire a dramatic licence for the large hall, while disavowing any intention of setting up in rivalry to the theatre. Nevertheless when Mr. D'Oyly Carte sent an opera company to the town in 1882 to perform Gilbert and Sullivan's "Patience", then still running at the Savoy Theatre, London, they appeared not at the theatre but at the Corn Exchange. The Mercury's hailing the event as "possibly the most brilliant theatre success ever achieved in Northampton" was indeed an insult to the Theatre Royal and a reflection of how Un-Royal it really was.

In 1876 it had appeared that a suitable use had at last been found for the Corn Exchange when skating was introduced there by the proprietor of the Victoria Hall Skating Rink, Exeter. Four hundred turned up on the first day. Skating hours were from 11–1, 3–5, and 7.30–9.30 except on Saturday mornings when the Corn Exchange served its nominal purpose. The bareness of the place was relieved by flags, evergreens and Chinese lanterns.

Then a snag developed. It was found that a patent was being infringed by the use without licence of the Plympton skates. In stepped Mr. H. J. Mulliner, a coach-builder whose name has passed into car history, to secure the area patent for the skates. He introduced skating at the Victoria Pleasure Gardens which he had opened adjacent to the new St. John Street Station, terminus of the Bedford–Northampton railway line. The land had a connection with the theatre for it was the old gardens of the Hospital of St. John. Mulliner moved his coaches from his old showroom to new buildings in Bridge Street and used the old one for the skating.

Some unusual competition came in March, 1869, from Mark Lemon, editor of Punch, who appeared as Falstaff in scenes from *Henry IV* at the

Town Hall, as he had done before the Prince and Princess of Wales. He was the first editor of that humorous journal in July, 1841, at £1 a week, and it was during a preliminary meeting that someone commented that the proposed paper would be like a good mixture of punch, nothing without Lemon. Thus Punch got its name. Lemon, who remained as editor for thirty-nine years, had three things in common with his three successors, Shirley Brooks, Tom Taylor and Francis Burnand—he was bearded, was a playwright, and was of ample girth. Their initials are among those carved on the famous "Punch" table, now in Tudor Street, in the Fleet district. Mark Lemon launched a revolution in pantomime with one he wrote for Madame Celeste at the Adelphi in 1857.

After his Northampton appearance the Mercury commented that they had been told to expect something good "but we were not prepared for so perfect and original an embodiment of it as Mark Lemon presented". Before it the paper had commented that a good deal of the interest the performances aroused in London was due to his reputation as the editor of Punch.

Penny Readings were a form of entertainment in town and village which appear in proliferation at this time. Organised usually by their betters, the working folk would go along to some convenient premises and listen to a few amateur songs and recitations. In many cases these replaced the touring entertainments of the strollers and were in any case more frequent and accessible. At Northampton the Penny Readings at the Mechanics Institute were very well attended. In the village of Wootton, just south of the town, the first of a series of Penny Readings was given in February, 1868, in a large barn lent by Mr. W. O. Harris, of Wootton Hall. The barn was "filled to excess, many being obliged to return, unable to gain admittance". On the programme were readings, glees and comic and sentimental songs. This form of entertainment is also mentioned among many other places at Brixworth, where there were readings varied with instrumental and vocal music and 230 were admitted but many turned away.

Over the Buckinghamshire border at Newport Pagnell a Penny Reading audience proved as noisy as some of those at our Theatre Un-Royal. "The audience was large, noisy and so very demonstrative that they encored not only every song but also every reading without the slightest judgment or discrimination. Of course, it was impossible to comply with their wishes which would have been just to repeat the entire programme." The next time the mob paid their pennies, they received stern words of warning from Mr. Thomas Coales who presided. "He impressed upon that portion of the audience likely to need such a caution the necessity of proper behaviour under the pain of being given over to the custody of a policeman who was present." This caution had the desired effect.

In December, 1863, the first Penny Readings organised by the Daventry Literary and Scientific Institute were held in the "lecture hall (late theatre)".

All sorts of other diversions arose, too many to deal with here and worthy sometime perhaps of a book on "How they were amused". At Melbourne Gardens (now Franklins Gardens and the home of the Saints rugby team) for instance there were bicycle races and the services of a gymnast instructor were free to all who paid the few coppers admission to the grounds.

And despite the various "depressions" in trade the working man was beginning to have just a little more money in his pocket and just a little more time to spend it. Not much. But some. Compared with the hours of work of the mid-twentieth century with its general five-day week and consequent two-day week-end and its three to four weeks annual paid holidays, conditions of a century ago were hard indeed. Paid holidays were unheard of. But things had improved a little. There were associations at work to reduce the hours of shops and to reduce the number of hours in the working week generally. There was an Early Closing movement as a result of the activities of which drapers, tailors, outfitters and general furnishing warehouses agreed to close on Thursdays at the early (!) hour of four o'clock, as from April, 1881.

Which alternative to the theatre provided the most serious competition in Northampton? Probably it was the music hall because you could drink and smoke there while being entertained. The general application of this point was referred to in comments in the Mercury on a London court case in the autumn of 1870, the result of which was that music halls might not display ballet dancing.

"The theatres are rejoicing over the interdict upon ballet dancing in musichalls. Places like the Alhambra and the Highbury Barn (both in London) have told heavily against the interests of the theatrical profession. Ballets, with freedom to drink and smoke, were found to be more effective than dramas at which the spectators were compelled to sit cigarless and thirsty. Paymasters of the Alhambra and such places have shown that leg pieces are the sort of spectacle people approve of most highly. Now the Middlesex magistrates have determined that the Terpsichorean feat of lifting your leg above your head shall no longer be performed upon music-hall stages." In default the Alhambra had started promenade concerts and military music . . .

But along with the competition within the town the theatre had to face challenges from without. You could now take a rail excursion to see a pantomime or other entertainment in London, Birmingham or Leicester. The new mobility brought its problems.

After half-a-century of waiting Northampton finally acquired a main-line railway station in 1881. Castle Station was opened on the historic site of the town's castle, where kings had held court. The castle remains were obliterated in a supreme act of Victorian vandalism.

"Northampton now becomes a suburb of London," said the Mercury. "A gentleman who begins business at 10 and finishes at 4 can now run up to town by train, complete his day's work and return to the bosom of his family in time for a fashionable dinner."

"DON'T LET YOUR KNICKERS CATCH ON FIRE"

A happening at the theatre on Thursday, April 14, 1870, would have received banner headlines in the newspapers had they been in the habit of using that sensational means of proclamation. As they weren't it didn't. In those days even the most newsworthy events merited a heading only slightly larger than the type size of the story over which they appeared.

In this case it really was "hot" news. Miss Davis, principal dancer, was the victim of a serious accident. We do not know in what role she was appearing, the name of the play or the company for at this time the theatre's productions did not appear in the advertising columns and the editorial columns as a rule therefore ignored the happenings at the theatre, unless something really unusual happened. Such as someone's knickers catching fire which, if you will pardon the expression and use of journalistic sensationalism, is what appears to have happened to the unfortunate Miss Davis.

She was dancing near the footlights (remember that this was before the days of electric footlights) when "the high heel of one of her boots caught in an irregularity in the flooring and she was thrown forward on to the footlights and her light dress was instantly in a blaze. Her struggles threw her over the orchestra into the pit where some gentlemen instantly wrapped her in their coats and extinguished the fire but not before she was terribly burned about the arms and body." In the excitement a lad jumped from the gallery to come to her aid, happily without injury.

A doctor who was sent for pronounced that the dancer was in a precarious state. Six weeks later she was still in bed.

The week after the accident a benefit performance was given for her and at the officers' mess of the local militia the Marquess of Exeter organised a subscription.

While there were bare flames about, it was inevitable that there should be accidents of this type from time to time. Four years earlier there had been a fatal outcome when Columbine caught fire at the Lyceum, Sunderland. A rubber tube connecting gas lights in the wings had become detached, the gas ignited causing a loud explosion and flames leapt to the top of the stage. Miss Louisa Ricardo, muslin skirt on fire, rushed from wings to stage where her father was appearing in a scene as a clown. From his private box,

Mr. Bell, lessee of the theatre, dashed out, pulled off his top coat and wrapped it round the girl. She appeared to have suffered no lasting effects, the show went on, but the next day she died.

It was not only in the theatre that ladies' clothes were being set ablaze. This was the age of the crinoline, a garment which might have been designed with easy ignition in mind, the hoops which supported the skirt ensuring a good supply of air while at the same time hindering attempts at putting out the undergarments.

Incidentally after reading the Miss Davis incident you may perhaps feel I have a knicker-fixation and that it was the lady's dress that caught fire. On the grounds of strict accuracy you may be right but my point can be validated.

This delicate question of ladies' clothing catching on fire was discussed by a London correspondent of the Mercury on February 22, 1864, six years before the Miss Davis incident. Suggesting that crinolines should be dispensed with during the new pastime of skating, the writer commented that legislation on ladies' skirts was a difficult matter.

"I suppose Lord Raynham will bring in a bill on the subject of ballet dancers and their skirts. In the meantime the Lord Chamberlain has declared that he can do nothing but make the managers take certain precautions to prevent such accidents as happened the other night to Columbine at the Britannia Theatre.

"That dresses can be made uninflammable there is no doubt and that managers can be made to supply such dresses is equally certain. But, as Mr. Webster pathetically pointed out the other day, the garments which usually catch fire are undergarments, with which the manager cannot interfere. So I suppose that, if the ladies of the ballet will not guard themselves against getting into a blaze, the managers cannot be expected to do more than provide means to put them out.

"And after all, the accidents in the theatre are a mere nothing to the accidents in private houses through this cause and the latter, of course, concern nobody except the victims and their friends. People in private life, however, are getting very nervous on the subject. Guards to the fire-grates are now matters of course where dancing is going on and I expect soon to see buckets of water carefully arranged in every ballroom, and servants posted with blankets, ready to catch the dancers as soon as they ignite."

The Mercury reported an accident of July, 1865, when a mother's crinoline dress caught fire as she sat by the grate with her five-year-old son in her arms. A passer-by heard her screams and rushed in—"I was able to quench the upper part of her dress but the hoops prevented my succeeding with her underclothing." On the other hand Mrs. Scott, a dressmaker, who fell into the canal at Bicester was saved by her hoops—the air trapped under her crinoline enabled her to float.

Conflagration was not the only problem with crinolines. Other accidents were sources of embarrassment. The Duchess of Manchester who looked most dignified when dressed up caught her hoops while climbing a stile and landed upside down, exhibiting a pair of scarlet knickers (also new-fangled at the time) to the astonished gaze of the Duke of Malakoff who is reported to have declared "C'etait diabolique!"

In a theatrical setting there was a crinoline catastrophe at Weimar, Germany, which turned high tragedy to low comedy. Christine Hebbel-Enghaus was playing Kriemhild in Hebbel's *Nieblungen*, clad in a crinoline. She was called upon to die but unfortunately chose to do so with her feet facing the audience, her bulging hoops thus exposing her underwear to their gaze.

In the streets of Northampton the voluminous dress was a difficulty which was raised before the Improvement Commissioners in December, 1866, when they decided that no person should be allowed to expose goods outside his house except on Saturdays. People had complained of the difficulty of driving through town on account of the large amount of parcels and boxes outside doorways.

Mr. Gurney said that in Gold Street (which led down to the theatre of which he was secretary) there was a great necessity of this rule as many carriers' carts stood there on Wednesdays and Saturdays. He had frequently seen ladies' dresses torn as they walked along the path. To which another member commented that the danger would be avoided if ladies were to wear less distended dresses.

Imagine by the way, what it must have been like to sit in the theatre next to ladies in crinolines!

Of course, the story of theatres is an incendiary one in other respects than clothes. Theatres are nearly as bad a risk as windows in Ireland. Had not the Theatre Royal, Drury Lane, and the Covent Garden Theatre both been burned down? In 1863 the Plymouth theatre was destroyed; two years later the theatre at Edinburgh and the Surrey Theatre at Sheffield. The Durham theatre had burned in 1869. There were three theatre fires in Glasgow—the Prince of Wales (1869), Royal Albert Hall (1876) and Theatre Royal (1879). The last-named year saw the fiery end of the East London Theatre and in 1880 two more theatres, at Huddersfield and Dublin, went down in flames, within a week of each other.

The Marefair theatre managed to avoid this fate. Its successor was less lucky, as we shall see, being ravaged by fire within three years of being completed. But a man who visited the Marefair theatre many times wrote in later life that he never did so without an uncomfortable feeling as to what might happen in the case of alarm by fire or other cause. "To reach the pit visitors had to tunnel down from the front entrance under the side stalls and enter that part of the theatre by doors on either side of the orchestra. Had anything happened to cause a stampede there must have been a terrible catastrophe."

Gas, which had been so effective in improving illumination, was at the same time a constant danger, especially in the footlights. The Marefair theatre, which had been the scene of the first gas lighting in Northampton, was in existence at the time of the first electric light demonstration in the town, though it did not this time take place at the theatre.

In September, 1882, the first demonstration of the new lighting miracle was to have been in the tent of Northamptonshire Horticultural Society at a Flower Show on Northampton Racecourse. Unlike the brilliant success of the gas evening in the theatre in the 1820's, it was a flop. Matters were put right by a demonstration a few days later on the Market Square, outside the offices of the Herald and Daily Chronicle.

This is perhaps a suitable moment to record that daily newspapers in Northampton had begun in 1880, first the Evening Mail (in the Guardian stable), then the Daily Echo (in the Mercury camp) and the Daily Chronicle.

The new electric light was to be a long time establishing itself, as slow as atomic power is today. Gas hit back with the incandescent mantle.

In the streets of Northampton horse-power in its four-hooved form, still reigned supreme. Horse trams had begun in June, 1881. To go into accidents affecting them would be to stray too far from the point. . . .

To get back to the point, and to gas. Gas was responsible for one of the most horrific theatre accidents of all time, at Exeter, in 1887, when after an escape of gas 130 were burnt, asphyxiated or trampled to death.

At Sunderland, in June, 1883, there was another cause for 183 children being suffocated at a conjuring entertainment. At the end of the performance some of the gallery crowd of 1,000 rushed to the lower part to claim prizes, a door became closed and they piled on top of each other.

A letter to the Albion nine years before had forecast something of this sort happening—but at the Northampton Mechanics Institute in the Corn Exchange, "in the case of alarm, say at the Penny Readings, when there are some hundreds of juveniles present. The means of egress are so dreadfully contracted that the two crowds meeting at the top of the stairs would tumble pell-mell over each other . . ."

Three months after the Sunderland horror, the invention of the safety bolt for theatres was announced—the sort with which we are now all familiar, responding to pressure from the inside but incapable of being opened from the outside.

In 1877, too, there had been a Select Committee on the question of fires, especially in music halls.

So with the hope that Miss Davis did recover sufficiently to get up on her points again we will leave the subject of accidents in the theatre and pass on to the topic of drink and the stage.

"THE BOOZIEST STREET IN BRITAIN"

For its length of under half-a-mile, Northampton's Bridge Street must surely have been one of the booziest streets in Britain. I cannot be precise on the exact date but at one time it had 29 public houses and hotels. Going down on one side were the Bodega, Hole In the Wall, Eagle and Child, Angel Hotel, Spread Eagle, Warwick Arms, Gunning Arms, Plough Hotel, Graziers' Arms, Tom Thumb, Malt Shovel, Globe, Cattle Market Tavern, Fleece Hotel, Half Moon, Magpie, Iron Founders Arms, and White Hart. Coming up the other side—which you probably couldn't, if you had paid a visit to all eighteen going down—were the Railway Tavern, Pomfret Arms, Crown and Anchor, Golden Horse, Black Horse, Pheasant, Bull and Butcher, Wagon and Horses, Saddlers Arms, Woolpack and the Bell Hotel.

This surfeit of drinking facilities partly resulted from the Whig Act of 1830 to free the drink trade. As I mentioned, this had meant that to open a beer-only public house you simply got a licence on demand, as simple as getting a dog licence.

Whether this easy tolerance of the trade played any part in producing the Inebriate Episodes at the theatre which I am about to describe is too controversial a subject to go into here, especially as I must take care not to upset any of my TT friends and patrons who have helped to make this book possible.

What I have done here is to take a number of events with the same theme and made them into an Alcoholic Bundle, in some cases out of chronological sequence, hoping at the same time that my readers will not take this as a sign of any dipsomaniac disposition on my part. In the cause of truth and completeness, however, I must fill in a gap in my previous book, *Death of a Theatre*, history of the New Theatre, in Abington Street, Northampton, in which I lamented its replacement by a supermarket. Among the reasons for my sadness was one that it was inadvisable to mention then, in 1960, when the last house had been only eighteen months previous. I did not at the time care to make a statement about the number of bottles of ale I consumed there after hours with various artists and other characters. Today, fifteen years after the final curtain I can presumably rely on statute-barred by time to avoid any summons for drinking after hours. Could one in any

OLD THEATRE,
MAREFAIR.

Box Plan at Mark's Library, where Seats may
be secured.

Prices of Admission:

Centre Boxes, 3s. Side Boxes, 2s. Pit, 1s.
Gallery, 6d.

DOORS OPEN AT 7,30 TO COMMENCE AT 8

W. MARK, Printer

AFTER THE FIRE at the Theatre Royal and Opera House, Northampton, in February, 1887, the Marefair Theatre was brought back into service, for one week only. This is the front of the programme issued that week, using the border from the Opera House programmes with "Old Theatre" inset. See Epilogue, Page 247.

THE NORTHAMPTON HEAVY MAN ONCE MORE TOLD HE IS NOT WANTED AT THE ST. STEPHEN'S THEATRE.—"A Day WILL come."

THE "DUNSTABLE ACTOR" is a well-known figure of fun. So too, in this A. Boyd cartoon of 1883, was the "Northampton Heavy". It appeared in the "Entracte Annual". (*Courtesy of Harry Greatorex*)

IN AN "ALIEN" THEATRE—W. Maugham, of the Princess Theatre, London, painted this
Act Drop curtain, among others, for the Marefair Theatre in 1876. How it has been preserved,
to be hung temporarily and photographed in November, 1973, in the Guildhall Road theatre
which succeeded it is told on Page 210. The lower picture gives an idea of the comparative
size of the two prosceniums. The curtain measures 17 ft. by 12 ft. 6 in. (*Photos by Bryan J.*
Douglas.)

ABOVE—Osborne Robinson's drawing of Northampton Repertory Theatre today, but with an
early drop curtain inserted. (*Northampton and County
Independent*)

RIGHT—Henry Compton, alias Mackenzie, who
was once a member of the Jackman Company, was
the father of Edward Compton whose company
opened the Theatre Royal and Opera House in
1884. Edward Compton was later joint owner of
that theatre, with Milton Bode.

OPPOSITE—The only surviving full frontal
picture of the Marefair Theatre premises, here
being used after it closed by Latimer and Crick,
Corn Merchants. Note the sign on the right-hand
side of the door "Ye Olde Playhouse". Today
nothing marks the site. (*Northampton Chronicle and
Echo*)

CONTRASTS IN TRANSPORT—In 1904 tram-lines were laid outside the former theatre, which is on the near side of the corner towards the right of the picture, opposite the Palace of Varieties—the former Thomas's Musichall, Alhambra etc.

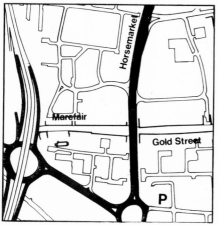

BUT TODAY (left) a dual carriageway is being completed along the line indicated, in the opposite direction, and Gold Street will be sealed off and pedestrianised. (*Above, Northampton Public Library; left, Northampton and County Independent*)

OPPOSITE—Harking back to the author's previous book, "Death of a Theatre", three of the four stone urns which surmounted the parapet of the New Theatre, Abington Street, now have a new home. Above, two are at the entrance to the Moulton home of Mr. Norman Chown; the other is in the St. George's Avenue, Northampton, home of the author. The fourth got broken on the way down. (*Photos top and lower left by E. C. Tippleston*)

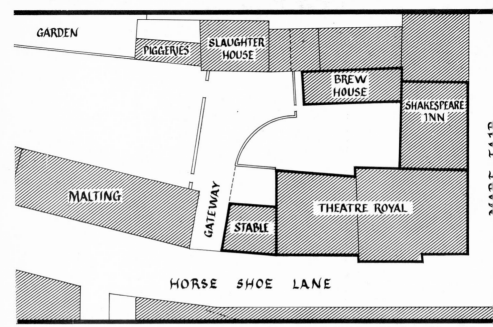

GARDEN

PIGGERIES

SLAUGHTER HOUSE

BREW HOUSE

SHAKESPEARE INN

MALTING

GATEWAY

STABLE

THEATRE ROYAL

HORSE SHOE LANE

A PLAN OF THE MAREFAIR THEATRE SITE, dated 1876, found in the archives of St. John's Hospital. A lease document also found there shows the last lessees in 1884 to have been Messrs. Abel, Cordeux and Eunson who paid £60 a year. (*Trustees of St. John's Hospital and their solicitors, Becke Phipps, per Mr. Eric Halliday*)

THE SCENE TODAY—The "Theatre Un-Royal" stood next to the Shakespeare Inn, where the road this side of it now runs. The widening took place in 1922. See Epilogue, Page 249. The Shakespeare Inn has so far survived but it too is due to be demolished for further road-widening. (*Photo by Roland Holloway*)

case be charged in relation to a building reduced to rubble and present whereabouts unknown?

To return to Mid-Victorian times. They decided to curtail the number of premises where one could get a drink, to put an end to the free-for-all in public house licences.

But first in our Alcoholic Catalogue comes an earlier event, the odd appearance of Gustavus Vaughan Brooke, central figure in the most memorable episode in the management of Charles Wilstone.

All 1863 Mr. Wilstone had refrained from advertising in the Mercury. Whether this was because he did not believe in it or for the more practical reason that he could not afford it we have no means of ascertaining but what we do know is that after eleven months without a single paid-for inch of space he dipped into his pocket and paid good managerial money to announce what was intended to be the highspot of his reign. It was, but not in the manner intended.

The Mercury described it as an extraordinary performance. Gustavus Vaughan Brooke was to play Othello, the role in which he had taken London by storm at the Olympic Theatre in January, 1848. But much water had passed under the bridge since that triumph by the former "Hibernian Roscius" (he played William Tell at the Theatre Royal, Dublin, when aged 13); and a great deal of brandy, stout and porter had passed down the gullet of G.V.B.

We have two accounts of what happened, one by the Mercury, the other by a correspondent of the Australian Magazine. It may be asked what a representative of the Australian Magazine was doing at the theatre at Northampton. The explanation is that Australia had an interest in Brooke, who had spent several years in that Continent as actor and manager, making and then losing considerable sums of money.

The Mercury reported that Brooke's name drew a good house but that impatience grew as a curtain which had been due to rise at half-past-seven was still down at eight o'clock. The Australian correspondent wrote in an issue two months later, about his visit to the "dingy tumble-down-looking place which does duty as a Theatre Royal" : "The house, dress circle excepted, was full; the pittites, solid-looking respectable people wearing, most of them, that expectant critical look which Charles Lamb regarded as the true mark of the old play-goer, but which is now as extinct as the dodo."

In manner factual the Mercury takes up the story. "At length the curtain bell tinkled . . . Mr. Brooke was welcomed with a round of applause. He was handsomely attired and the audience were prepared to appreciate his performance." But after a few lines Mr. Brooke's memory carried him no further. "I fetch my life and . . ." the next word was not at his tongue's end; "being" was heard all over the house from the prompter but Mr. Brooke did not catch it till it had been reiterated several times. A little farther on and he was again at a standstill—"siege" had utterly gone from his brain. However another very audible prompting got him going again.

"Then came the council scene in which Othello delivers the speech which is the very delight and realisation of an actor's ambition to speak— 'Most potent, grave and reverend signiors. . . .' Here, to the amazement of the audience Mr. Brooke again broke down; he lost his words and was incapable of taking them from the prompter. The break-down was so complete that the audience hissed; upon which Mr. Brooke, whose back was to them as addressing the signiory, wheeled suddenly round and exhibited a visage doubly disguised with paint and with something else and, balancing himself for a second or two, exclaimed 'Oh! Good night!' and made his exit.

"What was the matter was now obvious enough. Iago came forward and endeavoured to apologise and then on came Othello again and, more in the manner of an Ethiopian serenader than of the Moor of Venice, said 'I spose I may say a word'. 'Hear him, hear him; order, order' was the cry from all over the house. 'Well' said Mr. Brooke, balancing himself again, 'Here I am'. Nothing more being forthcoming, the hissing was renewed. 'Pon my honour,' said Mr. Brooke, 'Stradinary circumstance'. The uproar was renewed; for a few seconds Othello stood balancing himself and then, repeating 'I say Good night' made his final exit."

In his youth the Australian correspondent had been a great admirer of Mr. Brooke and he treated him still with great respect: "Very touching, very pathetic, were the reverential attempts of the actors to aid their fallen brother. All in vain. So the curtain fell. My last sight of the idol of my boyhood was the vision of a helpless man, head sunk upon his chest, arms hanging listless, form swaying backwards and forwards. With a big lump in my throat and deep pity in my heart I left the theatre. The real tragedy I had witnessed left me in no mood for mimic display."

The Mercury man stayed the course and prosaically described the sequence of events. "Manager Wilstone came forward to apologise. Iago was deputed to take the part of Othello while the manager read the part of Iago. But first, by common consent of an audience needing a little light relief from the tension, it was decided to take the farce 'Good For Nothing' first."

Othello, alias G. V. Brooke, who was indeed good for nothing on this occasion, took a cab and caught the train back to London, sleeping it off, no doubt, on the way. A couple of days later he was Othello-ing away in fine style again, in Nottingham. But in Belfast the following January the curtain went up to find him, as Cardinal Richelieu "reclining helplessly in his chair oblivious of all his surroundings".

At Northampton, where everyone had gone home with a free ticket for the following night, they reflected how sad it was that the great actor should stumble in the role which had taken him to the pinnacle in London.

In his "Recollection and Experiences" the actor Edmund Yates praised Brooke in his hey-day as Othello as the "best representative of the character I have ever seen, manly, soldierly, with a voice capable of the softest modulation in love or pity, now trumpet-toned in command". But stout, brandy and porter had made muddy the voice which had been magical. Brooke was a spent force, though he did occasionally, when in voice, rise to the heights.

His own end was both heroic and tragic. In January, 1886, he was setting out again for Australia, hoping to rebuild his fortunes, aboard the S.S. *London* when the ship went down in the Bay of Biscay. He refused an offer to board the only boat which got away in the heavy seas with sixteen survivors, thirteen crew and three passengers. He was last seen, after strenuous exertions at the pumps, leaning over the bulwarks, calmly awaiting his doom.

Ironically Brooke's last "lines" were in pencilled messages in two *bottles*. At the last he was clear-headed enough to take his final cue, write the messages on scraps of paper, and throw them into the sea. One landed at Brighton with this farewell : "11th January, on board the London. We are just going down. No chance of safety. Please give this to Avonia Jones, Surrey Theatre—Gustavus Vaughan Brooke."

Avonia Jones, also a tragedian, was his widow. As I have already mentioned, a few months after his death she played at Northampton on the stage where Brooke had given his "drunk scene".

A "drunk scene" of quite a different character was given in January, 1863, over the road at Thomas's Music Hall. The title was *Father Come Home or The Drunkard Reclaimed* and it was staged with "appropriate music, new scenery, mechanical effects, startling pathos etc." Considering what a gin palace the music hall was, it was perhaps an inappropriate place for this scena to be given. Or, looking at it another way, the message was being heard where it was most needed . . . one wonders how many fathers went home.

1869 was the year which saw an end to the free-and-easy system of handing out "pub" licences. From July 15 that year no new licence could be obtained without a certificate from the magistrates of the district. But still no licence to sell beer or wine for consumption *OFF* the premises was to be refused except on the grounds of the applicant's character or other special grounds. And all the existing licences were to continue to be renewed except in cases of misdemeanour or other special circumstance. Thus Northampton's Bridge Street continued to be awash with beer to within living memory.

Curtailment in drinking was largely due to the efforts of the Temperance movement. Northampton had had a Temperance Society since 1837, a few years after the Whig Act. But now the determined attack on "the drink" was taken up nationally by a body rejoicing in the name of the Central Association for Stopping the Sale of Intoxicating Liquor on a Sunday. From its headquarters in Manchester it sent forth teams of missionaries to all parts to hold revival meetings in The Cause.

At Northampton in 1870 there was such a gathering in the Town Hall under the neutral chairmanship of the Mayor, William Adkins. The chief speaker was to have been the Rev. T. A. Stowell but he got into the wrong train when changing at Rugby—I would like to think that it was not because he had had one too many—and finished up in London when he should have been holding forth at Northampton. One of those who did speak in favour of Never on Sunday was the Rev. Sidney Gedge, Vicar of All Saints Church, Northampton.

It might have been expected that such a meeting would be blessed with decorum and dignity but this did not happen. Because the opposition turned up, probably in a minority, but a very noisy minority. It is not beyond the bounds of possibility that they had been drinking. The Alhambra at its booziest heights of a Saturday night did not equal the uproar at the Temperance meeting at the Town Hall. Imagine the indignation of those who had taken the pledge when Mr. T. Plumb got up to say how surprised he was that ministers of the Gospel should want to fritter down to the last bit the fragment that was left of the working man's privileges. "Crimes committed in England," said Mr. Plumb, somewhat intemperately, "are not committed by drunkards. All the thieving, all the robbing and defrauding is done by cunning, contriving, temperate men."

There was a continual uproar in the hall and in the end the Mayor gave up the unequal struggle to keep order and left without any of the resolutions being put to the meeting.

A few years later the men of Temperance in Northampton had their day, however; indeed the cause can scarcely ever have had a single triumph of such a spectacular nature, unless it was when Prohibition reigned in the United States.

It was when British Workman No. 1 opened in Northampton on an April Monday in 1877. All the top Northampton teetotallers were there to trample on the corpse of the demon drink which they had vanquished right in its seamiest local lair—the Crow and Horseshoe, alias Thomas's Music Hall, alias the Alhambra.

Where King Alcohol had reigned on his tawdry throne, the Teacup would now stand primly supreme in its saucer. Where semi-bawdy music hall songs had been chorused, only the most moral ballads would now be intoned. Instead of staying open for the late night boozing working man, as the Alhambra had done, the British Workman No. 1 would open very early in the morning so that the British Working Man could, on his perhaps long tramp to work, drop in for a cheap breakfast to help him on his way.

The public house department had been turned into the temperance refreshment room; the old music hall was now the Temperance Hall, where "entertainment of an interesting and entertaining character will be given at intervals".

So many people turned up to the tea meeting on the opening day that there had to be two sittings. All the Good Templar Lodges in the town were represented. The evangelical atmosphere can well be imagined.

Reporting the opening, the Guardian said that the music hall had not enjoyed a high repute. Dedicated opponents of drink had gone much further, especially at court hearings on the subject.

By 1877, it must be remembered, a liquor licence was a very valuable piece of paper. New ones had to receive the sanction of the Secretary of State and to open a new public house the simplest course was to close an older and less profitable one. Provided, of course, that the magistrates could be persuaded to transfer the licence.

At this time the lease of the Crow and Horseshoe was owned by Northampton Brewery Company to whom it had been transferred from Phillips Brothers, the brewers who had shown a loss when William Thomas went bankrupt. The brewery company sought to move the licence to the Plough Hotel which they were then building in Bridge Street, specially to meet the requirements of those attending the nearby Cattle Market, opened in July, 1873, when the trade was moved from the Market Square.

At the Brewster Sessions the previous September Mr. E. B. Browne, for the Temperance folk, said that it had been suggested that the de-licensing of the old music hall was the removal of a nuisance but this did not justify it being planted elsewhere. There were already twenty-six indoor licensed premises in Bridge Street. At this time the new establishment was to be called the Union Hotel; the "Plough" was a second choice.

A prominent "T.T.", W. C. Hollowell, wrote to The Guardian: "I contend that the character of the Alhambra has been such for many years that the magistrates ought to have cancelled the licence years before. The owners of the place themselves became so ashamed of the house, so impressed with its corrupting influence that they determined that it should no longer be used as a public house in the ordinary sense of the word."

At the British Workman a cup of coffee and a small piece of bread and butter cost three-halfpence. Mr. George Bass(!), the president, said he thought this would compare with any XX (i.e. beer) in town. He added that it was not their purpose to drag people from their homes—home was the proper place for the working man to be after his toil.

Later that year another former public house became British Workman No. 2—the Prince Arthur, Barrack Road.

For reasons which are not entirely clear the Temperance reign in the former public house and music hall was brief. Whether it was bad management or whether insufficient working men dropped in for a snack on their way to work is not clear but as far as the entertainment hall is concerned by November, 1878, Mr. Charles Clarke was there giving variety programmes. At first he retained the name, as the Temperance Hall of Varieties, one of his first attractions being the perennial "Death of Nelson" tableau; then he called it the Star Hall of Varieties, disclaiming: "In no way connected with the British Workman No. 1."

By February, 1880, it had been taken over by a gentleman named Anidjah and re-named the Theatre of Varieties and a year later it was leased by a local auctioneer, Mr. T. S. Muddiman, as the Prince of Wales Concert (or Music) Hall. Under this title it was being run in August, 1881, by Mr. Hyram Travers. But drink had been banished and later owners struggled in vain to get a licence for "refreshments". [When Muddiman went bankrupt in 1887 reasons he advanced for his failure included "losses on a dog show and music hall".]

Finally, there was the court case in which the question of drink came up. A manager named Walter Shelley was sued in December, 1870, for two guineas wages which he was alleged to owe one of his actors. This is an instance where once again I can only spoil the effect by tampering with the contemporary account. From whatever grave he occupies the Victorian journalist who wrote the court report for the Mercury shall speak for himself, in his own words:

"At Northampton Petty Sessions, Walter Shelley, comedian, the Theatre Royal, was summoned by William Kennedy for 2 gns. due to him, at the rate of £1 5s. 6d. a week. Kennedy said that he had been engaged by

Shelley, lessee of the Theatre Royal, as an actor and also as a scenic artist. At his request he had also done duty as a labourer, shifting the scenes etc. He had also painted the Hamlets and Macbeths and all the Fine Arts on boards and carried them up to the wall against All Saints Church and then from art sublime he had descended to the work of scrubbing about as a labourer at the theatre.

"Mr. Shelley said he did not refuse to pay the man his wage but refused to pay him when he was in drink. The complainant was a good workman, a good scene painter and otherwise very useful to him. But for more than the last week he had been in a helpless state of intoxication. He was engaged to play a very important part as a magistrate and his stage manager would tell them that he was in a state of intoxication, hiccuped about the stage and acted in a way highly unbecoming to the Bench (laughter) and his stage manager would not allow him to play.

"Shelley was very much disgusted and annoyed because, although he had come into the town and lost all he had, he had striven to uphold the respectability of the theatre. The other ladies and gentlemen of the staff had done all they could to support him and there was not one to whom he did not owe money—from Lady Macbeth to the man who picked up the skull and bones in the tragedy of Hamlet. But he hoped to be able to satisfy their claims. The complainant was one of his staff of artistes and was a very useful man until he took to drinking."

Faced with a legal decision of such nicety the magistrates took a typical legal attitude by deciding that the matter was outside their jurisdiction. As the actor, cum scene shifter, cum artist, cum floor swabber, was one of the "artistes" the case did not come within the provisions of the Master and Servant Act. No doubt Mr. Shelley would endeavour to pay Kennedy but they had no power to say when he should pay.

This was the only Mercurial mention of the theatre for months—no advertisements, no editorial, nothing.

Scene Two

THE CLOSING COMPANIES

It is perhaps fortunate that we have these interludes to provide a touch of farce and tragedy, a change of theme, to enliven the story of the last few years of the Marefair theatre for it might otherwise be a pedestrian progression of the names of the touring companies who provided the entertainment.

It would indeed be mere tedium to chronicle the names of all the shows and companies during the last decade of the theatre's life, post-Byron, as one might term it. For whereas that gentleman's approach to the stage was highly individual, the companies which followed were highly conventional and entirely predictable. This was the start of the hey-days of the touring companies and they were the same whether playing in Nottingham or Newcastle or Northampton. Now all local link was lost. The provincial theatre in the true sense of the word was dying if not already dead, inasmuch as it was not at all provincial, no longer local.

The stages of the provinces probably witnessed higher standards of performance than ever before if only because it was no longer a question of a man like Old Henry Jackman having to cast half the parts from among the members of his own family, but of companies hand-picked in London to suit a particular play or style of play and then setting out for a repetitive tour which might last years.

Attracted though they might be by the talented folk they now saw, some of whom they would not have seen under the old system, audiences in the provinces could no longer regard the players as their own. The loss of local individuality in the cause of progress is a theme repeated a thousand-fold during the past century.

By 1880 the provinces relied almost entirely upon the touring companies; today the circle has turned; the touring company has all but disappeared, replaced by television drama, and for live plays the provinces rely largely upon their own local repertory theatres and companies.

One of those who fought to install the touring companies was, by an odd quirk of fate, a Robertson, a member of the family which had been involved for so many years in the operation of the Lincoln and Nottingham and Derby Circuits. T. W. Robertson was the eldest of the twenty-two children of William Robertson, last manager of the Lincoln Circuit. The youngest of that vast brood was named Madge and was also to go down in theatrical history, as Dame Madge Kendal, honoured as an actress. Oddly enough "T.W.", though practically born on the stage, turned out to be no actor. His first plays were also flops. Then he hit upon the idea that was to make his name, a concept so simple that it sounds silly. He would write plays in which people spoke and acted as they do in real life. His titles were also "different" in that they were brief, indeed some monosyllabic, in contrast to some of the lengthy and alternative titles of the past.

Society was the first and *Caste* the most notable. Indeed *Caste* was virtually the first "significant" play that century, in that it marked a turning point towards realism. Some called it the "tea-cup school". Props were real as well as the characters; doors had handles and even a window might open instead of being done by the scene painter.

The natural home of the Robertson plays was the Prince of Wales Theatre, under Marie Wilton, with a splendid, sympathetic company. All the plays produced there succeeded. Those initially staged elsewhere drooped and were at best creditable failures. These included *War* at the St. James Theatre which was not even a creditable failure, being withdrawn after a fortnight, the day before Tom Robertson died at the age of forty-two. The month was February, 1872, and it was said that the jaunty tone of the play did not accord with British concern at the recent Franco-German War.

More than once Tom Robertson wrote the syndicated "London Sketches" column which appeared in the Mercury and it was in that column that Northamptonians could read a tribute to the man who was a great-nephew of the Robertson whose company opened their theatre in 1806. He was summed up as the playwright who had been welcomed by those who "think the stage should be something more than a vehicle for the exhibition of costumes and scenery".

Four of the Robertson plays were brought to Northampton in June, 1878, by Craven Robertson and the Caste Company. They performed *Caste* on Monday and Saturday; *School* on Tuesday and Thursday; *Ours* on Wednesday; and *Society* on Friday. As the villain of *School* Mr. T. Sidney was reported to have received the greatest possible compliment by being hissed and hooted off the stage. Seemingly the ears of a Northampton audience were not yet attuned to the finer overtones!

Craven Robertson was one of "T.W.'s" younger brothers and was to die at an even earlier age—the year following the Northampton visit, aged thirty-three.

T. W. Robertson had fought the provincial managers on the question of touring companies. When they would not accept the innovation or only at prohibitive odds, Robertson and his partner took the companies to alternative halls and as this emptied the theatres, the managers had to give in.

Two other companies who appeared with success at Northampton were successful for other reasons, one for the magnetic personality of its manageress and star and the other on the fantastic popularity of a single musical play.

The "star" with the powerful personality was Madamoiselle Beatrice, a French actress who first brought her company to the town in January, 1873.

A number of her plays were translated from the French and all had some powerful "moral". Madamoiselle Beatrice was said to kneel in prayer in the wings before each performance. She seems to have had a remarkable aura and presence and strangely enough it lived on beyond her death. The company was taken over by one of its members and continued to visit Marefair, usually in the December-January period, until January, 1884, and later played at the Theatre Royal and Opera House, Guildhall Road.

More than one visit was paid by Mr. C. Bernard's *Les Cloches de Corneville* Company, which presented this piece only. There were forty performers in the touring company which came first in August, 1880, when the show had clocked up 700 nights at the London Globe, and in January, 1881 and December, 1881, by when the 1,000 mark had been passed in London.

The bills of 1873 included great basinfuls of the Bard, far more than a provincial company of today would find it politic to serve up. Mr. Henry Loraine, "leading legitimate actor of the day" did *Hamlet* on Monday, *Othello* on Tuesday, *Richard III* on Wednesday and *Macbeth* on Saturday. The same year Mr. Pennington, "London tragedian", provided *Hamlet* on Monday, *Macbeth* on Wednesday, *Richard III* on Thursday and *Julius Caesar* on Saturday. On three nights *Aladdin* was second course. But for Mr. Laurence Smyth's Company, a few years later, it was The Bard and Nothing But The Bard—"The evening will be devoted exclusively to the performance of a Shakespeare work in order that it may be thoroughly and adequately represented." No farces or after-pieces here. Not even a comic song.

Many of the other companies were associated with one or more particular West End successes. Wybert Reeve appeared in *Woman in White* (the cast also included Eliza Saville); there were the Garrick Comedy Company (*David Garrick, The American, Twixt Cup and Lip*); Wilson Barrett's Company (*Proof, The Old Love and the New, No Escape*): Mr. Henry Dacre's Company (*Pink Dominoes, Truth, Olivette* and *Les Cloches de Corneville*); Mr. George Leitch's Company (*The Madman, Sithors to Grind*); York and Groves Comic Opera Company; Mr. Albert Dunmore's Company (*British Born, Our Boys*); Mr. Alfred Hemmings' Company (*Crutch and Toothpick*); Mr. William Duck's Company (*The Money Spinner, Courtship, Our Boys*); Mr. Henry Davenport's Company (*New Magdalene, The Lady of Lyons*); Mr. Arthur Garner's Company (*Stolen Kisses*); Messrs Holt and Wilmott's Company (*New Babylon, Taken from Life*); Mr. Alfred Parry's Company (*Queen's Evidence*); Herr and Mrs. Bandmann's Company; Mr. J. L. Shine's Comedy and Burlesque Company (*Don Juan*, as played 200 nights at the Royal Theatre, London); the Drury Lane Operatic Recital Company; Mr. Joseph Eldred's Comedy Dramatic Company; Miss Emma Rainbow and Company; Mr. Victor Stevens and his Comedy and Burlesque Company; Miss Sarah Thorne's Company; M. Lasseur de Tremblaye's Grand Opera Bouffe Company; Mr. Elliott Galer's Company (he was later lessee of the Leicester theatre); and, the last company to appear before the 1884 close-down, Mr. and Mrs. E. F. Edelsten's Company (*Recommended to Mercy*).

Some of the most crowded houses of the closing years were not for theatricals but for religious services. Held on Sunday evenings these were services "for the people"—people who would not attend the more conventional dispensaries of spiritual succour.

It was in 1861 that a proposal had been made, nationally, to use playhouses for the purpose. Nottingham had been in the forefront, services beginning at the Theatre Royal in that city in November, 1860. As is not uncommon with new ideas, the innovation did not meet with universal approval. A typical anti reaction was that of the Era weekly newspaper which protested against "this unseemly mixture of sacred and secular associations". Using a theatre for services was as incongruous as if plays were given in churches.

Nevertheless the idea caught on and in 1883 the Rev. Harry Jones, Rector of St. George's in the East, London, declaimed : "We want no more bricks and mortar, but flesh and blood, the rough and ready mission room and not the prim church. It has been found, however, that neither mission rooms nor open air preaching, nor house-to-house visitations adequately reach the class whom it is sought to bring within the sound of the Gospel. Accordingly, about twenty-two years ago the proposal was made to hire theatres, music-halls and other places where the masses of the people habitually resort, for special services on Sunday."

If anyone was sceptical of the benefits of Special Services in Theatres he invited them to go along and see and hear for themselves.

Certainly the Marefair theatre services seem to have been packed. Not only were they successful but they were to a degree ecumenical. The chairman might be a Church of England parson (perhaps from nearby St. Katharine's or St. Andrew's, both now demolished) and the speaker a Nonconformist minister.

When the Rev. W. Noblett, curate of St. Andrew's, spoke on the eve of leaving town, the chairman was the Rev. J. Oates, pastor of Doddridge Chapel, who commented that the town could not afford to lose its good men —"People say that this town is a very bad place and the worst in the United Kingdom but I fling back the perfidious falsehood and declare that Northampton is one of the most orderly, respectable and well-conducted towns in Great Britain." Well, they couldn't both be right. . . .

The services had that eternal problem of the size of the collection. At one meeting the chairman appealed for "increased pecuniary assistance". To some extent it fell on deaf ears for the collection that night was £1 5s., compared with £1 7s. 9½d. the week before.

Sometimes the services were moved to the Prince of Wales establishment. Abstinence from alcohol was a principal theme of the first meeting there when Mr. J. T. Wilson quoted passages from Shakespeare to prove that the Bard did not believe in alcohol but had a high regard for water.

The last manager of the Theatre Royal served for nearly five years, taking over in the autumn of 1879. He was of course, simply a manager, booking shows and arranging all the details, not a Thespian. He was Mr. J. Tebbutt.

Scene Three

SCHEMING FOR A
NEW THEATRE

There had been a number of attempts to replace the Theatre Un-Royal by something a little better. At least, there had been a lot of talk about it, going back as far as 1861.

In that year, just before the end of the Jackman and Morgan tenure a newspaper report announcing this fact stated: "It is proposed to build a new theatre in the north part of the town at an estimated cost of £2,500 to be raised by shares, the holders of which will have the usual privileges. Messrs Jackman and Morgan offer to become shareholders and lessees of the new theatre."

Less than forty-eight hours after the final J. and M. performance a meeting, convened by circular, was held at the George Hotel, where the meetings to formulate plans for the 1806 theatre had been held. But history was not to repeat itself. It was a small gathering which heard Jackman and Morgan put their views forward and "Under existing circumstances it was deemed advisable that the matter should stand over for a time." That was the end of the project as far as I have discovered. What site, if any, was in mind remains a mystery.

In 1875 the owners of the Marefair theatre themselves grew so disenchanted with it that they contemplated knocking it down and building another on the same site. Having taken a lease for a further forty years they felt that they would be justified in erecting "A more commodious and comfortable structure better suited to the requirements of a town with a population of nearly 50,000" to quote the Albion. The paper added that though the old theatre had probably suited the requirements of the town of sixty years before it was now a disgrace to any respectable community. The exterior presented no attractive features; the inside had such a poverty-stricken air that every time the Albion went inside the place it experienced a strong feeling of disgust; its situation was bad; and the ground on which it stood was so cramped and confined that the paper marvelled that any speculators could be found to put money into a building on the same spot when so many other more suitable and more central sites might be had.

As regards the site the Albion recalled that the earlier Playhouse had been in St. Giles Street. "What unfortunate circumstance drove it to the west of the town it is hard to say. Most probably because the site was then more central, for Northampton in 1806 had a population of about 8,000 while in 1875 it numbers six times as many, showing that the town has necessarily largely extended and this may account for the present site being anything but central."

There was another powerful argument to consider against re-building on the same site though this being Northampton it was to take a further half-century to fructify. "The Improvement Commissioners ought to secure the land on which the present theatre stands to widen the disreputable entrance to a populous neighbourhood."

In the event the re-building plan came to nought.

A substantial attempt to build a new theatre was made by Mr. Henry Cooper, well known in the district for his Shakespeare readings. His target was to raise £8,000 and when, in March, 1881, he had already been promised £3,000 hopes were high. The projected site was that of the old County Gaol, now displaced by a more modern prison.

The site had been bought by Mr. John Watkins and he was willing to sell part of it for the purpose. An offer to lease the new theatre was made by Mr. Henry Neville, of the Olympic Theatre, London, partly as a reaction to the disgust he felt at the accommodation offered for actors when he visited the old theatre with Mr. Wilson Barrett's *Proof* Company in July, 1881. He offered a rental of £400 a year.

But the inflow of funds slowed down, only £3,700 was in the kitty by October, and the following March the scheme was abandoned. In the Northamptonshire Guardian a columnist called "Man About Town" noted : "We must bide our time and wait until the growth of the population and enterprise justifies the resurrection of this or some similar project."

Another plan was put forward by Mr. Henry Dacre, a touring manager, who favoured a site to the south of the old gaol and offered to put up £1,500 of the £6,000 required. He had, in fact, talked of a new theatre for ten years, supported by Mr. Thomas Arlidge, printer and proprietor of the short-lived Albion.

The site favoured by Mr. Cooper was sold for another cultural purpose. The Town Council's Museum and Free Library Committee bought it to house a museum and reading room.

Two interesting points emerge from this. That if the project had gone through, Northampton's theatre would have been on the other side of the street from where the Theatre Royal and Opera House was in fact constructed in 1884, and where it still stands as the home of Northampton Repertory Players. Secondly that the whole area is now planned to accommodate Northampton's new cultural centre, to meet the needs of a town doubling within a couple of decades.

Meanwhile the old gaol did briefly get a touch of the entertainment for in March, 1881, the yard was covered over with corrugated iron sheeting so that it could serve as a circus ring for a visit by Keith's Circus. Clowns cavorted where convicts had been confined and the surface which had seen hangmen carrying out their carefully-timed performances witnessed the whip-cracking commands of the ringmaster.

The Guardian had suggested an alternative use for the old prison site—as a covered market.

Where meetings had malingered, caucuses collapsed, where civic enterprise was totally absent, as so often happened in our history one business man made up his mind to get on with it, dip into his own pocket and build the much-needed new theatre. Not, of course, that he was out to benefit the town directly; he merely thought it was a good business proposition. The business man was John Campbell Franklin who announced his intentions in July, 1883—that he was to raise a mortgage of £2,500 on the site (adjacent to his Franklins' Hotel) and that the rest was to come from subscribers who were to get four per cent. The cost of the building: £4,500. It is a testimony to Mr. Franklin's energy and purposefulness that within ten months the theatre was up and open. The builder was under penalty to finish by March 1; in fact the hammers were still going a few hours before the first curtain on Monday, May 6, 1884.

The site was between Guildhall Road and Cow Lane, since re-named as Swan Street. The leading theatre architect of the day, Mr. C. J. Phipps, was commissioned to design the house of which a special feature was to be that the benches of the pit would occupy the entire floor, extending under the balcony and dress circle.

To the reader of today the biggest surprise is that Phipps guaranteed that the minimum capacity would be 1,500 while at high pressure it would probably hold as many as 1,700. The mind fairly boggles at the idea of such numbers being crowded into the same building which today, in proper seats, caters for precisely 503 including the boxes, plus an estimated 100 in the gallery.

Apropos the physical size of the theatre (105 feet including 35 feet for the stage and average width 46 feet) the Echo Reporter commented: "The conviction has been forcing itself upon the public mind for some time past that big theatres are big mistakes. Hence, all those erected in the Metropolis have been of moderate dimensions. The expression of the softer passions is sacrificed in larger theatres. The origin of the ranting, roaring, rumbustious style of acting of the English school was doubtless owing to the vast area of our old playhouses."

Some day it may be possible to publish the story of the Northampton Theatre Royal and Opera House from its opening in 1884 to 1927 when the Northampton Repertory Players took over the fortunes of the house, saving it from demolition.

The first twenty-one years of their distinguished stewardship has already been accounted in Aubrey Dyas's Adventure in Repertory. Some day, too, it may be possible to bring up to date the story, continuing it from 1948 to the present day. Suitable dates for either or both of these projects would be 1977, when the company attains its golden jubilee, or 1984, when the building reaches its centenary.

I need (literally) to insert here: if it is allowed to reach its centenary. For on February 13, 1974, the very day this book finally goes to press in the middle of the Miners' Strike, I have opened my Chronicle and Echo to find the headline: "Rep. May Have to Come Down." Despite being now on the Board of Northampton Repertory Company this is the manner in which I, along with the other members, have heard for the first time of this possibility, resulting from a plan put forward by some members of the Leisure and Recreation Advisory Committee of Northampton Town Council. This local authority is in effect giving a dying gasp for it reaches its own date for interment on April 1, the day this book is due to be born, along with new forms of local government. The "knock-down" suggestion is part of a scheme to build an Arts Complex, embodying a new theatre.

Leaving aside the question of old world courtesy in failing to inform the Board of the theatre in advance, I scarcely have time for reflection or space for comment, but feel bound to speculate whether February 13 may not turn out to be as significant a date in Northampton's theatre saga as April 1 (when, in 1960, the proscenium of the New Theatre was pulled down by a bulldozer with a crash and in a cloud of dust) and also on whether the title for my intended history of the Opera House (or Theatre Royal, or Repertory Theatre, or Royal Theatre—confusing, isn't it?) may not turn out to be "Death of *Another* Theatre". It is only fair to say that, to the best of my present knowledge, it is not planned to build a super-market on the site of this second, possibly, doomed Northampton theatre. Though absolutely nothing would surprise me in this age of vandalism.

For the moment we will leave the Northampton Theatre Royal and Opera House on that opening night of Monday, May 6, 1884, with the Compton Comedy Company performing *As You Like It* and manager Isaac Tarry, amateur actor and auctioneer, making his inaugural speech:

"I may perhaps be allowed to congratulate the town upon at last possess-ing a theatre which, to say the least of it, is some degrees more worthy of its patronage than that which it has supplanted. I don't want to be un-generous or to kick a fallen foe, but I think that even those who have vested interests in the little Temple of the Muses in Marefair will be ready to admit that it ceased long ago to be able to supply the wants of an increased and ever-increasing population like that of Northampton."

The Press, which has provided so much of the material for this book, shall have the last word: "It was difficult for anyone present in the new building for the first time to realise that he was in Northampton—a thoroughly handsome and spacious theatre has replaced the old-time uncomfortable habitat of the drama."

EPILOGUE

NIGHT OF THE FIRE

...which sets out the manner in which the new theatre was the subject of a Conflagration, which led to the unexpected, but sadly brief, revival of the Little Temple of Thespis. How corn of another variety was subsequently dispensed there. And other matters, bringing our entertainment to a melancholy conclusion. If you have enjoyed it, tell your friends; if not, keep quiet!

MONDAY,

FEBRUARY 14, 1887.

WEDNESDAY,

THURSDAY,

SATURDAY,

THE FINAL WEEK—The story
of how the "Old Theatre" came
into use again for one week only
after a fire at its successor is told in
this series of advertisements in the
Daily Chronicle.

NIGHT OF
THE FIRE

Yet still, one short spell of glory remained for the "little Temple of the Muses in Marefair".

Between its unsung last night in April, 1884, and February, 1887, it had become a Church Army barracks. A service was actually in progress on Sunday, February 13, that year when the news arrived that the following week it was to become a theatre again. The Church Army Captain conducting the devotions took his cue like a true professional and immediately offered up a prayer that this might be averted.

As far as I can make out, the Church Army were due for an exodus in any case, as Latimer and Crick, corn merchants from the opposite corner of Horsemarket and Marefair, had acquired a tenancy or lease.

At all events, a week later a Church Army parade was on its way down Gold Street to a new meeting place in a schoolroom in Horseshoe Street and came to a halt outside the Old Theatre, as it was now termed. One of the members addressed the troops : "The Devil has taken away from us the Old Theatre but the Lord, bless his name, has found us a new place to meet in."

It was a tragedy that had brought the actors back to Marefair. After the week's performances of *Jim the Penman* the company of Mr. Balsir Chatterton had moved their gear to St. John's Street Railway Station, nearby, in the late hours of Saturday and early hours of Sunday, when a fire was found to have broken out in the Theatre Royal and Opera House.

Messrs. Shiel Barry and Hogarth's Comic Opera Company, with the popular *Les Cloches de Corneville*, were due the following week but when they arrived it was to find the stage devastated, along with the dressing rooms, scenery, drop scene etc. In the orchestra pit all that remained of Mr. Nind's bass viol was the carved head.

Thus the old theatre had its chance for brief reincarnation. Instead of being overcome by the tragedy to his beloved theatre Mr. Isaac Tarry, the manager-cum-auctioneer, threw his energies into ensuring that the show went on. The lowly alternative accommodation was given a dust-up, new scenery was prepared, the licence was transferred, and the place was ready

18—TU * *

THE THEATRE ROYAL AND OPERA HOUSE, which supplanted the Marefair
theatre, after the fire of February 13, 1887, which led to the temporary re-opening of
the "Old Theatre". (*Photo copy by Bryan J. Douglas*)

for the Monday night performance which seems to have been a great
success.

There was a good house, Miss Bouverie of Delapre Abbey took a party,
as so many Bouveries had done before, during more than a century; for
special mention the Daily Chronicle singled out the centre boxes, where
"the muster was exceedingly gratifying" in contrast to their one-time
"cheerless and deserted appearance".

Tarry made a pleasant little speech, betraying signs of emotion as he
declared that he would rather that his own house, with all its contents, had
been burnt down, than that the theatre in Guildhall Road should
have been destroyed. Many in the audience were nostalgic on this historic
occasion, and it was intended that the theatre should fill the gap until the
Opera House could be restored. But, as so often it has failed, Northampton
as a whole did not respond. Before the end of the week the "Roger's Local
Commentary" column of the Daily Chronicle carried this note : "One regrets
to find that there is some justification for the rumour which has been
circulated that through want of patronage at the Old Theatre a renewal of
the licence after this week will not be asked for. In other words playgoers
must do without their theatre-going until the restoration of the Opera
House. It was to be hoped that Mr. Franklin's friends would have rallied
round him in his temporary home but after the miserable houses (since the
first)—and with such a company—the determination of the management
is to be easily understood."

Isaac Tarry put a good face on it, advertising that it was because the
stage of the Old Theatre was inadequate for the production of the plays
engaged for the next two months that the season would end that Saturday
night.

The Mercury had a slightly different version. "We are given to understand that Mr. Tarry will not continue in occupation of the Old Theatre in Marefair longer than this week. The fact is that the place is so small and the companies Mr. Tarry has booked are so expensive that it could not possibly pay to hold performances there. Besides the inconveniences of the Old Theatre are innumerable."

On Tuesday, Wednesday and Friday *La Mascotte* was performed and on Thursday and Saturday *Les Cloches de Corneville*. Thus, on Saturday, February 19, there was the very last performance at the theatre, eighty years after the first.

Perhaps the most astonishing thing is to compare the prices. In 1806 it was 3s. in the boxes, 2s. in the pit and 1s. for the gallery. And in 1887? Centre boxes 3s., side boxes 2s., pit 1s., gallery 6d. How's that for stability?

After this second and final last night there was a gap in theatre-going until the Opera House re-opened on Monday, May 2.

The Old Theatre served several different and multiple purposes, book-shop, corn chandlers, for a further thirty-four years.

Finally, in the 1920s the Corporation of Northampton decided to widen Horseshoe Street and therefore bought the place from the Master and Co-Brethren of St. John's Hospital, along with the Trustees who now over-looked the activities of the charity.

The Master was Canon John Rowden Hussey, Vicar of St. Matthew's Church, Northampton, the "Arts" church built by the Northampton brewer Pickering Phipps which was later to house the controversial works of Graham Sutherland, "Crucifixion", and Henry Moore, "Madonna and Child".

The names of the trustees of the charity who signed the place over to the local authority reads almost like a Northampton roll of honour of that day :

William Harvey Reeves, Mayor, Spencer Parade (who was to appear in Gilbert and Sullivan's *The Mikado* at the New Theatre, Abington Street, in 1929, with Northampton Amateur Operatic Company. He had been with them in the 1899 and 1904 performances of the same work at the Opera House).

Henry Butterfield, proprietor of the Northampton Herald and Daily Chronicle, of Cliftonville.

Samuel Smith Campion, King Edward Road, proprietor of the Northampton Mercury and Daily Echo.

Charles Lewis, Harlestone Road.

Sir Henry Randall, The Hall, Monks Park.

Christopher Smythe, Little Houghton House.

George Smith Whiting, Kettering Road, furniture dealer.

Abraham John Chown, East Park Parade.

Lee Fyson Cogan, Sheep Street.

Alfred George Slinn, Lower Thrift Street, umbrella dealer.

Charles Saunders Wilson, Derngate, dealer.

Sir William Ryland Dent Adkins, K.C., M.P., Cheyne Walk.

Col. Henry Wickham, Cotterstock Hall.

Francis Hugh Thornton, Kingsthorpe Hall.

Brigadier General H. E. Stockdale, Milton Manor.

Not only were the old theatre premises involved in the deal but the Shakespeare public house, C. W. King's butcher's shop, and some warehouses and stables. The old documents of the St. John Charity, prior to 1887, had been lost (some of the earlier ones could feasibly have been destroyed to conceal the evidence!) so a declaration had to be sworn by the Clerk to the Trustees, Albert Edward Phipps.

On the corner opposite, Gold Street–Horseshoe Street, the former site of the Crow and Horseshoe/Thomas's Music Hall/Alhambra/British Workman No. 1/Theatre of Varieties/etc. etc. later became in turn the Palace of Varieties, where Charlie Chaplin, Stan Laurel and Gracie Fields appeared, and the Majestic Cinema. Today it is occupied by Bells Corner shop premises, wherein the old auditorium and stage still survive in one of the showrooms. This site is yet another theme from this book which deserves a volume on its own.

But meantime, as I write, the former St. John's properties which survived the road-widening—the Shakespeare and C. W. King's—are under a compulsory purchase order to widen Horseshoe Street still further, in forming a dual carriageway and to stop off traffic from going up Gold Street (see maps).

When the last pints are drawn at the Shakespeare—if they have not already been drawn by the time this appears—and the demolition hammers come into play again it will seem that a last link between the spot and the old theatre will have gone.

No longer will one be able to go into the public and drink a toast to Old Henry Jackman and all the other Thespians who fought their audiences for attention so close by over a period of fourscore years.

AUTHOR'S CURTAIN SPEECH

(Prepared in advance, as are all author's speeches, to meet either extreme of situation. On the one hand plaudits so deafening that the speech cannot be heard; on the other, representing an attempt to quell the embittered mob intent on dismantling the theatre interior.)

Before allowing the audience to get out of hearing, until the next performance (i.e. book, should it prove possible to produce another by the same means—if you want to help, send me a fiver) the author wishes to be allowed the prerogative of the condemned—a few last words. They amount to: I TOLD YOU SO:—

"My previous book 'Death of a Theatre', published in 1960, urged that Northampton Town Council ought to have prevented the demolition of the town's New Theatre, then a mere 47 years old—a premature death indeed —and its replacement by a supermarket.

"That this should indeed have been the case I imagine few will today dispute for since the book was published it has been decided that it is absolutely and urgently essential that the town of Northampton should double its size. This piece of instant decisionery was not known, of course, in 1960 when the theatre came tumbling down, its proscenium falling on April 1, a singularly appropriate date.

"It is not inappropriate to ask how any informed decisions about the future needs of the town could be arrived at at that time, about entertainment or anything else, when the major factor to be taken into account was not then known—that there were twice the number of people to be catered for in the future, in every facet of life. It may pertinently be asked what sort of 'planning' (with a small 'p') this was.

"Had the Northampton Town Council had the savvy (or cultural courage, if you prefer that sort of terminology) to buy both theatres instead of only one (they did purchase the Repertory Theatre) not only would they have made a very fine property investment (the Abington Street site must have quadrupled in value since 1960) but by letting the theatre for bingo for part of the time they could have shown sufficient profit to allow its use free or at minimal charge to the organisations of the town, such as Northampton Musical Society (which has had to perform out of town for lack of a venue) or Northampton Amateur Operatic Company which, at the time of drafting these lines, for a second time faces the possibility of losing a home for its productions—if the A.B.C. Cinema is 'twinned'.

"Someday, a new auditorium is promised, as part of an Arts Centre. The question of when remains unanswered and in view of the present activities of the Arabs with Oil, the Miners with Coal, and the Power Workers with Electricity, the prospects are not bright. But even if it is built it could never match up to the fine atmosphere of the old, New, theatre.

"And, so farewell" (with appropriate Thespian or Churchillian gesture, according to mood of audience) "until the next time, I hope . . ."

Northampton
January, 1974

"MEDAL" or commemorative disc
issued to mark the erection of the
"Theatre Un-Royal" (*Northampton*
"Chronicle and Echo").

Patrons

Sincere thanks are expressed to the Patrons listed below. By pre-paying (or pre-ordering in the case of libraries and some other organisations) it is they alone who have made the publication possible. The very first subscription was from Mr. Cecil Madden, M.B.E. : it was, indeed, directly as a result of his urgings that the venture was begun. The second subscription was especially pleasing, being from Miss Meg Toyer, who was co-author of "Death of a Theatre". Another was from Mrs. F. Driver, who, in a door-step campaign, personally sold 75 copies of that book.

Patrons and others helping in the production of "Theatre Un-Royal" do not, of course, necessarily agree with any views expressed in the text.

At the time of publication a further publishing venture is being formulated. It is hoped to publish either "Drama That Smelled or A Pre-1806 History of the Theatre in Northampton and Hereabouts" or a history of Northampton Theatre Royal and Opera House, 1884–1927. As will be seen, these books would take up the story of the periods immediately before and after "Theatre Un-Royal". Much promising material is already to hand.

Whichever project appeared to be most likely to show promise of fruition would be proceeded with. It will again depend entirely upon the number of Patrons who can be persuaded to trust the author and publisher with their money in advance. With costs mounting as they are the sum asked for this enterprise is £5. Subscriptions will be acknowledged and there is a guarantee that if the project founders the money will be available for return to the subscribers. The address is 54 St. George's Avenue, Northampton, and cheques should be made out to "Northampton Theatre History". The money will be kept in a Trust Account and not spent on preliminary expenses.

Here, then, is the list of those who turned the present book from an idea into 280 pages of text and pictures :

W. S. ABBOTT
(Tendring, Essex)
HARRY ADAMS
(New Duston)
DOM EDWIN B. ADDICOTT
(Hardingstone)
BERYL J. ADDINGTON, L.G.S.M.
H. R. ALFORD
(Corby)
GEORGE V. ALLINSON
(Ecton)
A. W. ALLURED
D. B. ANDERSON
H. J. APPLETON (Mrs.)
(Oxendon)
GRAHAM ASHLEY
(London)
R. W. ASHBY
(Muscott))
CAPTAIN W. ASHBY
(Aynho)
WALTER ASHTON
(Whitfield)

H. H. ATTERBURY (Mrs.)
(West Haddon)
MARY ATTERBURY (Mrs.)
(West Haddon)
LESLIE AUSTIN-CROWE
DR. RONALD AYLING
(Edmonton, Canada)
FRED AYRES

J. T. B.
IDRIS W. BAILEY
BOB BAKER
(Market Harborough)
ANDRE BALDET
HARRY BANKS
DEREK J. BARBER
K. M. D. BARKER (Miss)
(Wembley)
O. E. BARNES, M.A., F.R.G.S.
(Great Houghton)
COL. DENNIS BARRATT, E.R.D.
(Great Billing)

JOHN BARRONS
(Rickmansworth)
MRS. A. M. COWPER BARRONS
(Rickmansworth)
MR. and MRS. D. G. BARTLETT
WALLY BATEMAN
(Ashton, Roade)
GILBERT BATES
STANLEY JAMES BATTAMS
(Blisworth)
PATRICIA BEADON
THE DUKE OF BEDFORD
(Woburn)
MR. and MRS. M. BELGION
(Titchmarsh)
J. C. BENNETT
DIANA K. BERESFORD (Mrs.)
(Oundle)
BRIAN BERRILL
CLIFF BILLING
HENRY BIRD
(Hardingstone)
GORDON BOSWELL
(Hardingstone)
TED BOTTLE
(Coalville)
NORMAN BOWLES, F.S.V.A., F.C.I.A.
(Ickleham, Middx)
PETER BRINSON
(London)
J. FRANCIS BROWN, C.B.E.
(Great Houghton)
J. FRANCIS BROWN, C.B.E.
(London)
LT.-COL. K. C. BROWN
(Ashton, Roade)
O. F. BROWN, M.B., B.S.
(Milton Keynes)
A. L. DE BRUYNE
(Edinburgh)
H. BULLARD
(Duston)
F. BURBIDGE
(London)
ALAN BURMAN
E. M. BURR
(Falcon Manor School)
J. A. BYRNES
(Elizabeth, New Jersey, U.S.A.)

JEREMY H. CALDERWOOD
(Harpole)
H. O. CAPELL (Mrs.)
"CHARLIE CARLSBERG"
F. C. L. CARRESS
(Thrapston)
BRIAN J. CARTER
(Milton Malsor)
THE REV. CANON J. L.
CARTWRIGHT, M.A., F.S.A.
(Peterborough)
I. M. CHAMBERLAIN (Mrs.)
J. H. CHANDLER
(Stamford)
LT.-COL. JOHN CHANDOS-POLE
(Newnham)

LADY CHAPMAN
(London)
PHILIP E. CHARLTON
(Walton-on-Thames)
M. H. CHATBURN (Mrs.)
RICHARD C. CHATBURN
H. L. CHENEY
(Wellingborough)
DAVID CHESHIRE
(London)
CYRIL A. CHOWN
MRS. M. J. CHUDLEY
(Creaton)
MR. and MRS. W. V. CHURCH
ALBERT CLARKE
(Great Billing)
F. A. CLARKE
THOMAS J. CLARKE
(Hackleton)
S. E. CLAYSON
FRANK and PEGGY CLOWES
J. L. COALES
(Newport Pagnell)
ALDERMAN T. H. COCKERILL
MR. and MRS. F. W. COLES
(Wootton)
DR. R. B. COLES
A. C. A. COLTON (Mrs.)
(Higham Ferrers)
DOROTHY S. COOK
(Courtney Hope)
E. H. COOPER
J. B. CORRIN
L. and A. B. CURTIS
(Boughton)

MR. and MRS. DON DARBY
(Towcester)
GLADYS DAVIES (Mrs.)
(Little Brington)
R. D. G. DAVIES (Miss)
DOUGLAS DAY
C. M. DELANEY (Miss)
HUGH B. DERBYSHIRE
(Scaldwell)
CELIA DESBOROUGH (Miss)
(Great Billing)
ERIC DEVEREUX
(Wootton)
C. E. DIAMOND
(Thrapston)
PHILIP DICKENS
(Great Houghton)
W. A. DICKENS
J. E. DOLBY
LT.-COL. DENIS M. DORR
(Wellingborough)
BRYAN J. DOUGLAS
MARION DOWSE
(Moulton)
F. DRIVER (Mrs.)
(Rhyl)
PETER DULAY
(London)
MAURICE L. DUNMORE

D. DURHAM
(Hardingstone)
R. C. T. DYER

OLIVE ELLIOTT (Miss)
(Harpole)
TOM ELLIOTT
JAMES ELLIS
(South Hadley, Mass., U.S.A.)

THE REV. J. W. H. FAULKNER
(Bedford)
RICHARD FIELD
(Wigan)
A. C. FINNIMORE (Mrs.)
G. FISHER (Mrs.)
(Stoke Bruerne)
ALISTAIR FOOT (Mrs.)
(Pinner)
DEREK FORBES
(Hertford)
SIR EDWARD FORD
(Eydon)
ERIC F. J. FORD, Secretary, Shaw
Society (Dagenham)
PAUL and SHIRLEY FORSYTH
RICHARD FOULKES
SALTER FOX
(Newtown, Mon.)
WILFRED H. FOX
(Pattishall)
J. W. FRAME
GERALD FREEMAN
(Horton)
H. C. R. FROST

COUNCILLOR JOHN JAMES
GARDNER
H. W. GEARY
(Kettering)
NORMAN E. GIBBS
(Harlestone)
MARGARET GLADYS GILBERT
L. J. GILES
CHRISTOPHER J. GLAZEBROOK
SIR GERALD GLOVER
(Pytchley)
JULIA GORDON-LENNOX
DR. ANDREW N. GRAHAM, M.B.,
F.R.C.Psych.
COLIN GRAHAM (Mrs.)
(Staverton)
DEREK GRAY
(Kettering)
LARRY GRAYSON
(Nuneaton)
HARRY N. GREATOREX
(Swanwick)
DAVID M. GREEN
(Staverton)
MICHAEL GREEN
(Ealing)
LT.-COL. T. R. L. GREENHALGH
(Overstone)

C. T. GROOM
(Overstone)
PHILIP M. L. DE GROUCHY
(Southampton)
R. J. W. GUBBINS
R. A. GUINNESS
(Hardingstone)

T. C. HADLAND
(Horton)
S. B. HADLEY
(Boughton)
GARTH R. HALESTRAP
BRIAN G. HALL
VINCENT S. HALTON
LIONEL HAMILTON
SIR WILLIAM HART, C.M.G.
(Turweston)
VICTOR A. HATLEY
ALFRED HAWTIN
K. I. HAYWARD (Mrs.)
(Harrington)
MICHAEL HENLEY
(Chapel Brampton)
NORA HERON
(Courteenhall)
LADY HESKETH
(Easton Neston)
LORD HESKETH
(Easton Neston)
ROBERT HEYGATE (Mrs.)
(Lichborough)
BETTY M. HILL (Mrs.)
(Hinwick)
BARRY L. HILLMAN
GEORGE HOARE
(Boughton)
MR. and MRS. J. HOCKENHULL
(Great Doddington)
NORMAN L. HODSON
(Desborough)
G. H. B. HOLLAND
S. E. HOLLAND
(Milton Keynes)
H. A. HOLLOWAY
(Walgrave)
RICHARD HOLLOWELL
(Cogenhoe)
DONALD HOPEWELL, M.A., Ll.B.,
Hon.Ll.D.
(Moreton Pinkney)
DOROTHY HUCKELL (Mrs.)
BARRY HUGHES
WINSTON F. HUGHES
BELINDA HUMFREY
(Lampeter)
STUART H. G. HUMFREY
S. H. G. HUMFREY (Mrs.)

TONY IRESON
(Kettering)
SIR GYLES ISHAM, Bart.
(Lamport)

VERNON W. JACKSON
(Wellingborough)

JEAN JACKSON-STOPS (Mrs.)
(Wood Burcote)
MR. and MRS. M. JAFFA
R. A. JAMESON (Mrs.)
(Earls Barton)
COL. R. C. JEFFERY, T.D., D.L.
(Great Addington)
MARCUS JELLEY
DENNIS JEYES
(New Duston)
ARTHUR JONES, M.P.
FELICITY JONES (Mrs.)
(West Haddon)
MICHAEL JONES

GERALD KENDALL
(Scaldwell)
PAUL KERTI
(Kettering)
IVAN J. KIGHTLEY
(Great Billing)
SYDNEY KILSBY
M. KIRKBY (Miss)
E. R. KNAPP
(Duston)
ELIZABETH L. KNIGHT
(Ecton)
J. KNIGHT (Mrs.)
MAY KNIGHT (Mrs.)
(Old)
W. FRANK KNIGHT
(Hackleton)
P. J. KOTTLER
(Gayton)

ERIC LAWE, F.I.I.P., A.R.P.S., P.P.ofA.
H. C. (BERT) LAWRENCE
HARRY LESLIE (CAPELL)
(Blackpool)
EDWARD LEWIS
MARGARET LEWIS (Miss)
(Moreton Pinkney)
PETER LEWIS
(Daily Mail)
PHILIP & JEAN LINER
(New Zealand)
G. LINNELL
(Canterbury)
JOHN LITTLE
(Overstone)
D. J. LLOYD
(Mosely)
PROFESSOR WILLIAM B. LONG
(New York)
PHIL LYMAN
(Nether Heyford)

A. J. MACDONALD-BUCHANAN
(Great Harrowden)
MAJOR SIR REGINALD
MACDONALD-BUCHANAN,
K. C.V.O., M.B.E., M.C.
(Cottesbrooke)
ANGUS MACKAY
(London)

DR. DONALD M. MACKAY
(London)
DR. D. H. G. MACQUAIDE
CECIL MADDEN, M.B.E.
(London)
PAUL MANN, F.R.S.A.
(Sherington)
W. MANN
(Plymouth)
A. W. MARKHAM
ARTHUR A. J. MARSHMAN,
F.R.I.B.A., F.R.S.A.
(Horton)
C. C. MARSTON
(Milton Malsor)
A. C. MASON
(Deene Park)
IAN MAYES
(Hardingstone)
GRAHAM MAYO
RALPH MEAKINS
RON MEARS
(Kettering)
JOAN L. MERRITT
(Little Houghton)
MARTIN T. MERRITT
(Little Houghton)
BILL MIDDLETON
M. MILLBURN (Miss)
MR. and MRS. A. J. MINNEY
(Kettering)
MR. and MRS. C. N. MINTY
(Walgrave)
W. ROWAN MITCHELL
DR. JOE MOLONEY
F. A. MOORE
(Kettering)
MR. and MRS. F. MOSS
RUBY L. MUNDIN
NANCY MUNKS (Mrs.)
(Rottingdean)

HAROLD J. NASH
M. V. NASH (Miss)
DAME ANNA NEAGLE, C.B.E.
H. NECUS
J. C. NETTLETON (Mrs.)
PETER NEWCOMBE
(Blisworth)
F. H. W. NIGHTINGALE

DES O'CONNOR
(London)
J. RAYMOND OWEN
(Rugby)

R. T. PAGET, Q.C., M.P.
DR. B. W. PAINE
(Higham Ferrers)
R. A. PALMER
W. E. PARKER
G. H. PAYNE
(Rushden)
KENNETH R. PEARSON
(Mayor of Northampton 72-3)

W. J. A. PECK
(Rushden)
DR. A. C. PERCIVAL
(London)
A. DYAS PERKINS
A. E. PERKINS (Mrs.)
RUTH G. PERKINS (Miss)
F. P. PHELAN
G. H. PICKERING
(Hallaton)
W. E. PIGOTT
(Eastbourne)
SIDNEY C. PITTAM
ALDERMAN JOHN POOLE
RAYMOND P. POOLE
(Boughton)
J. A. H. PORCH
(Maidwell)
DAVID POWELL
ROY PLOMLEY
(London)
GRACE PRATT (Mrs.)
MR. and MRS. S. I. PHILIPS
DAVID J. PRIOR
(Thrapston)
V. P. PRESTNEY-ARCHER (Mrs.)
JIM PURVIS

RONALD RADD
JACK READING
(London)
DR. ERNEST REYNOLDS
SQUADRON-LEADER JOHN
RICHARDS
(Oakham)
G. W. RISDALE
(Andover)
K. H. RISDALE
(Rushden)
JOHN ROAN
ERIC ROBERTS
(Overstone)
MR. and MRS. FRANK ROBERTS
MR. and MRS. C. C. ROBINSON
(Chapel Brampton)
COLIN ROBINSON
(Whiston)
ELISABETH ROBINSON (Mrs.)
(Whiston)
OSBORNE ROBINSON, O.B.E.
(Whiston)
MR. and MRS. REX ROBINSON
WILLIAM ROGERS
(Nether Heyford)
ARNOLD ROOD
(New York)
SYBIL ROSENFELD
(London)
P. ROUYER
(Bordeaux)

PROFESSOR ERIC SALMON
(Tunbridge Wells)
MOLLIE SANDS
(London)

C. B. SAVAGE
B. A. SCHANSCHIEFF
LORD GEORGE SCOTT
(Weekley)
VALERIE SCOTT (Mrs.)
(Walton-on-Thames)
DENISE H. SCOTT (Miss)
(Walton-on-Thames)
ANTONY SHAW (Mrs.)
ANN SHORE
(Barton Seagrave)
VIDA SLINN (Mrs. Eric Slinn)
MR. and MRS. JOHN SMITH
(Towcester)
M. ROYDE SMITH
THE EARL SPENCER
(Althorp)
N. G. SPENCER
(East Haddon)
HENRY G. SPOKES
(Milton Malsor)
VICTORIA SQUIRES
(Duston)
EELIN STEWART-HARRISON
(Carbondale, Illinois, U.S.A.)
CHARLES E. STOPFORD
GRACE STURGIS (Mrs.)
(Finedon)
W. D. SUMMERLY
(Kettering)
SIR SPENCER SUMMERS
(Banbury)
V. H. SYKES
(Raunds)
MAJOR J. S. SYMINGTON
(Guilsborough)
F. O. SYMON (Miss)
(Echunga, S. Australia)

MARIE TAYLOR (Mrs.)
(Long Buckby)
D. NORMAN TAYLOR
WILFRID TEBBUTT
(Kettering)
PHIL THOMAS
ANNE TIBBLE
(Guilsborough)
R. L. TIMMS
ERIC TIMS
(Wellingborough)
ROGER JAMES TIVEY
(Aldwincle)
MEG TOYER (Miss)
V. TRAVIS (Miss)
FRED TUCKLEY
ARTHUR TUSTIN
(Spratton)

W. WADDELL (Mrs.)
SIR HEREWARD WAKE, Bart.
(Courteenhall)
COUNCILLOR DAVID A.
WALMSLEY
RICHARD B. WALTERS
OSWALD BARRETT WARD

PETER J. WARD
(Enon, Ohio, U.S.A.)
GRETA WARWICK (Mrs.)
ELIZABETH WATT (Miss)
(Aynho)
L. G. WEBSTER
WALTER WEBSTER
(Guilsborough)
REBECCA WESTAWAY (Mrs.)
(Naseby)
DR. JOHN WESTON
MICHAEL L. WHITE
THE REV. HARRY WHITTAKER
ETHEL WHITTINGHAM (Miss)
DOROTHY WIGGINS (Mrs.)
JEAN WILCOX (Mrs.)
PETER WILCOX
(West Haddon)
P. W. WILKINSON
(East Haddon)
DON WILSON
(Boughton)
LYNN WILSON
(Holcot)

P. T. M. WILSON
(Chairman, Anglia Building Society)
SHEILA and TERRY WILSON
SYLVIA T. WOODGER
JOSEPH E. WRIGHT
(Nashville, Tennessee)
P. J. WRIGHT
(Stanwick)

JOHN R. YATES
(Old Swinford, Stourbridge)

PATRONS DECEASED

It is regretted that the following
Patrons have died since subscribing :-

THE DUKE OF BUCCLEUCH
WILFRID S. CHURCH
GEORGE FOSTER
BEN HARRIES
ALDERMAN JIM LEWIS
JOAN WAKE (Miss)

LIBRARIES AND OTHER ORGANISATIONS

ABBEY MINSTRELS

ABINGTON VALE HIGH SCHOOL FOR GIRLS

ALLEN-LYMAN SECRETARIAL BUREAU

ARTS THEATRE CLUB, NORTH-AMPTON

AYLESBURY COLLEGE OF FURTHER EDUCATION

BACAL CONSTRUCTION CO. LTD.

BEDFORD COUNTY PRESS

BEDFORD COUNTY RECORD OFFICE

BEDFORD PUBLIC LIBRARY

BEDFORDSHIRE COUNTY LIBRARY

BELFAST PUBLIC LIBRARY

BRISTOL PUBLIC LIBRARY

BRITISH LIBRARY, LENDING DIVISION (Boston Spa, Yorks.)

BUCKS COUNTY LIBRARY

CHELTENHAM PUBLIC LIBRARIES

UNIVERSITY OF CHICAGO

MALCOLM A. LOVE LIBRARY, CALIFORNIA STATE UNIVERSITY

CHRONICLE AND ECHO, NORTHAMPTON

UNIVERSITY OF COLORADO

ROYAL LIBRARY OF COPENHAGEN

CORBY OPERATIC SOCIETY

DALHOUSIE UNIVERSITY (Halifax, Nova Scotia)

UNIVERSITY OF DURHAM

EAST MIDLANDS ARTS ASSOCIATION

EDINBURGH UNIVERSITY

MARC FITCH FUND

FOLGER SHAKESPEARE LIBRARY (Washington D.C., U.S.A.)

GALLERY (Higham Ferrers) LTD.

GRANTHAM PUBLIC LIBRARY

HILLINGDON BOROUGH LIBRARIES

HOARE & COLE LTD.

UNIVERSITY OF ILLINOIS AT URBANA-CHAMPAIGN

INDIANA UNIVERSITY

KENT COUNTY PUBLIC LIBRARY

KETTERING CIVIC SOCIETY

KETTERING AND DISTRICT THEATRICAL SOCIETY

KETTERING GRAMMAR SCHOOL

KETTERING PUBLIC LIBRARY

KETTERING SECONDARY GIRLS SCHOOL

KING'S LYNN PUBLIC LIBRARY

LEICESTERSHIRE COUNTY LIBRARY

LEICESTER UNIVERSITY CENTRE (Northampton)

CITY OF LINCOLN PUBLIC LIBRARY

LINDSAY AND HOLLAND COUNTY LIBRARY

LITERATURE GROUP OF NORTHAMPTON ARTS ASSOCIATION

LIVERPOOL CITY LIBRARIES

LONDON LIBRARY

UNIVERSITY OF LONDON

UNIVERSITY LUND OF SWEDEN

LUTON PUBLIC LIBRARY

MANCHESTER UNIVERSITY

RAYMOND MANDER & JOE MITCHENSEN THEATRE COLLECTION

W. MARK & CO. (1935) LTD.

MASQUE THEATRE, NORTHAMPTON

MERCURY AND HERALD

MILITARY ROAD COUNTY PRIMARY SCHOOL, NORTHAMPTON

MINNEAPOLIS PUBLIC LIBRARY

UNIVERSITY OF MINNESOTA

MOTLEY BOOKS LTD.

NEWARK-ON-TRENT PUBLIC LIBRARY

NORTHAMPTON AMATEUR OPERATIC COMPANY

NORTHAMPTON CAMERA CLUB

NORTHAMPTON COLLEGE OF EDUCATION

NORTHAMPTON COLLEGE OF FURTHER EDUCATION

NORTHAMPTON COLLEGE OF TECHNOLOGY

NORTHAMPTON AND COUNTY INDEPENDENT

NORTHAMPTON GRAMMAR SCHOOL

NORTHAMPTON MERCURY COMPANY LTD.

19—TU * *

SMITH COLLEGE, WERNER
  JOSTEN LIBRARY, NORTHAMP-
  TON, MASS.
NORTHAMPTON PUBLIC LIBRARY
NORTHAMPTON REPERTORY
  PLAYERS
NORTHAMPTON SCHOOL FOR
  GIRLS
NORTHAMPTON TRINITY
  GRAMMAR SCHOOL
NORTHAMPTONSHIRE COUNTY
  LIBRARY
NORTHAMPTONSHIRE EVENING
  TELEGRAPH
NORTHAMPTONSHIRE RECORD
  OFFICE
NORTHAMPTONSHIRE RECORD
  SOCIETY
NOTRE DAME HIGH SCHOOL
NOTTINGHAM PUBLIC LIBRARY
NOTTINGHAM UNIVERSITY
OVERSTONE SCHOOL FOR GIRLS
OXFORDSHIRE COUNTY LIBRARY
PENNSYLVANIA STATE
  UNIVERSITY
PETERBOROUGH MUSEUM
  SOCIETY
PETERBOROUGH CITY LIBRARIES
PORTLAND STATE UNIVERSITY
  (Oregon, U.S.A.)
READING PUBLIC LIBRARY
ROYAL SHAKESPEARE THEATRE,
  STRATFORD-UPON-AVON
RUSHDEN PUBLIC LIBRARY
UNIVERSITY LIBRARY,
  ST. ANDREW'S, SCOTLAND
C. B. SAVAGE LTD.
SCOTT BADER COMMONWEALTH
  LTD.

SHAKESPEARE BIRTHPLACE
  TRUST, STRATFORD-UPON-
  AVON
UNIVERSITY OF SHEFFIELD
SHEFFIELD CITY LIBRARIES
SILHOUETTE SLIMMING CLUB
SOCIETY FOR THEATRE
  RESEARCH
SOUTHLANDS COLLEGE
  (Wimbledon)
SPENCER GIRLS HIGH SCHOOL,
  NORTHAMPTON
STAMFORD PUBLIC LIBRARY
STEVENS & BROWN LTD.
STRATFORD-UPON-AVON PUBLIC
  LIBRARY
SUNDERLAND PUBLIC LIBRARIES
UNIVERSITY COLLEGE OF
  SWANSEA
HENRY TELFER LTD.
UXBRIDGE LOCAL HISTORY AND
  ARCHIVES SOCIETY
VICTORIA & ALBERT MUSEUM,
  LONDON
WALTHAM FOREST PUBLIC
  LIBRARY
UNIVERSITY OF WARWICK
WARWICKSHIRE COUNTY
  LIBRARY
WELLINGBOROUGH PUBLIC
  LIBRARY
CHARLES WELLS LTD.
  (Bedford, owners of Swan and Castle,
  Buckingham, Page 125.
WESTMINSTER CITY LIBRARIES
WHITE'S OFFICE EQUIPMENT
  LTD.
WYCOMBE PUBLIC LIBRARY

Index